Robot Building for Beginners

David Cook

Apress®

Robot Building for Beginners

Copyright © 2009 by David Cook

ISBN-13 (pbk): 978-1-4302-2748-9

ISBN-13 (electronic): 978-1-4302-2749-6

President and Publisher: Paul Manning
Lead Editor: Steve Anglin
Technical Reviewer: Scott Preston
Editorial Board: Steve Anglin, Mark Beckner, Ewan Buckingham, Gary Cornell, Jonathan Gennick, Jonathan Hassell, Michelle Lowman, Matthew Moodie, Jeff Olson, Jeffrey Pepper, Frank Pohlmann, Douglas Pundick, Ben Renow-Clarke, Dominic Shakeshaft, Matt Wade, Tom Welsh
Coordinating Editor: Jim Markham
Copy Editor: Ralph Moore
Compositor: Bytheway Publishing Services
Indexer: Potomac Indexers
Artist: April Milne
Cover Designer: Anna Ishchenko

Distributed to the book trade worldwide by Springer Science+Business Media, LLC., 233 Spring Street, 6th Floor, New York, NY 10013. Phone 1-800-SPRINGER, fax 201-348-4505, e-mail orders-ny@springer-sbm.com, or visit www.springeronline.com.

For information on translations, please e-mail rights@apress.com, or visit www.apress.com.

Apress and friends of ED books may be purchased in bulk for academic, corporate, or promotional use. eBook versions and licenses are also available for most titles. For more information, reference our Special Bulk Sales–eBook Licensing web page at www.apress.com/info/bulksales.

For everyone who looks at the everyday objects around them and sees the potential of what they could become.

Contents at a Glance

Contents

About the Author

David Cook has shared his robot-making experience with readers for over ten years as the host of the popular web site, RobotRoom.com, and in his two Apress books. Like many other enthusiasts, David began with inspiration from NASA's Sojourner landing on Mars.

By day, David's profession is software development. His career started in writing award-winning video games for the early Apple Macintosh computers. Then, he created and managed Motorola public-safety applications for police officers, emergency medical technicians, and firefighters.

Presently, David is a development manager at SmartSignal Corporation. SmartSignal produces predictive analytics software that listens to sensors at a variety of power plants across the globe. The application alerts plant operators to emerging concerns before they become problems. In doing so, David and the SmartSignal team prevent black-outs, lower costs, and increase efficiency (which is good for the environment).

About the Technical Reviewers

 **Scott Preston** lives in Columbus, Ohio with his wife Emily, daughter Lilu, and dog Castle. Scott has been developing web applications since graduating from Ohio State University in 1996. In 2006, Scott left consulting to focus on his own business, Preston Research. Scott is also a member of the Java Community Process, Central Ohio Java Users Group, and founder of The Columbus Robotics Society. He wrote his first book, *The Definitive Guide to Building Java Robots*, published by Apress in 2005, and co-authored *Real-World-Ajax*, published by SYS-CON Media in 2006. Scott continues to build advanced robots in his basement and publish and discuss them at **www.scottsbots.com**.

Acknowledgments

Thanks to the fine people at Apress:

- Ralph Moore edited the second edition with record speed, yet took the care to proof every word, even fixing some sentences that were originally untouched from the previous edition.

- Scott Preston was the technical editor. A number of his suggestions clarified complicated steps, inserted tips, or specified another part supplier.

- April Milne and Jerry Votta of the art department replaced my telestrator-style chicken scratches with clean, consistent overlays on dozens of illustrations.

- Steve Anglin, the Assistant Editorial Director, was always in ear shot (or e-mail shot) to remove obstacles from the book's path to production.

- Jim Markham is the friendly and incredibly productive Coordinating Editor. Although this book wouldn't have happened without Steve, it would have taken another six months if not for Jim.

I also want to extend my thanks to all the people from the first edition: Gary Cornell, Dan Appleman, Grace Wong, Stephanie Rodriguez, Sofia Marchant, Jim Munro, Dave Baum, and Tom Gavin.

Thanks to my family, Rachel, James, Sam, Pumpkin, Raisin, and Bones for their love and understanding–even when I spend too much time at the computer or machining in the basement.

Finally, a big hello to everyone at SmartSignal: Stacey, Trung, Jon, Nasser, Chad, Matt, Bryan, Greg, Rich, George, Dave, Patrick, Bob, and Jim.

Introduction

I wrote this book because I love building robots. I want you to love building robots, too.

It took me a while to learn about many of the tools and parts in amateur robotics. Perhaps by writing about my experiences, I can give you a head start.

It's amazing that so many brilliant minds work in the virtual universe now, rather than with what can be touched. Hopefully, you'll join the select ranks of inventors who create things that are physically real, even if homemade.

Intended Audience

This book is aimed at teenagers or adults who have an avid interest in science and dream of building household explorers. No formal engineering education is assumed.

The robot described and built in this book is battery-powered and about the size of a lunchbox. It is autonomous. That is, it isn't remote controlled.

You'll begin with some tools of the trade, work your way through prototyping, robot bodybuilding, and eventually soldering your own circuit boards. By the book's end, you will have a solid amateur base of understanding so that you can begin creating your own robots.

"Where's the stuff about the killer saws?"

This book isn't about destructive robots. However, the fundamental techniques presented here can provide a good foundation before tackling monster projects, if you so choose.

"Houston, we have a problem."

If you're an experienced engineer and would like to learn more about multi-dimensional vision systems, FPGAs (field-programmable gate arrays), or seven-degrees-of-freedom robot arms, then this book is probably under your head.

Thumb through the pages to see if there's anything that gets your brain juices flowing.

Not Ready to Learn How to Solder?

If you're younger, have a limited financial budget, negligible free time, or aren't ready for drilling and soldering, then I highly recommend you begin with LEGO MINDSTORMS. The LEGO robot kit has limited electrical potential, but is very friendly and should have you building interesting robots quickly.

The most recent version of the kit is LEGO MINDSTORMS NXT. The prior versions of LEGO MINDSTORMS Robotics Invention System (1.0, 1.5, and 2.0) are no longer manufactured. However, they are often available at garage sales and online auction sites for a lower cost than the NXT version.

If you decide to go the LEGO route, pick up a LEGO MINDSTORMS kit, some batteries, and an Apress MINDSTORMS book.

Beyond LEGO But Still Not Ready to Solder?

If you want an easily constructed kit that is more advanced than LEGO, consider the Parallax Boe-Bot robot. It comes with a BASIC processor, circuit board, motors, wheels, body, instruction books, CD-ROM, tutorial, and either a USB or RS-232 serial port. Boe-Bot doesn't require soldering.

If walking robots are more your style, check out the Parallax Penguin. Or, if you want a preassembled (ready-to-go) robot, look into the Parallax Scribbler.

Parallax also has robots based on the more-advanced Propeller processor, such as the Stingray. It is more appropriate for those with a software programming background.

Arduino is a very popular open source brain board, similar to the Parallax BASIC Stamp or Propeller. Both Solarbotics and SparkFun Electronics carry a wide variety of Arduino-based boards that you can connect with prototyping wires, rather than soldering.

Note Regarding Part Lists

Whenever possible, descriptions of tools and parts mentioned in this book are accompanied by listings of resellers, part numbers, and approximate prices. No favoritism to a particular supplier or part is intended.

Prices are listed in US dollars. Keep in mind that prices change and that part numbers may no longer be accurate after this book is published. Bummer!

Book errata, updates, and an up-to-date parts list is maintained at http://www.robotroom.com/SandwichStuff.html#PARTS

Getting Updates and Seeing What's New

I have a web site, www.robotroom.com. Please drop by and visit. You'll also find other robots I've built as well as links to robot-related clubs and sites.

CHAPTER 1

∎∎∎

Welcome Robot Inventor!

You've chosen a stimulating and rewarding hobby. It's more expensive than insect collecting, but less expensive than stock-car racing.

Think of it: One day your hands will be giving birth to new life forms. Initially, they'll be rudimentary, but like all handcrafted art, each piece will be unique. And like any great artist, your pieces will gradually become more complex and more wonderful.

Despite decades of public fascination with the concept of robots, helpful personal robots remain an unfulfilled dream. Other than industrial robots, most advancements in the field of robotics are actually due to somewhat unrelated consumer products, such as personal computers, CD players, toys, remote controls, and household appliances.

Disheartening? No. It's exciting to be involved in a field that's rife with world-changing potential. You can make a difference because there is still so much room for new inventions. So, welcome to robotics and let's get started!

Four Disciplines

Robotics comprises at least four major branches of learning:

- Electrical Engineering (circuits and sensors)

- Mechanical Engineering and Machining (gears, motors, and body)

- Computer Science (pseudo-intelligent behavior)

- Arts (expression, style, and fun)

You don't need to be an expert in each field in order to build a decent robot. However, if you happen to have a background in one field, your creations will naturally revolve around that strength. Along the way, robotics provides an exciting opportunity to learn new skills and find hidden talents.

Think of the Renaissance artist and scientist, Leonardo da Vinci. If he were around today, he'd be making robots.

Anatomy of a Homemade Robot

Robots come in a wide variety of shapes and sizes. The point at which an electronic or mechanical object becomes a robot is open to debate. Movement seems a basic requirement to be a robot, as do sensors and some form of intelligence.

Figure 1-1 shows a typical homemade robot. This robot is capable of finding opposition robots (or any objects) on a table and knocking them off. It does so without any human control. Would most people identify this as a robot?

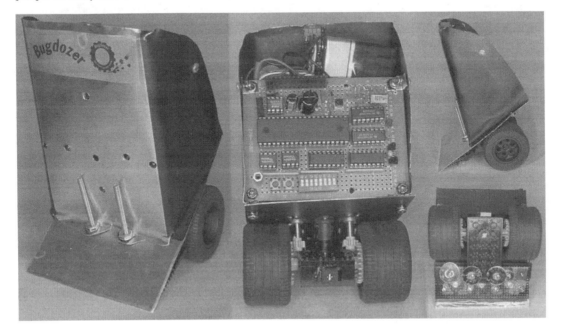

Figure 1-1. Multiple views of the battered champion sumo robot, Bugdozer

People are more likely to identify an object as a robot when it has the rudimentary sections of a living being. People look for eyes and a mouth (generally a face), legs, and a torso, as though they were examining an insect or exotic animal.

From an anatomical perspective, robot parts generally fit into one or more of the following categories:

- Brains

- Electrical Power

- Sensors

- Action and Feedback

- Body/Aesthetics

As a robot doctor, you'll become familiar with robot guts. The next sections of this chapter describe some common things you'll find under a robot's hood.

Brains

Robots can be built without a brain, such as those robots operated by a human via remote control or a joystick. Robots can also be built with distributed brains, where simpler chips handle individual parts (such as a leg or an arm) without knowing anything about what the rest of the body is doing. Or, robots can even be built with the brains located away from the body, such as on a laptop computer.

But, all in all, the top choice for robot brains is the microcontroller chip (see Figure 1-2). Microcontrollers are very similar to microprocessors, which are found in personal computers. A microcontroller differs in that it is almost like an entire tiny computer merged into a single piece.

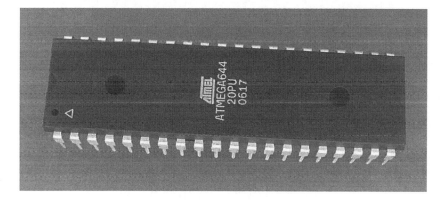

Figure 1-2. An Atmel ATmega644 microcontroller

Microcontrollers have small amounts of memory and storage space built directly into the chip. Where the PC microprocessor dedicates its pins to high-speed memory, a microcontroller has a diverse variety of input and output pins. These pins can connect directly to sensors, buttons, and other odd devices.

Unsung heroes, microcontrollers surround us, yet few people know about them. Microcontrollers are in automobiles, household washers, dryers, VCRs, and other appliances. The multi-billion-dollar market for microcontrollers makes them inexpensive and plentiful.

That's right, one day your robots are going to have the brains of a dishwasher! Put some wheels on a Maytag® and you've got a great robot.

To make things easy, the robot built in this book uses a simple comparator chip instead of a microcontroller. The follow-up book, *Intermediate Robot Building* by David Cook (Apress, 2010), includes a robot with a microcontroller brain.

Electrical Power

Although robots can be built with gasoline-powered engines and pneumatic actuators, at some level almost every robot contains electronic components. The electrical power supply consists of a raw power source, a regulating circuit to stabilize and process the source, and a switch to activate and deactivate.

Power Source

Except in extreme circumstances, hobby robots are supplied power from popular consumer batteries (see Figure 1-3). Consumer batteries are safe, inexpensive, readily available, reliable, and standardized. The main robot presented in this book uses a 9 V battery for those reasons.

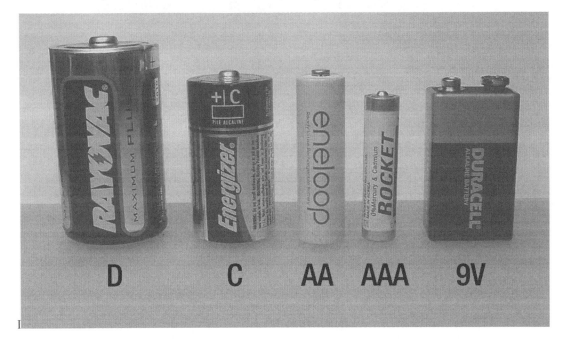

Figure 1-3. Common battery sizes

Rechargeable batteries are preferable. Although their initial cost is higher, they'll save the experimenter a lot of money in the long run.

Solar power is also an option. Because light isn't constantly available, rudimentary solar-powered robots operate in repeating charge and discharge cycles, powering off between bursts of activity. More sophisticated solar-powered robots recharge batteries during optimal lighting conditions, with the batteries maintaining power to the brains during dark conditions.

Power Regulation

Most robots have a small portion of their bodies dedicated to keeping a steady, specific level of power available to all of the electronics. This is called power regulation (see Figure 1-4).

As batteries are used up, they provide less and less power. Unless stabilized, this would result in a robot that moves at different speeds and has different light brightness and sensor readings based on battery freshness.

Figure 1-4. *Power regulating circuit based on a Microchip MCP1826S, which is the modern equivilant to the classic 7805*

Another reason for power regulation is that some parts of the robot need more power than other parts. For example, motors require more power than logic chips or blinking lights. The power regulation module steps down (or, conversely, boosts) the battery power to the range needed by each major part. To reduce the complexity of the robot presented in this book, all of its parts can operate at the varying voltages of the battery. As such, no voltage regulator is necessary.

The aforementioned follow-up to this book, *Intermediate Robot Building*, compares several voltage regulating technologies, and provides recommendations for complete power supplies.

On/Off Switch

Most robots have power switches (see Figure 1-5). This allows the robot to be disabled for maintenance or storage.

Interestingly, solar-powered robots usually *don't* have a power switch. Those robots wake up in the morning sunshine and dance all day.

Sensors

There are more sensors in a single crease of your brow than there are in any robot ever built. With the exception of the pixel elements of a vision module, most homemade robots end up with fewer than a dozen sensors of four or five major types.

Figure 1-5. A heavy-duty power switch

A complicated homemade robot might have infrared object detection, touch switches, brightness sensors (see Figure 1-6), a battery tester, tilt switches, and perhaps a temperature probe. Even with so few inputs, the robot can do really interesting things.

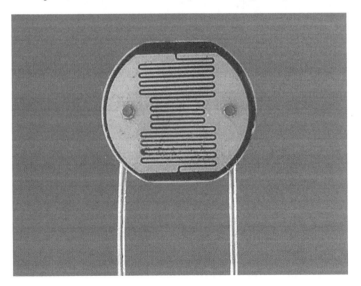

Figure 1-6. Cadmium-sulfide sensor for light detection

Pushbuttons

Switches and pushbuttons (see Figure 1-7) are a subset of sensors. They "sense" a push.

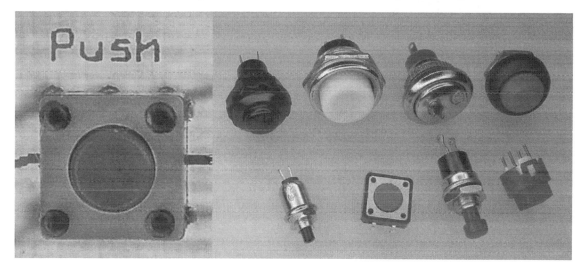

Figure 1-7. (left) *A tiny pushbutton mounted to a circuit board etched in my basement.* (right) *A selection of pushbuttons in various shapes, sizes, colors, and firmness.*

On most robots, a couple of pushbuttons are usually dedicated for human input. Buttons can trigger a change in modes or the beginning of an experimental sequence. Alternatively, crafty engineers can discard dedicated buttons and instead wave a hand in front of various sensors to indicate a desired action.

Action and Feedback

Robots perform actions coordinated with the processing of sensor information. Most often the action is in the form of movement. However, sounds, displays, indicator lights, and other forms of feedback are also actions, which are usually intended to provoke humans to act.

Movement

Most homemade robots move around with only a pair of wheels (see Figure 1-8). Unlike an automobile's four wheels and one motor, a robot's two wheels and two motors provide agile turning and sufficient force without the additional weight of elaborate drive trains.

Mechanical legs are a blast to see in action, but are more complicated to actually build. There are some simple wire-feet and six-legged variations that are easier to implement, although with less dexterity.

Figure 1-8. Pair of tiny pager motors attached to wheels via belts

Motor Controller

Like the power regulator, a motor controller section (see Figure 1-9) is required on most robots. The sudden starting and stopping (and stalling) of motors involves bursts of power; much more power than the brains can supply by itself. So, a portion of the robot is dedicated to managing the enabling of the motors and is responsible for protecting the rest of the electronics from backlashes and surges.

Figure 1-9. Motor control circuit with MOSFET chips and Schottky diodes

Indicator Lights

Lots of tiny lights adorn most robots. LEDs (light-emitting diodes) indicate power status, motors engaging, sensor detection (see Figure 1-10), and decision-making. This display of the robot's state makes error correction and design improvements a lot easier. Of course, the lights also make a robot look more fascinating.

Figure 1-10. A row of LEDs for target detection

LEDs are simple to use. They're inexpensive, lightweight, cool to the touch, and are being produced in an increasing variety of colors.

Miscellaneous Components

You'd be amazed at how quickly the connections to the brains can get used up. A few support chips are commonly used to gather connections together before reaching a microcontroller. Support chips can also preprocess signals (such as from sensors and buttons) to decrease the workload of the brains.

A lot of other stuff is needed, too! Wires, connectors, capacitors, resistors, diodes, and other components (see Figure 1-11) play important roles in bringing circuits together.

Body

Unless you're building a jellyfish or paper-bag robot, all of the parts must be attached to a primary frame. Surprisingly, many designers fail to pay enough attention to the robot's body. They end up with a mess that either collapses under its own weight or limps around in an awkward way.

Not only does a good body hold the pieces together, but it also protects them against injury. An unfortunate number of homemade robots turn out to be too delicate, with wires hanging out and circuit boards exposed.

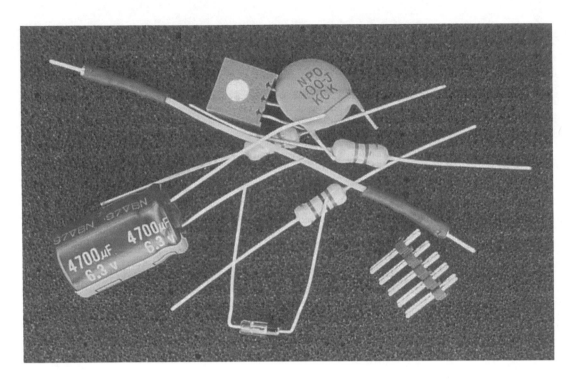

Figure 1-11. Wires, connectors, capacitors, diodes, and resistors—oh my!

Aesthetics

The other important aspect of a body is visual appeal (see Figure 1-12). No matter how technically amazing your robot, the finishing touches in appearance greatly affect how onlookers perceive the robot. Never underestimate showmanship.

Building Up

Because robots are complete entities, a lot of work must be invested before the creature begins functioning. There are a few techniques that you may find useful to extend your patience and increase your enjoyment.

Taking Small Bites

Even a small robot is a large project. It is easy to become overwhelmed.

After coming home from work or school, or when the weekend comes around, focus on a *small* piece that interests you. Perhaps get a motor to spin backwards and forwards. Perhaps attach a wheel to that motor. Simply pick out and buy a few parts from a catalog.

Figure 1-12. Line-following robot made from a candy container

At the end of day, hold up the piece that you worked on and spend some time admiring it. If it didn't turn out so well, think about all the things you learned.

Recognize your steady accomplishments and reward yourself for gradual progress. Don't be a visionary, be a builder.

Making Modules

Avoid the temptation to build an entire robot in one sitting or one piece. Instead, build individual modules (see Figure 1-13) that become a robot when connected together. That way, if a module turns out well, you can use the module's design over and over again for subsequent robots. If a module turns out to be ineffective or becomes damaged, only that portion needs to be replaced.

Because the time investment in a single module is small and manageable, it's easier to finish something substantial. Some people claim they built their robot in a weekend. Well, not really. They aren't counting the time spent purchasing, learning, designing, altering, or creating the subunits.

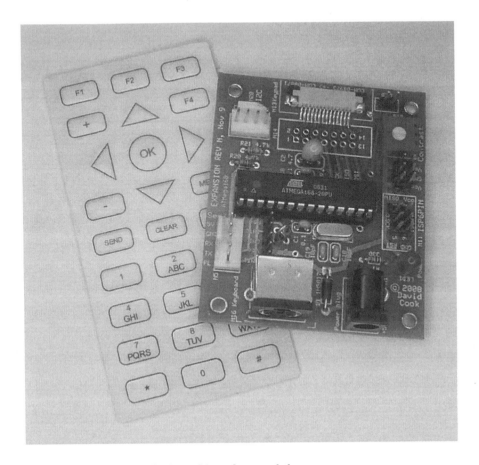

Figure 1-13. *A reusable keyboard interface module*

Keeping It Fun and Keeping It Light

If you find yourself frustrated and about to stomp on a stubborn contraption, simply set it aside. This is a hobby, right?

Draw a cartoon bubble saying "I'm too wily for you, human!" and tape it to the robot. Prove your greater intelligence by challenging the inert blob to a game of chess.

On the other hand, let's say the robot is finished and working well. Before the grand unveiling, take a careful look to see if anything is missing. Any empty spots? Maybe it needs a smiley face and googly eyes (see Figure 1-14). Stickers, paint, flags, and blinking lights are also attractive finishing touches.

Be sure to name your robot something clever or thought provoking. Avoid numbers, movie monikers, and clown names ("M1734," "R2-D2®," "Fuzooo"). Instead, how about "Graham Cracker," "Conqueror," or "Neighborhood Menace"?

At the premiere ceremony, consider playing some music. Are celebratory beers in order? Mood lighting?

Figure 1-14. *A face to reckon with*

Finding Camaraderie and Support

The World Wide Web has ushered in a new era of information sharing. Datasheets that describe a component in complete detail can be obtained instantly from the web sites of manufacturers and resellers. A quick search results in a plethora of robot-related material. Posted pictures and movies can be very informative and inspiring.

Local robot clubs are even better resources. For the social aspect, you get to meet new friends, both humans and robots. More importantly, informal discussions often provide insight or help with problem solving. Many clubs hold monthly or annual contests. If you have a competitive personality, these opportunities can be highly motivational. Although prize values are still relatively low, you might receive cool items you might not have purchased for yourself.

The physical locations of clubs can be found on the Web. Keyword searches work well. Most of the larger associations provide lists of links to other clubs. So, finding one organization, even if it's out of your area, can possibly lead to a club in your area.

If you can't find a local club, consider forming one. It's easy to do—just have people meet at a public library, museum, or community center.

Involve your family in your hobby. Not only will they be more genuinely appreciative of your accomplishments, but their presence can also make the whole experience more deeply enjoyable. When I went to my first robot contest in Illinois, I was struck by the family-friendly atmosphere. There were children of all ages, husbands and wives, grandfathers, grandmothers, and friends.

Onward and Upward

The next few chapters cover some important basics such as catalogs, safety, obtaining a multimeter, and numbering.

The heart of this book is dedicated to each component, tool, and step of building a line-following robot. It begins with a description of line-following track requirements and an inspection of the completely assembled line-following robot. Then, each chapter revolves around a piece or stage of designing and building the robot. You'll be instructed on the exact purpose and alternatives to each component.

If you complete each experiment, you'll have built your own copy of the line-following robot by the end of the book. You hold in your hand the complete blueprints and set of instructions to actually build the robot from scratch, without any prior knowledge of electronics, mechanics, or programming.

I chose a line-following robot as the primary subject for this book due to the overwhelming number of requests I've received from beginners on that topic. By focusing on a single design, the book covers every related detail and subject in depth. There are a number of robot books that provide an enormous range of robot projects, but without the details necessary for a beginner to actually build any of them.

The line-following robot won't be zooming around the track until the final chapters. However, there are modularized circuits and milestones to provide you with accomplishments along the way. Even if you choose not to build the line-following robot, it's actually a perfect base model that you can rearrange to build a robot with a completely different purpose.

The final chapters include ideas and suggestions for where to proceed from here in the wonderful world of robotics.

CHAPTER 2

■ ■ ■

Where to Obtain Tools and Parts

Lots of different parts and lots of different tools are needed to build high-quality robots.

If something is frustrating or difficult to make, or is otherwise turning out badly, then either you are using the wrong tool or you are using it incorrectly. In fact, some jobs are literally impossible without the right instrument. Using the correct tools in the correct manner makes almost any job fast and easy.

The same principle applies to parts. There are an infinite number of materials that you can employ to build a robot or provide a particular feature. It's important to choose materials that will make your robot more robust, adaptable, and less expensive.

Often, the greatest barrier is not knowing that a tool or part exists.

Ordering Free Information

A good place to start is to order some free catalogs. Take a few minutes, now, to order complimentary printed catalogs (see Figure 2-1) from most of the retail companies listed in Table 2-1. It's going to take a few weeks to receive the publications, so you might as well have the companies start the process while you enjoy reading the rest of this book.

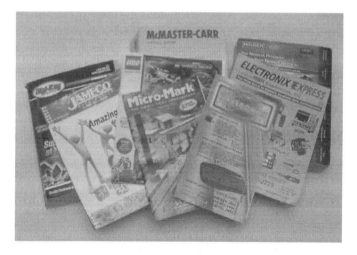

Figure 2-1. Some component and tool catalogs

Although online sites are useful for ordering and for more detailed information, the printed catalogs are better for browsing and lazy reading. They also make for pleasant surprises when they arrive in the mailbox.

Table 2-1. Retail Companies, Most with Printed Catalogs

COMPANY	CATEGORY	WEBSITE
Digi-Key	electronics	www.digikey.com
All Electronics	electronics, surplus	www.allelectronics.com
B. G. Micro	electronics, surplus	www.bgmicro.com
Jameco Electronics	electronics	www.jameco.com
Electronix Express	electronics	www.elexp.com
Electronic Goldmine	electronics	www.goldmine-elec.com
Mouser Electronics	electronics	www.mouser.com
Marlin P. Jones	electronics, surplus	www.mpja.com
Micro-Mark	tools, materials	www.micromark.com
McMaster-Carr	tools, materials	www.mcmaster.com
MSC Industrial Supply	tools, materials	www.mscdirect.com
Small Parts	tools, materials	www.smallparts.com
Micro Fasteners	fasteners (screws)	www.microfasteners.com
Solarbotics	kits, parts	www.solarbotics.com
SparkFun	kits, parts	www.sparkfun.com
Tower Hobbies	R/C, batteries, motors	www.towerhobbies.com
LEGO Shop At Home	kits, parts	shop.lego.com

With the exception of LEGO, the companies in Table 2-1 carry products from many different manufacturers. Most manufacturers themselves also have catalogs. As you begin to discover a personal preference for a particular manufacturer's parts, check the manufacturer's web site to see if they have any free printed material or even free sample parts.

Discovering Hidden Messages

Besides their obvious content, catalogs also provide an unintentional education. Since every square inch of printed page costs money, the companies try to condense data as much as possible. Sometimes what's not there is as important as what is there.

Considering Columns

If you want to know the most significant differences in a family of parts, just check out the table columns the catalog companies publish to compare them.

Hmm, if color, wavelength, dimensions, and brightness are all listed for LEDs, then those must be some of the most distinguishing characteristics between types of LEDs. Weight isn't listed, because that isn't a common concern for LEDs.

Counting Pages

Another subtle message contained in a parts catalog is the number of pages devoted to a family of parts. If surface-mount capacitors take up a lot of space in a particular catalog, you can infer that enough people are buying enough of those parts to be worth listing them.

The amount of space given to a variation of parts can also be noteworthy. If there are twenty lines of text dedicated to one variation of a part, but only one line of text for another part, perhaps the one-line variation has an unnoticed limitation.

On a sad note, if your favorite parts or packages seem to be receiving less and less coverage from subsequent catalogs, perhaps something is changing in the industry. It might be worth investigating whether that particular piece of technology is fading away.

Comparing Prices

The price list also tells a story. The chips listed in Table 2-2 all provide the identical logic function. So why the huge range in price?

Table 2-2. Single-Unit Prices for the Same Chip Function

Chip	Price
7400	109 cents
74LS00	56 cents
74HC00	45 cents

74AC00	50 cents
74AUC00	88 cents

Researching the plain 7400 chip reveals that it uses the most power, provides poor high-output current, and has no feature better than the other chips. Why is it the most expensive? Because it's obsolete. It's a really old design. If you're among the few people who still want that part, the lack of sales volume is going to cost you.

The lowest price on this list happens to be for a technology, 74HC00, that is very popular and has fully matured. Rounding out the bell curve is the newest technology, 74AUC00, which isn't selling yet at a high enough volume to bring down the price.

Of course, there are exceptions. With labor-intensive or rare-material parts, higher prices may be an indication of better quality parts rather than obsolescence or the latest technology.

Saving Money

You can spend money more efficiently by:

- purchasing in larger quantities

- ordering from catalogs rather than retail

- looking for discounts for purchasing online

- avoiding handling fees for minimum order amounts by bundling smaller orders

- considering the shipping costs

When purchasing inexpensive components, think about purchasing in quantities larger than you need for a single project. In quantities of 100, many components are half the price of a single piece (see Figure 2-2). Some components cost so little (such as resistors) that they often aren't available in quantities fewer than 10.

Consider informally organizing a group to buy a larger quantity of a particular item. Not only will each individual lower the unit cost of their parts, but also the group splits the shipping costs.

I try to support my local electronic, hardware, and hobby stores so that they will be there when I need them. There are some items, such tools and body materials, that are better to examine in person. However, for electronic parts, the costs are often exorbitant and the selection is limited in retail locations.

Most catalog companies offer better prices than retail stores because the stock is consolidated and is warehoused at a few low-rent locations. Since customers aren't walking through the aisles, the products can be stored more densely and needn't be packaged attractively.

Online companies can further reduce costs over catalog companies by decreasing the size of printed catalogs or eliminating them altogether. In addition, online order systems don't have the labor and toll costs of phone orders. Thus, even many catalog companies offer additional discounts for orders placed online.

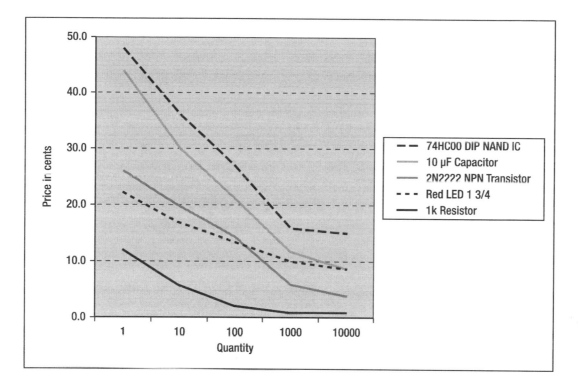

Figure 2-2. Sharp drop in component price with quantity

Watch out for minimum order amounts. Most online and catalog companies charge a handling fee below a certain total order size. The minimum order size is often $20 to $25. Also, consider the cost of shipping. It tends to have a significant base price that grows relatively slowly with weight.

In summary, by consolidating smaller orders into a single purchase and by buying in larger quantities, the per-unit price of components can be dramatically reduced. Simply plan ahead or combine orders with friends or local club members.

CHAPTER 3

∎∎∎

Safety

Building a robot is a sign of great intelligence. Retaining your health while doing so is a sign of greater intelligence.

Robotics involves a number of potentially harmful or dangerous situations. This safety chapter is meant to introduce readers to a broad variety of concerns regarding the hobby. Now, here are a few examples of potential dangers that may be encountered in the activities described in this book:

- Heat sources (burns, fires) during soldering and installing heat-shrink tubing

- Spark or ignition sources from batteries

- Bodily harm (cuts and so on) during drilling and cutting

- Chemical exposure in solder, solder flux, glues, and electrical components

- Eye injury during drilling, cutting, soldering, stripping, and snipping

- Inappropriate tool and component access by children

Benefiting from Age and Experience

Robotics is a great hobby to share with a parent or child. However, many of the tools, chemicals, forces, and power associated with robotics can be dangerous. Minors should only attempt to build robots with the assistance of an adult.

Following Instructions

Always read and follow the instructions provided with equipment and materials. A cynic would suggest the manufacturer's warnings are only designed to reduce the company's liability, but that's fine if it keeps you out of the emergency room.

There's an added benefit to reading the manuals: You might learn a technique that improves the effectiveness of the tools or describes a feature you didn't know about. Remember, the information is coming from the experts.

If you're fortunate enough to have access to a laboratory or machine shop, follow their shop rules. The rules are designed not only to keep everyone safe, but also to protect the equipment and to produce a high-quality product.

Keep manuals and safety sheets with their associated equipment. That way you know where to look if you lend the tool to someone or are having difficulty using it yourself.

Reread instructions every so often. As part of my research for this book, I reread some tool manuals and was delighted to learn some things I had either forgotten or missed on first reading.

When in doubt, ask for help.

Reading Chemical Labels

The labels for chemicals are as important as the instructions for tools.

Of additional benefit are Material Safety Data Sheets (MSDS), which often aren't included with the chemical at the time of purchase. The MSDS lists all hazards and the appropriate preventions and solutions. These sheets are available from the manufacturer and often the distributor. The sheets are commonly posted on the Web.

Donning Safety Glasses

A single errant shard in an eye can eliminate your depth perception and half of your vision. A chemical splash can impair or destroy both your eyes. Together with a sharp brain and steady fingers, your eyes are fundamental to building great robots.

Wear your safety glasses! (See Figure 3-1.)

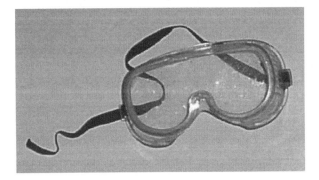

Figure 3-1. Safety goggles protect your eyes

There was a woman up the block from me who made a little extra money by sewing. One day, the needle from her sewing machine shattered during ordinary use, sending a piece of the needle into her eye. Freak accident? Yes, but it goes to show that you can't rely on your sense of what is dangerous to determine when an activity might bring about an eye hazard.

I always wear safety glasses whenever I work around machinery or chemicals. I also wear safety glasses when snipping wires or cutting sheet metal.

Hanging Glasses and Placing Them Face Up

A tip from your high-school shop teacher: Never place your safety glasses face down. The lenses will become greasy, soiled, or scratched. The decreased visibility results in a lower likelihood of your using the glasses and an increased likelihood of your removing them "just long enough" for a close inspection.

Instead, hang the glasses some place that you'll be reminded to put them on before using the equipment.

Wearing Other Safety Clothes

Wear appropriate gloves and long-sleeved clothing to protect yourself against irritation, minor scratching, chemical burns, or even poisoning. I always wear long pants, long-sleeved shirts, chemical-resistant gloves (see Figure 3-2), a dust mask, and safety glasses when working around chemicals.

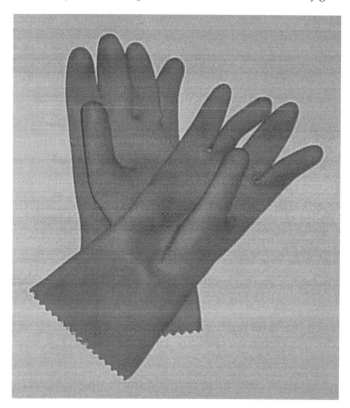

Figure 3-2. Resistant gloves protect your hands against chemicals

Thick leather steel-tipped boots with puncture-resistant soles are appropriate when working with metals or large, heavy materials.

Insuring Adequate Ventilation

Oh, man—somebody open a window! Try to use chemicals outside. If that's not possible, open a window. If the room lacks windows, obtain proper ventilation equipment such as an exhaust fan. In cases of recurring or extreme exposure, consider using a respirator.

Seemingly benign materials can irritate your nose, throat, and lungs when reduced to an airborne form. Wear a dust mask (see Figure 3-3) when sanding or drilling.

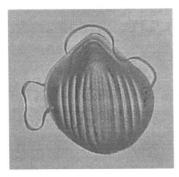

Figure 3-3. Even an inexpensive dust mask can help protect your nose, throat, and lungs

Everyone knows that smoking is bad for you. But, sometimes people forget about the potential for smoking to act as an ignition source for flammable chemicals or fumes. This is especially a danger in poorly ventilated rooms.

Storing Properly

Store chemicals and tools up high and lock them securely to keep them away from children.

Place chemicals and raw materials away from heat sources, such as soldering irons, heat guns, stoves, furnaces, and water heaters (think of the pilot light). If you transfer chemicals to a different container, or simply expose something to a chemical during use, be sure to label the item properly, including all appropriate warnings.

Talking About Your Activities, Materials, and Tools

Speak to your friends and family members about the items and chemicals you have. This is especially important if you are prone to stealing your spouse's Tupperware® bowl for etching copper circuit boards (not me, of course). You don't want the bowl reclaimed for its original purpose.

Washing Before Eating

After any soldering, painting, sanding, chemical or otherwise soiling job, don't eat or drink anything until you've had a chance to clean yourself up. At the very least, wash your hands with soap and water.

Avoiding Nasty Elements

In years past, matter was chosen based primarily on its beneficial attributes. However, as environmental and material sciences progress, the negative characteristics of a particular matter is being given more significant consideration. Many seemingly benign or marginally acceptable substances are now found to be too dangerous or polluting.

Toxic elements are of serious concern. Unlike compounds, elements can't be destroyed by chemical reactions, such as fire or incineration. However, when disposed of properly, many can be recycled or chemically neutralized.

Lead

Lead is being banned from an increasing number of products including electronic components and assembly. Airborne exposure to lead is the worst, followed by ingestion, with the least absorption through touch.

High levels of lead can cause death in adults, but even moderate blood levels cause permanent loss of IQ in children. To give you a sense for the danger, the current "safe" level of lead in blood for children is only one-tenth the level acceptable for non-pregnant adults.

Avoid purchasing products containing lead, including lead-acid or lead-gel batteries, even at surplus sales. Don't throw away items containing lead, but instead take them to a local hazardous waste collection site for proper disposal or recycling.

Like most technicians, I learned to solder using standard 60/40 (60% tin and 40% lead) solder. It flows well. However, I made the switch to a tin-silver lead-free alternative (see Figure 3-4).

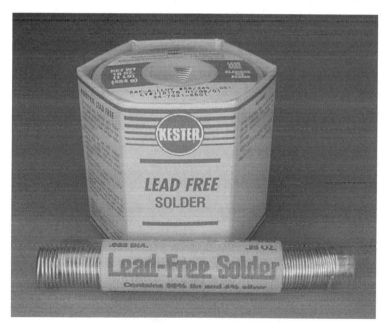

Figure 3-4. Use lead-free solder

When lead-free solder is purchased in the small 16-ounce rolls, the cost is insignificantly higher than leaded solder. Initially, if lead-free solder seems more difficult to apply cleanly, it may be because you aren't accustomed to it. With the correct temperature and practiced technique, lead-free solder works as well and even forms a stronger bond.

Flux, the cleaning material within solder, is irritating and a potential carcinogen. So, being lead free doesn't completely eliminate all dangers. Adequate ventilation and clean-up helps here.

Mercury

Old-fashioned mercury tilt switches are sure cool to look at (see Figure 3-5). However, mercury is a particularly toxic element. Small amounts can poison you, as well as make their way into rivers and streams.

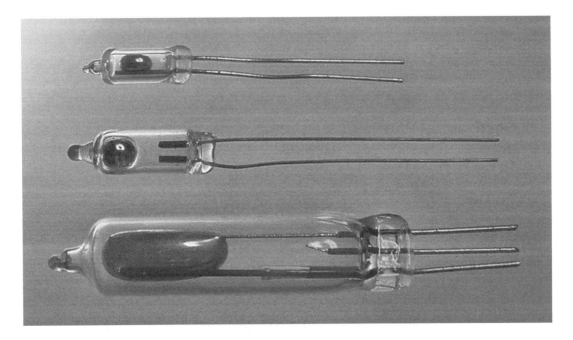

Figure 3-5. Three glass tilt switches with noxious liquid mercury

Don't purchase or use items containing mercury. Mercuric-oxide, silver-oxide, and even zinc-air batteries contain mercury. As long as people continue to buy products with mercury, they'll continue to be manufactured. If you use a mercury switch in your robot and the switch shatters, spewing mercury all over your robot, how are you going to clean it up? The robot is covered in toxin.

Don't throw away items containing mercury, but instead take them to a local hazardous waste collection site for proper disposal or recycling. Most types of consumer batteries are accepted at local hardware stores (or Target or Wal-Mart) for disposal and recycling at no charge. Seriously, a few minutes of your time here can make a significant impact on the environment.

Cadmium

Cadmium is also a hazardous element. Don't buy nickel cadmium (NiCd, NiCad) batteries, even at a surplus sale. Nickel-metal hydride (NiMH) batteries are a superior replacement, in several ways.

Take items containing cadmium to a local hazardous waste collection site for proper disposal. Again, many local retail stores accept batteries for disposal at no charge.

Purchasing Safer Parts Labeled RoHS

The European Union has a regulatory initiative called RoHS (Restriction of Hazardous Substances). This initiative is also being adopted in various forms by states and countries throughout the world. The purpose is to reduce the usage of certain harmful elements and compounds. Manufacturers that comply with the requirements can label their product RoHS.

This initiative is being adopted broadly across the electronics industry. In particular, you'll notice seemingly identical components with part numbers that differ by only a single digit or letter. The difference is usually that the newer part has either been certified or modified to be RoHS-compliant.

Ironically, rather than leading to increased costs, RoHS parts are often slightly less expensive. I don't know whether this is due to the reduced disposal costs related to the less-hazardous waste, or whether the remaining limited supply of the non–RoHS parts is being demanded by downstream manufacturers that specified the old part number in their products.

In any case, RoHS is good for you because you get the same great functionality with less nastiness. And, it's good for the environment.

Shocking

Electricity is the lifeblood of a robot. Too much electricity or its passage through a vulnerable location can be harmful to the robot as well as the designer.

AC vs. DC

Billions of AC (Alternating Current) appliances are used safely everyday. However, those appliances were designed by people with more experience and education than the ordinary hobbyist has.

Alternating current itself isn't the problem; it's the high voltage and never-ending current available from the outlet. As such, this book avoids projects related to AC.

Instead, stick to low-voltage DC (Direct Current) applications. In fact, all of my robots run from standard consumer batteries. Although a capacitor charged by a pair of 9-volt batteries can still wake you up, and obviously 12-volt car batteries can kill under the wrong conditions, the overall risks are dramatically reduced in comparison to the household outlet.

Using Rechargeable Batteries and Professional Transformers

Rechargeable batteries have become very practical in recent years, not only from an environmental standpoint, but also financially. Specially designed rechargeable lithium batteries and nickel-metal hydride (NiMH) batteries are readily available.

Beyond safety, an advantage of using batteries is that the robot can roam freely. Tethers (power lines or other cables) tend to get tangled and confine the device to a clumsy, short range. Inevitably, either you'll end up tripping over the lines, or they'll get jammed in the robot's wheels.

If you need steady, long-term power, then purchase a voltage-adjustable DC power supply (see Figure 3-6). Although the power supplies connect to AC, these "wall warts" were designed by professionals and usually have built-in thermal and current overload protection inherent to their DC voltage regulators. In short, they're usually safer than the converters you could make on your own.

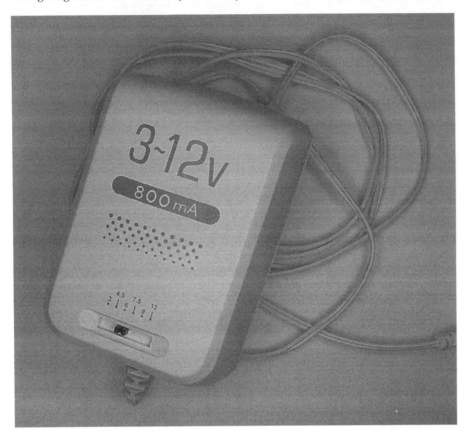

Figure 3-6. An AC-to-DC transformer with adjustable voltages from 3 volts to 12 volts

Connecting Through Circuit Breakers and GFCI Outlets

Now's a good time to check your house's fuse box to see if the previous owner jammed pennies into any of the fuse holes.

With power tools and electronic experiments, it's better to run them through an outlet strip with a built-in power switch and circuit breaker (see Figure 3-7). That way, even if the circuit breaker fails to trip, you can quickly cut power without having to touch the rampaging device.

Figure 3-7. A circuit breaker built into an outlet strip

GFCI (Ground Fault Circuit Interrupter) outlets are often found in bathrooms and kitchens. Unlike circuit breakers that detect too much total power, GFCI outlets disable power when not all of the electricity being sent out from the outlet is returning. This is more likely in wet conditions, where the water provides an electrical path from the device to your body. Like circuit breakers, GFCI outlets can be lifesavers.

Another place to consider a fuse or circuit breaker is on the robot itself. The portions of the circuit with regulated power go through a voltage regulator chip. So, check their datasheets to make sure your regulator chips have built-in thermal and current overload mechanisms (most do).

For circuits on the robot that connect directly to the battery, such as the motors, use a fuse or circuit breaker to prevent damage or fire.

PPTC (Polymeric Positive Temperature Coefficient) switches (see Figure 3-8) resist power flow when overheated by too much current. A few seconds after the fault is corrected, they cool down and automatically reconnect the power. They're lightweight, inexpensive, and can be placed deep within a robot since the user doesn't need to press a button to reset the circuit breaker.

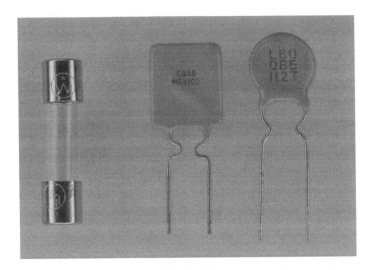

Figure 3-8. A classic single-use fuse (left) *versus PPTC self-resetting circuit protection devices* (right)

Saving the Ground Prong

Never cut off the third prong from a power cord (see Figure 3-9). The grounding prong is there to protect you from shocks in the event that a device's internal power wire comes loose and touches a metal portion of the case.

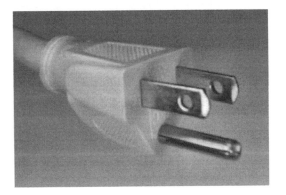

Figure 3-9. Grounded three-prong plug

With the advent of the third prong, the metal case can safely dispose of the electricity back into the outlet instead of into the person touching the device.

- If you have access to the proper three-prong outlet but have an inadequate reach, use a three-prong heavy-duty extension cord.

- If you have the proper connection but not enough outlets, use an outlet strip.

- If you don't have a working three-prong outlet, have a licensed electrician install one. A trip to the hospital is going to be a lot more expensive.

Rooms with just a few two-prong outlets are becoming a thing of the past. Not only did such conditions become fire hazards as people added on "octopus" adapters, but also, buyers started paying attention to electrical details when purchasing a home or facility. Thanks to changes in local electrical codes and ordinances, these issues usually aren't present in newer homes.

Disconnecting Power

Always physically disconnect power from the robot's circuits before working on it. On larger robots, not only should the batteries be disconnected, but they also should be literally removed from the robot during maintenance. This is safer for the builder and it prevents physical damage to power sources. Either way, use test probes to ensure no power remains.

Use a high-wattage resistor (or a rubber-handled screwdriver if you're desperate) to discharge large capacitors, as they may continue to store enough power to be harmful even after the primary power source is removed from the circuit. Large, charged capacitors are one of the reasons that television sets and computer power supplies can be so dangerous to service.

Never touch a live circuit with **both** hands—you want to avoid creating a path through your heart. You should also wear rubber-soled or other insulating-soled shoes. An electrical path from a hand through your chest and out a foot can be deadly.

Ground paths work because the electricity makes its way through the path of least resistance. If the electricity finds a low-resistance (think "metal") route directly to ground, most or all of the electricity is going to use that path rather than your body.

One last point: human skin is much more conductive when wet. Don't service your robot or anything electronic if you or the circuits are moistened. That includes rain or sweaty hands (gross!).

Steering Clear of Dangerous Robots

We've got enough problems in this world without people creating deadly robots. Cutting tools, spikes, hammers, projectiles, and spinning masses all seem like a pretty bad idea on something you're going to debug. "Oops! Sorry about your arm. I guess I've got those wires backwards."

Sizing Up Motors

Consider the total size of your robot and the power of the motors needed. Even if intended for good purposes, moderate-sized motors can produce significant force. Pick up a copy of any industrial-robot trade magazine and you'll see they're full of advertisements for laser beam screens and other safety devices that immediately disconnect the power to robots when humans (or materials) get too close. Wonder why?

Motors and power components tend to get hot during use. Think about the amount of electrical work being performed by each piece and the amount of current it is receiving. Every electronic or mechanical part wastes a portion of the power it receives as heat. The more power something receives, the more total heat it's likely to generate.

Lighting Up

A vividly lit area is a joy to work in. Additionally, bright lighting makes it easier to spot mistakes, especially in circuit boards. If the workpiece is easy to see, it reduces the likelihood of leaning way into the piece or squinting.

Whenever possible, purchase fluorescent lights (see Figure 3-10). Not only are they energy efficient, but they run cooler. (Hmm, are those two factors related?) A nice desk-mounted adjustable table lamp is a must.

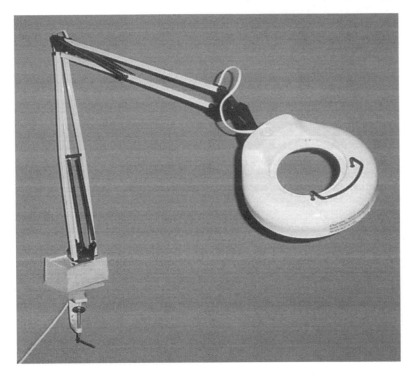

Figure 3-10. *Desktop adjustable lamp with fluorescent bulb*

Staying Rested and Level-Headed

Fatigue and frustration can cost you and your robot. Plan ahead to finish your robot well before a competition. Those "all nighters" should be a source of shame, not of pride, little grasshopper.

Relax, take breaks, and enjoy your hobby.

■ ■ ■

CHAPTER 4

Digital Multimeter

We're still covering basic prerequisites to building a robot, such as safety and where to buy parts. In this chapter, you're going to learn about a vital piece of measurement equipment that every robot builder has by their side, the digital multimeter. Multimeter features are broken into groups: must-have, nice-to-have, and optional. The chapter concludes with an analysis of three multimeters.

A multimeter is a required tool for robot building. You will need a multimeter to perform the experiments and build the projects in the chapters that follow. (See Figure 4-1 for an example of a multimeter.)

With a multimeter, you can:

- determine if an unexpected amount (too much or too little) of power is being used

- determine if a part is damaged or worn out

- determine what type of part something is

- determine the value (electrical denomination) of a part

- manually read sensors and chips to aid designing and debugging

The capabilities of digital multimeters (also called DMMs) have rocketed while prices have dropped. A perfectly acceptable digital multimeter can be had for under $20. A really great digital multimeter can be had for $150.

What follows are brief descriptions of the features available on multimeters. Don't worry too much about what the fancy symbols (μ,Ω) stand for, as they're written that way so that they'll match the catalogs and advertisements.

If this information seems overwhelming to you, just buy (or borrow) any cheap, digital multimeter until you've learned enough to make a more educated purchase.

Must-Have Features

Here are the features your multimeter must have:

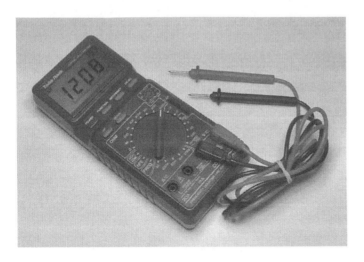

Figure 4-1. Digital multimeter with test probes

Digital

Digital meters display measured values on an LCD (liquid-crystal display) similar to a calculator (see Figure 4-2). No guessing or interpretation is needed. Analog meters have a needle that swings back and forth, with line markings underneath (see Figure 4-3). Because digital meters are so easy to read and so inexpensive, don't use analog.

Figure 4-2. LCD of a digital multimeter

Digits

3½ digits means that numbers up to 1999 can be displayed (with a floating decimal point). 3 ¾ digits means that numbers up to 4999 can be displayed. 4 digits means that numbers up to 9999 can be displayed. In practice, 3½ digits are all that's needed. Every digital multimeter meets this requirement.

DC Voltage

Measured in volts, DC voltage indicates how much pressure or force the electricity has. A range of 0.2 V (200 mV) to 48 V is usually all that's needed for tabletop robots. Every basic multimeter meets this requirement.

Figure 4-3. Needle display of an old-fashioned analog multimeter

DC Current

Measured in amps, DC current indicates how many electrons are speeding by per second. A range of 0.0002 A (200 µA) to 2 A is usually all that's needed. Every basic multimeter meets this requirement.

Resistance

Measured in ohms, resistance indicates how much something opposes electricity going through it. A range of 1 Ω to 2,000,000 Ω (2 MΩ) is usually all that's needed. Every basic multimeter meets this requirement.

Probes or Leads

The meter should come with the cables (see Figure 4-4) needed to connect it to the parts to test. Every basic multimeter meets this requirement. Ironically, really expensive pieces of equipment, such as many oscilloscopes, require probes that are sold separately.

Overload/Fuse Protection

Almost every multimeter includes protection to prevent permanent damage to the device if too much voltage or current is applied to the probes. UL (Underwriters Laboratory) Listing mark or CE (Conformité Européenne) marking is a good sign (see Figure 4-5). However, be aware that despite protection on the probe inputs, many meters are still vulnerable to damage through their transistor, capacitor, or data ports.

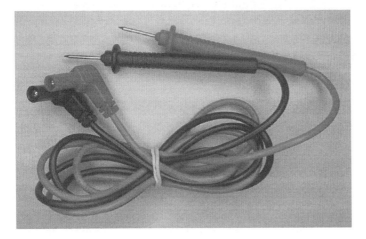

Figure 4-4. Test probes or test leads

Figure 4-5. Underwriters Laboratory listing mark and Conformité Européenne marking

Nice-To-Have Features

Here are features that are worth paying extra for, if you can afford to do so:

Capacitance

Measured in farads, capacitance indicates the number of electrons the multimeter can store. A range of 0.000000000020 f (20 pF) to 0.01 F (10,000 μF) is desirable. Many multimeters have this feature, but the range is usually less broad.

Diode

Measured in volts or millivolts, diode test mode indicates how much electrical pressure is required to turn on a semiconductor. This is an important feature because it can help classify different diode types and test and identify transistors. It can even light up LEDs. Most multimeters have this feature.

Continuity

Measured in ohms, continuity indicates whether an electrical connection exists between two points. Many multimeters have this feature, which usually includes an audible beep so that you don't need to look at the display to see when something is connected.

If an audible continuity feature doesn't exist on your multimeter, you can use the resistance setting instead, although you'll need to look at the display rather than listen for a beep.

Frequency

Measured in hertz, frequency indicates how many times something is occurring per second. A range of 0.1 Hz to 50,000,000 Hz (50 MHz) is desirable (see Figure 4-6). If the meter has a frequency function, get one that at least measures up to 45,000 Hz (45 kHz). Some multimeters have this feature, but the range is usually less broad.

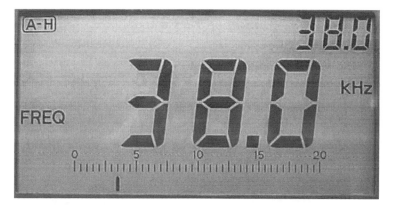

Figure 4-6. Meter displaying 38-kHz frequency measurement

Duty Cycle

Measured in percentages, duty cycle indicates how often a measurement is high as opposed to how often a measurement is low. This turns out to be an important measurement in robotics, as it is the key to PWM (pulse-width modulation). Only some multimeters have this feature, which often appears in frequency mode.

37

Autoranging

Normally a user must manually dial the meter to select the expected maximum value to be measured (see Figure 4-7). Autoranging automatically determines the range and subsequently bumps it up or down as necessary, which is nice. Autoranging can be annoying if the measurement is occurring on the border between two ranges, because the device will keep switching between the modes unless the multimeter also has some sort of range-hold button. Only the mid-range and high-end multimeters have the autoranging feature, which you can easily identify by uncluttered dials (see Figure 4-8).

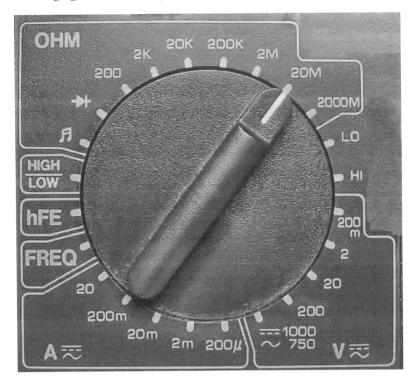

Figure 4-7. Dial with groups of manual range settings

Auto Power Off

It's common to forget to turn off the multimeter as your mind considers the task at hand. I'm often surprised to see the on switch still engaged when I'm putting my meter away. Luckily for the battery, my meter has auto power off. This feature can be annoying if it shuts off after too short of a delay, but most meters won't turn off if the measurement value changes enough.

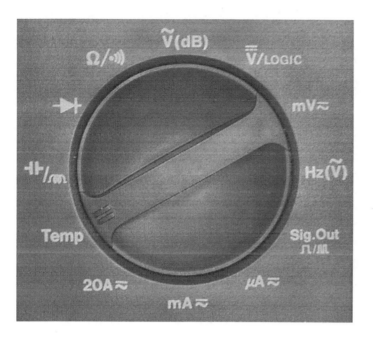

Figure 4-8. Dial simplified because of autoranging

Transistor

A transistor mode measures the h_{FE} (or β), which indicates the amount of amplification or gain of a transistor. The bipolar type of *npn* or *pnp* is usually determined by the user inserting the transistor into different socket holes (see Figure 4-9). You can use the multimeter's diode feature to determine bipolar transistor types if the multimeter doesn't have this transistor-test feature. See Chapter 16 for detailed steps on testing with a transistor socket or diode feature.

Dual Display

A dual display includes a small, second set of digits in a corner of the display so that other measurements or calculations can be displayed at the same time as the ongoing value. This is almost a requirement for maximum, minimum, and the other calculated features, since the ongoing value is otherwise not displayed. Many meters have this feature.

Maximum

A maximum mode displays the maximum value measured. This is actually a nice feature to test that a part isn't ever exceeding a specified range. While the meter continuously measures, you can exercise the various parts of a circuit, pausing every so often to view the maximum value read by the meter. This way you don't need to watch the display all the time. Many multimeters have this feature.

Figure 4-9. Transistor test socket

Minimum

A minimum mode displays the minimum value measured. See the Maximum feature, previously described. Many multimeters have this feature.

Stand

Most meters have a foldout piece to prop the meter up at an angle on the desktop (see Figure 4-10). This makes it easy to read the display while working on the robot.

Optional Features

Here are some bonus features that are available on some multimeters, but not absolutely necessary to have:

Inductance

Measured in henries, inductance indicates the amount of opposition to changes in electrical flow. Very few multimeters have this feature; otherwise, it would have made the nice-to-have list.

Figure 4-10. Multimeter held at readable angle by built-in stand

RS-232/USB Data Interface

A data interface (see Figure 4-11) communicates measurements to a personal computer or external device. This can be very useful for generating test logs. However, since the data from a multimeter is updated only a few times per second, this feature can't be used to make a multimeter into a true oscilloscope.

Figure 4-11. Connecting a multimeter to a personal computer with RS-232 DB9 (left) *or optical USB* (right)

Check to see if the computer software is included. If available separately, consider purchasing the software at the same time as the multimeter, just in case the software becomes unavailable when that multimeter model is discontinued.

Only some multimeters have the data interface feature.

Scope

A scope mode graphically plots measured values over a period of time. This can be an extremely useful feature for examining the quality and grouping of data pulses and timing signals. Unfortunately, the resolution and maximum speed limit of multimeter-based scopes is rather limited at this time. A true, high-speed oscilloscope with a generous display is a different beast. Few multimeters have a scope feature, and their price is greatly increased.

Backlight

A backlight lights up the meter's display from behind. Useful at night or in dimly lit areas. When turned on, the meter's battery drains much faster and some units can emit a high-pitched whine detectable by people with sensitive ears. Mainly higher-end or graphic-intensive units have backlighting.

Stopwatch/Single Pulse Width

A stopwatch measures the time between events. It can be useful for checking circuit timing or servo commands. Few multimeters have this feature.

Temperature

Measured in degrees Celsius or degrees Fahrenheit, a temperature mode indicates how hot or cold something is. It could be useful to answer the age-old question "Does this feel like it's getting hot to you?" Only some multimeters have this feature.

Sound

Measured in decibels, a sound mode indicates how loud or quiet something is. It could be useful for motor, speaker, or microphone volume testing. Few multimeters have this feature.

Count

A counter measures the number of times something occurs, regardless of length of time. Many multimeters have this feature.

Bar Graph

Digital meters don't react instantly to changes in measured values. Instead, they average their readings over a short period of time and update the display only a couple of times per second (analog-nostalgic supporters point to this weakness). So, some digital multimeters supplement their display with a bar graph, which is a rapidly updating single-axis line (see Figure 4-12).

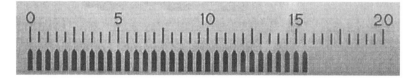

Figure 4-12. Digital bar graph allows DMMs to approach responsiveness of analog meters

Data Hold

Data hold prevents the screen from changing from the currently displayed value. Most meters continue to display the current measured value but place the held value somewhere else on the screen. Many multimeters have this feature.

Data Auto

A data-auto mode periodically moves the measured value to the smaller portion of the dual display. This makes it clear when the ongoing value is changing, since the small and large display won't have the same value for a few seconds.

High/Low/Logic

A logic mode interprets the DC voltage measurement as a logical signal, indicating low, high, or an improper value in between (see Figure 4-13). It's better to do this in your head using the meter's voltage mode. Depending on the parts you choose, the robot's chips may accept a certain voltage as "high" that the meter may consider "low." This is especially likely with the recent advent of low-voltage chips. Most multimeters have this logic mode feature.

Figure 4-13. Meter transitioning through logic states

Memory

Similar to the memory feature available on most calculators, memory mode on a multimeter can store one or more measured values. When only a single value is frozen and stored elsewhere on the display, this feature is simply another name for data hold. Some multimeters have a multi-memory feature, but it's not terribly useful except in graphic scopes.

Relative

A relative mode shows the difference between the last value measured and the current value. This shows the change in value, rather than the absolute value. Some multimeters have this feature.

Offset

An offset mode shows the difference between the value stored in memory and the current value being measured. Some multimeters have this feature.

Limit Testing/Compare

A limit mode displays whether the measured value exceeds a specified maximum or minimum value stored in memory. Some multimeters have this feature.

Holster or Rubber Boot

A rubber boot (see Figure 4-14) protects the meter from scuffs and bumps that might otherwise damage or crack the meter's primary case. The meter is almost always operated with the boot installed, unless space is a serious issue.

Figure 4-14. Rubber boot (edge cover) for meter

If a rubber boot is available but not included with the meter, it might be best to purchase the boot at the same time as the meter. The boot may no longer be available when the meter is discontinued.
Most multimeters have a boot available.

AC Features

Unlike DC (Direct Current) that comes from a battery, AC (Alternating Current) comes from a standard household outlet. Because of the danger from the higher voltage and current capacity of household outlets, this book only involves DC.

AC Voltage

Measured in volts, AC voltage indicates how much peak-to-peak pressure or force the electricity has. Every basic multimeter has this feature.

True RMS

True RMS accurately measures average AC voltage despite disturbances and fluctuations (noise) commonly present in household and industrial power. Many multimeters now have this feature.

AC Current

Measured in amperes, AC current indicates how many electrons are speeding back and forth per second. Every basic multimeter has this feature.

Obtaining Hook Probe Adaptors

The standard test leads that come with most multimeters are appropriate for probing circuit boards and briefly touching wires or connectors.

Hook adaptors (see Figure 4-15) and alligator clips are available that slide over each probe and clip to the circuit being tested, resulting in hands-free connections to jumper wires and IC pins. The hook adaptor tends to be preferable for most low-voltage digital circuits.

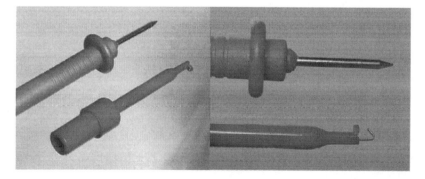

Figure 4-15. Hook adaptor for standard probe

A pair of hooks can be more perilous in that the multimeter becomes physically attached to the circuit or test points. The hooks make it more difficult to suddenly withdraw the leads in the event of high voltage or other error.

On the other hand, a single hook connected to ground can actually be safer than no hooks at all. This allows the technician to hold only a single, hookless probe, making a pathway across the heart less inviting and allowing the technician to concentrate on a single point.

Because hook probes are referred to extensively throughout this book, it would be helpful for you to purchase a pair (see Table 4-1).

Table 4-1. *Test Hook Adaptors*

Supplier	Part Number	Price	Color
MPJA.com	7161-MI	$0.50	1 red
MPJA.com	7163-MI	$0.50	1 black
Radio Shack	270-334	$3.49	(2) 1 black and 1 red

Comparing Actual Multimeters

Described in this section are various advertised specifications for three digital multimeters. Don't expect to buy these exact models, because multimeter part numbers and branding are constantly changing. Instead, try to understand the specifications so that you can find an existing model that meets your needs.

I've deciphered the jargon and analyzed an inexpensive model, a moderately priced model, and a higher-end model. See if you can guess the prices for them.

Understanding the Features of a Low-End Multimeter

Figure 4-16 shows the absolutely cheapest meter I could find, the DT-830B. It appears to have several siblings with slightly rearranged cases and model numbers.

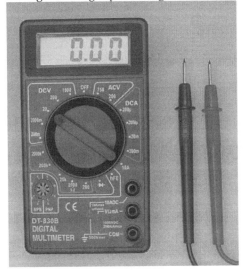

Figure 4-16. *An inexpensive digital multimeter*

Display: 1999	Means the same thing as 3½ digits.
DC Volts: 200mV	Lowest DC voltage setting is 200 millivolts. That's just fine. That means the meter's going to be able to measure voltage levels lower than 0.2 volts, as the lowest setting on the dial measures up to 0.2 volts.
±0.5% + 2	Indicates the lower setting ranges can be measured accurately within half a percent, and the last digit may be off by ±2 decimals. For example, with a reading of 1.05, the actual value may be as low as 1.05 - (1.05*0.005) - 0.02 = 1.024 or as high as 1.05 + (1.05*0.005) + 0.02 = 1.075. That's fine for amateur robotic work.
2/20/200/1000V	The upper ranges on the dial measure up to 1000 V. That's more than enough for household robots. All together, there are five ranges on the DC voltage section of the dial: 0.2, 2, 20, 200, 1000.
±0.8% + 2	Indicates the highest setting range (1000 V) can measure accurately within eight-tenths of a percent, with the last digit being off possibly by 2 decimals. That's acceptable for amateur robotic work. I question why you're measuring something that is 1000 volts!
AC Volts: 200/750V ±1.2% + 10	Indicates only two ranges for AC (household outlet) voltage. This feature isn't needed for battery-based robots. Notice that this meter's accuracy is much worse for AC.
DC Current: 200µ/2m/20mA /200mA±1.0% + 2	Lowest current setting is 200 microamps (0.0002 amps). That's just fine. That means the meter is going to be able to measure current levels lower than 0.0002 amps, as the lowest setting on the dial measures up to 0.0002 amps.
10A ±2% + 2	Most multimeters leap at some point between low-current measurement and high-current measurement. When you switch the meter to measure high current, you need to move the positive (red) test probe to the high-current socket. Internally, the high-current socket connects to a fuse with a different rating. The disappointing aspect about this meter is that it can only measure up to 200 mA in low-current mode. Somewhere up around 500 mA would be preferable. This means you'll need to use the less accurate (but otherwise capable) 10 A range for all measurements that are likely to be above 150 mA (so that you don't blow the 200 mA fuse).
Resistance: 200/2K/20K/200K/2M ±0.8%	Five ranges. Good minimum and maximum. The low end isn't indicating that it can't measure 1-ohm resistors. It means you can turn the dial to the 200-ohm setting for the best accuracy of measuring low-value resistors.
HFE: 1 ~ 1,000 Transistor Test	That's a nice feature. It can test the gain of transistors.
Diode Test	Good for testing LEDs.

The ad said this meter has a capacitance test and a back light, neither of which is true. But, you can determine that from just looking at the photograph. There is no capacitance mode on the dial and there is no button for a backlight.

There are some features that I'd miss if I had only this multimeter: continuity test with buzzer, capacitance, frequency, duty cycle, autoranging, auto power off, rubber boot, and built-in stand.

In person, I discovered this meter has a very cheap plastic case, the probes don't fit tightly in the sockets, the battery snaps are soldered to the PCB (removing/adding the battery can break the meter), and the 200 mA fuse is soldered to the board (significant work to replace when you eventually accidently test more than 200 mA). Yet, this is perfectly fine as a disposable meter or for students who plan to take only one electrical engineering course. You'll understand why I'm so forgiving when you read how little this digital multimeter costs.

Understanding the Features of a Mid-Range Multimeter

The VC97 Auto Range digital multimeter (see Figure 4-17) has all the features and more of the previously described multimeter.

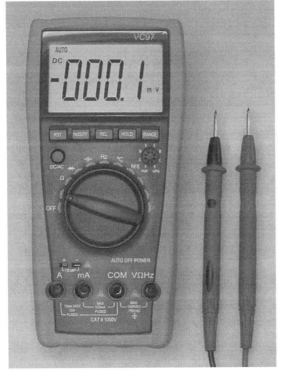

Figure 4-17. Moderately-priced digital multimeter

3¾ Digit	This meter can display numbers up to 3999.
Large display and units	Easier to read, particularly if the meter is off to the side of your work area. This meter also shows the units adjacent to the value on the display (mV, V, mA, A, µF, Ω, and so on) to indicate the mode and range. Nice touch.
Autoranging	This is an especially useful feature for resistance and capacitance if you're sorting a pile of components. I strongly recommend that you obtain an autoranging meter. They aren't that much more expensive than most manual-dial meters. This is the very best reason to step-up from the low-end meter.
Temperature measurement probe (-40°C to +1000°C) included	Some devices don't include the temperature probe, which could be difficult to obtain later. The temperature range is wonderfully broad, as is true with almost all meters that support temperature measurement.
Frequency/Duty Cycle	An important feature to have, especially if you're tuning object-detection circuits. The manufacturer says the meter can measure up to 30 MHz, which is much higher than most meters.
Capacitance	The meter tops out at 200 µF, which is a little lower than desired for electrolytic capacitors, but is perfectly acceptable for most capacitors.
Auto power off	This saves plenty of batteries.
500 mA low-current mode	This is a much more reasonable limit than the 200 mA limit in the previously discussed meter.
Continuity test	Beeps when a connection is made. This is very useful as it allows you to concentrate on examining the circuit you're probing, rather than constantly looking away at the multimeter display.
Rubber boot	Helps protect against breakage if you drop it.

The advertisement for this meter includes the amusing specification "Strong antimagnetic and anti-jamming performance." I have no idea what that means, but those sound like features I definitely want in my meter. ☺

In person, I found this meter to be well made and enjoyable to use. The test probes are higher quality than most. There are a number of features and modes that I haven't mentioned that are accessible via the soft buttons under the display. One quibble is that it doesn't have an off button. Instead, the dial must be turned to "off," which is located on the end of the dial rather than the middle.

The meter uses a pair of AAA batteries. Many meters are moving away from 9 V batteries to AA or AAA. This has an unfortunate consequence: those meters are unable to test blue and white LEDs in their diode test mode because over 3 V is required to do so.

Understanding the Features of a Higher-End Multimeter

The VA38 meter is shown in Figure 4-18. It has all of the features of both of the previously described multimeters and some additional plusses.

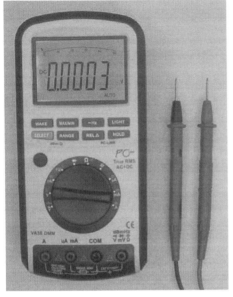

Figure 4-18. *Higher-end digital multimeter*

40,000 count display	The display has five digits, which is quite a lot. The high number of digits in the display suggests this meter is capable of higher accuracy and precision than lower-end meters.
DCV accuracy 0.03%	This is an order of magnitude more accurate than the least-expensive multimeter in this chapter, which was 0.5%. However, since the tolerance of most robot circuits is fairly rough and wide, the increased accuracy is really only necessary for professional designers.
True RMS	Accurately measures the voltage of alternating current even if the signal shape is a little odd. Not of much value in DC circuits unless it's going to be used to measure some input or output signal. In that case, an oscilloscope would be better.
50 segment bar display	I'm not sure this is valuable. I never use it.
Backlight	It has a beautiful bluish-white backlight. Although I rarely use a meter in the dark, it is nice to know that this meter has that capability should I need it.

9 V battery	The diode test lights up blue and white LEDs.
Stand-alone power button	You don't need to turn the dial to another mode to turn off the meter. I can set up the meter, power it off when I want to take a break, and then power it back on when I return without having to reselect the correct measurement mode.
Optical USB data output	This meter has a USB cable, unlike older multimeters that require a PC with a now-obsolete RS-232 port. The other end of the USB cable connects optically to the meter—which means the information is transmitted with light rather than an electrical connection. This avoids problems with the computer or household power contaminating the meter readings. The meter comes with the PC software, rather than being available separately for an additional cost. (Most commercial multimeter software is written only for Microsoft Windows. Keep that in mind if you use Linux or a Mac.)
Complete with integrated protective holster, zipper pouch, and high-quality test leads	It's important to check to see if these items are included. Some higher-end meters require you to purchase these items separately.

Interestingly, like most higher-end meters but unlike most mid-range meters, this doesn't include a transistor socket or temperature measurement. The more expensive meters focus on accuracy and precision (number of digits) instead of trying to be all-in-one tools. In fact, laboratory professionals often use highly accurate, highly specialized stand-alone tools (a voltmeter, an ammeter, an LCR meter, and so on) rather than combination multimeters.

Comparing Prices with Features

Here are the prices I paid for the digital multimeters, including shipping:

$6.50 - Low-end DT-830B

$32.00 - Mid-range VC97

$165.00 - Higher-end VA38

Honestly, $6.50 for a digital multimeter! The least expensive meter would be acceptable for someone on a budget or as a spare. Just don't expect it to last very long. It measures the most important attributes with reasonable accuracy, although you will miss capacitance and frequency measurement. Often times, low-end meters like this are given away for free with a certain-size order. Look for those deals before actually buying a cheap meter.

The mid-range meter includes almost everything you could ever want for amateur robotics. You may have to hunt around on eBay to find this price, or expect to pay closer to $50. If you can afford to do so, aim to purchase an autoranging meter with these types of features. It will significantly increase your productivity and satisfaction.

The higher-end meter is very accurate. It's definitely constructed out of higher-quality materials. However, the resolution and accuracy are wasted, since only rough values are necessary for building, testing, and debugging homemade robot circuits.

Even more expensive meters with (believe it or not) fewer features are available. Those ultra-high-end meters (> $1000) provide amazing resolution and accuracy at a steep price. For certain specialized tasks, these certified meters are indispensable. However, for most people, a moderately priced multimeter and moderately priced oscilloscope would be a better purchase.

Proceeding Without a Meter

It is imperative to obtain a digital multimeter before proceeding too much further into this book. Although it is possible to simply read about the experiments, you will receive a more effective education with first-hand experience. Nearly every electronic component described in later chapters is accompanied by a procedure for testing the part on your multimeter.

CHAPTER 5

■ ■ ■

Numbers and Units

Here is the last building block before you're introduced to the line-following robot. This chapter describes the numbering systems and abbreviations common in robotics. It's important to get at least a basic sense for these things, although you can always turn back to this chapter later if you run across something you don't understand.

Choosing the Metric System

Scientists use the metric system because it is well defined in universally constant ways and easily converts by multiplying and dividing by ten. As a robot scientist, you should use the metric system for your own work. This also permits you to be snobby towards those Neanderthals who still use the old-fashioned Imperial system.

This book uses the metric system except where a manufacturer specifically designs or specifies a part in a non-metric measurement. For example, if the manufacturer makes a board with holes spaced 0.1 inches apart, then that is how it is described. Although inches could easily be converted to metric, 2.54 millimeters isn't really the official specification for that board.

Another example: If a contest limits robots to 8½ by 11 inches, it's preferable to continue to communicate in those terms, as people in the United States readily understand that's the size of an ordinary piece of paper. The same audience doesn't immediately recognize those dimensions in metric, 21.59 by 27.94 centimeters. In addition, some numeric precision can be lost in the conversion between inches and centimeters.

Reducing Powers of a Thousand

Long numbers are difficult to read (see Figure 5-1). If a circuit calls for a component of the value 10000000, the reader may accidentally install something significantly higher or lower by merely miscounting the number of zeros.

To avoid errors, the number of digits in long numbers is usually reduced in a standardized way.

Figure 5-1. Quick! How large of a number? 158 million? 15 million? 1.5 million?

Table 5-1. Metric Powers of a Thousand

Amount	Multiplier	Prefix	Abbreviation
trillion	1,000,000,000,000	tera-	*uppercase* T
billion	1,000,000,000	giga-	*uppercase* G
million	1,000,000	mega-	*uppercase* M
thousand	1,000	kilo-	*lowercase* k
thousandth	0.001	milli-	*lowercase* m
millionth	0.000001	micro-	*Greek* μ or *lowercase* u
billionth	0.000000001	nano-	*lowercase* n
trillionth	0.000000000001	pico-	*lowercase* p

Referring to Table 5-1, instead of writing 10,000,000, it can be reduced to 10 M.

```
10,000,000 = 10 million = 10 mega = 10 M
```

Notice that the million multiplier has six zeros (see Table 5-1) and we removed six zeros from our original number. So, the M is just taking the place of the six zeros we chopped off.

If, for some reason, it is helpful to retain some of the zeros (such as for comparison's sake), a smaller multiplier can be used:

```
10,000,000 = 10,000 thousand = 10,000 kilo = 10,000 k
```

Notice that the thousand multiplier has three zeros (see Table 5-1) and we removed only three zeros from our original number. So, the k is just taking the place of the three zeros we chopped off.

A larger multiplier can be used, in which case the original number slides below the decimal point:

```
10,000,000 = 0.01 billion = 0.01 giga = 0.01 G
```

In each case, the actual value remained the same:

```
10,000,000 = 0.01 G = 10 M = 10,000 k
```

Usually the entire number is written out only if it helps make a point: "Install a 10,000,000-ohm resistor, not 10,000 ohm!"

Not only can the powers-of-a-thousand system reduce the number of digits, but also it can group parts together. 1200000, 32000, 13200 becomes 1.2 M, 32 k, and 13.2 k. This makes it easier to see that the last two components are similar because they both are in the "k" range.

Don't worry if this system seems confusing at first. It won't take long for you to pick it up.

M & m

There are two letter "m"s used as abbreviations. The million abbreviation is uppercase "M" (see Figure 5-2), the thousandths abbreviation is lowercase "m".

Figure 5-2. One million represented by 1 M

Be careful not to mix these up, because there's a huge difference in values:

```
1 M = 1,000,000,000 m
```

A sales representative sent me an e-mail asking how much power a specific wireless device transmitted through the antenna. I replied with an e-mail stating "600 mW" (that's 0.6 watts; one-hundredth of an ordinary 60-watt light bulb).

After a bit, it occurred to me there might be a miscommunication. I called the sales representative and asked what she told the customer, she replied "600 megawatts." Wow, that's ten million light bulbs.

Alternative for Greek Micro

One last comment on powers-of-a-thousand: The abbreviation for millionths is the Greek letter mu, μ. If "μ" is not available in a font, the letter "u" is often substituted (see Figure 5-3). For example: 10 u is the same as 10 μ (which is the same as 0.00001)

Figure 5-3. Some markings use the English letter "U" instead of the Greek letter "μ."

Abbreviating Units

Besides abbreviations for multipliers, there are also abbreviations for the units or types of measurements:

Table 5-2. Units Common in Robotics

Measurement	Units	Abbreviation	Usually Refers To
length or distance	meter	m	component dimensions, material thickness
resistance	ohm	Ω	resistors, motor coils
voltage	volt	V	batteries, motors, chips
current	ampere or amp	A	circuits, power supplies, motors
power	watt	W	circuits, motors
frequency	hertz	Hz	crystals, chips, signals
capacitance	farad	F	capacitors
inductance	henry	H	inductors
amplification	beta factor	h_{FE} or β	transistors
luminous intensity	candela	cd	LEDs
mass	gram	g	motors, batteries
torque	newton-meter	Nm	motors
capacity	amp-hour	Ah	batteries
temperature	Celsius	°C	chips, sensors, solder
rotational speed	revolution per minute	rpm	motors

Frequently, the multiplier (see Table 5-1) is combined with the units (see Table 5-2). For example, older personal computer processors are rated in MHz (megahertz). The M part represents millions (see Table 5-1), the Hz parts represents hertz (see Table 5-2).

Another ordinary example is millimeters, abbreviated mm. The first m represents thousandths; the second m represents meters. So, a millimeter is one-thousandth of a meter, or 0.001 meter.

Too Little

On most parts, the values and units are printed directly on the case (see Figure 5-4). For example, on a large motor, you might see "24-volt DC permanent magnet reversible motor, 0.5 amp no load, 8-ohm coil, Part #54321, manufactured December 6, 2001 by McCloskey and Son Corporation, Visit our Web site! Say, that reminds us of a funny story…"

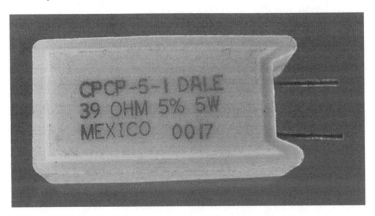

Figure 5-4. A part with plenty of room for a descriptive label

However, as part sizes shrink, less space is available to print the component values directly on the part. Manufacturers employ a few tricks to squeeze in the most vital information.

Guessing Missing Units

When specifying a value, normally the units must not be omitted. 200 doesn't mean much. Is that 200 Ω (ohms) or 200 V (volts) or 200 F (farads) or 200 A (amps)? I don't want to touch three out of four of those.

If the units are missing from a small part (see Figure 5-5), you can make an educated guess based on the type of part (see Table 5-3).

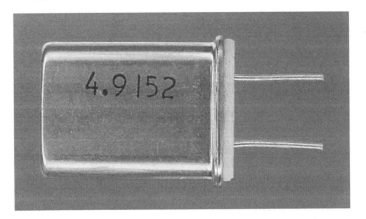

Figure 5-5. Missing multiplier and units (should be 4.9152 MHz)

Table 5-3. Missing Units

Type	Units
Battery	volts (V)
Large capacitor	microfarads (μF)
Small capacitor	picofarads (pF)
Crystal	megahertz (MHz)
Inductor	henrys (H)
Oscillator	megahertz (MHz)
Potentiometer	ohms (Ω)
Resistor	ohms (Ω)

Expanding from Three Digits

Here's a little trick: On some parts, not only are the units missing, but only three digits are printed (see Figure 5-6). The last digit indicates the number of zeros to tag onto the end of the first two digits.

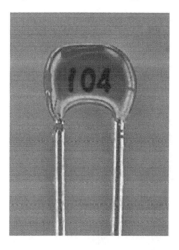

Figure 5-6. Not much room for a label (104 represents 100000 pF)

For example: 223 represents 22000, 501 represents 500, 475 represents 4700000. Any guesses as to what 100 represents? 10. (So, they usually just print 10.)

Converting Colors to Numbers

Not only are many parts small, but some are cylindrical too (see Figure 5-7). To overcome that printing challenge, color stripes indicate value (see Table 5-4).

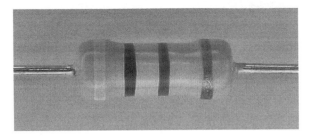

Figure 5-7. Color bands of yellow, violet, brown, and gold (470 at 5% Tolerance)

Table 5-4. Color Value Bands

Color	First Band	Second Band	Third Band
Black	0	0	× 1
Brown	1	1	× 10
Red	2	2	× 100
Orange	3	3	× 1000 *(kilo-)*
Yellow	4	4	× 10000
Green	5	5	× 100000
Blue	6	6	× 1000000 *(mega-)*
Violet	7	7	..
Gray	8	8	..
White	9	9	..

For example, a part with a yellow (4) stripe, a violet (7) stripe, and a brown (x 10) stripe would be 47 × 10 = 470. A part with red (2), red (2), red (× 100) would be 22 × 100 = 2200.

Looking at the color table (see Table 5-4), it may occur to you that on a small, cylindrical, poorly printed object, it may be quite difficult to distinguish red stripes from orange stripes or black stripes from brown stripes. You're correct—use good lighting or measure with a multimeter.

If the color table seems difficult to remember (the middle section is in rainbow order), a common compact cardboard color code calculator can come in handy (see Figure 5-8).

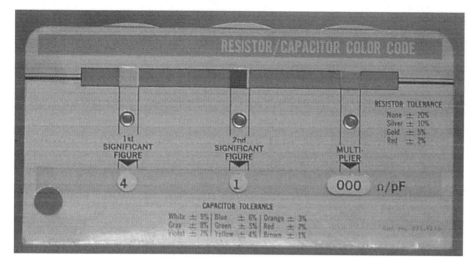

Figure 5-8. Turn the cardboard wheels to calculate color codes.

Although the calculator will remain useful for odd values, it turns out there are only a few popular values that you'll use on a regular basis. You'll quickly memorize these patterns: brown-black (10 something), red-red (22 something), and yellow-violet (47 something).

If the part has four color bands, the last indicates the tolerance (see Table 5-5).

Table 5-5. Color Tolerance Bands

Color	Tolerance
(none)	20%
Silver	10%
Gold	5%
Red	2%
Brown	1%

Tolerance refers to how far away the part may be from the specified value. A 5% (gold) tolerance on a 1000 value part means it could be as low as 950 and as high as 1050. A particular piece could be exactly 1000, but the manufacturer simply doesn't guarantee it.

There can be five or even six bands on some fancier parts. The additional bands can represent reliability, additional significant digits, or the amount of change with temperature. Most hobbyists are unlikely to encounter or need such parts.

Determining Component Values with a Multimeter

If a marking or color band doesn't immediately describe a value to you, there's no reason to waste time guessing or looking it up in a table. Simply connect the part to your multimeter! (Instructions on testing specific parts appear throughout coming chapters.)

Another reason for checking a part with a multimeter is that few parts match the printed value. In fact, a 10 µF capacitor could legitimately be 8 µF or even 18 µF (see Figure 5-9). Fortunately, most circuits tolerate a wide range.

Figure 5-9. *A multimeter shows the capacitor marked 10 µF is actually 11 µF*

An extra benefit of checking a part with a multimeter is the possibility of discovering a damaged part before soldering it into a robot. If the multimeter reads a really low or really high value, it suggests a bad part.

Base Subjects Covered

Thus far, this book has reviewed robot anatomy, construction attitude and approach, obtaining components, safety, multimeters, numbering, units, and labeling. All of these subjects arise during actual robot design and building, so it's advantageous to have had this background.

In the next chapter, your reading persistence pays off with the detailed introduction of a line-following robot.

CHAPTER 6

■ ■ ■

Robot Line-Following

Sandwich, the robot featured in this book, is a robot that follows lines (see Figure 6-1). It's a rewarding project, because you can quickly lay out different courses, obstacles, and tunnels, and your robot immediately entertains you without any reprogramming.

Figure 6-1. Sandwich, the line-following robot

A line-following robot usually contains the same building blocks that are universal to all robots. I have simplified Sandwich's line-following design to the point that only the most rudimentary forms of each module are necessary.

Even with a basic design, a decent robot still isn't particularly simple. There's a lot to learn and a lot to build. Only after understanding the individual components, circuits, and techniques will you be ready to combine them into a robot.

This chapter introduces the project goals. The following chapters walk you through component parts in detail. The line-following robot acts as a context for discussing many of the parts and circuits, but the part-specific information applies to all robots.

Defining the Course Conditions

By making life easy on the robot, we'll make life easy on ourselves. Since this is a controlled scientific experiment, there's nothing wrong with reducing the environmental factors or variables that the robot is required to deal with.

Surface Materials

The terrain must be flat and smooth, like a linoleum floor. Also acceptable is short, solid carpeting like commercial or non-patterned Berber loop-pile. Although softer flooring can reduce the robot's speed, the flooring is gentler on the robot's wheels and any parts that drag. On the other hand, sidewalk concrete quickly grinds down parts.

Do not permit obstacles, doors, or domesticated animals (including children) to interfere with the robot's path.

Course Lighting

Indoor lighting conditions without heavy shadows are essential. Although you can make a robot to handle both indoor and outdoor driving, you would need additional electronics.

Defining the Line

The width of the line to be followed should average from 1.8 cm to 2.54 cm (from ½ inch to an inch). The line must contrast well with the floor. Both the line and the floor should be solid colors, not patterns. In fact, solid white on solid black would make the robot happiest (see Figure 6-2). The line and floor must remain the same color throughout the course.

It doesn't matter what shade of floor you have because the robot is designed to follow either a darker line on a lighter floor or a lighter line on a darker floor.

Picking Line Marking Material

How should you make your line? Painting the line can work very well. With paint, there is a wide variety of colors and glosses to choose from and you can control the line width. Some long-term upkeep may be necessary, but generally a painted line tends to be very durable. However, painting entails preparation time and is permanent.

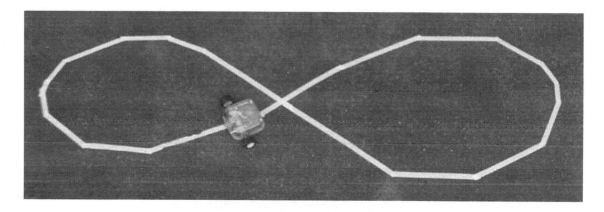

Figure 6-2. A course made with ordinary masking tape on a flat, dark surface

Alternatively, wide-head marker pens work well on poster board. Make sure the lines are wide enough and cover the background thoroughly. Spotty, faded, or broken lines can cause the robot to drive off course.

For household courses, most people prefer tape lines. You can create, adjust, and remove non-permanent tape courses quickly. Tape rolls are easily obtained and come in the desired range of widths. Glossy (shiny) white cloth tape or flat (non-shiny) black cloth tape provides the highest contrast and thus is easiest for the robot to follow. Ordinary semi translucent masking tape may not adequately cover the color and pattern of the floor underneath it.

Watch out for glossy dark materials. The shine reflects more light than you may realize, and it may not appear dark to the robot's sensors.

Tape lines can leave a sticky residue when removed. This is especially true in hot conditions or if the tape remains in place for too long. Blue masking tape (see Figure 6-3) or other low-adhesion varieties are much cleaner than ordinary off-white masking tape. For this reason, I use blue masking tape most often.

Warning: A mother contacted me regarding the difficulty of removing old tape from new hardwood flooring. She recommended the book include a warning. Now it does.

- Avoid walking on tape, because it grinds it into the floor.

- Test tape in a discreet location to ensure you can remove it without residue.

- Don't allow tape to remain in place more than a week (or whatever the manufacturer recommends).

An interesting aspect of blue masking tape is that it isn't quite light and it isn't quite dark. The upside to this is that blue masking tape can be followed as a light line when placed on a dark background and a dark line when placed on a light background. The downside is that the maximum contrast is less than an actual white or black line.

There are two disadvantages to blue masking tape. First, the blue color reflects very little infrared, and therefore is not suitable for use as a light line for robots with infrared emitters. Second, unless firmly applied, blue tape can catch on the robot and get pulled up. Very-low-adhesion tape often suffers from this problem.

Figure 6-3. Ordinary off-white masking tape (bottom) *and blue painter's masking tape* (top)

Curving and Crossing Lines

Straightaways are easy for any properly operating line follower. Sharp turns, however, can derail even a competent robot.

With reasonable brains and an array of sensors or a vision system, you could build a line-following robot to handle turns 45° or greater and also broken lines (see Figure 6-4). However, for the example robot, limit turn angles to 22.5° or less. Lines should always be contiguous.

Figure 6-4. Unacceptably sharp turns: (left to right) *135°, 90°, and 45°.* (far right) *broken line*

Given a series of smaller turns over a longer distance, you can guide the robot in any direction (see Figure 6-5).

Figure 6-5. Acceptable 180° turn made gradually from 22.5° segments

The better the surface contrast and the slower the robot's pace, the steeper the turns the robot can perform. Feel free to experiment with increasingly difficult arrangements. After all, the worst thing that can happen is that the robot wanders away.

Many designers fret over line crossings or line splits in the course (see Figure 6-6). It's possible for some robots to head between the lines as the brightness averages out. But, the robot circuit presented in this book isn't confused by such intersections, and quickly settles into one path choice or the other.

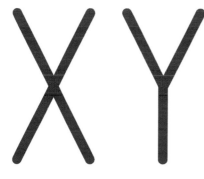

Figure 6-6. A crossing and a split

It's fun to watch the robot choose between equally split forks in the road. It doesn't always pick the same route. In fact, on multiline crossings, I've seen the robot take a wide turn and head off in the most remote direction. Perhaps it's just bored, but usually a shadow or bad hop explains the decision.

Summarizing Course Conditions

In summary, the Sandwich robot follows a moderately thick, easy-to-see line around an obstacle-free flat floor. The course should feature gradual turns on a high-contrast surface illuminated evenly by indoor lighting.

Picking the Robot's Size

It would be cute to build a really tiny robot. Maybe one that fits into the palm of your hand (see Figure 6-7). Unfortunately, very small robots are difficult to assemble and work on. Small details require steady hands, patience, and experience. Like a miniature dollhouse, all of the parts on a small robot need to be equally small. This limits part choices and options.

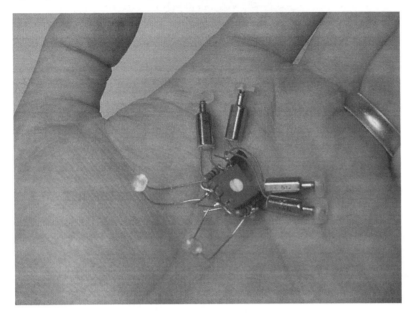

Figure 6-7. A palm-sized line-following robot

At the other extreme, large robots are usually heavy, requiring larger motors to move. Large motors need a lot of power, which leads to a bigger battery. To support all the weight, the body must be constructed of stronger materials, which are harder to cut and drill.

Perhaps the best size for an amateur robot is around the size of a lunchbox. Plenty of parts fit those dimensions, standard consumer batteries provide enough power, and plastics and soft metals have enough strength for the forces exerted. Topping it all off, lunchbox-size robots fit well within the home.

This is not to say you'll forever be stuck crafting small creatures. With the successful completion of a few moderate designs, you can expand your work into the dimensions you desire. At that point, you'll already have experience with all of the robotic fundamentals, allowing you to concentrate on the unique obstacles that occur with other proportions.

Seeing Sandwich

There are many possible designs for a line-following robot. I'm presenting Sandwich's design because it contains the fewest and simplest parts possible, while still being cool and capable.

All of the components are currently being produced, so you don't have to use salvage. However, you can choose to make a couple of the pieces yourself from raw materials.

This robot is named Sandwich because its body is based on a sandwich container. Even if you choose a different shape, you can still apply the same circuit and techniques. Depending on the motors and containers you have lying around, your robot may turn out looking very different but with approximately the same line-following capabilities.

Examining Sandwich

At first glance, Sandwich may appear to be a very complicated robot (see Figure 6-8). That's exactly the impression you want people to have. Blinking lights, colorful wires, production-quality wheels, metal screws, and a rounded case all add sophistication without adding much real work. Half of the battle is showmanship.

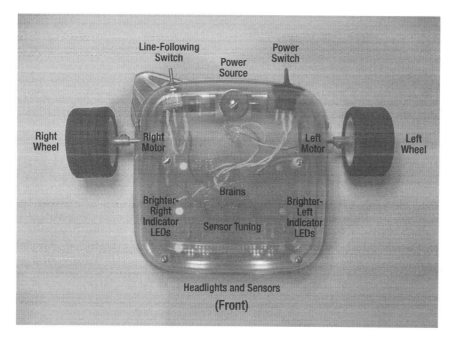

Figure 6-8. Overhead view of Sandwich, a line-following robot

Don't be fooled or overwhelmed by it. This robot breaks down into smaller modules that are easily recreated. The next sections of this chapter describe the modules and switch functions.

Line-Following Switch

At the rear of the robot is a toggle switch (see Figure 6-9). This switch has three positions: left, center, and right.

Figure 6-9. Rear-mounted line-following toggle switch in center (motors off) position

When the switch is in the left position, the left motor is connected to the left sensors and the right motor is connected to the right sensors. This allows the robot to follow dark-colored lines. When the switch is in the right position, the motor wires are crossed. The left motor is connected to the right sensors and the right motor is connected to the left sensors. This allows the robot to follow light-colored lines.

Believe it or not, switching the motor connections is all that it takes to follow different line brightnesses. No fancy algorithms or circuitry!

Power Source and Power Switch

Also at the rear of the robot is a battery and a power switch (see Figure 6-10). The battery is an ordinary 9 V consumer battery.

Figure 6-10. Rear-mounted power switch (left) and battery (right)

Sensors and Headlights

Underneath the front of the robot are two headlights and four brightness sensors (see Figure 6-11). The headlights allow the robot to drive in darkness. By lighting the floor evenly, the headlights help prevent the robot from thinking a shadow is a dark line.

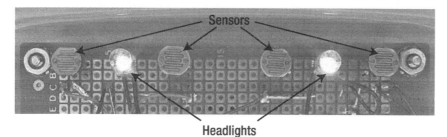

Figure 6-11. Front-mounted sensors and headlights

The four sensors are arranged in pairs: two sensors for the left side and two sensors for the right side. Technically, each side only requires a single sensor, but the leftmost and rightmost sensors act as safety nets in case the line sneaks by the middle sensors on a sharp turn.

Placing the Robot on the Center of the Line

When positioning the robot, the sensors should be centered over the line (see Figure 6-12). This way, the amount of light received is equally balanced between the left and right pairs of sensors.

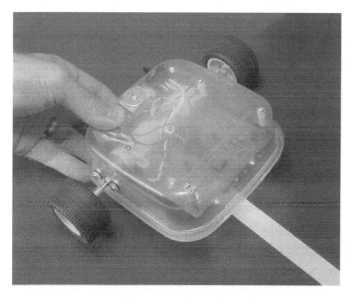

Figure 6-12. Placing the robot with sensors centered on the line

When the robot detects an imbalance of brightness, it knows it's off center. It then applies power to either the left or right motor to turn itself until the brightness is balanced again.

Adjusting Sensor Balance

At the front of the robot is a small hole leading to a sensor adjustment dial (see Figure 6-13). A tiny screwdriver fits into the hole to turn the dial.

Figure 6-13. *Front-mounted sensor adjustment dial*

There are a number of reasons why a sensor adjustment dial is necessary. First, it would be very difficult to find four perfectly matched brightness sensors. Second, during soldering, one sensor is inevitably placed a little bit higher than another. Third, as the parts age or become soiled with dirt or dust, they may no longer provide the same sensitivity that they did originally.

With the adjustment dial, you can balance the left pair of sensors against the right pair. Since adjustments need to be made when the robot is already in place on a track, the dial must be accessible with the robot assembled. However, the dial needs to be recessed so it isn't nudged accidentally during handling. An internally mounted dial with an access hole ends up being the solution.

Fine-tuning dials are wise features to have.

Brighter-Side Indicators

If the robot isn't following a line or otherwise isn't responding correctly, it's important to have some indication of what the robot thinks it is seeing. Also, it would be impossible to properly adjust the sensor balance dial without some feedback from the robot as to which pair of sensors was seeing more light.

Three yellow LEDs light up on the right side when the right sensors see more brightness than the left sensors. Conversely, three green LEDs light up on the left side when the left sensors see more brightness (see Figure 6-14). When completely balanced, both sets of LEDs light up or blink off and on.

Figure 6-14. Brighter-left indicator LEDs as seen from left-side of robot

Two different colors were chosen so that you can tell which side is lit up even in the dark when the position of the body isn't visible. Three LEDs are used so that the indication is visible from any angle.

The Brains

This robot isn't exactly the smartest cookie in the package. It simply turns on a motor and indicator light if one set of sensors is brighter, or turns on the other motor and indicator light if the other set of sensors is brighter.

To accomplish this feat of genius, a chip called a comparator is used (see Figure 6-15). It compares two signals and flips a switch one way or another. That's it.

Figure 6-15. Comparator (center) flanked by two transistor switches (left and right)

Unfortunately, a motor and three lights consume more power than the comparator chip can provide. So, transistors provide power to each side of the robot as the comparator directs.

The Muscle

The motors are fixed in a forward position without the ability to swivel for steering. Tiny steering columns are tricky to make at home and difficult to obtain in the sizes desired for a robot.

However, the robot can control its direction by varying the amount of power applied to each motor. Power to both motors drives the robot forward. Power only to the left motor causes the robot to turn right, pivoting around the right wheel. Power only to the right motor causes the robot to turn left, pivoting around the left wheel.

Sandwich has two wheels. If the robot had four wheels, it would be very difficult for it to pivot. Mainly the robot would go straight. On the occasions that it did turn, it would make a horrible vibrating noise as one pair of wheels was dragged horizontally rather than in the forward direction they want to roll.

There are other wheel arrangements possible, such as a single caster or ball roller on the front or rear, making a three-wheel robot. There are even omni-directional wheels available, containing multiple sets of perpendicular rollers. Although not a critical factor for small, lightweight robots, wheel formation becomes more significant with heavier or faster robots.

Mounting the two wheels toward the rear causes the front lip of the robot to drag on the ground. This isn't a big problem, although the plastic does scuff up a bit. Generally the plastic slides quite well in any direction. This makes for reasonably smooth forward movement and agile turning.

Sometimes the front of Sandwich skips and hops due to uneven or gritty terrain. With fresh batteries and tall wheels, Sandwich occasionally stands up on its rear and pops a wheelie! Even though that's a blast to watch, it causes the robot to momentarily lose sight of the line, sometimes causing it to head off course.

Fitting and Changing Wheels

LEGO makes fantastic wheels. A wide variety of shapes, styles, and sizes are available from LEGO kits in retail stores, from online auctions, or from the LEGO Shop At Home web site. The prices are reasonable and no one produces higher-quality parts.

Most wheels consist of a tire (the outer rubbery part) and a rim with hub (the inner hard part). Almost all LEGO hubs are compatible with LEGO cross axles (see Figure 6-16).

Figure 6-16. LEGO wheel (left) *and coupler on motor* (right)

If there was a piece that could connect a motor to a standard LEGO cross axle, then your robot would have access to almost the entire line of LEGO wheels. It turns out that you can make such as part, called a coupler (see right side of Figure 6-16).

With a coupler, you can quickly slide different wheels on and off the robot, without needing tools. This is great for experimenting. It can also save you from a disaster if you suddenly discover the wheels you originally planned to use are too short or too wide.

Sandwich Body

I confess that Sandwich wasn't the first line-following robot I built for this book. The earlier model (see Figure 6-17) is good, but is more difficult to build. It has an aluminum base and bracket that have to be cut to size. Also, the sensors are exposed in front and bend every time the robot smacks into something. The electronics, wires, and gears are also exposed, which makes picking up the robot a delicate endeavor.

Figure 6-17. Wavy, the predecessor of Sandwich

Using a consumer storage container solves all of those problems. For Sandwich, I chose a reusable/disposable square 2.5-cup plastic container from Ziploc (see Figure 6-18). Plastic containers are lightweight, inexpensive, easy to drill, and available at local grocery stores.

Most disposable food storage containers are made from polypropylene thermoplastic. Polypropylene is highly resistant to chemicals and moisture. It can resist boiling heat, although it will become brittle in freezing temperatures.

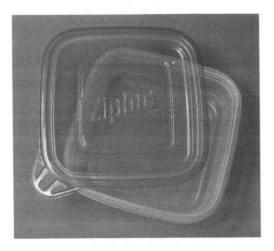

Figure 6-18. Ziploc brand square 2.5 cup container

Connecting It Together

In Sandwich, no tape, rubber bands, or glue are used to connect the parts to the robot's body. Many hobbyists overuse these fastening methods, resulting in a sloppy or fragile robot. Additionally, it's awkward to disassemble pieces connected in that manner.

Physical Connections

Whenever possible, use ordinary screws to connect parts to the body (see Figure 6-19). Screws have tremendous holding strength, they're durable, fairly inexpensive, look impressive, and you can remove and install them over and over. You can buy fasteners of all shapes and sizes at your local hardware store, or online at MSCDirect.com, MicroFasteners.com, or McMaster.com.

Figure 6-19. Common #4-40 round slotted machine screw

To whatever extent you can, use the same type and the same size screws throughout your robot. That way, you won't need to carry around a tool chest filled with a variety of screwdrivers to service your robot.

Electrical Connections

On Sandwich's main circuit board, all of the parts are connected with solder. This makes for a strong connection, though nearly permanent.

For electrical connections coming into the board, such as the power switch or motors, use a removable connector (see Figure 6-20). Not only is servicing a breeze, but you can pull parts for testing or even interchanging them with other robots.

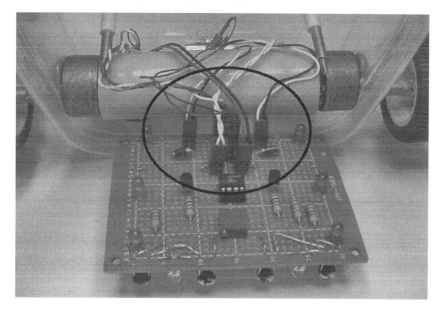

Figure 6-20. Wires connect to a circuit board with Molex KK connectors

Obtaining a Kit

Suppliers of individual parts are listed throughout this book, in the relevant chapters. However, you can save money and get a head start on the Sandwich robot by purchasing a kit (see Figure 6-21). Solarbotics sells part #K SAND for $49.95. This ensures that you have the correct components and reduces the time it would have taken to track down pieces from various vendors.

Of course, you still have the option of modifying the kit as desired, by substituting your own parts or decorations. In any case, you will need to supply a piece of plastic or container to hold the robot together.

Building Up

You should now understand the line-following course requirements and the basic functional anatomy of Sandwich.

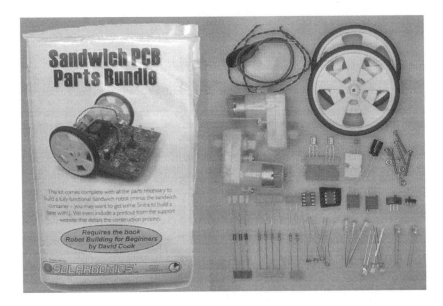

Figure 6-21. The Sandwich PCB Parts Bundle includes motors, wheels, printed circuit board, and electronics.

If you haven't soldered, drilled, or worked with electronics before, it may seem like a huge leap to get from here to actually building the robot. Don't distress. The coming chapters break down each element, telling you what to buy, how to test, and how to prototype the line-following circuit.

Even if you've decided you don't want to build a line-following robot, please read the next chapters carefully. Although Sandwich forms the framework for each topic, the subject matter and techniques taught are applicable to all robots.

CHAPTER 7

■■■

Nine-Volt Batteries

Sandwich, the line-following robot, uses a 9 V battery for power. In fact, most of my robots use 9 V batteries because the batteries are so small and lightweight. In this chapter, you're going to learn how to test a 9 V battery (see Figure 7-1) and find out about the differences in battery brands and chemistries.

Figure 7-1. Alkaline 9 V battery

How many volts in a nine-volt battery? Yes, it's sort of a trick question. Although the answer is somewhere around nine volts, the actual voltage varies based on what the battery is made of and how much of the battery's power has been used up.

During this stage, it's not necessary to understand exactly what "voltage" is. However, if you'd like, you can think of voltage as water pressure coming out of a water pump. A pump with more pressure can spray water harder than a pump with less pressure. Likewise, a battery with more voltage can spray electricity harder than a battery with less voltage.

The unit for voltage is volts or simply the letter V. So, 9 volts and 9 V mean the same thing.

Testing Battery Voltage

Now you're going to learn how to test a 9 V battery's voltage with a multimeter. Robot builders measure battery voltage quite often. After all, you don't want your robot starting out on an adventure with weak batteries.

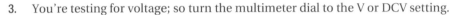

■ **Caution** This book presents directions applicable to most multimeters. However, you should always read and follow the instructions provided with the test equipment you're using.

Setting Up a Multimeter for Voltage Testing

1. Connect the black-colored test lead to the multimeter terminal (hole) marked COM (see Figure 7-2).

2. Connect the red-colored test lead to the multimeter terminal marked V. (Depending on the meter, there may be additional markings alongside the V, such as Ω.)

3. You're testing for voltage; so turn the multimeter dial to the V or DCV setting.

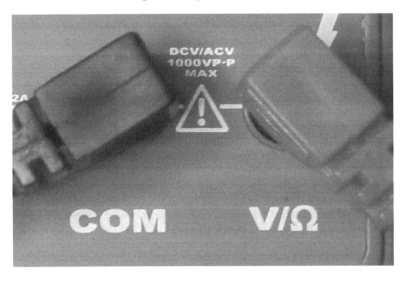

Figure 7-2. Common and voltage test lead terminals on multimeter

If your meter is manually ranged (has several ranges in the V section of the dial), choose a number above 9 (see Figure 7-3). Autoranging meters usually don't have any ranges on the dial since those kinds of meters automatically pick the maximum range.

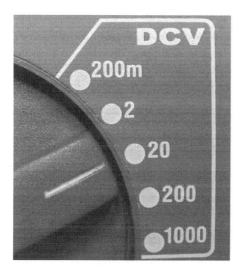

Figure 7-3. Dialing a DC voltage range above 9

To protect the meter, you must always select a number that's bigger than the maximum you expect to test. Since you expect to see a little more or less than 9 volts on a 9 V battery, pick a range a little more than 9.

Although it's not harmful to dial too large of a number, like 1000, the resolution of the meter isn't as descriptive. In other words, the quality of the reading is not going to be as good if you tell the meter it's testing a number between 0 and 1000 when you know the meter is actually going to be testing a number between 0 and 10.

4. Do not touch the metal tips of the probes to anything at this point. If the meter isn't already turned on, press the power-on button.

The meter should now be displaying zero (see Figure 7-4). The number on the display may bounce around a little, but it should be near zero.

Figure 7-4. Meter displays no voltage

5. Touch the metal tip of the black test lead to the battery's negative terminal (the larger snap, which is usually marked "-").

6. Touch the metal tip of the red test lead to the battery's positive terminal (the smaller snap, which is usually marked "+"). See Figure 7-5.

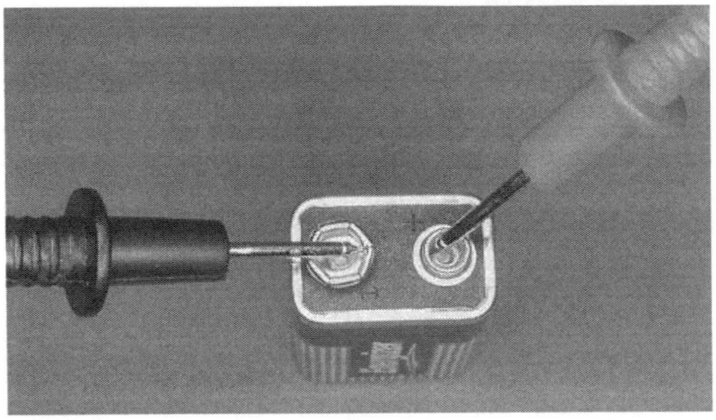

Figure 7-5. Probe tips touching battery terminals

Interpreting Test Results

If the multimeter display shows a negative number (see Figure 7-6), then something has gotten reversed. Check that the test leads are connected to their proper terminals on the battery and on the meter. Switch the probes if necessary. Don't worry if you got a negative number, that doesn't hurt the meter at all.

Figure 7-6. A negative number indicates a mixed-up connection

If the display shows zero, some connection isn't making full contact. Make sure the leads are fully inserted into the meter terminals. Make sure the metal tips are touching the metal portion of the battery terminals.

If the meter displays a positive number (see Figure 7-7), then you're measuring the battery correctly. Depending on the type of battery and the capacity remaining, a valid voltage of a 9 V battery should be between 5 and 10 volts.

Figure 7-7. A positive number indicates a proper measurement

When you remove either probe from either battery snap terminal, the meter will display zero again. It's worth noting that, **in all cases**, both probes must be touching the part in order to measure it.

9 V Battery Characteristics

Depending on their chemical makeup and age, the voltage and other attributes of a 9 V battery can differ considerably (see Table 7-1).

Table 7-1. Typical Characteristics of 9 V Batteries

Chemical Type	Fresh	Rated	Halfway	Discharged	Mass	Capacity	Price
Super Heavy-Duty	9.8 V	9 V	6.5 V	4.8 V	37 g	400 mAh	$1.50
Lithium	9.7 V	9 V	8.1 V	5.4 V	35 g	1200 mAh	$7.00
Lithium Polymer (Rechargeable)	8.4 V	8.4 V	7.4 V	6.5 V	28 g	500 mAh	$15.00
Alkaline	9.5 V	9 V	7.4 V	4.8 V	45 g	595 mAh	$3.00
NiMH 8.4 (Rechargeable)	9.6 V	8.4 V	7.5 V	7.0 V	40 g	250 mAh	$6.00
NiMH 9.6 (Rechargeable)	11.2 V	9.6 V	8.6 V	8.0 V	45 g	230 mAh	$8.00

It may now occur to you that it's a bit of a misnomer to call the battery **size** "nine volt" since the actual voltage varies quite a bit from nine. Somehow the name for the size got mixed up with the voltage. Other consumer batteries avoid this problem with names like "AA," "C," "D," and so on.

The Fresh column in Table 7-1 is approximately the voltage you may find when you test a brand-new (or newly recharged) battery not connected to a circuit. Voltage always reads a bit lower when testing a battery attached to other electronic parts. A fresh battery settles down to the officially rated voltage with age or after a short amount of use.

The Rated column describes the official voltage the manufacturer claims for this size of the battery. In all cases except rechargeables, the manufacturers state the batteries are designed to provide approximately 9 V.

The Halfway column was generated by taking the total number of hours the battery lasted until the discharged voltage was reached, and then looking at the voltage at half that time. This gives a sense of the voltage when half of the battery capacity has been used up.

In the Discharged column, the manufacturer arbitrarily picks this voltage number. For example, it isn't as though an alkaline 9 V battery suddenly stops working below 4.8 volts. However, at some point you need to call the battery "dead." By the way, some sneaky manufacturers may claim a battery is longer lasting just by choosing a lower final acceptable voltage.

Realistically, many consumer devices stop performing adequately when their 9 V battery falls below 7 V. Although you'll usually design your homemade robot to operate at even lower voltages, the power output of most batteries drops like a rock at the end of their lives. So, even a low-voltage design won't be able to extend useful battery life indefinitely.

Referring again to Table 7-1, the Mass column reflects the differences in battery masses due to differences in chemical makeup and case materials. For example, a plastic case weighs less than a steel or aluminum case. These differences also suggest a potential opportunity to shave a little weight from a robot by the choice of battery.

The Capacity column is stated in mAh. "mA" is the abbreviation for milliamps and "h" is the abbreviation for hours. Basically, the capacity value indicates how much electricity can be circulated for an hour. If the device uses less electrical current, the battery will last longer than an hour. If the device uses more electrical current, the battery will last less than an hour.

9 V Battery Recommendations

Recommended

Nickel-Metal Hydride

NiMH (nickel-metal hydride) rechargeable batteries (see Figure 7-8) are preferable for robot experimentation and testing because you can recharge the batteries hundreds of times.

■ **Note** Technically, single-use (non-rechargeable) batteries are called *primary* batteries. Rechargeable batteries are called *secondary* batteries.

Unfortunately, rechargeable batteries have a lower run time (total capacity) compared to non-rechargeable batteries. Also, every day they lose some percentage of their electricity, even when not in use. However, because you can recharge them, simply top them off immediately before a robotic demonstration.

Figure 7-8. Nickel-metal hydride rechargeable 9 V batteries. Left: *low-end 8.4 V 150 mAh.* Right: *high-end 9.6 V 260 mAh.*

When purchasing NiMH 9 V-size batteries, look for the rated voltage and the rated capacity (mAh). For most uses, you want to purchase 8.4 V-rated batteries rather than 7.2 V-rated ones (most manufacturers have discontinued making these). You may want to have a 9.6 V-rated battery available to add a little more speed or pushing power in competitions. But, be aware that the 11.2 V fresh voltage of these batteries may be too high for some robots and may not work in many battery chargers.

A higher-capacity (mAh) battery outlasts a lower-capacity battery of similar chemistry. It also retains a higher voltage for a longer period of time during usage. All things being equal, a robot using a 260 mAh battery would continue operating 73% longer than if it were using a 150 mAh battery.

Retaining Charge When Not in Use

The newest NiMH batteries are much better at retaining their charge when not in use (see Figure 7-9). As such, you can use them immediately upon taking them out the package, because much of the manufacturer's charge has been retained.

The batteries are advantageous to the robot builder, as you can have a stock of nearly charged batteries without constantly keeping them in the charger.

Lithium-Polymer

Li-poly (lithium-polymer) rechargeable batteries (see Figure 7-10) are similar to li-ion (lithium-ion) batteries used in laptops. You can recharge them hundreds of times, they retain their charge better than NiMH, are lightweight, can provide high current, and have capacities that nearly match alkaline batteries. As such, I switched from NiMH to lithium-polymer during robot competitions.

The disadvantages of lithium-polymer batteries are that they are more expensive and that you **must** use a charger specifically designed for lithium-polymer batteries.

Figure 7-9. *"Ready-to-use" rechargeable batteries*

Figure 7-10. *Lithium-polymer rechareable 9 V batteries*

Alkaline

Alkaline batteries (see Figure 7-11) are the most common and are readily available. These batteries retain their charge for years (when not in use), have a high starting voltage, and tend to keep a reasonable voltage during use. For medium or high-current electrical draw, alkalines are the longest-lasting non-rechargeable consumer batteries.

Unfortunately, 9 V alkaline batteries aren't rechargeable. After they're used up, they must be discarded into the recycling bin. This practice can get very expensive.

Figure 7-11. *Some popular brands of alkaline 9 V batteries*

Specialized Use
Lithium

Lithium batteries (see Figure 7-12) have a couple of nice benefits: they're lightweight, they work well even at cold temperatures, and they stay fresh for many, many years. So, these batteries might be good for a high-altitude balloon robot or a multi-year test project.

Figure 7-12. *Non-rechargeable lithium 9 V batteries*

Lithium 9 V batteries have a couple of downsides: they're expensive, they can't provide significant bursts of electricity (no more than 80 mA or 120 mA depending on brand), and their high-rated capacity (1200 mAh for 9 V) only holds true if you use the electricity in very small amounts. These minuses make lithium unsuitable for most motor-driven robots.

Don't confuse **single-use** lithium batteries with **rechargeable** lithium-ion or lithium-polymer batteries. The rechargeable varieties offer higher current bursts without the same caveats.

Not Recommended

Carbon and Zinc

Poor "heavy-duty" battery! The greatest benefit I could come up with is they are the least expensive to buy for a single use. This might make a good choice for a robot that dives off cliffs or unsuccessfully explores lava pits.

Despite their low initial cost, the total lifetime price of carbon-zinc, magnesium-carbon, and zinc-chloride batteries (see Figure 7-13) is much higher than rechargeable batteries. This is because the rechargeable batteries can be recharged, but the carbon and zinc batteries cannot.

Figure 7-13. Classic and super heavy-duty 9 V batteries

Heavy-duty battery capacity is seriously eroded at higher discharge rates, so the respectable 400 mAh rating is hideously reduced in power-hungry robots. Older-technology carbon and zinc batteries have a short shelf life (they self-discharge faster).

Carbon and zinc battery voltage slopes down steadily during use, which decreases the useful battery life if the device requires a higher voltage. Ironically, the sloping voltage turns out to be useful for predicting remaining capacity.

Nickel-Cadmium

For environmental reasons, nickel-cadmium (NiCd or NiCad) batteries are not recommended (see Figure 7-14). Additionally, NiCd batteries have a lower capacity and accept fewer recharges than NiMH batteries. The major brands no longer make NiCd batteries.

e² Titanium and Ultra

The top two manufacturers of alkaline batteries have both introduced premium versions of their alkaline batteries (see Figure 7-15). These enhancements are basically marketing gimmicks. The companies charge a notably higher price for an unnoticeable change in performance. (Ouch!)

Figure 7-14. *Nickel-cadmium rechargeable 9 V battery*

Figure 7-15. *Tweaked alkaline 9 V batteries*

Battery Brand Names

Stiff competition has ensured that there's no performance difference between most popular battery brands. Instead of brand name, pay attention to battery chemistry (alkaline, NiMH, and so on), price, and freshness date.

Watch out for batteries with a voltage rated at less than 8.4 volts. For example, some NiMH rechargeable 9 V-size batteries are only 7.2 volts. The cause? Instead of seven internal cells, those batteries contain only six cells and some filler (see Figure 7-16). Tsk. Tsk.

Although a lower voltage is detrimental to many applications, it does provide a lower-weight and a lower-power battery in a standard form factor (case style). For example, if your robot doesn't need all 9 volts, substituting the lower-voltage battery can save some weight or slow down a robot that fails because it operates too quickly.

Figure 7-16. Polystyrene foam filler in a less-powerful battery

Using 9 V Batteries in Robots

Generally speaking, the higher the voltage, the faster the motor's speed and the greater the motor's push.

The first time I set Sandwich down onto a track, I was disappointed in the robot's line following. The motors were too fast for sharp turns. So, I switched from a fresh 9.5 V alkaline battery to a 7.2 V rechargeable. The lower voltage produced lower motor speed. The slower speed had a dramatically positive effect on the line following.

Alternatively, another robot was a little too slow and a little too weak in a robot Sumo contest. The motors were nominally rated for 12 volts, so it was safe to upgrade to a fresh 11.2 NiMH battery.

By using a standard-size battery in your robot, regardless of whether it is 9 V, AA, AAA, C, D, or whatever, you can switch between battery chemistries to adjust performance. That's a good trick to remember. It is a lot easier and faster to switch batteries than to rebuild your robot or alter the software five minutes before a competition.

Mounting Batteries

Batteries tend to be one of the heavier parts in a robot. For this reason, the battery in Sandwich is mounted near the wheel axle (see Figure 7-17). That way, most of the battery weight is on the tires (adding traction) rather than on the front part (which drags).

Figure 7-17. Battery mounted near rear axle

Since a robot's battery is going to be replaced often, you want to make sure it is placed in a location that is easily accessible. I made a mistake in my mini-Sumo robot, Bugdozer. The batteries are stored underneath the wires and circuitry (see Figure 7-18), requiring most of the robot to be disassembled to swap in a fresh power source.

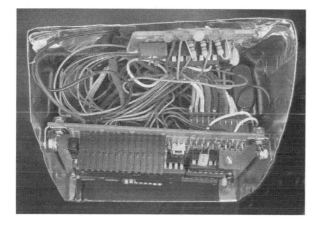

Figure 7-18. Spot the copper tops! There are two batteries hiding inside this robot. Your job: find them.

There are a number of ways to physically connect a 9 V battery to a device. Most consumer products have specifically designed compartments formed into their cases. Unless you have access to some wonderful tooling or injection-molding machinery, custom compartments are not viable options for your robots. At the opposite end of the spectrum, masking tape is ugly and unreliable.

Rubber bands are okay for securing batteries, though not ideal. I've successfully used hook and loop fasteners, commonly called by their brand name, Velcro. The only problem with hook and loop fasteners is that one fastener strip needs to be permanently adhered to the battery. A new fastener strip needs to be attached to each replacement battery thereafter.

Preformed metal clips are available (Jameco #105794 or Mouser #534-080 or #534-095). They have a screw hole in the middle (see Figure 7-19) that makes it easy to secure against a frame. Use a washer (a flat, circular disc—see Figure 7-17) on the other side of the robot's body so that the force of battery removal doesn't rip the screw through the body wall.

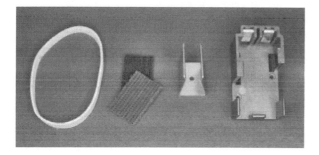

Figure 7-19. Methods of mounting a 9 V battery: (left to right) *rubber band, hook and loop fasteners, clip, molded part*

A word of caution about metal clips: they tend to grab tightly against the battery, causing scrapes on the battery's case during installation and removal. The damage is purely superficial, and a little masking tape around the ends of the clip eliminates the problem.

Molded plastic parts can cradle a battery and provide an electrical connection. If you have room on your robot for such a part, it's preferable because the battery is less likely to slip out.

Powering Forward

You've now got a power source and you know how to test it. With a little bit of thought given to battery location, you can find it a spot in your robot. Looking ahead, the 9 V battery will supply power to each of the upcoming experiments.

CHAPTER 8

■ ■ ■

Clips and Test Leads

The components on Sandwich's circuit board are permanently soldered together. You'll learn about that later. But what do you do if you want to make a quick connection for a simple experiment? No, don't use electrical tape. It's too loose and sticky!

This chapter covers a simple method for making a few temporary connections. It also describes a multimeter test that you can perform to check if an electrical connection has been made.

The Gators Are Hungry Tonight

Alligator clips have spring-closing "mouths" that grip parts (see Figure 8-1). Squeezing the center of the clip causes the mouth to open and release whatever it's holding. When you let go of the clip, the mouth closes and can hold onto things.

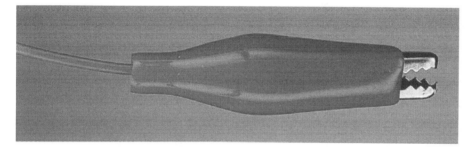

Figure 8-1. Alligator clip with insulated shroud

Alligator clips are friendly. They have a lighthearted name and you can pinch their mouths open and shut like they are eating or saying hello.

A pair of clips attached by a wire is called a jumper lead or clip test jumper (see Figure 8-2). The wire itself is usually flexible copper surrounded by an insulating colored plastic casing. Now you've got something that can grip a part on both ends and connect them with a wire.

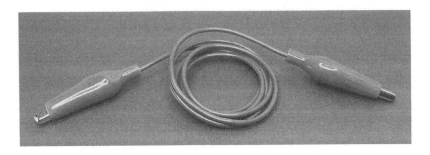

Figure 8-2. *A jumper lead is alligator clips with a connecting wire.*

Obtaining Hook Clips

Clips are available in many sizes and colors (see Figure 8-3). Beyond the "alligator" style, there's the mini IC hook, which is smaller and tends to hold onto wires a little better (see Figure 8-4). For these reasons, you'll probably use hooks more often than alligator clips.

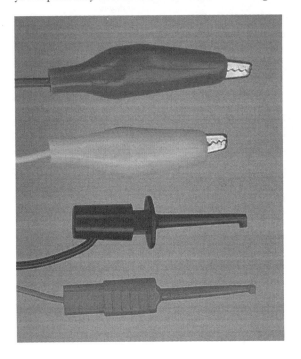

Figure 8-3. Top to bottom: *large alligator, medium alligator, mini IC (hook), micro IC (hook)*

Figure 8-4. Close-up of hook

Sometimes the end of a hook bends flat during use. It becomes more like a letter 'L' than a letter 'J.' It's not supposed to be that way. Bend it back. When the hook retracts, it should fit into the hole in the end notch.

Purchase at least five medium alligator and five mini IC hook jumper leads (see Table 8-1). They are available in a variety of colors. Try to obtain red, black, and at least one other color.

Table 8-1. Alligator and Hook Jumper Leads

Supplier	Part Number	Price	Description
All Electronics	MTC-5	$6.50	(5) Black, red, green, yellow, and white long IC hook
All Electronics	MTL-10	$2.95	(10) Two sets of five colors alligator
Jameco	10444	$4.49	(10) Two sets of five colors alligator
Jameco	135299	$10.95	(5) Black, red, green, yellow, and blue mini IC hook
Mouser	548-285	$6.06	(10) Two sets of five colors alligator
SparkFun	CAB-00501	$8.95	(5) Black, red, green, yellow, and blue mini IC hook

Testing Jumpers

You're now going to learn how your particular multimeter displays an electrical connection or lack of connection. Then, you'll make a test connection with an alligator jumper lead.

Setting Up a Multimeter for Continuity Testing

1. As always, connect the black test lead to the COM terminal of the multimeter.

2. Connect the red test lead to the Ω or ohm terminal of the multimeter. Most likely the test leads will be in the same places they were when you were testing the voltage of the 9 V battery.

3. If your multimeter has a continuity feature, turn the dial to that (see Figure 8-5). A continuity test checks to see if a continuous (unbroken) connection exists between the two probe tips. A continuity setting is nice because it usually beeps when a connection is complete, so you don't need to look at the display.

Figure 8-5. Multimeter dial set to continuity

(alternate) If your multimeter doesn't have a continuity feature, turn the dial to the lowest ohm range (see Figure 8-6). This measures resistance. A short wire like the jumper lead should have almost no resistance to electricity flowing through it.

Figure 8-6. Multimeter dial set to lowest ohm range

Testing an Open Connection

4. Do not touch the metal tips of the probes to anything at this point (see Figure 8-7). If the meter isn't already turned on, press the power-on button.

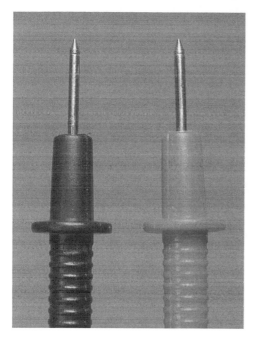

Figure 8-7. Multimeter probe tips not touching

A meter with a continuity feature should now display open and should not be beeping. Some meters display "0L mV" instead of the word "open" (see Figure 8-8). Check your meter manual.

Figure 8-8. Multimeter displays open (no connection) and very high resistance

If you don't have a continuity feature, the meter should display 0L or ∞ (infinity) or some very large number in the megohm (M) range.

Since the probe tips aren't touching each other, this connection is "open."

Testing a Shorted Connection

5.   Touch the probe tips together (see Figure 8-9).

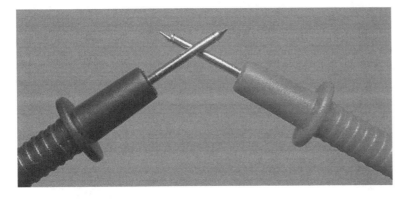

Figure 8-9. Touching the probe tips together to make an electrical connection

A meter with continuity should now display short (see Figure 8-10) and should beep annoyingly. Some meters display "0 mV" instead of the word "short." Check your meter manual.

Figure 8-10. Multimeter displays short (connection) and almost zero resistance

If you don't have a continuity feature, the meter should display zero Ω (ohms) or a very small number.

Ever heard of a "short-circuit?" Well, this one is pretty short. The electricity from the meter goes out of one probe and then directly into the other!

Experiment with the ohm ranges and the continuity setting of your meter. You want to get a good sense for what the meter displays when there is a connection and what it displays when there isn't a connection.

Testing an Alligator Connection (Shorted)

6. Instead of touching the multimeter probe tips together directly, connect them with an alligator jumper lead (see Figure 8-11). Using a single jumper, attach one alligator clip to the tip of the black probe and the other alligator clip to the tip of the red probe.

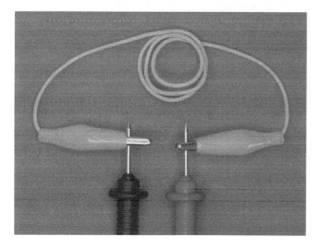

Figure 8-11. Making a connection with alligator jumper leads

You should get the same value displayed on your meter whether you touch the probe tips together directly or whether you connect them with a jumper. The alligator clips and wire are just as good at allowing electricity to flow through them as touching the probes together directly.

During use, alligator clips may become loose or grimy and fail to make a solid connection. The wire between the clips may rip and detach. In those cases, if the jumper lead no longer conducts a continuous connection, you can test for it on your multimeter. A broken connection will read "open" or some ohm value greater than touching the probe tips together.

Think of the wire in the alligator jumper lead as electrical pipe. Electricity flows through the copper wire (or any metal) like water flowing through a pipe. Unlike water pipes, if you disconnect one end of the wire, the electricity doesn't spill all over.

Discovering Unintended Connections

The continuity mode (and also the ohm mode) of a multimeter has a very beneficial use in robotics. It can detect if an unintentional electrical connection exists between various robot body parts and circuits. Although you won't perform these steps now, here are some example steps you might take to test a robot.

1. Turn the robot's power off. Remove all of the batteries, if possible.

2. Connect the black test probe of the multimeter to one piece of the robot. If you prefer, you can use an alligator clip to connect the probe tip to the piece being tested. Doing so is a lot easier than holding the black test probe in place. Also, a hook clip may be able to reach spots that would be awkward for a test probe.

3. Touch the red test probe tip to each metal part throughout the robot, as thoroughly as desired.

If an electrical connection exists between the part connected to the black test probe and the part being touched by the red test probe, the meter will beep (or display "short" or a low ohm value or whatever). It doesn't matter how long or how complicated the connection is. If there's an electrical connection between the parts, the multimeter can detect it.

One of my line-following robots, Sweet, uses a metal candy container for a body. After drilling holes for the sensors and screws (see Figure 8-12), I didn't consider that cutting away the paint coating had exposed the metal in the container to the robot's circuits. When I proudly powered on the robot, the circuits went crazy. Fortunately, I only lost a $15 chip that day.

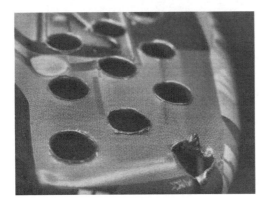

Figure 8-12. Exposed metal on drill holes causes unintended electrical connections

I should have probed the robot a bit with the continuity mode of my multimeter before powering up. By quickly checking the motors, each circuit board, major screws, battery connections, and body, I would have noticed that direct electrical connections had mistakenly occurred between metal parts of the circuit board and metal parts of the robot's container.

Plumbing with Jumpers

In the last chapter, you learned that a 9 V battery works like an electricity pump. In this chapter, you learned that alligator clip jumper wire (or any other piece of metal) acts as electrical pipe. All you need now is something worth hooking up to the pipe.

CHAPTER 9

■ ■ ■

Resistors

Sandwich, the line-following robot, uses many resistors on its circuit board (see Figure 9-1). These resistors are so vital that Sandwich could not operate without them. In this chapter, you'll learn how to identify, purchase, and test resistors. In later chapters, you'll put resistors into use in the same way that they're used on Sandwich.

Figure 9-1. Five resistors on Sandwich's circuit board

Limiting Power with Resistors

The main water supply hookup to your home is a fairly large pipe. But the pipe leading to your showerhead is a lot smaller.

Obviously, the smaller pipe saves some space, but it also acts to decrease the amount of water delivered to that location. You would not be pleased to begin your day with a shower blasting you with the full force of your water main! (Well, I don't know you personally; perhaps you could use that much of a shower.)

Besides the displeasure of getting overwhelmed by a watery blast, a lot of water would get wasted. You don't need that much water to effectively take a shower.

Resistors limit or divide up the flow of electricity. In doing so, they prevent waste and deliver the specifically requested amount of electricity to each part.

Obtaining a Resistor Variety Pack

Resistors are so useful and inexpensive that you'll want to obtain a wide assortment of values. A good place to start is with a ½-watt, 5% tolerance, carbon-film variety pack (see Figure 9-2).

Figure 9-2. 100-piece assortment of ½-watt, 5% tolerance, carbon-film, through-hole resistors

Table 9-1. Resistor Assortments

Supplier	Part Number	Price	Number of Resistors
Electronix Express	13RK5001	$8.50	365
Jameco	107837	$9.95	350
Jameco	107879	$29.95	540 + cabinet
Digi-Key	RS150	$16.95	365

Any of the resistor packs in Table 9-1 are perfectly adequate for a start. The Jameco #107879 includes a cabinet, which is nice.

Understanding Size and Tolerance

I recommend starting with ½-watt through-hole resistors because their larger physical size makes it easier to see the color code bands. If you want to use the smaller ¼-watt through-hole resistors instead, that's fine. Until you become an expert, don't buy surface-mount (SMT or SMD) resistors. Those are too small to experiment with (see Figure 9-3).

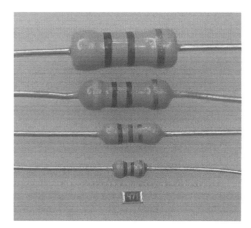

Figure 9-3. Top: *1-watt, ½-watt, ¼-watt, and $^1/_8$ watt through-hole.* Bottom: $^1/_{10}$-watt surface-mount

5% tolerance means that a 100 Ω resistor could be as low as 95 Ω or as high as 105 Ω. That's plenty accurate for homemade robots. You can spend a little more money and purchase 1% tolerance metal-film resistors, but your robot isn't going to notice the difference. Many of the high-precision resistors have more than four color bands, which makes it more difficult for a beginner to decipher the value.

Cut It Out

Components often arrive connected together by tape bands (see Figure 9-4). This is because most components are manufactured in long reels so that they can be fed into robotic part-placement machines. A reseller purchases a full reel and then cuts off lengths according to your order.

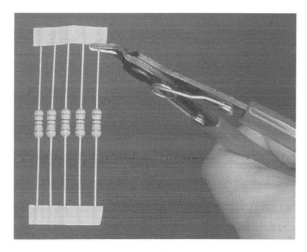

Figure 9-4. *Cutting resistors away from reel tape*

You could try peeling off the tape, but it leaves a sticky residue on the ends of the wires. The residue can prevent a clean metal-to-metal connection when prototyping. The residue can also gum up sockets and holes.

Instead, use a wire cutter to cut both ends of the resistor from reel tape. Don't use scissors because the cutting edges will become dulled and damaged.

If you absolutely need the full resistor wire length, you can pull the part from the tape and clean the ends of the resistor thoroughly. Resistors are hardy components; the cleaning won't harm them at all.

Obtaining a Wire Cutter Tool

A wire cutter is an essential tool (see Figure 9-5). Not only can it cut components free from tape reels, but also it cuts raw wire, shortens tall component leads in solderless prototype boards, and trims excess material from circuit boards after soldering.

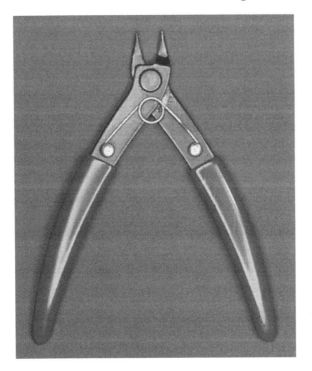

Figure 9-5. Flush wire cutter or nippy cutter

It may be worth buying a cutter from a local store rather than from a catalog (see Table 9-2), so that you can experience how a particular model feels in your hand.

Table 9-2. Wire Cutters

Supplier	Part Number	Price
All Electronics	FC-14	$4.50
Electronix Express	0602MS01	$4.95
Jameco	159274	$4.95
Jameco	146712	$6.49
Micro-Mark	80333	$12.49
SparkFun	TOL-08794	$1.95

Resistance and Ohms

The unit associated with resistance is ohms. This is abbreviated with the symbol Ω. So, 100 ohms is the same as 100 Ω. There isn't any difference.

It doesn't matter if you understand or have a feel for ohms yet. Recall that resistance is like the smaller pipe sizes and tiny holes in your showerhead. A larger ohm number represents larger resistance, which is sort of like a narrower pipe.

Most electronic parts can't take the full force of the battery. They need something to reduce the flow; that's what resistors do.

Measuring Resistance

1. If your meter isn't already on the 200 range (or thereabouts) for ohms, switch the dial now.

2. As always, connect the black lead to the COM terminal of the multimeter.

3. Connect the red lead to terminal marked Ω or ohm or whatever the specific instructions are for measuring resistance on your particular meter.

4. Turn on the meter.

It would be helpful to use alligator-clips or hook adaptors (if you have them) for your meter test probe tips. It's somewhat difficult to touch each end of a resistor with both probe tips at the same time without the resistor rolling away.

5. Find a 100 Ω resistor. The color bands are brown, black, brown, gold. There's no such resistor as gold, brown, black, brown (backwards). If you think you've found one, you're reading in the opposite direction.

In a prior chapter, the color-code table indicates that brown is 1, black is 0, brown is × 10, and gold is 5% tolerance. That is $100 \pm 5\ \Omega$.

■ **Note** The symbol ± means plus or minus. In this example, 100 plus 5 is 105 and 100 minus 5 is 95. So, the value of the resistor could be anything from 95 to 105.

6. Touch or connect the black probe tip to one end wire of the resistor (see Figure 9-6). It doesn't matter which ends you choose.

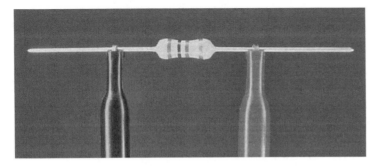

Figure 9-6. Hook test probe adaptors holding a 100 Ω resistor

7. Touch or connect the red probe tip to the other end wire of the resistor.

Interpreting the Resistance Displayed on the Meter

If you're lucky, the meter is displaying 100 Ω. More likely, the meter is showing a number slightly above or below 100. That's perfectly normal. (I can't tell you how many resistors I went through to get that near to 100 Ω for the picture in Figure 9-7.)

Figure 9-7. Meter displaying resistance of approximately 100 Ω

If your meter is displaying 0L or some very large number, double-check the setting you've chosen on the dial. Is it ohm? Is the range more than 100? Wiggle the test probe connections to make sure everything is firmly connected. Check the colors of the resistor again; perhaps your third band isn't brown (times 10)?

A resistor that's undergone aging, temperature extremes, shock, or other abuse may be damaged out of the expected value. However, it is really unlikely that a fresh, 5% tolerance, 100 Ω resistor would be beyond the appropriate 95 Ω to 105 Ω range. You can always try a few other resistors to be sure.

Experiencing Resistance Ranges

1. Find a 470 Ω resistor. The color bands are yellow, purple, brown, gold.

2. If you have a manual-ranging multimeter, choose an ohm range **below** 470 on your meter. We're goofing around for a minute here.

3. Hook up the 470 Ω resistor as you did the 100 Ω resistor (refer back to Figure 9-6).

Unlike an improper voltage range, choosing too low of a maximum range on the ohm-portion of the dial does not harm your multimeter at all. However, the manual-ranging meter will be unable to display a measurement of the resistance. On my meter, 0L is displayed instead of the proper value (see Figure 9-8).

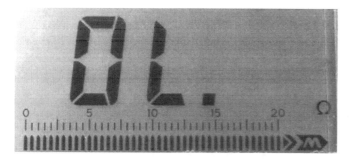

Figure 9-8. The resistor value is above the selected range on the multimeter

This is one of the annoying aspects of a manual-ranging meter. In order to determine the resistance of something, you either have to make an educated guess (by looking it up in a color-code table) or you have to flip through the ohm ranges on the dial until you get a reading.

Because of the need to constantly try different ranges on the dial of a manual-ranging meter, it's more difficult to sort a box of resistors. That same task is a breeze on an autoranging meter.

If you have an autoranging multimeter or have now chosen the correct range on your manual meter, you may find that your meter displays the value of the 470 Ω resistor as 0.470 kΩ more or less (see Figure 9-9). This value is still correct. The k stands for 1000. If you multiply 0.47 by 1000, you'll get 470.

As multimeters get smarter or more expensive, they do a better job of displaying numbers in user-friendly ranges. If your meter doesn't present all numbers nicely, be prepared to think twice when a decimal point appears on the meter.

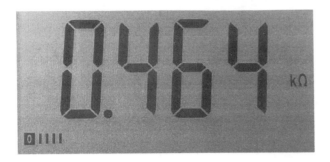

Figure 9-9. Non-friendly display of an in-range resistor value on a multimeter

Looking Up Resistor Values Online

The benefits of measuring a resistor using a multimeter are that you don't need to decipher the color bands and you know for sure the actual value of the resistor. But, the process is time-consuming. Robot Room features a visual resistor calculator (see Figure 9-10) where you can either select the colors or enter the resistance value. Go to: http://www.robotroom.com/Calculators/Resistor/Resistor-Color-Code-Calculator.aspx

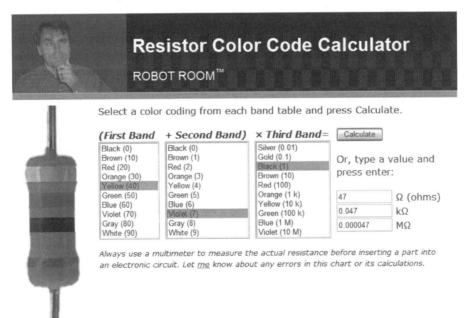

Figure 9-10. Online resistance calculator

Labeling and Storing

Measure and sort all of the resistors in your variety pack. If the resistors are attached by reel tape, keep them together and write the value on the tape (see Figure 9-11).

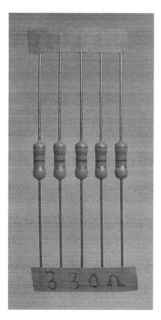

Figure 9-11. Resistors still connected to reel tape with hand-written value at bottom

I like to store my resistors in groups based on their third (multiplier) color band. That is, I organize resistors together that have a value between 0 and 99 (black), 100 and 999 (brown), 1 k and 9.9 k (red), 10 k and 99 k (orange), 100 k and 999 k (yellow), and 1 M and up (green, blue). Checking for a single color band makes them easy to sort and to find values that are out of place.

Obtaining Storage Cases

Buy a bunch of plastic storage cases with movable compartment separators (see Figure 9-12). It's easier to stack cases if they're all the same size, and, as a robot builder, you're going to have lots and lots of different parts. You'll want to be able customize the size of the individual compartments within the cases to fit the size of your parts.

You can find inexpensive storage cases at hardware stores and variety retailers, or tackle boxes at sporting-goods stores. Most parts (resistors, capacitors, switches, wire, screws, potentiometers, connectors, sockets, motors, magnets, and so on) don't need to be stored in any special kind of materials or plastic.

Choose a sturdy case that closes firmly and whose inner walls reach from the bottom to the top of the case. If the container should fall, you don't want your neatly sorted parts to jump over short compartment walls and become disorganized.

Figure 9-12. Components sorted in a storage case or organizer

Resisting the Temptation to Skip Ahead

Now you've got a broad collection of resistor values at your disposal. You'll never build a robot without them. However, before you can start using them in a circuit, you'll need to learn about one more part... LEDs.

CHAPTER 10

■■■

LEDs

In this chapter, you're going to learn about LEDs. You'll see how to select them, test them, and why no self-respecting robot would reject them.

Light Emitting Diodes (LEDs) are modern miracles. They're long lasting, impact resistant, inexpensive, cool to the touch, lightweight, and come in a wide variety of colors and sizes. LEDs are perfectly suited for battery-powered devices due to their low-voltage and low-current requirements.

When pronouncing "LED," speak the letters individually, like "el," "eee," "dee." Don't say it like a word, such as "led."

Learning About LED Attributes

Because of their usefulness, LEDs are available in different sizes, shapes, colors, and viewing angles. They also have various levels of brightness and efficiency.

LED Sizes

The most familiar LED size is T 1 ¾. This terminology comes from the days of miniature incandescent bulbs. The "T" refers to the bullet shape. The 1 ¾ refers to the approximate diameter in 1/8ths of an inch. What an odd standard!

The standard T 1 ¾ size is the least expensive and is available in the widest variety of colors (see Figure 10-1). However, the smaller T 1 size is more modern looking and uses up less space. Surface-mount LEDs are smaller still, but are more difficult for a hobbyist to experiment with.

LEDs are increasingly being advertised by their metric horizontal diameter. For example, a T 1 ¾ LED is often listed as 5 mm (millimeters). Although the T 1 ¾ descriptor implies the shape, the millimeter diameter is more accurate since LEDs are actually manufactured in millimeters, not eighths of an inch.

Using Calipers to Measure LED Diameter

It won't take long for you to get a feel for LED sizes, since there are only a few common sizes. However, you can always check by using a caliper.

Figure 10-1. LED sizes: surface-mount (1.5 mm), small - T 1 (3 mm), standard - T 1 ¾ (5 mm), and jumbo - T 3 ¼ (10 mm)

A caliper measures small dimensions. The left side of Figure 10-2 shows a T 1 ¾ LED placed in the jaws of the caliper. The digital display reads 5.00 mm. SparkFun Electronics sells a digital caliper for $29.95 (part #TOL-00067). You can also find them on eBay or machining web sites for approximately the same price.

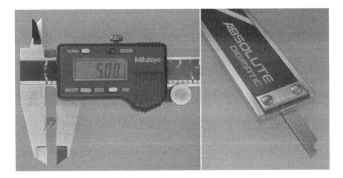

Figure 10-2. Measuring an LED diameter with calipers (left). The other end of the calipers protrudes for measuring the depth of a hole (right).

Although not required equipment, calipers are useful for many tasks in robotic engineering. For example, calipers can measure the thickness of aluminum sheets, the distance between wires on a component, or the depth of a screw hole (see right side of Figure 10-2).

LED Shapes

Discrete (individual) LEDs come in a variety of shapes and mounts (see Figure 10-3). The classic bullet shape ("T") still dominates, but side view and square styles are available.

Figure 10-3. A variety of discrete LED shapes

The LED's shape acts as either a collimating lens (light straightening—like a narrow-beam spotlight) or as a light distributor. If you shave down the dome of an ordinary T 1 ¾ LED (use medium-grain sandpaper and then polish with extra fine sandpaper or paste) you'll end up with a peculiar glowing circle instead of a directed beam (see Figure 10-4).

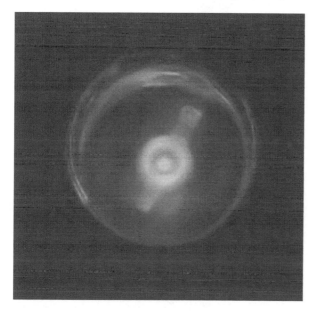

Figure 10-4. Homemade pinpoint LED

Multiple LEDs are often combined into a group package (see Figure 10-5). A numeric LED (often found in clocks) is nothing more than seven individual LEDs arranged into the number "8." By lighting up specific LEDs, it can form a variety of numbers and letters.

Figure 10-5. Multi-segment numeric and bar-graph LEDs

LED Lens Clarities

There are three popular lens clarities (see Figure 10-6).

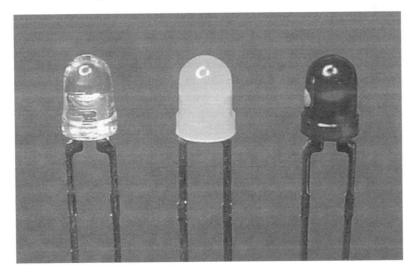

Figure 10-6. Water-clear, white-diffused, and color-diffused lenses

Water Clear

Water-clear LED lenses are sometimes simply called "clear." The lens is a transparent epoxy that tends to bend light unevenly like water. Water-clear LEDs are likely to be a bit brighter since the clear lens itself neither absorbs nor disperses the light. The light output is usually straight ahead like a spotlight.

114

Water clear is a good choice for an indicator that will be viewed head on but shouldn't be too apparent from the sides. (A traffic light, for example.) Water clear is excellent for a long distance beam, such as an intruder alarm. Sandwich, the line-following robot, uses them because they focus most of their energy on the floor in front of the robot, like headlights.

White Diffused

White-diffused LED lenses are a milky or hazy epoxy. The light spreads out throughout the LED body, making it equally bright and visible from all sides. The amount of "head-on" light is reduced since the semi-opaque lens absorbs some of the light and spreads the light over a larger viewing angle. Because the LED is dim white when off, there's a significant visual difference when the LED lights up with color.

White-diffused lenses are excellent for indicators that need to be visible from the sides as well as the front. Power, ready status, target acquisition, and error lights are good examples.

Colored Diffused

Color-diffused LED lenses are sometimes called "red diffused" or whatever the particular color. A color-diffused lens spreads light uniformly much the same as a white-diffused lens. Unlike the white lens, the epoxy is tinted so that the LED color is obvious even when the LED is off. This is useful if a bunch of LEDs are adjacent to each other ("Is the red LED turned off?"). However, since the color doesn't change from the off state to the on state (only the brightness), it's more difficult to tell in a bright room if the LED is lit.

Early LEDs were so weak in their light output that they couldn't act as spotlights and couldn't light up a white-diffused lens. As such, colored lenses were the manufacturers' best solution. Colored lenses provided consistent color quality with decent illumination.

Today, colored lenses remain the most common and least expensive. However, with the technological improvements in brightness, the trend is heading toward very lightly tinted water clear and diffused.

LED Viewing Angles

It's valuable to know the viewing angle characteristic of a particular LED, as it gives you a sense of how the light beam will spread out. A large viewing angle indicates an LED that is more visible from the sides. Datasheets often show the viewing angle in graph form, which is much more informative than a single number.

Only clear lens LEDs are described with viewing angles, since the color-diffused or white-diffused lenses naturally distribute the light throughout the entire LED.

LED Colors

LEDs became available in commercial production quantities in the 1970s, beginning with the color red. The 1990s marked significant improvements in brightness and efficiency, as well as the introduction of a pure, affordable blue. High-quality white LEDs appeared about that same time because they're really blue LEDs with white-emitting phosphor.

Red, orange, yellow, and yellow-green remain the least expensive. True green, blue, and white are coming down in price, but can still be more expensive than the price of red. Violet and ultraviolet are also available.

LEDs emit most of their light in a narrow band of color. As such, mixed colors like brown would necessitate multiple dies that are finely tuned. That would be a difficult feat to consistently replicate in production quantities. It will be a while before there's a selection of colors resembling a case of crayons ("burnt umber?"). See Figure 10-7 for what's available now.

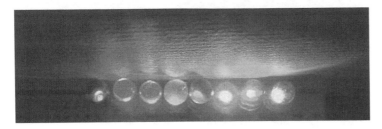

Figure 10-7. *A spectrum of colors from infrared to blue, with white on the end. (This image isn't particularly helpful in a grayscale book. But, trust me, it looks lovely.)*

Relating Color to a Wavelength

In advertisements and datasheets, LED color is often described by a dominant wavelength measured in nanometers (nm). Sometimes this is referred to with the abbreviation λP, for peak wavelength.

When the wavelength of an LED is indicated, use Table 10-1 to see where the color lies within the range. For example, 655 nm is a good red, but 635 nm looms a bit towards orange. (This is fine, if orangish-red is the color you desire.)

Table 10-1. *Approximate Color Ranges*

Color or Hue	Approximate Wavelength Range
Infrared (IR)	above 700 nm
Red	700 nm to 630 nm
Orange	630 nm to 590 nm
Yellow	590 nm to 570 nm
Green	570 nm to 500 nm
Blue	500 nm to 450 nm
Violet	450 nm to 390 nm
Ultraviolet (UV)	Below 390 nm

■ **Fun** If you want to start trouble, assemble some artists, physicists, philosophers, and psychologists into a locked room and ask them "What are the primary colors?" and "What are their wavelengths?"

You can experience the problem for yourself: The next time you see a rainbow, mentally try to slice it into neat chunks of colors. Where does blue end and green begin?

Indicating Color via the CIE Standard Colorimetric System

The Commission Internationale de l'Eclairage (CIE) is headquartered in Vienna, Austria. In 1931, the organization published a scientific method for specifying a color based on a standard observer. In their colorimetric system, any color can be described exactly by three values: X, Y, and Z.

Although LEDs are rarely advertised using the CIE system, the specification sometimes appears in datasheets. Instead of absolute XYZ, usually relative x and y chromaticity coordinates are indicated. Software can convert the CIE values to wavelengths or on-screen colors.

LED Brightness

LED brightness is often advertised in beam millicandela (mcd). This refers to how intense the light is at a peak angle. To increase a mcd rating, the manufacturer need simply shape the reflector cup and lens to aim the light like a spotlight. More of the light is then concentrated at a narrow angle, making it more intense (brighter).

The mcd rating is barely useful if you really need a bright spot, since you don't know how wide and evenly distributed the bright spot is. Lower-quality LEDs often have a halo shape with a dark hole in the center.

The mcd rating is completely misleading if you're concerned with overall light output. Lumens (lm) is the measurement unit that sums up all of the light, regardless of direction. The manufacturer can't play with lumen numbers by redirecting the light in a single direction because the total light remains the same.

■ **Note** The United States Environmental Protection Agency (EPA) now requires that consumer light bulbs indicate their value in lumens. Unfortunately, this mandate doesn't apply to LEDs.

Lux or footcandle (fc) measurements describe how much light falls in a given area at a given distance away. It doesn't tell you how much total light is coming out of an LED from all sides, nor does it say how evenly distributed the light is.

Super Ultra High Brightness to the Max

LEDs are often advertised in categories such as high brightness, super brightness, and ultra brightness. These terms are purely subjective and there isn't any industry standard. Sorry, but they're meaningless.

LED Efficiency

Efficiency is how much electricity goes in compared to how much light comes out. LEDs are becoming more and more efficient with advances in technology. This is particularly important to battery-powered robots.

For visible light, efficiency is measured in lumens per watt (lm/W). Recall that lumens measures total light output, regardless of direction. Take your total light (lumens) and divide that by your total power (watts) and that tells you how much power was used for each drop of light.

Unfortunately, few manufacturers specify lm/W. This makes it very difficult to tell if a "high-efficiency" LED really is more efficient. However, in most cases, true "high-efficiency" LEDs do illuminate better at lower power levels.

Extreme Close Up of an LED

Most LEDs have two wires, called leads (see Figure 10-8). You must connect positive voltage to the anode lead and negative voltage to the cathode lead. An ordinary LED won't light if the leads are connected in reverse. Not only that, but the diode-characteristic of an LED prevents electricity from even passing through it in reverse.

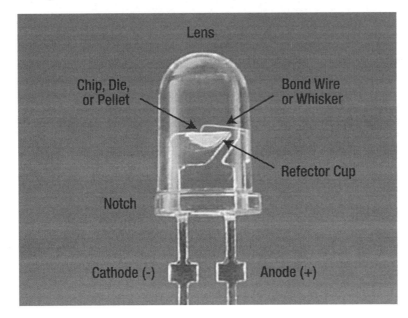

Figure 10-8. Anatomy of an LED

To determine which lead is the cathode, look for a flat or notched side on the bottom of the otherwise round lens. Also, the cathode lead wire is usually shorter than the anode lead wire.

Most often (but not always), the cathode is connected to the side with the reflector cup (see Figure 10-8 and Figure 10-9). The reflector cup is a tiny, rounded mirror that aims light forward.

Figure 10-9. View of a reflector cup and die

Inside the reflector cup is a die (see Figure 10-10), also called a chip or pellet. This is the part of the LED that actually emits light. The manufacturer adjusts the chemistry of the die to control the LED's color.

Figure 10-10. Glowing die with a view of the bonding wire and bonding site

A bond wire (also called a whisker) connects the die to the anode lead. The bond wire is very thin! With some clear LEDs, you can actually see the shadow of that wire (and sometimes the shape of the die) when you aim the LED at the ceiling.

Identifying Multicolor LEDs

Placing more than one die into an LED allows it to emit more than one color (see Figure 10-11). The lens is usually water-clear or white-diffused, because it wouldn't make much sense to tint the lens with a single color for an LED that can display two or more colors.

Figure 10-11. Side view of a two-color (red and green) tri-state LED

Multicolor LEDs are useful for conserving space or for showing multiple statuses. For example: white is off, red is error, green is ready.

Bicolor

Bicolor usually refers to a multicolor LED that has two leads. When the electricity flows in one direction, the LED lights with one color. When the electricity flows in the other direction, the LED lights with the other color.

Since electricity can't flow in opposite directions at the same time, only one color can be lit at a time. However, you can switch the flow back and forth really quickly. To human eyes, the result will be a third color that is a mix of the first two.

Tricolor or Tri-state

Tricolor usually refers to a multicolor LED that has three leads, instead of two (refer back to Figure 10-11). One lead for the first color, another lead for the second color, and a third lead that they share. If they share the cathode (-), it's called common cathode. If they share the anode (+), it's called common anode.

Because one wire is dedicated to each of the two LED colors, they can be enabled at the same time. This permits three colors (one on, the other on, or both on) plus "off."

Full Color

Full-color LEDs are the Holy Grail! These RGB LEDs contain red, green, and blue dies within the same LED. By electrically adjusting the brightness of each die, you can mix the primary colors together to create almost any color.

RGB LEDs have four leads (see Figure 10-12): one lead for red, one lead for green, one lead for blue, and one lead to share. That makes them more complicated to hook up.

Figure 10-12. Red, green, and blue in a single LED can make almost any color

In the last ten years, the cost of an RGB LED has dropped to $1/10^{th}$ the price. You can find them at almost every electronics reseller. For example, SparkFun Electronics sells a 5 mm full color LED for $1.95 (clear lens #COM-00105, diffused lens #COM-09264)

Testing an LED

The most obvious way to test an LED is to connect it to a circuit (next chapter) and see if it lights up. However, if your multimeter has a diode test function, you can safely test LEDs and learn a few things about them.

Setting Up a Multimeter for Diode Testing

1. On the multimeter, the black lead should be connected to the COM terminal.

2. The red lead is usually connected to Ω terminal, but you should check your multimeter's manual.

3. Turn the multimeter dial to the diode symbol, which looks like an arrow crashing into a wall (see Figure 10-13). This indicates a component that allows electricity to flow in one direction (the arrow) but not the other direction (the wall). The diode setting is appropriate for LEDs, because the "D" in "LED" stands for diode.

Figure 10-13. Diode setting on multimeter dial

4. Power up the meter and note what the display indicates. Some meters show "0L" or "OPEN" or something else to indicate that no electricity is currently passing between the probes.

5. Select an ordinary **red** LED. The color is important for this test.

6. Find the cathode lead of the LED. Usually that's the shorter of the two wires, but check for a flat notch at the bottom of the LED lens to be sure. Connect the black probe to the LED's cathode (-) and connect the red probe to the LED's anode (+) (see Figure 10-14). It's a lot easier if you use hook adaptors on the multimeter test probe tips. Don't worry if you connect the LED in reverse. It's not harmful.

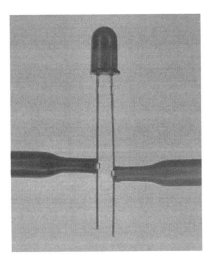

Figure 10-14. LED connected to hook adapter probes for testing

Interpreting LED Test Results

If the multimeter display doesn't change values when the LED is connected, it's likely the LED has been put in backwards (see Figure 10-15). If that's not the problem, double check that all the meter leads are firmly connected to the meter terminals and that the probes are making good contact with the LED leads.

Figure 10-15. Open circuit indicating a test error or damaged LED

If there isn't a problem with the test setup, it could be that the LED is damaged. It's unlikely that a fresh red LED is going to be broken. However, electrically abused LEDs are likely to have their bond wire melted or some other form of disconnection. In those cases, the LED's internal circuitry is permanently broken open and can't pass power through.

There's also a problem if the meter displays a voltage rating around zero (see Figure 10-16). It is very likely that the LED's anode and cathode leads are accidentally touching each other or that the multimeter test probe's tips are accidentally touching each other.

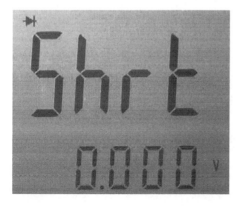

Figure 10-16. Short circuit or zero volts indicate a test error or damaged LED.

If there isn't a problem with the test setup, it could be that the LED is damaged. A diode voltage value below 400 mV (0.4 V) indicates the power is passing almost directly from the anode to the cathode without passing through the die. This is called a short circuit. It's unlikely that an LED would kick the bucket this way. An open or partially open circuit is more common.

If all goes well, the multimeter will display a red LED's voltage value as being somewhere around 1.6 volts (see Figure 10-17). A lot of meters display this rating in millivolts (mV). For example, 1632 mV is the same as 1.632 V.

Figure 10-17. Multimeter displaying normal LED value

■ **Tip** Take a close look at your LED as the multimeter tests it. The LED may be lit up dimly. (You may need to cup your hands around the LED to block the room's lighting.) This is a good trick for proving that the LED is working and also to give you a sense of the LED's efficiency. Poorer-quality LEDs won't light up at all or will have just a glimmer. High-efficiency LEDs will be quite noticeable.

If you haven't already, try reversing the LED leads to see what the meter displays when an LED is hooked up backwards. It should be "open" or "0L." If the LED works in both directions, it's likely a bicolor.

Try a bunch of different kinds of LEDs. You may notice that the physical size of the LED doesn't affect the voltage rating displayed. However, the color does!

Colors nearer to red (including infrared) generally have a lower voltage value and colors nearer to blue have a higher voltage value. In fact, many older or cheaper meters' diode modes usually can't go high enough to test the 2.5 volts required by true green, blue, and white LEDs. That's why I had you start by testing a red LED.

Forward Voltage Drop

The voltage value displayed on the meter is called the forward voltage drop. That is, if the electricity is moving in the correct direction (forward), then this is how much voltage the LED consumes (drops).

Obviously, voltage usage is valuable information for any component you want to use in your robot. This gives you an idea of minimum battery voltage requirements and how many you can string together for a given battery.

When purchasing LEDs, beware of those listed as having forward voltages (V_f) above 4 V. For example, some blue LEDs are listed at 5 V to 5.5 V. Advanced robot circuits operate at 5 V or lower and many microcontrollers won't guarantee their outputs will always exceed 4.5 V. This makes it impossible to illuminate 5.5 V LEDs without additional circuitry.

Variety Pack

Order some assorted packages of LEDs (see Table 10-2). A mixed bulk bag is an inexpensive way to become familiar with sizes, colors, shapes, and lenses. Also, because you may damage some LEDs in your early experiments, it's more comforting to blow a $0.09 red than a $2.99 blue.

Before buying a large quantity of a single kind of LED (as opposed to a variety pack), it's best to begin by ordering only a few of that type to insure the overall light output and quality meet your needs. You'd be surprised how off-color and spotty some LEDs can be.

Table 10-2. LED Assortments

Supplier	Part Number	Price	Number of LEDs
Electronic Goldmine	GP27	$2.49	50 assorted (although some surface-mount)
Electronic Goldmine	GP36	$2.49	15 uniquely shaped assorted
Jameco	18041	$7.95	100 standard assorted
Electronix Express	32LEDGRAB	$5.90	100 variety assorted grab bag
Electronix Express	3200LPK	$12.95	75 variety assorted
Electronix Express	3200LPKD	$19.00	105 deluxe assorted

Brightening Your Way

Sandwich, the line-following robot, lights up with eleven different LEDs (see Figure 10-18). Three green LEDs and three yellow LEDs indicate the brightest path. Three red LEDs sit inside the motor tube to illuminate it from the inside, purely for fun. Two white LEDs act as headlights, for following lines at night or through tunnels.

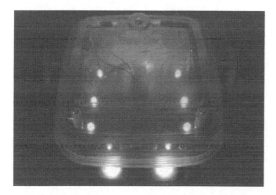

Figure 10-18. Eleven LEDs light up Sandwich.

The green, yellow, and red LEDs tend to be inexpensive. In fact, all of the colored LEDs combined cost less than the white LEDs. I could have chosen something other than white to light the path, but it wouldn't have reflected as well off of all possible path colors.

Not only do cool-looking LEDs bring attention to your robot, but also they can be tremendously helpful in diagnosing a problem when used as indicators. It's a good idea to have a bunch lying around.

You've read through ten chapters of the book. Perhaps the battery, alligator clips, resistors, and LEDs provide enough parts to build a circuit? Let's find out.

■ ■ ■

CHAPTER 11

Power On!

Building and Testing a Power Indicator Circuit

Nearly all robots need a power indicator light. It's a very simple circuit to build.

In this chapter, you're going to make a power indicator using the parts and tools you've read about in the previous chapters. You'll learn a little about the role of each component and how to use the multimeter to test that the circuit is working as designed.

A circuit description generally includes a parts list, schematic, and wiring diagram, as well as photographs and step-by-step building instructions. As you gain experience, you'll discover that all circuits reuse common techniques and patterns, so their accompanying documentation mostly focuses on the core concepts or tricky portions.

Introducing the Parts List

A parts list is a brief description of each of the components that are in a circuit. Sometimes tools will be mentioned in a parts list, but usually not. Small circuits typically don't include parts lists, as the illustration or diagram of the circuit provides enough information to figure out the required inventory.

Here's the parts list for the power indicator circuit:

- Multimeter for testing

- 9 V battery, preferably rechargeable

- Three alligator clip jumper leads, preferably red, green, and black

- 1 kΩ resistor (brown, black, red, and gold color-code bands)

- Red LED

Testing the Parts Before Assembly

Before building, be sure to test all of your parts with a multimeter. This isn't vital when you're connecting stuff together temporarily with alligator clips. However, it's sensible to test each part if you're going to permanently solder them, especially if any expensive parts are involved.

From the prior chapters, you know how to use your multimeter to test for the following requirements:

- The battery's voltage should be between 7 V and 10 V. A reading of 9 V is optimal.

- The alligator jumpers should have less than 1 Ω resistance (good continuity).

- The 1 kΩ resistor should be between 950 Ω and 1050 Ω.

- The red LED should have a voltage drop between 1.4 V and 2.0 V.

Reading a Schematic

A schematic illustrates the logical connections between all of the parts (see Figure 11-1). Different types of parts have different symbols. The symbols don't look much like the real life object, but after you've seen a few schematics, you'll begin recognizing the symbols.

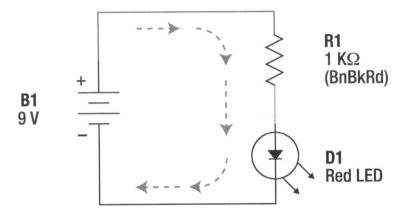

Figure 11-1. Power indicator circuit schematic

Each part is labeled with a letter and number. The letter relates to the type of part, like "R" for resistor. This is a nice hint if you don't recognize the schematic symbol.

Along with the letter, there's a number that ensures that each part is labeled uniquely. If two resistors appear in the schematic, they would be labeled R1 and R2. The number doesn't necessarily suggest anything about the location or value of the part; it simply gives it a distinctive name.

A bit of significant information about the part is usually displayed in the schematic along with the part label. Referring to the schematic in Figure 11-1:

B1 – 9 V battery. Notice the location of the positive (+) and negative (-) indicators. The symbol for a battery is two or more horizontal lines of different widths.

R1 –1 kΩ resistor. "(BnBkRd)" is my shorthand for indicating that the resistor's color-code bands are brown, black, and red. The last band, tolerance, is usually omitted as most resistors are gold (5%) or better nowadays. The symbol for a resistor is a sharp, squiggly line.

D1 – Red LED. I used the letter "D" because an LED is a diode. It would have been perfectly acceptable to use "LED1." In fact, "LED1" is preferable in circuits that contain other types of diodes. Notice the symbol inside the circle is the arrow crashing into a wall, just like on the multimeter dial. The two arrows coming out of the circle represent light emissions.

Center arrows – (five arrows in the middle) Sometimes arrows are drawn to show the flow of electricity though a circuit. In this conventional depiction, electricity comes out of the positive terminal of the battery, through the resistor, through the LED, and into the other end of the battery.

Building the Power Indicator Circuit

You're now going to build the power indicator circuit by connecting the parts together with alligator clips (see Figure 11-2).

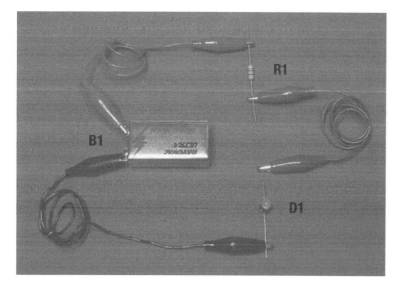

Figure 11-2. *Photograph of the assembled power indicator circuit*

1. Connect one red alligator clip to the positive terminal of the 9 V battery.

2. Connect the other red alligator clip (the other end of the same red jumper) to one lead (wire) of the resistor. It doesn't matter which end of the resistor is connected.

3. Connect one green alligator clip to the other end of the resistor.

4. Connect the other green alligator clip to the anode lead of the red LED. See the earlier chapter if you don't remember how to locate the anode lead.

5. Connect one black alligator clip to the cathode lead of the red LED.

STOP! The last connection is going to be to the other end of the battery. But, you should always check your circuit before making the final connection to the battery. With only one connection to the battery so far, no electricity is flowing.

For a moment, pretend you're a lazy drop of electricity. The battery is a pump shoving you (electricity) out of the battery and into the wire pipe. You don't like being outside of the battery. Your mission: Get back to the battery as quickly and easily (you're lazy) as possible. If you can find any shortcuts, take them. Jumping through the air is not easy, so that's not a shortcut.

Are any metal pieces touching any other metal pieces by accident? Those are great shortcuts.

Make sure that the electricity has no choice but to go out the battery, through the red jumper, through the resistor, through the green jumper, through the LED, and then into the other end of the battery. This is the path you want the electricity to take in its quest to return to the battery.

Ready?

6. Connect the remaining black clip to the negative terminal of the 9 V battery.

Do You See The Light?

Hopefully you're patting yourself on the back for a job well done. You've got a beautiful red light.

If the red LED isn't lit, check all of your connections. Alligator clips tend to slip off.

If the red LED still isn't lit, perhaps it's in backwards. No harm done. Disconnect both ends of the LED, flip it around, and reconnect both ends.

Experimenting with the Power Indicator Circuit

After admiring your red LED for a while, here are some things to try:

- Disconnect the red LED and put a different color or size in its place.

- Reverse the resistor connections. It won't make any difference; the resistance won't change. Resistors are non-polarized. That is, resistors don't care which end is connected to the negative or the positive. This is a fairly boring experiment since nothing happens differently when the resistor is flipped, but that alone is worth noting.

- Reverse the LED connections. It won't light in the wrong direction. LEDs are polarized. That is, they **do** care which end is connected to the negative and the positive.

- Disconnect any one of the alligator clips. The LED turns off. It doesn't matter where you disconnect a circuit; if the entire branch or loop isn't connected to both ends of the battery, it stops working. (Because the pipe cuts off before reaching the other end of the battery, there isn't anywhere for the electrical drops to go. With nowhere to go, there isn't any room for more drops to get squeezed out. It's a bad traffic jam on a dead-end street.)

Understanding the Roles of Each Component

Each part of the power indicator circuit provides a vital function.

The battery, B1, is the pump. It takes electrons (electricity drops) and sends them around and around the loop.

The alligator clips and wire leads are the pipes. They deliver the electrons to the desired parts.

The resistor, R1, protects the "delicate" LED from the full force of the battery. Recall that resistors are like narrower pipes or skinny holes that only let a desired maximum amount of electricity through.

The resistor's restriction of flow also prevents waste. We only care that the LED lights up, we don't want to use any more battery power than that.

The red LED, D1, is the purpose of the circuit. The battery, wires, and resistor are only there to provide for the LED's needs.

Measuring the Power Indicator Circuit

Within a circuit, there are two useful measurements that you can make: voltage (pressure) and current (flow).

Measuring In-Circuit Voltage

Testing voltages throughout a circuit is the most common test you'll perform. This tells you whether each part is receiving the desired range of "pressure." Too little voltage and the part won't operate; too much voltage and the part will break.

1. Set up your multimeter as you would to measure battery voltage (see Figure 11-3). Use a hook or alligator clip adapter on the black (COM) test probe. However, the red test probe should be a bare metal tip since you're going to move it around a lot.

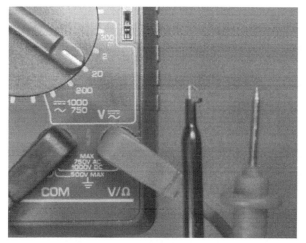

Figure 11-3. Multimeter setup for measuring voltage at various locations in a circuit

2. Turn on your LED circuit. The measurements are going to be made with the power on.

3. With the black alligator clip still attached, connect the multimeter's black test probe hook to the negative terminal of the 9 V battery (see Figure 11-4). The black test probe will stay there as you touch the red test probe tip to various other locations on the circuit.

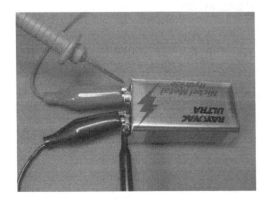

Figure 11-4. Black probe hooked onto negative battery terminal. Red probe can be moved freely.

4. When you touch the red test probe tip to the positive terminal of the battery, the multimeter should indicate the battery's voltage as expected. My battery is 9.15 V.

5. Touch the red test probe tip to the clip at the other end of the red alligator jumper. You shouldn't see any change in voltage. Remember, the jumper wire is just a pipe; it shouldn't use up any voltage.

6. Touch the red test probe tip to the top resistor lead. You still shouldn't see any change in voltage. The resistor lead is also a pipe.

7. Touch the red test probe tip to the lower lead of the resistor (see Figure 11-5). Finally some action! The voltage should drop significantly. My circuit is 1.8 V at this point.

Figure 11-5. Red probe detecting the voltage at the point after the resistor

What happened? The resistor did its job. It reduced the voltage to an amount acceptable to the LED coming up. (That's not exactly a technically accurate explanation, but good enough for now.)

8. Touch the red test probe tip to each of the green alligator clips and then to the anode of the red LED. The voltage should still be 1.8 V (or whatever you saw earlier). The green jumper and anode wire are pipes. They aren't using up voltage.

9. Touch the red test probe tip to the cathode of the red LED. The voltage should drop to zero at this point. The red LED used up all of the remaining voltage.

10. Touch the red test probe tip to the black alligator clips. Zero voltage. Touch the red test probe tip to the negative terminal of the battery (same as the black test probe hook). Zero voltage. No matter what parts you install in a circuit, by the time the electricity reaches the other end of the battery, the voltage is always zero.

Measuring Voltage "At" a Point

The test method you've just been using answers the question, "What's the voltage *at* such-and-such a point?" To check the voltage at a particular point, always connect the multimeter's black test probe to the negative terminal of the battery and touch the red test probe to the point in question.

As you make your way down the circuit, the voltage decreases as each major part uses up some voltage.

Measuring Voltage "Drop" or Voltage "Across" a Part

Often you'll be interested in how much voltage a particular part uses up by itself. One way of determining this is to perform a little math.

Here's what I calculated for my circuit:

The voltage before the resistor is 9.15 V. The voltage after the resistor is 1.8 V. So, the resistor uses 7.35 V.

The voltage before the LED is 1.8 V. The voltage after the LED is 0 V. So, the LED uses 1.8 V.

You don't need to calculate these numbers. You can test the voltage usage of an individual part with a multimeter. The meter dial stays the same from the last voltage measurement, except now the red test probe goes above the resistor and the black test probe goes below the resistor (see Figure 11-6). The meter should display 7.35 V (or whatever you calculated for your circuit).

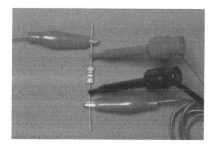

Figure 11-6. Red and black test probes detecting the voltage dropped only by the resistor

■ **Caution** Don't test the resistor's resistance with the multimeter's Ω mode while the resistor is in the circuit!! Only use voltage mode in a circuit, not Ω mode. Otherwise, you might damage your meter.

In Ω mode, the multimeter actually supplies its own voltage to the test resistor and measures how much of the voltage is consumed by the test resistor in comparison to a known-value resistor inside the multimeter. As such, the multimeter is not expecting voltage to already exist across the test resistor. If a high-enough voltage already exists, the external electrical pressure can break through the unsuspecting circuit inside the meter.

On the other hand, a multimeter in voltage mode expects external voltage to be in the circuit, because that's exactly what the multimeter is supposed to be measuring. So, as long as you dial a reasonably high-enough voltage range on the multimeter dial, the multimeter's electronics are designed to expect and thus withstand external voltage.

Test the voltage used by the LED by placing the red test probe above the LED and the black test probe below the LED (see Figure 11-7). The meter should display 1.8 V (or whatever you calculated for your circuit).

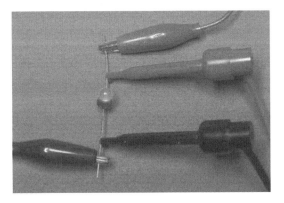

Figure 11-7. Red and black probe detecting the voltage dropped by the LED

In an earlier chapter, you tested the LED using the diode mode of the multimeter. The amount of voltage being used up by the LED in a circuit will usually be a little higher than the multimeter diode mode indicated.

■ **Caution** Don't test the LED with the multimeter's diode mode while the LED is in the circuit!! Only use voltage mode in a circuit, not diode mode. Otherwise, you might damage your meter.

In diode mode, the multimeter actually supplies its own voltage to the test diode, just like it supplies its own voltage to test resistors in Ω mode. External voltage in the diode may be high enough to melt unprepared circuits inside the meter.

Summarizing Circuit Voltage

The wires (alligator jumpers and component leads) didn't use any voltage. The LED used about the amount of voltage the meter's diode mode said it would. The resistor used up the remaining voltage.

Depending on where you place the test probes, the multimeter can measure the voltage at a particular point or the voltage used across a single part.

Measuring Current Flow

The second most common test you'll perform on a circuit is current flow. Voltage measures how much **force** each drop has; current is a count of how **many** drops are going through the circuit. Current is a vital measurement for determining how long your batteries are going to last.

1   Disconnect the multimeter test probes if they are presently connected to the circuit.

2   As always, the black test lead is connected to the COM terminal on the multimeter.

3   But, the red test lead now needs to be unplugged from the V terminal and connected to the A or mA terminal on the multimeter (see Figure 11-8). Check your meter manual for exact instructions.

Figure 11-8. *Multimeter setup for mA current flow*

4   For this measurement, both the red and black probes should have hook adaptors on the ends.

5   Rotate the meter dial to the mA, A, or amp function. If you have a manual ranging meter, you'll want to choose some number over 20 mA (milli). If you prefer, you can start at a higher range and work your way down.

Previously, when measuring voltage, the meter test probes always connected on top of an existing part. You didn't need to disconnect anything in the circuit to make the measurement. However, to measure current flow, the meter needs to have all electrical drops pass through the meter to be counted. Think of it like a subway turnstile. Nobody is allowed to continue through the circuit until they pass through the meter.

6   Hook up your power indicator circuit and make sure the LED is lit.

7   Now, disconnect the red alligator clip from the positive terminal of the battery and connect it to the black test probe hook (see Figure 11-9).

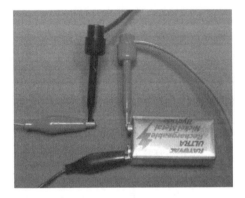

Figure 11-9. Power indicator circuit connection for current-flow measuring

8   Connect the red test probe hook to the positive terminal of the battery.

With this setup, all of the electricity that leaves the battery is going into the meter's red probe, through the meter for counting, out the meter's black probe, and into the red alligator clip. With this arrangement, the meter is guaranteed to count every drop of current pushed out by the battery and used by the circuit.

If all goes well, the red LED should be lit and the meter should be displaying between 5 mA and 10 mA. My circuit measured 7.2 mA (see Figure 11-10).

Figure 11-10. Multimeter displaying 7.2 mA of current flowing through circuit

If the LED doesn't light, check all of the connections and the dial settings. If the value displayed on the meter is negative (like -7.2 mA) then you've got the black and red test probes reversed.

Calculating Battery Life

Assuming you have a fresh 9 V battery in your circuit, you can now determine how long it will last. Usually the fresh battery capacity is published on the package or on the manufacturer's web site. If you don't know the official capacity rating of your 9 V battery, you can assume 595 mAh for alkaline and 150 mAh for rechargeable.

Take the mAh (milliamp hour) battery capacity and divide it by the mA (milliamp) current usage of your circuit. This tells you how many hours the battery can power your circuit.

For example: I have a 150 mAh rechargeable battery and my power indicator circuit is using 7.2 mA.

```
150 mAh / 7.2 mA = 20.8 h
```

That's almost 21 hours.

Extending Battery Life

If you can reduce the current flow, you can extend the battery life. Recall that resistors not only protect the other parts from the force of the battery, but that resistors also prevent wasted power.

Instead of the 1 kΩ resistor, try substituting a 2.2 kΩ resistor (red, red, red, gold color bands). That's slightly more than double the resistance. It's twice as good as resisting flow. Go ahead and try that now.

The multimeter should reflect the decrease in current flow due to the 2.2 kΩ resistor. My circuit went from 7.2 mA down to 3.4 mA. That means the battery life is now 44 hours:

```
150 mAh / 3.4 mA = 44 h
```

However, the LED isn't as bright as it was.

Try some other resistor values (see Figure 11-11). You can pick values as large as you want, but don't go below 470 Ω. Watch the meter and observe the brightness of the LED.

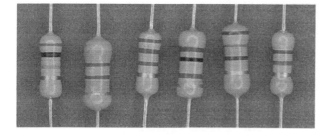

Figure 11-11. Resistor values for experimenting: from 10,000 Ω down to 470 Ω

As the Ω value increases, the battery life increases but the LED dims (see Table 11-1). As the Ω value decreases, the battery life decreases but the LED brightens.

Table 11-1. Resistance Versus Battery Life and Brightness

Resistance	Band Colors	Current	Battery Life	LED Brightness
10,000 Ω	brown, black, orange, gold	0.7 mA	200 hours	Very dim
4,700 Ω	yellow, violet, red, gold	1.6 mA	94 hours	Dim
2,200 Ω	red, red, red, gold	3.4 mA	44 hours	Acceptable
1,000 Ω	brown, black, red, gold	7.2 mA	21 hours	Good
680 Ω	blue, gray, brown, gold	10.5 mA	14 hours	Bright
470 Ω	yellow, violet, brown, gold	15.1 mA	10 hours	Very Bright

It is important to note that the LED's brightness depends on the current flowing through it, not the voltage. Many electronic parts work this way. They are said to be "current driven."

Selecting Resistors

When I first started experimenting with electronics, I couldn't figure out how people chose the values for resistors. Somehow I thought there would be one absolutely correct value for a specific use.

Within a particular range, resistor value selection is a matter of taste. It depends on the designer's perception of performance. If the LED is bright enough at 2,200 Ω, that will save on battery life. If battery life isn't an issue but brightness is, perhaps 1,000 Ω is a better choice. Resistor values are negotiable.

How bright can the LED get? According to the manufacturer's datasheets, the maximum rated current for my LED is 30 mA.

You could move the multimeter test probes to immediately before the LED to test the amount of current going through the LED. You'd reconnect the red alligator clip to the positive terminal of the battery. Then you'd disconnect the green alligator clip from the LED anode and connect the meter probes in between (see Figure 11-12).

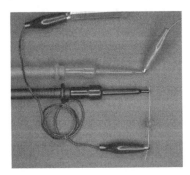

Figure 11-12. Counting current between the green clip and the LED

But, since there isn't any return path to the battery except for the one that goes through the LED, the count of electrons coming out of the battery is the same count as those going through the LED and returning into the other end of the battery. All the current that leaves the battery must pass through the LED. So, there's no reason to move the multimeter probes to determine the amount of current flowing through the LED.

Calculating Current

Here's a simple formula that allows you to predict how much current a circuit will use before you build the circuit.

```
(V / Ω) × 1000 = mA
```

Let's see if the formula matches our test results. For my circuit, the voltage at the resistor is actually 9.15 V and the resistor's resistance is actually 1020 Ω.

```
(9.15 V / 1020 Ω) × 1000 = 8.97 mA
```

Oh no! Something's wrong. 8.97 mA is predicted but only 7.2 mA was measured.
Ah ha! The resistor doesn't use all 9.15 V; the LED uses some. The resistor only uses 7.35 V.

```
(7.35 V / 1020 Ω) × 1000 = 7.2 mA
```

Perfect.

Minimum Resistor for LED Formula

Here's a formula that allows you to determine the lowest value resistor you can use to protect an LED. You need to test your battery's voltage and test the LED in the multimeter's diode mode. You need to look up the LED's maximum forward current rating on the manufacturer's datasheet.

```
(battery voltage - LED voltage) / (maximum LED current in mA / 1000) = minimum resistor
```

For the power indicator circuit:

```
(9.15 V - 1.8 V) / (30 mA / 1000) = 245 Ω
```

The calculation reveals a 245 Ω minimum, but earlier I warned you not to go below 470 Ω. Well, that provided a bit of safety in case your battery had a little more voltage or your LED used a little less voltage.

Don't Measure Voltage with Probe in Current Terminal

To test current, you had to pull the red test lead from the V terminal on the multimeter. You put the red test lead into the mA, A, or amp terminal. This formed a pipe in the multimeter to let the electricity flow through and get counted.

Let's say you now decide to test the voltage of the resistor but you forget to put the red test lead back into the V terminal. You put the red and black test probes above and below the resistor. Poof! Suddenly your light emitting diode becomes a smoke emitting diode.

■ **Note** Just kidding. The LED dies without drama.

What happened? Because the multimeter has become a pipe to test for current, the electricity can now get around the resistor (see Figure 11-13). It's like the resistor isn't in the circuit anymore. The LED takes the full force of the battery, destroying it.

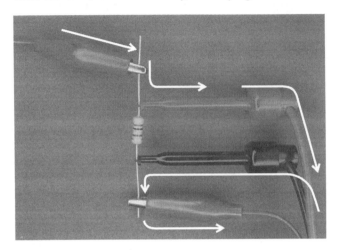

Figure 11-13. Electricity accidentally getting around the resistor through multimeter amp mode

Don't laugh. You're going to do it one day.

The point is, be sure to switch your red test lead back to the multimeter's V terminal before you test for voltage. Or, an even safer practice is to get in the habit of always putting the meter's red test lead back into the V socket and turning the dial to voltage mode as soon as you're done measuring current.

Circuit Summary

Important things described in this chapter:

- A schematic is a symbolic illustration of the parts in a circuit.

- Each part in a schematic is labeled with a letter and number so that it can be referred to without confusing it with any other part in that particular schematic.

- You can test voltage at any point by connecting the black test probe to the negative end of the battery and touching the red test probe to the point to be measured.

- You can test voltage used by (dropped across) a particular part by connecting the red test probe immediately before and the black test probe immediately after the part to be measured.

- You can test the current used by an entire circuit by changing the multimeter mode, switching the red test lead terminal, and connecting the test probes in line with the positive terminal of the battery.

- Battery life is directly proportional to the amount of current a circuit uses.

- The amount of current that passes through it controls the brightness of an LED.

- You can adjust current by changing resistor values.

- Too much current can destroy an LED, so always use a resistor to protect it.

Alligator clips work satisfactorily for short, simple circuits that contain only a few parts. However, sometimes clips slip off and sometimes the exposed pieces of metal accidentally touch each other. Sometimes the circuit even becomes a giant tangled ball.

There is a much better way to quickly create test circuits. Read on!

CHAPTER 12

■ ■ ■

Solderless Prototyping

Sandwich, the line-following robot, has a fairly simple circuit. Even so, at least 30 or 40 electrical connections need to be made. Consider what you have planned for your ultimate robot and you'll see that alligator clips are not going to be sufficient. In this chapter, you'll learn about a popular technology for experimenting.

Needing A Better Way

When designing a robot circuit, mistakes will be made. Also, most builders throw in some new items with each creation in an endeavor to advance their knowledge. These two factors necessitate some sort of test phase, which is called prototyping. This is the time to try things before committing to a final design.

For electronic circuits, something is needed to allow easy switching of parts and rearrangement of wires to encourage experimentation. The prototyping technology should be inexpensive, stable, and accept the same components as the final device.

All in all, a few alligator clips are acceptable for temporary connections to either batteries or measurement equipment. Beyond that, engineers look to more stable methods of making connections.

Solderless Breadboards

The solderless breadboard (see Figure 12-1) is a great prototyping solution. As the name implies, a solderless breadboard doesn't require any soldering. Wires and components are simply pushed into holes on the board to connect them together. No mess; no fuss. You can us the holes, wires, and components over and over again.

I always try out a new part or module design using a solderless breadboard. Although I often begin by thinking I'm fairly certain how a circuit is going to be built, a number of improvements are subsequently made because it's so easy to try variations on the breadboard.

Even after soldering together a final circuit, my original prototypes usually sit intact on their solderless breadboards. As long as I have spare parts (and spare breadboards), I retain the original for later experiments, debugging, or brainstorming.

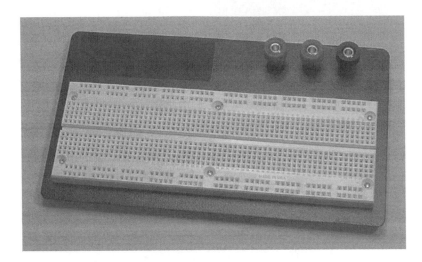

Figure 12-1. 840 tie-point solderless breadboard with base and three binding posts

Connecting with Holes

Technically, the holes in a breadboard are called tie points. When a wire is pushed into a hole, it makes contact with a solid metal strip underneath (see Figure 12-2). When another wire is pushed into a hole on the same strip, the wires are connected. The metal strip acts as a connecting pipe that allows electricity to flow from one wire to the other.

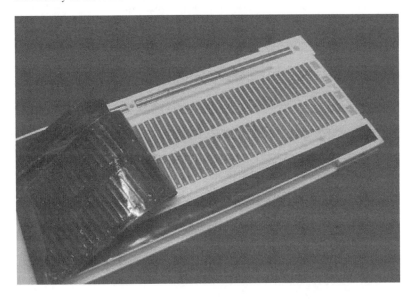

Figure 12-2. Exposed view of metal strips underneath the holes

The holes are spaced every tenth of an inch. Underneath, each hole has individual metal prongs to firmly grip the wires or components that are inserted. Ideally, the component wires should have diameters from 0.38 mm to 0.81 mm (0.015 inches to 0.032 inches). Smaller wires tend to slip out or connect intermittently. Larger wires tend to jam and damage the hole or metal prongs.

5-Position Group

Most of the holes on the breadboard are physically connected in groups of five. Any and all wires pushed into the five holes are electrically connected to each other (see Figure 12-3).

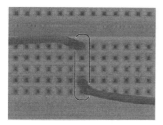

Figure 12-3. Two wires connected within a 5-position group

Put a wire in each of the five holes of the 5-position group and all five wires will then be connected. Or, put just a couple of wires in and they'll still be connected to each other, with a couple of empty holes remaining.

Adjacent groups are independent of each other. A wire in one 5-position group is **not** connected to a wire in an adjacent 5-position group (see Figure 12-4).

Figure 12-4. Two wires disconnected because they're in different 5-position groups

However, if you want to, you can connect 5-position groups together. Simply push each end of a single wire into a hole in each group (see Figure 12-5). This wire is now connecting together the two metal strips underneath. Anything connected to one strip is now also connected to the other.

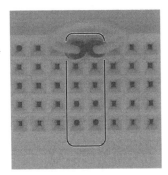

Figure 12-5. Using both ends of a wire to connect groups together

Center Gap

There's a gap in the center of the board. A wire in one 5-position group is **not** connected to a wire in a 5-position group across the gap (see Figure 12-6).

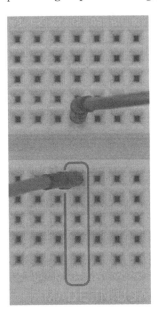

Figure 12-6. Two wires disconnected because they're across the gap from each other

The gap is designed for a DIP (Dual Inline Package), as demonstrated by Figure 12-7. DIP refers to the case style and size, not the manufacturer or the function of the part.

Figure 12-7. Center gap designed for DIPs

Place a DIP so that each pin connects to its own 5-position group. When properly placed, it just so happens that the middle of the part crosses over the gap. This makes it easy to insert a tool to pop out the part.

The part is in the wrong orientation if several DIP pins are left hanging in the gap (see Figure 12-8). Obviously, this makes it difficult to connect wires to the pins. Even worse, when placed in the wrong orientation, several DIP pins are connected to the same 5-position group.

Figure 12-8. Improperly placed DIP with pins in the gap

25-Position Distribution Bus

At this point, you've probably got the board figured out. Everything is in groups of five. Well, what's the deal with the two leftover rows running the length of the top and bottom?

The two horizontal rows of holes at the top and bottom of the breadboard are called distribution buses (see Figure 12-9). Although they appear to be horizontal groups of five, they are actually connected underneath to a metal strip that is much longer, 25 holes.

Figure 12-9. Two wires connected on a distribution bus

It's named the bus because it's long with many points along the way, like a real bus line. Getting on at one end can take you halfway across town, or you can get off at points in between.

There's a good reason why there are two rows of distribution buses at both the top and bottom of the board: Many parts in the circuit need nearby access to power. You can connect one of the bus rows to the positive end of the battery and the other bus row to the negative end of the battery. Now all the parts have convenient power access.

Depending on the length of a breadboard, the buses may be disconnected in the middle of the board. If you want the buses to run the entire length of the board, just connect the middle of each row with wire (see Figure 12-10).

Figure 12-10. Extending buses by connecting with wire

Binding Posts

The fancier breadboards have binding posts (see Figure 12-11). They are not absolutely necessary, but the posts do make it easy to quickly connect and disconnect a power source without wear and tear on a breadboard hole or fragile wire.

Figure 12-11. Three binding posts: Middle post has banana plug and wire

Plastic caps insulate the binding posts. The caps are usually different colors. For consistency, use red for positive power and black for negative.

The plastic caps twist up to expose a small hole in the metal post. You can insert a wire through the post hole and screw the cap back down to hold the wire in place. You can then push the other end of the wire into a hole in the breadboard.

Atop the post is a jack (connection hole) for a banana plug.

Banana Plugs

Banana plugs? You bet. Banana plugs kind of look like bananas on the ends, to the same extent that alligator clips look like alligators on the ends.

The nicer banana plugs include jacks in the middle and rear (see Figure 12-12) so that you can insert and connect additional banana plugs. A pair of insulated banana plugs connected by a wire is called a banana test lead.

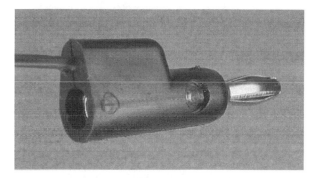

Figure 12-12. Banana plug with a jack in the middle and the rear

Banana plugs are often found on test equipment, like meters and scopes, and also found on laboratory power supplies.

Hungry for Breadboards

Breadboards are available in a variety of sizes (see Figure 12-13). The boards are usually classified by the number of tie points (holes). I probably have half a dozen of the 840 tie-point boards, as well as a couple of smaller 270 tie-point and larger 3220 tie-point boards. The 840-size makes a fine starter board (see Table 12-1).

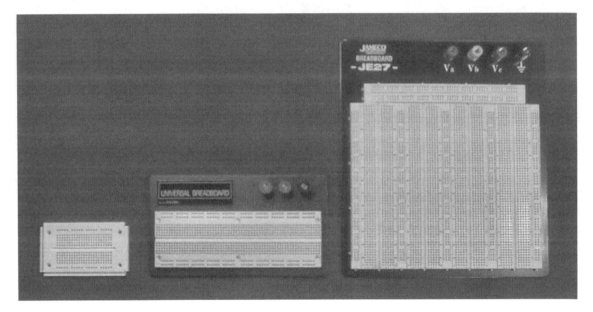

Figure 12-13. Solderless breadboards with 270, 840, and 3220 tie points

Table 12-1. Better-Quality Solderless Breadboards

Supplier	Part Number	Price	Tie Points	Binding Posts	Description
SparkFun	PRT-07916	$3.95	170	none	Colored : PRT-08800 to PRT-08803
Electronix Express	03SB02	$24.50	840	Three	3M Solderless Breadboard
Digi-Key	922309	$27.57	840	Three	3M ACE309 Solderless Breadboard
Jameco	20812	$33.95	3220	Four	Breadboard, Solderless

The "where to buy" lists that appear throughout this book serve as examples of the characteristics of parts you might want to consider. The lists usually aren't supposed to be exhaustive. However, the breadboard price list (see Table 12-1) is exclusive. I don't recommend buying any other boards than these, as some of the other boards I've tried have been unusable.

The metal strips in junky breadboards don't line up well with the holes (see Figure 12-14), causing parts to bend or resist as they are inserted or removed. A bad solderless breadboard makes the whole experience frustrating.

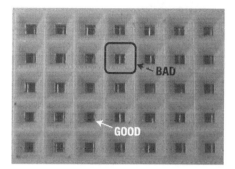

Figure 12-14. Poorly aligned tie-point prongs make holes almost unusable

■ **Tip** The holes in factory-fresh solderless breadboards tend to require a bit of exercising until they're conditioned. But after some use, the holes will hold firmly yet allow smooth insertion and release.

Solderless Breadboard Wire

Although solderless breadboards tolerate a range of wire diameters, the best is insulated solid #22 AWG (American wire gauge - a size standard, not a company) hook-up wire.

For solderless breadboards, use solid wire instead of stranded (see Figure 12-15). Stranded wire consists of numerous smaller wires twisted together. The individual wires tend to separate and bend when being inserted into breadboard holes.

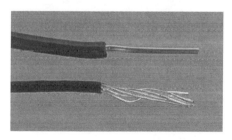

Figure 12-15. Insulated #22 AWG wire: solid (upper) *and stranded* (lower)

Ordinary copper (reddish-brown color) wire or tinned copper (silvery color) wire are equally good choices for breadboards.

Use #22 AWG size wire. Smaller diameters are a little loose in the holes and the wire tends to bend when being pushed in. Larger diameter wire jams the holes, often permanently forcing open the prongs of the metal connection underneath.

Use insulated wire. The rubber-like coating prevents unintended connections between portions of wires that accidentally touch. Also, the insulating coating is available in a variety of colors, which helps distinguish individual wires from each other (see Figure 12-16). At the very least, purchase red for positive power, black for negative, and some other color for signals (see Table 12-2).

Figure 12-16. Spools of colored, insulated #22 AWG copper wire

Table 12-2. Insulated #22 AWG Copper Hook-Up Wire

Supplier	Part Number	Price	Length	Color
Electronix Express	270022BK	$1.05	25 feet	Black
Electronix Express	270022RD	$1.05	25 feet	Red
Electronix Express	270022GN	$1.05	25 feet	Green
Electronix Express	270022BL	$1.05	25 feet	Blue
SparkFun	PRT-08022	$2.50	25 feet	Black
SparkFun	PRT-08023	$2.50	25 feet	Red

SparkFun	PRT-08024	$2.50	25 feet	Yellow
SparkFun	PRT-08025	$2.50	25 feet	Grey
SparkFun	PRT-08026	$2.50	25 feet	White
SparkFun	PRT-08027	$2.50	25 feet	Brown
Jameco	36792	$6.95	100 feet	Black
Jameco	36856	$6.95	100 feet	Red
Jameco	36822	$6.95	100 feet	Green
Jameco	36881	$6.95	100 feet	White
Jameco	36920	$6.95	100 feet	Yellow

Choosing Jumper Wire

Jumper wires (see Figure 12-17) of various types connect components and tie-point groups together on a solderless breadboard. It's called jumper wire because it jumps from point to point, or at least it allows electricity to do so.

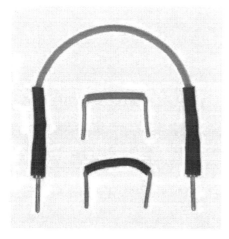

Figure 12-17. Jumper wire: Reinforced (top), *ready-made* (middle), *handmade* (bottom)

Obtaining Reinforced Jumper Wire

Reinforced jumper wire has sturdy metal posts on both ends covered in a rubber insulator. The rigidity and size of the posts makes it very easy to insert and remove the wire from the holes. The height of the posts extends over the top of components. The length of the wire allows for greater reach.

Common lengths for reinforced jumper wire are 50 mm (millimeter), 100 mm, and 200 mm. The 100 mm length is the most practical, although the shorter and longer lengths come in handy every once in a while.

The rubber-covered posts are finger friendly. They fit snugly, yet no tools are needed to move them around. Definitely stock your prototyping lab with lots of reinforced jumper wire (see Table 12-3).

Table 12-3. Reinforced Jumper Wire

Supplier	Part Number	Price	Length	Description
Electronix Express	2700WK1	$9.50	3 ½ to 7 ½ inches	(30) black, yellow, red, white
Jameco	126360	$3.95	2 inches	(10) Two each of yellow, white, red, black, and blue
Jameco	126342	$5.95	4 inches	(10) Two each of yellow, white, red, black, and blue
Jameco	126325	$6.95	8 inches	(10) Two each of yellow, white, red, black, and blue

Obtaining Flat, Ready-Made Jumper Wire

Ready-made jumper wire kits contain a wide variety of jumper lengths (see Figure 12-18). The lengths are designed to reach across a specific number of holes, although in practice they always seem a little bit long or a little bit short. The insulation color indicates the length of the wire.

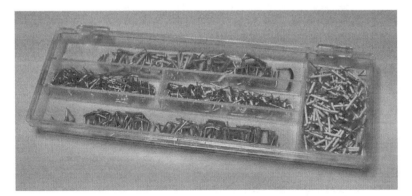

Figure 12-18. Pre-stripped, pre-formed jumper wire kit

The wire is formed to fit flush against the breadboard, which makes for a neat appearance. The short height also permits access to components since the wire isn't crossing all over the place. The downside, however, is the wire *can't* cross over a component or another wire. A mix of the flat kit jumper wire (see Table 12-4) and tall-reinforced jumper wire is optimal.

Table 12-4. Flat Jumper Wire Kits

Supplier	Part Number	Price	Number of Jumpers
Electronix Express	2700MJW70	$4.50	140
Electronix Express	2700WJW60B	$9.50	350
Jameco	19290	$16.95	350
Digi-Key	923351	$32.14	350

Electronix Express has a nice combination package of 350 flat jumpers and 30 reinforced jumpers (various lengths) for $16.95, part # 2700RJW90.

Making Your Own Jumper Wire

You can make your own jumper wire. In doing so, you can get exactly the length you need with an insulation color that indicates the function (rather than the color indicating the length). However, it's not as convenient as the ready-made wire, and doesn't survive reuse as well as the reinforced jumpers.

Stripping the Insulation Off of the End of the Wire

To make your own jumper wire:

1. Begin by stripping off about 7 mm of the insulation from the end of solid #22 AWG wire (see Figure 12-19).

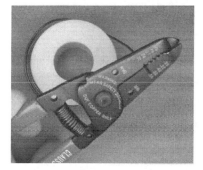

Figure 12-19. Numbered-notch wire strippers removing insulation from #22 AWG solid wire

155

Choosing Wire Strippers

A large variety of wire stripper tools exist. I prefer those with numbered notches (see Figure 12-19) for each wire diameter rather than the adjustable or automatic wire strippers (see Figure 12-20). The numbered notches are exact, so you needn't worry about cutting into and damaging the wire itself. Also, no adjustment wheels need to be dialed to match the wire diameter—simply slide the wire into the correct notch. Table 12-5 lists some suppliers of notched wire strippers.

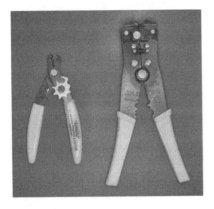

Figure 12-20. Adjustable and automatic wire strippers

Table 12-5. Wire Strippers

Supplier	Part Number	Price	Gauge Range	Description
SparkFun	TOL-08696	$4.95	20-30	Wire Strippers
Jameco	159291	$9.95	20-30	Wire Stripper Tool
Electronix Express	060245-125	$15.75	22-30	Professional Wire Stripper
Micro-Mark	14221	$17.85	22-30	Micro-Size Wire Stripper

Cutting the Wire to Length

2. After stripping off one end of the insulation, cut the wire to the desired length. Don't forget to consider the amount of insulation you're going to strip from the other end of the wire.

Cutting the wire is faster if your stripping tool also has a cutter built in, as most do. If not, use flush wire cutters or nippy cutters.

3. After cutting, strip off about 7 mm of insulation from the other end of wire.

Bending the End of the Wire

4. You can bend the wire into the desired shape with your hands. However, holding the wire in the tip of needle-nosed pliers and bending against the flat edge can achieve nice square corners (see Figure 12-21).

Figure 12-21. Bending wire with the help of needle-nose pliers

This bending trick also works well on component wires, such as resistors. That's it. Your jumper is ready (see Figure 12-22).

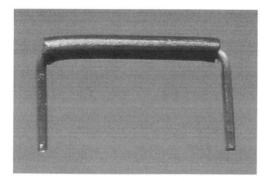

Figure 12-22. Completed homemade flat jumper wire

Selecting Electrical Pliers

Besides wire strippers, a pair of needle-nose pliers is a tool you should not be without (see Figure 12-23). As with all tools, purchase the highest-quality tool you can afford. Fine tools are an investment that pays off every time you use them.

Look for smooth movement, clean edges, and grips that feel comfortable in your hands. Hold the pliers up to a light with the jaws closed. The light that seeps through the cracks between the jaws indicates places that aren't coming together completely. Check the tip for horizontal alignment.

Needle-nose pliers should be long and skinny. That's how they get their name.

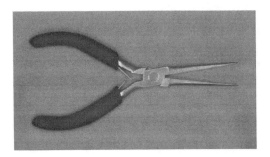

Figure 12-23. A pair of needle-nose pliers

Obtaining Smooth-Jaw Needle-Nose Pliers

Obtain a pair of smooth (non-serrated/no teeth) jaws for breadboarding, wire bending, and delicate work (see Table 12-6). Because non-serrated jaws are smooth (see Figure 12-24), they don't rip or cut into wire insulation and they can slide under components without damaging them.

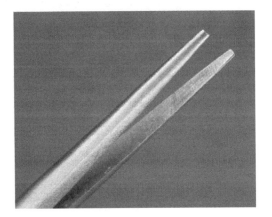

Figure 12-24. Smooth jaws

Table 12-6. Smooth-Jaw Needle-Nose Pliers

Supplier	Part Number	Price	Description
Electronix Express	0602NNP1	$1.95	6-inch mini needle nose pliers
Electronix Express	0602NNP2	$2.50	7-inch mini needle nose pliers
Micro-Mark	82827	$20.95	5-inch long needle nose pliers

Smooth, long, slim, needle-nose pliers are good for removing flat jumper wire from a solderless breadboard (see Figure 12-25). This is especially valuable as the board fills up with wires and components that human fingers can no longer reach.

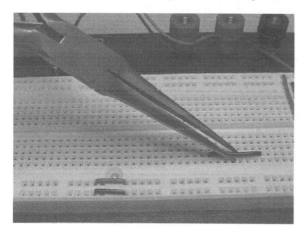

Figure 12-25. Removing a flat jumper wire with needle-nose pliers

Obtaining Serrated-Jaw Long-Nose Pliers

Serrated (see Figure 12-26) long-nose pliers are better suited for more muscle-intensive work, where a sure grip of the item is important but scraping and scuffing of the item doesn't matter (see Table 12-7).

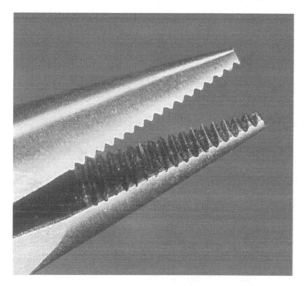

Figure 12-26. Serrated jaws

Table 12-7. Serrated-Jaw Pliers

Supplier	Part Number	Price	Description
Jameco	177608	$4.95	4.7 inch long nose pliers
SparkFun	TOL-08793	$1.95	4 inch long pliers

Making The Connection

With solderless breadboards, you've got a wonderful technology for designing circuits. In the coming chapters, not only will you recreate this power indicator circuit, but also you'll create and test the entire line-following robot circuit before soldering it together.

CHAPTER 13

■■■

Solderless Breadboard Setup

In this chapter, you'll prepare an 840 tie-point solderless breadboard for experimentation (see Figure 13-1). You'll install a battery, power switch, and an LED power indicator. You can use this basic setup over and over again for trying out robot circuits and modules.

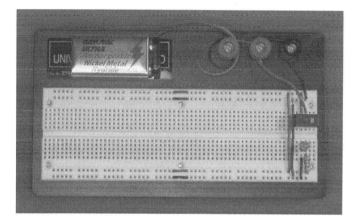

Figure 13-1. *Solderless breadboard after completed setup*

Considering Power Sources

There are a lot of good options available for supplying power to a circuit on a breadboard.

Continuous power is available by attaching the circuit to a wall outlet through an ordinary power adaptor (otherwise known as a wall wart). Replacement adjustable-voltage supplies are available at most consumer electronics retailers and some hardware stores. Or, you can salvage a fixed-voltage supply from a consumer device, such as an answering machine or old cable modem. I choose to power circuits from an outlet if they consume a lot of current or are going to be hooked up for long periods.

However, most of the time, I choose 9 V rechargeable batteries. They're portable, safe (low power, low maximum current), small, and I don't have to drape power supply cables across my desk. A 9 V battery provides plenty of power for most digital circuits. It's beneficial to test circuits on a breadboard using the same power source that they will experience on the robot.

Obtaining 9 V Battery Snap Connectors

Although you could attach the battery to the breadboard using alligator or hook clip jumpers, a 9 V battery snap connector is preferable because it's less likely to slip off. I highly recommend a solid, rigid 9 V connector rather than an ordinary, flexible connector (see Figure 13-2). The flimsy connectors are difficult to remove from the battery and tend to wear out quickly, often ripping or falling apart. See Table 13-1 for a supplier of rigid clips.

Figure 13-2. Solid (top) *versus flimsy* (bottom) *9 V battery snap connectors*

Table 13-1. Solid, Rigid 9 V Battery Snap Connectors

Supplier	Part Number	Price	Description
Jameco	216452	$0.35	6-inch Safety
Mouser	123-5006-GR	$0.43	6-inch Molded
Digi-Key	BS6I-MC	$0.48	6-inch I-Style Molded
Mouser	123-7016	$0.83	6-inch Premium 24 AWG

Connecting Power to Binding Posts

You could push the ends of the 9 V snap connector's wires directly into the desired breadboard holes. However, the battery often falls when the breadboard is moved, causing one or both 9 V wires to pull out of their respective holes.

A better solution is to connect the 9 V wires to the binding posts (if available on your breadboard). Obviously, the black wire connects to the black post, and the red wire connects to the red post. Any red post will do if you have more than one.

Because only a short amount of the plastic insulation is already stripped off of the end of the snap connector's wires, strip off a little bit more. Then insert the bare ends into the binding post holes (see Figure 13-3).

Figure 13-3. *Inserting the 9 V snap connector's wire (stripped) into a breadboard post*

Make a short length of red and black #22 American wire gauge (AWG) copper wire and insert them into their respective post holes. You should wrap the wire ends around the metal portion of the post to achieve a reliable connection. Place the short lengths of #22 wire into the desired holes of the breadboard. (Skip ahead to Figure 13-8 for a photograph of the battery and post connections as viewed from a different angle.)

Electricity will flow from the battery terminal, through the snap connector wire, to the post, to the #22 wire, and finally to the breadboard hole.

An advantage of attaching the power source to the binding posts is that you can conveniently connect a multimeter to the banana jacks atop the posts to check voltage. Also, you can disconnect the 9 V battery from the snaps and connect a wall adaptor to the binding posts.

■ **Caution** Never connect a battery and a wall power source to the same circuit at the same time. If you still want to leave the batteries connected to the circuit, rechargeable and non-rechargeable batteries will require specifically designed protection to avoid destruction when the wall power is applied.

Choosing a Power Switch

How suave is it to lunge after your out-of-control robot and rip out the batteries? Polished robot designs have power switches. Easily accessible power switches are vital during prototyping, as the circuits may suffer a few shorts and power overloads during development.

Unfortunately, few switch sizes are compatible with breadboards. Either the switch leads are too thick or they are spaced apart at a distance other than 0.1 inch. As such, you can't push the switch into the breadboard holes. Bending or trimming the power-switch leads is rarely successful, as the switch needs to be firmly in place or else it falls out when you physically try to use it.

I'm aware of a couple of switches with solderless breadboard dimensions (see Figure 13-4). They're so indispensable that you should have a dozen on hand. The EG1218 switch is more compact, which can be advantageous as your robot's circuit board runs out of space. The 600SP1S2 switch is a little easier to toggle because of its larger size. Table 13-2 lists suppliers of breadboard-compatible switches.

Figure 13-4. Breadboard-compatible switches: EG1218 (left) *and 600SP1S2* (right)

Table 13-2. Breadboard-Compatible SPDT Slide Switches

Supplier	Part Number	Price	Description
Mouser	612-EG1218	$0.78	E-Switch EG1218 SPDT Slide Switch
Digi-Key	EG1903	$0.73	E-Switch EG1218 SPDT Slide Switch
Solarbotics	SWT1	$1.35	E-Switch EG1218 SPDT Slide Switch
SparkFun	COM-00102	$1.50	E-Switch EG1218 SPDT Slide Switch
Electronix Express	17SLDH251	$1.30	E-Switch 600SP1S2 SPDT Slide Switch

Understanding SPDT

Slide switches are activated by sliding the actuator back and forth. The term SPDT stands for single pole, double throw.

Think of SPDT like a tall metal pole standing in the middle, separated from wires on the left and on the right. When the actuator is slid to the left, the metal pole is thrown onto the left wire, connecting the pole and left wire. When the actuator is slid to the right, the metal pole is thrown onto the right wire, connecting the pole and right wire.

Other than for a brief second, the metal pole is not standing completely disconnected in the middle. It either slams down on the left side or slams down on the right side. At no time do the left and right wires touch each other. Nor can the pole touch both the left and right wires at the same time.

Adding a Power Switch to the Breadboard

You want to connect the negative (black) wire directly to the breadboard's power distribution bus. However, you want the positive (red) wire to go through the switch so that you can easily disconnect it, stopping the flow of electricity.

Up to this point, you have negative battery power connected to the black binding post with a #22 black wire coming out. Insert the black wire to the rightmost hole on the second row from the top (see Figure 13-5). This row is a distribution bus, so now negative power is available to the many holes in that row.

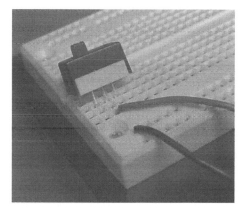

Figure 13-5. Placing a switch into solderless breadboard holes (viewed from above the upper-right of the board)

Positive battery power is connected to the red binding post with a #22 red wire coming out. Instead of connecting the red wire directly to the first row at the top, connect it to a 5-position group just below the distribution bus (again, see Figure 13-5). This way you can have the switch connect and disconnect positive power from the remainder of the circuit.

Place a SPDT power switch so that the middle lead is in the same 5-position group as the positive power wire (also Figure 13-5). The placement of the middle lead of the switch and the positive wire creates a connection between them.

Connecting Power Buses

Use a small red jumper wire to connect the left lead of the switch to the uppermost row on the breadboard (see Figure 13-6). Positive power and negative power are now connected to the upper two rows, but positive power first passes through the switch.

165

Figure 13-6. Adding a wire to connect the top row to positive power through the switch

When the switch actuator is slid left, positive power is connected. When the switch actuator is slid right, positive power is disconnected. It doesn't matter that negative power is connected the whole time.

Adapting Multimeter Probes Using Jumper Wire

Because of their thickness, it's not possible for bare multimeter probe tips or hook adaptors to reach the metal strips beneath the breadboard holes. Using a hook adaptor, connect a piece of ordinary copper wire or a reinforced jumper wire to the multimeter probe tip (see Figure 13-7). Now you can check the voltage in any group or hole by inserting the wire.

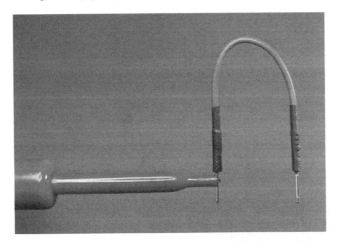

Figure 13-7. Multimeter probes with hook adaptors holding a reinforced jumper wire

To determine if the top rows are properly connected to the battery's power, use a wire on each multimeter probe to check the voltage of the top two rows (see Figure 13-8). Flip the switch back and forth to see that the voltage changes from zero to full (approximately 9 V).

Figure 13-8. *Testing the voltage of the upper bus using probes hooked to jumper wire*

Connecting the Lower Bus

Connect the top row of the upper bus to the top row of the lower bus with red jumper wire (see Figure 13-9). Connect the bottom row of the upper bus to the bottom row of the lower bus with black jumper wire. Now battery power is available uptown and downtown!

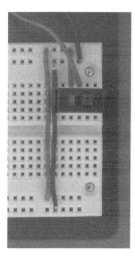

Figure 13-9. *Jumper wires delivering power to lower bus rows*

Split Down the Middle

The buses on an 840 tie-point breadboard don't extend all of the way across the board; they're split halfway. Use jumper wire on the top two rows and bottom two rows in the middle of the breadboard (see Figure 13-10).

Figure 13-10. Jumper wires connecting the left side to the right side of the breadboard

With the voltage feature of a multimeter, check that battery power is now distributed in the upper and lower rows (distribution busses) all across the breadboard.

Installing a Power Indicator LED

Recall the LED power indicator circuit you built earlier with alligator-clip jumper leads. Basically, it consisted of a resistor hooked to positive power and then to an LED. The other end of the LED was connected to negative power. The LED turned off whenever the battery was disconnected at any point in the loop.

Since you've distributed power throughout the board, you can add the power indicator circuit wherever you'd like. I chose the lower-right corner because there's just enough space there.

Insert one lead of a 1 kΩ resistor into any hole that has positive power. Insert the other resistor lead into a 5-position group (see Figure 13-11).

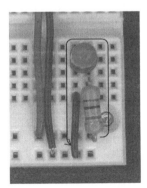

Figure 13-11. LED power indicator circuit connected to lower bus

In that same 5-position group, insert the anode of a red LED. Note that the LED isn't receiving the full force of the battery because power is supplied to the group only through the protective (current limiting) resistor.

Insert the cathode of the red LED into an adjacent 5-position group. Connect the adjacent group to any hole that has negative power by using a black jumper wire.

The red LED should light when the power switch is turned on. The LED should extinguish when the power switch is turned off.

Checking Voltages at Certain Points

You should check the voltages of the breadboard power indicator circuit to be assured they are similar to the same circuit assembled with alligator-clip jumper leads.

Recall that to test voltage at a point, the black multimeter test probe must be connected to negative power. Since you've connected the battery's negative terminal to the black binding post and to the bottom row of both upper and lower buses, you can connect the black test probe to any of those locations.

In Figure 13-12, I chose to connect the black test probe to the bottom row of the lower bus. I could have chosen any hole on the bottom row of the board because they are all connected to negative power.

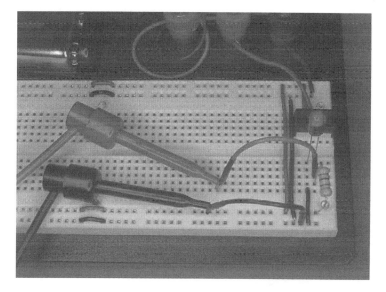

Figure 13-12. Multimeter probes with jumpers testing voltage at the LED's anode

This is why distribution buses are so valuable. You can add individual modules and mini circuits anywhere on the board and it will be as if they all were connected directly to the battery. Of course, the 5-position groups aren't connected to the buses, so you can deliver the desired voltage and current to them based on your choice of resistor or other part.

With the black test probe connected to negative power, insert a wire connected to the red test probe into the 5-position group that contains the LED anode (see Figure 13-12). You should get a reading of 1.8

V (or thereabouts), just as you did when the power indicator circuit was put together with alligator-clip jumper leads.

Trimming Leads

After testing a part or circuit on a breadboard, you may want to cut down the part's leads. Short, flush parts stay out of your way and there isn't the risk of their leads accidentally brushing against other wires.

The LED and resistor of the breadboard power indicator are good candidates for trimming down. Chances are you'll leave those parts in the breadboard for almost all experiments.

Demystifying the Robot's Power Switch

The power switches on most robots are no different than the power switch you installed on your breadboard. Robot power switches may look more striking, handle more voltage, or make multiple connections at the same time. However, robot power switches still employ the same technique of making and breaking a connection to the positive terminal of the power source.

In fact, nearly all robots deliver power to their circuits and modules using a power bus, just like a solderless breadboard. Figure 13-13 is a photograph of the underside of Sandwich's circuit board. It has an array of holes, just like a solderless breadboard. Toward the middle, there are two long lines that all the various circuits are tapping into. Those are the positive and negative buses.

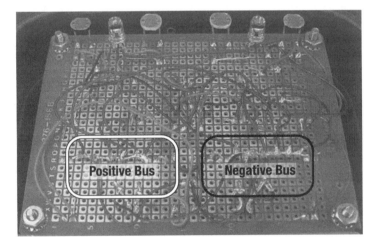

Figure 13-13. Sandwich's circuit board with power buses

The negative terminal of the 9 V battery is always connected to the negative bus on Sandwich's circuit board. The power switch has one end connected to the positive terminal of the 9 V battery and the other end to the positive bus. All of this is just like on your solderless breadboard.

When you flip the robot's power switch on, the power flows from the positive terminal of the battery through the switch to the positive bus, through the various circuits, into the negative bus, which leads back to the negative terminal of the battery.

I admit that Sandwich's board is pretty messy. Also, some of the parts, like the switches, have been stretched off the board via wires. But the only significant difference between Sandwich's breadboard and a solderless breadboard is that Sandwich's parts are soldered together rather than pushed into little group holes.

Ready for More

Your solderless breadboard has been prepared. It's ready to supply power to its wide-open spaces with a flick of a switch. You know how to test voltage at any point to make sure the values are in the ranges that the parts can accept.

Are you ready to learn about some new parts, such as sensors, and add them to your breadboard?

■ ■ ■

CHAPTER 14

Variable Resistors

The brightness sensors and balancing dial at the front of Sandwich are variable resistors. In this chapter, you'll learn about variable resistors and you'll prototype the first portion of the line-following circuit. Along the way, you'll run across techniques for simplifying schematics.

Thus far, the resistors you've experimented with have had fixed values. That is, their resistance stays the same all the time.

For the LED power indicator circuit, the brightness of the LED is based on the value of the resistor installed. To change the brightness, you need to remove the resistor and replace it with a resistor of a different value. It would be nice if the circuit had a resistor that could alter its value so that you could change the brightness of the LED without having to switch parts.

Potentiometers

Potentiometers (see Figure 14-1) are variable resistors. Their resistance changes by turning a control knob or dial. You've probably operated potentiometers plenty of times without even knowing it. For example, potentiometers commonly control stereo volume as well as analog television brightness and contrast.

Figure 14-1. A variety of potentiometers

You can adjust all potentiometers down to zero ohms (no resistance). The value printed on the potentiometer indicates its **maximum** value. For example, you can adjust a 500 Ω potentiometer from 0 Ω up to 500 Ω. You can adjust a 10 kΩ potentiometer from 0 Ω to 10 kΩ.

There are a wide variety of potentiometer sizes and packages available. However, like switches, only a small subset of potentiometers fit into a solderless breadboard. The other potentiometer sizes tend to have oddly spaced or thick leads.

Trimpot

Trimpot is short for trimmer potentiometer. Sometimes they're called trimmers. They're lightweight, take up very little space, and most fit into solderless breadboards (see Figure 14-2).

Figure 14-2. A breadboard-compatible single-turn trimpot

Unlike full-size potentiometers, trimpots don't have finger-friendly control knobs. Instead, they're adjusted with a small screwdriver. This can be a pain when you want to make an adjustment; however, it does reduce the likelihood of accidental changes. Trimpots are often used for values that won't be adjusted very often and are usually set by a service technician as opposed to a consumer.

Trimpot dials are more delicate than full-size potentiometers. Trimpots wear out after as little as a hundred turns, as opposed to tens of thousands of turns for a full-size potentiometer. This shouldn't be an issue since trimpots are adjusted less often.

Recall Sandwich's sensor balancing dial. The robot needs to be in place on a track to determine if the left pair of sensors sees the same values as the right pair of sensors. However, the dial rarely needs tweaking after the initial adjustment is made to compensate for manufacturing variations or soldering inconsistencies. For those reasons, Sandwich has a tiny hole for a screwdriver to access a trimpot (see Figure 14-3) instead of a full-size, externally mounted potentiometer.

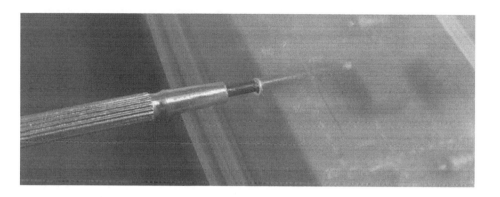

Figure 14-3. Adjusting Sandwich's trimpot with a flathead screwdriver through an access hole

Turning the Dial

Most potentiometers have single-turn dials. That is, they rotate from their minimum value (0 Ω) to their maximum value (printed on the case) within one rotation of the dial. With only a single rotation, you can quickly change the value and you can easily tell by the dial angle when the potentiometer is at the beginning, middle, or ending of its range.

Multiturn potentiometers (see Figure 14-4) take many turns (25, for example) to adjust through their entire range. This makes it possible to fine-tune an exact value, since each twist of the screwdriver only tweaks the resistance a little bit. Also, if the dial slips a little bit on its own due to vibration or temperature changes, a multiturn potentiometer changes value less than a single turn potentiometer.

Figure 14-4. A breadboard-compatible multiturn trimpot

An easy way to identify a multiturn trimpot is to look for a metal screw offset to the side of the trimpot (see Figure 14-4) instead of a plastic dial in the center (see Figure 14-2). Multiturn trimpots are more complex internally, and therefore more expensive than single-turn trimpots.

You will want to make very fine adjustments to the line-follower's sensor balance. Also, you don't want the value to change much due to vibrations as the robot moves. Therefore, a multiturn trimpot (see Figure 14-3) would be a good choice for the line-following robot's sensor balance.

Obtaining Assorted Trimpots

It's worthwhile to have a variety of sizes and ranges of trimpots. Table 14-1 lists suppliers of assorted kits.

Table 14-1. Assorted Value Trimmer Potentiometers

Supplier	Part Number	Price	Quantity	Case Description
Electronix Express	32CSP2	$14.95	20	¼ square
Digi-Key	3386C-KIT	$65.95	75	Single turn (see Figure 14-2)
Digi-Key	3296W-KIT	$139.00	75	Multiturn (see Figure 14-3)

Trimpots are also available individually or in bulk packets of the same resistance value. After determining your favorite resistance values and dial style, consider stocking up. I like 500 Ω, 2 kΩ, 10 kΩ, 25 kΩ, 100 kΩ, and 1 MΩ.

If you only want a pair of 20 kilohm multiturn potentiometers used in the Sandwich robot, the part numbers are: Solarbotics RT20k, Electronix Express 18MPT20K, Mouser Electronics 652-3296W-1-203, or Digi-Key 490-2881.

Testing Potentiometers

The maximum resistance value of the potentiometer usually appears printed on the casing as a three-digit code. The third digit is the number of zeros to add to the end of the first two digits. For example, "501" is 500 Ω. "103" is 10,000 Ω. "254" is 250,000 Ω.

To measure a potentiometer, set up your multimeter the same way as you would to measure the resistance of a normal fixed resistor. An important difference is a potentiometer has three leads, not two.

Measuring the Maximum Resistance of a Potentiometer

To determine the maximum resistance of any kind of potentiometer, connect the multimeter test probes to the first and third leads (see Figure 14-5). This should be approximately the same as the value printed on the potentiometer's case.

Turning the potentiometer control dial has no effect on the resistance between the first and third leads. Swapping the black and red test probes on the potentiometer makes no difference, just like a fixed resistor.

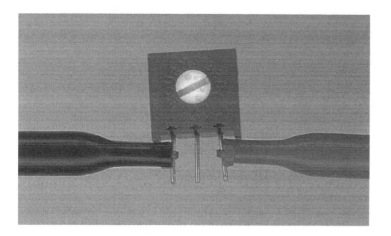

Figure 14-5. Hook probes connected to the first and third pins of a trimpot to measure maximum value

Measuring the Variable Resistance of a Potentiometer

Connect the multimeter test probes to the first and middle leads of a potentiometer to display the changing resistance as the potentiometer control dial is turned (see Figure 14-6). As the dial is turned to the left, the resistance to the first lead decreases and the resistance to the third lead increases. The reverse occurs as the dial is turned to the right, the resistance to the first lead increases and the resistance to the third lead decreases.

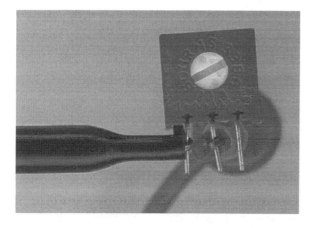

Figure 14-6. Hook probes connected to the first and middle pins of a trimpot to measure varying values

When dialed all the way to one extreme, the resistance between the middle pin and either the first or the third pin should be 0 Ω. When dialed all the way to the other extreme, the resistance should be the maximum value printed on the potentiometer's case.

Linear Versus Logarithmic/Exponential

Turn the potentiometer dial to the middle. Is the measured resistance approximately half the maximum value? If it is, then the potentiometer is probably a linear taper. This means that the resistance changes at a steady rate as you turn the dial. That's desirable for most robotic applications.

If the resistance value halfway through the dial is much more or much less than half the maximum value, then the potentiometer is probably a logarithmic or exponential taper. That's less desirable for most robotic applications. Logarithmic taper potentiometers are often used in stereos to increase the volume in multiples to reflect the perceptions of human hearing.

Variable Brightness LED Circuit

The schematic in Figure 14-7 is very similar to the LED power indicator schematic shown earlier in the book. The battery (B1) and the LED (D1) stay the same.

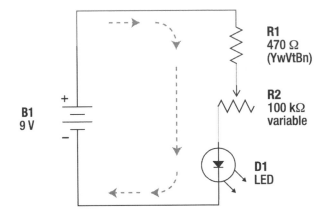

Figure 14-7. Schematic of a simple circuit to vary the brightness of an LED

However, a potentiometer (R2) now appears between the fixed resistor (R1) and the LED (D1). Notice that the schematic symbol for a potentiometer looks somewhat like a fixed resistor, except there's an arrow in the middle. You can imagine this arrow sliding back and forth on the resistor, jumping in at some value in between.

Also noteworthy is that the letter "R" is assigned to the potentiometer (R2) because it is in the resistor family, even though it has a variable resistance. Recall that "D" is assigned to an LED (D1) because it is in the diode family, even though it is a light-emitting variation.

Since you've got a potentiometer whose resistance spans a broad range, why bother to include a fixed resistor (R1)? After all, a 100 kΩ potentiometer provides all the usable values of 470 Ω and up.

Unfortunately, the user has the ability to turn the potentiometer all the way down to no resistance (0 Ω). Without a minimum value enforced by the fixed resistor (R1), the LED would be connected to the full strength of the battery and would be destroyed. Unless you're designing a self-destruct button, you generally want to guard against extreme ranges on adjustable controls.

■ **Tip** Whenever you install a potentiometer, ask yourself what would happen if it were dialed to zero and what would happen if it were dialed to the maximum. Consider the voltages and currents under those extremes, and then test the design with a multimeter to be sure they're within the values that the surrounding components can tolerate.

Building the Variable Brightness LED Circuit

Make sure power is disabled on the solderless breadboard. Never connect or disconnect parts to a live (powered on) system.

The *variable brightness LED* circuit (see Figure 14-7) is easy to build on a breadboard. See Figure 14-8 for a photograph of an actual example.

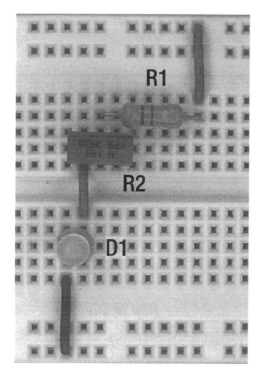

Figure 14-8. Variable brightness LED circuit built on a solderless breadboard

Note that the fixed resistor (R1) goes into the same 5-position group as the center lead of the trimpot (R2). The first lead of the trimpot (R2) is connected to the LED (D1), but the third lead is not connected to anything.

Power up! Turn the trimpot dial with a small screwdriver and observe the brightness of the LED. If you have a very efficient LED, the light may remain visible even when the trimpot dial is turned all the way to the right. If you have a poor-efficiency LED, the light may not be visible even when the trimpot dial is halfway.

Try different values of trimpots. Recall that R1 is protecting the circuit against too much current, so you're free to experiment with any value potentiometer.

Brightness Balancing Circuit

Take a look at the schematic in Figure 14-9. Where did the battery go?

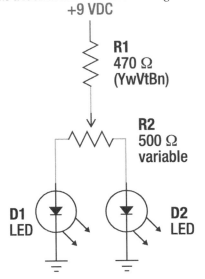

Figure 14-9. Schematic of brightness balanced LEDs

The circuit has been simplified by substituting the words "+9 VDC" for the battery. This takes up less space and focuses attention on the heart of the circuit. Also, this doesn't falsely lead you to believe you *must* use a battery. For example, a wall adapter power supply providing the same voltage would be fine.

What happened to the bottom of the schematic? The LEDs are each connected to three evershortening horizontal lines. Again, a simplification. These are the power return lines. It's less distracting to show abbreviated return lines rather than having them cross all over the illustration.

The schematic is cleaned up and simplified by eliminating the battery and chopping all of the power return lines. For such a small circuit, it may not seem like much, but this commonly accepted technique really tidies up large schematics.

Building the Brightness Balanced LEDs Circuit

Looking at Figure 14-10, it may strike you that the actual built circuit looks a lot like the schematic (see Figure 14-9). This is yet another reason for drawing the schematic without the battery or power return lines.

Figure 14-10. Brightness balanced LEDs circuit built on a solderless breadboard

In this circuit, an LED (D2) has been connected to the third lead of the trimpot (R2). The maximum value of the trimpot has been decreased to only 500 Ω.

When the trimpot dial is in the center, the resistance is split evenly between the two LEDs, 250 Ω each. As the dial is turned left and right, the resistance is delivered unequally between the two LEDs. The brightness of one LED increases and the brightness of the other LED decreases. It's like the speaker balance control on a stereo.

Cadmium-Sulfide Photoresistors

Cadmium-sulfide photoresistors (see Figure 14-11) are extremely popular in robotics. They're lightweight, inexpensive, fascinating to look at, and mimic the visible-light responsiveness of the human eye.

■ **Note** Thorough readers with good memories will dredge up my advice not to purchase or use components containing the element cadmium. Despite my research, I haven't been able to locate a suitable replacement photoresistor without cadmium. "Well, it's not got much cadmium in it."

Figure 14-11. Standard cadmium-sulfide photoresistor

Cadmium-sulfide can be abbreviated CdS. Sometimes, photoresistors are called photocells or photoconductors. It's the same component no matter the name.

Potentiometers change resistance in response to rotations of their dials, whereas photoresistors change their resistance in response to the amount of light shining on them. Pretty cool!

Obtaining Assorted Photoresistors

Encapsulated photoresistors (see Figure 14-12) are available for outdoor or rugged uses. An opaque metal case and clear plastic lens protect the sensor against moisture, dust, and soil. The opaque metal also prevents light coming from the rear from affecting the resistance.

Figure 14-12. Encapsulated and exposed ceramic cadmium-sulfide photoresistors

Like potentiometers, photoresistors are available in a variety of resistance ranges and physical sizes. Larger photoresistors change resistance more slowly, but are generally more sensitive to the true lighting conditions as they have a larger "eye" to experience more of the lightness or darkness.

Table 14-2 lists suppliers of assorted photoresistors. It's much cheaper to buy an assorted bagful rather than specific values. I highly recommend buying several Electronic Goldmine (http://www.goldmine-elec.com/) bags, because of the variety and low price.

Table 14-2. *Assorted Cadmium-Sulfide Photoresistors*

Supplier	Part Number	Price	Quantity	Description
Electronic Goldmine	G14025	$3.00	20	Assorted sizes, encapsulated and plain
Jameco	169578	$21.95	100	Small, plain only

Experiencing the Variable Resistance of a Photoresistor

Attach a photoresistor to your multimeter using the same method as measuring a fixed resistor (see Figure 14-13). Watch the resistance change as you bring the photoresistor towards a light or cover it with your hand. Really, this is worth trying.

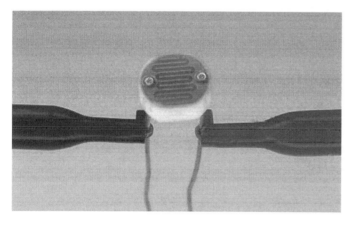

Figure 14-13. *Hook probes connected to a cadmium-sulfide photoresistor to measure varying values*

Light-Controlled Circuit

Substitute a photoresistor for the potentiometer in the variable brightness LED circuit presented earlier in this chapter (see Figure 14-7). See Figure 14-14 for a photograph of the revised circuit built on a breadboard. As the room darkens, the LED also darkens. As the room brightens, the LED also brightens. Putting your finger over the photoresistor also does the trick.

Remember when you had to choose a resistor size to compromise between LED brightness and battery life? With a photoresistor, the circuit can automatically brighten the LED so that it's visible in daylight, but conserve battery power in dim areas where the LED is perfectly noticeable.

Photoresistors are commonly found in automatic nightlights and streetlights. In these applications, the photoresistors are hooked up to circuitry that turns on a bulb when the ambient lighting gets dark.

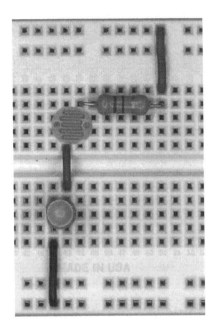

Figure 14-14. Light-controlled variable-brightness LED circuit built on a solderless breadboard

Balanced Brightness-Sensing Circuit

Sandwich, the line-following robot, uses four cadmium-sulfide photoresistors in pairs to detect the amount of light at front of the robot. Figure 14-15 is an exact schematic of the robot's brightness-sensing circuit.

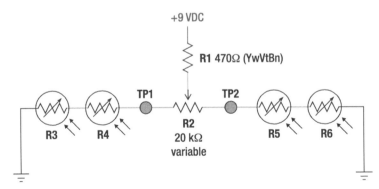

Figure 14-15. Balanced brightness-sensing circuit

Part List for Balanced Brightness-Sensing Circuit

- -- – 9 VDC power supply

- **R1** – 470 Ω resistor (yellow, violet, brown)

- **R2** – 20 kΩ trimpot

- **R3, R4, R5, R6** – Roughly 100 Ω bright to 450 kΩ dark cadmium-sulfide photoresistors

Brightness-Sensing Pairs

R3 through R6 are photoresistors (notice the variable resistor symbol with a circle drawn around it and "light" arrows coming in). Each photoresistor changes resistance depending on the amount of light it receives. R3 and R4 are paired to sense the right side of the floor beneath the robot. R5 and R6 are paired to sense the left side of the floor beneath the robot.

A pair of photoresistors can detect a physically wider area than can a single photoresistor. Another advantage to using a pair is that you can hand–select them to average out manufacturing discrepancies in minimum and maximum values.

Matching Photoresistors

Individual photoresistors have appreciably different overall resistance ranges even if they look the same or came from the same production batch. This is especially true if purchased in mixed bags. It's important to match similar resistance groups and sort them into their own piles. You can balance your line-following robot with photoresistors that are slightly different, but not with photoresistors that are radically different.

Photoresistor matching is a simple process. Connect a photoresistor to your multimeter and hold it up to a light. Write down the Ω value. Now hold the photoresistor under a table (or other dark area) and write down the new Ω value. As you make your way through a pile of photoresistors, you'll get a sense for how closely the high and low values can match.

Your primary goal in testing the photoresistors is to knock out any defective ones. These will not change value or will have really low or really high values—especially compared to the rest of the lot.

Your secondary goal is to roughly match the photoresistors. Again, stick one up to a light bulb, count to 5, and record the value. Stick it under a dark desk, count to 5, and record the value. Good enough.

Because of the balancing potentiometer (R1) and the striking contrast of the line on the floor, the photoresistors don't have to be matched exactly. Truth be told, the four photoresistors for Sandwich were picked at random from a previously defective-removed lot. And Sandwich performs beautifully. Subsequently built Sandwich clones had more carefully matched values, but show no differences in performance.

In order of testing, Table 14-3 shows the values I found for otherwise identical-looking photoresistors.

I would pair photoresistors 'C' and 'H' on one side of a line-following robot and photoresistors 'G' and 'D' on the other side. The sensor order would be 'C,' 'H,' 'G,' and 'D.' 'C' and 'H' have a combined range of 230 Ω to 834 kΩ, whereas 'G' and 'D' have a combined range of 234 Ω to 800 kΩ. In the center of the robot, 'H' and 'G' have similar ranges. On the sides of the robot, 'C' and 'D' also react similarly.

Table 14-3. Sample Photoresistors Values

Label	Resistance Pressed Against Light bulb	Resistance Under Dark Desk
A	123 Ω	260 kΩ
B	130 Ω	338 kΩ
C	115 Ω	400 kΩ
D	124 Ω	370 kΩ
E	105 Ω	440 kΩ
F	128 Ω	470 kΩ
G	110 Ω	430 kΩ
H	115 Ω	434 kΩ
I	119 Ω	550 kΩ

You don't have to go to all of this effort. But imagine the bad luck of a robot comparing photoresistor 'A' with photoresistor 'I.' Both photoresistors react the same to light lines, but the resistance of photoresistor 'I' would be double that of photoresistor 'A' when looking at the same dark surface.

None of the photoresistors in Table 14-3 are bad or damaged. A bad photoresistor I ran across ranged from 4 MΩ in light to greater than 40 MΩ in darkness. That's extremely different than the other photoresistors. If you find a part like that, dispose of it properly before it gets into one of your creations. In an assorted grab bag, expect as many as 10% of the photoresistors to be faulty.

Resistance-Balancing Potentiometer

Referring back to Figure 14-15, R2 is a 20 kΩ potentiometer. As the dial is turned, it splits the resistance supplied to each branch that leads to each pair of photoresistors. R2 works the same way it did in the brightness balanced LED's circuit (see Figure 14-9).

In the middle of its range, R2 provides 10 kΩ resistance to the left side and 10 kΩ to the right side. Jamming it in one direction provides 20 kΩ resistance to one side and 0 Ω resistance to the other (or vice-versa). Table 14-3 shows that the maximum anticipated difference in bright ranges isn't very much, so R2 provides plenty of resistance to equalize the photo-resistance of both sides in bright conditions. The robot has headlights to run in dim conditions so dark balancing isn't necessary.

Current-Limiting Resistor

In Figure 14-15, R1 is called a current-limiting resistor. Because all of the other resistors are variable, there might come an occasion when a combination would resist so little that lots of electricity from the battery would be wasted.

For example, if R2 were dialed down so that 0 Ω was supplied to one pair of photoresistors and that pair was looking at a bright floor (around 100 Ω each) then only a total of 200 Ω resistance (0 Ω + 100 Ω + 100 Ω) would exist through that path. The formula for determining current is:

```
(V / Ω) × 1000 = mA
Thus: (9 V / 200 Ω) × 1000 = 45 mA
```

But, by adding a 470 Ω resistor (R1), the worst case becomes 670 Ω (470 Ω + 0 Ω + 100 Ω + 100 Ω).

```
Thus: (9 V / 670 Ω) × 1000 = 13 mA
```

With R1, this branch of the circuit draws ¼ the power in the worst case, yet provides the same function. R1 doesn't have much of an effect in the average case because R2 is dialed to around 10,000 Ω. In that case, the current drawn is less than 1 mA for each path.

If you're careful to not adjust the potentiometer to either end of its dial, then R1 is technically unnecessary. Still, it's nice to know R1 is there so that you can dial the potentiometer to any value without possibility of component harm or extreme battery waste.

When you create your own designs, be sure to add a minimum-value fixed resistor to any path that is otherwise controlled by variable resistors.

Test Points

The schematic (see Figure 14-15) features test points, labeled TP1 and TP2. No components physically exist at TP1 and TP2; they're just good spots to attach a multimeter for testing voltage. In fact, it turns out that these test points are *great* spots to test voltage.

Calculating the Voltages

When the battery is connected, the electricity flows through R1 to R2 and then splits into two paths. Considering just one path for the moment, the electricity then flows through R4 and R3 and then it finally returns to the battery.

We know the voltage starts out around 9 V and always ends up at 0 V when it reaches the other end of the battery. Along the way, how does the voltage get apportioned between the components?

1. Add up all of the resistance in the path. We're going to assume the photoresistors are looking at bright light (100 Ω) for this example.

```
R1 Ω + R2 Ω + R4 Ω + R3 Ω = total Ω of the path
This example: 470 Ω + 10,000 Ω + 100 Ω + 100 Ω = 10,670 Ω
```

2. For any resistor of interest, divide its resistance by the total to determine what share of the voltage it will use.

```
R1 Ω / total Ω = R1's share
This example: 470 Ω / 10,670 Ω = 0.044
```

3. Determine the amount of voltage being used in the path.

```
V at beginning - V at the end = total V used in the path
This example: 9 V - 0 V = 9 V
```

4. Multiply the resistor's share by the voltage used in the path to determine how much voltage is used in that resistor.

```
R1's share × total V of path = V of R1
This example: 0.044 × 9 V = 0.4 V
```

Let's check the value for R2:

```
R2 W / total W = R2's share
This example: 10,000 Ω / 10,670 Ω = 0.937
R2's share × total V of path = V of R2
This example: 0.937 × 9 V = 8.43 V
```

What's the deal with that? R2 has the largest resistance, so most of the voltage (pressure) was used up getting through it. Thus far, R1 and R2 have used up 8.83 V out of 9 V.

```
R4 Ω / total Ω = R4's share
This example: 100 Ω / 10,670 Ω = 0.00937
R4's share × total V of path = V of R4
This example: 0.00937 × 9 V = 0.08 V
```

And R3:

```
R3 Ω / total Ω = R3's share
This example: 100 Ω / 10,670 Ω = 0.00937
R3's share × total V of path = V of R3
This example: 0.00937 × 9 V = 0.08 V
```

Evaluating Test Point 1

Now that all of the voltages used along that path have been calculated, it is possible to determine the voltage at test point 1 (TP1). The battery starts out at 9 V. R1 and R2 use 8.83 V combined. So, around 0.17 V must be remaining by the time the electricity reaches TP1 (see Figure 14-16).

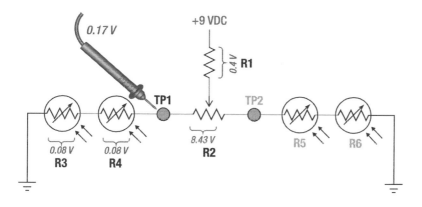

Figure 14-16. Voltages used by each resistor on one branch of the balanced brightness-sensing circuit

As the floor in front of the robot becomes darker, the photoresistors increase in resistance. If instead of 100 Ω, each the photoresistors reach 6,000 Ω each, the share of voltage used by each part changes.

1. Add up all of the resistance in the path. We're going to assume the photoresistors are looking at darker flooring (6,000 Ω) for this example.

```
R1 Ω + R2 Ω + R4 Ω + R3 Ω = total Ω of the path
This example: 470 Ω + 10,000 Ω + 6,000 Ω + 6,000 Ω = 22,470 Ω
```

2. For any resistor of interest, divide its resistance by the total to determine what share of the voltage it will use.

```
R1 Ω / total Ω = R1's share
This example: 470 Ω / 22,470 Ω = 0.021
```

3. Determine the amount of voltage being used in the path.

```
V at beginning - V at the end = total V used in the path
This example: 9 V - 0 V = 9 V
```

4. Multiply the resistor's share by the voltage used in the path to determine how much voltage is used in that resistor.

```
R1's share × total V of path = V of R1
This example: 0.021 × 9 V = 0.19 V
```

Plugging in the values for the other resistors results in:

```
R2 V = 4.0 V
R4 V = 2.4 V
R3 V = 2.4 V
```

As less light reaches the sensors (R3 and R4), their resistance increases. As their resistance increases, they use up a greater portion of the voltage in that path. As such, the voltage at TP1 increases (see Figure 14-17).

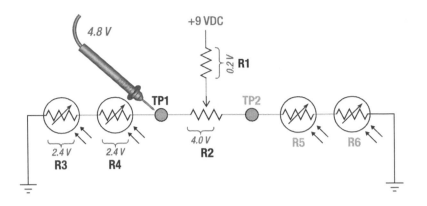

Figure 14-17. Voltage changes at TP1 when sensors have less light

The voltage at TP1 and the voltage at TP2 vary based on the amount of light seen by the pair of photoresistors on their respective sides. Not only does this circuit balance the sets of photoresistors, but it also converts their variable resistance into variable voltage.

Converting Resistance to Voltage with a Voltage Divider

Combining a variable resistor (such as a photoresistor sensor) with other resistors and taking the voltage value between them is called a voltage divider. The balanced brightness-sensing circuit is nothing more than voltage dividers dividing up voltages among bunches of resistors. **Along with current-limiting resistors, voltage dividers are among the most important and most often used techniques within a circuit.**

Chips are good at reading voltages. The next time you have a chip and you'd like to connect it to a variable resistor, think of voltage dividers. And the next time you think of voltage dividers, think of two or more resistors and measuring in between them.

Building the Balanced Brightness-Sensing Circuit

Assemble the balanced brightness-sensing circuit on a solderless breadboard (see Figure 14-18). Build it on the far-right side of the board so space remains for the other line-following circuits to be added in the next chapters.

The trimpot (R2) will probably be marked "203," which represents 20,000 Ω. Before adding the trimpot to the circuit, dial it to its halfway point. (Attach the trimpot's first and second leads to a multimeter as you turn the dial to watch the resistance settle to around 10,000 Ω.)

After the circuit is complete, check the voltage at TP1 with power turned on. Recall that to test voltage at a point, you connect the multimeter's black test probe to the negative bus and connect the multimeter's red test probe to the point of interest (in this case, TP1).

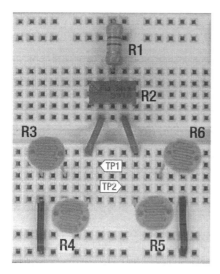

Figure 14-18. Balanced brightness-sensing circuit built on a solderless breadboard

If you bring R3 or R4 toward a light bulb, the voltage at TP1 decreases. If you cover either R3 or R4 with your finger, the voltage at TP1 increases. In fact, you can witness a change in voltage by merely casting a shadow over the sensors as you move your hand back and forth.

After experimenting with TP1 for a while, switch over to TP2. Sensors R5 and R6 provide the voltage effect for TP2. Even so, you may notice that covering R3 and R4 produces a slight increase in voltage.

Because R1 is shared by both pairs of sensors, R1's voltage usage is affected by the resistance of all four sensors. When R1's voltage usage decreases because of one set of sensors, the other set of sensors takes up the slack, thus increasing the voltage at that pair's test point. It's not a consequential effect for line following. However, it is noteworthy that when two paths have a component in common, their values can affect each other.

Inability to Balance the Brightness-Sensing Circuit

As designed, changing the dial on the trimpot (R2) affects the voltages at TP1 and TP2. If you have two multimeters, you can connect one to each test point and adjust the trimpot until the voltages match.

You can attempt to swap a single multimeter between the test points. However, you're likely to cast dissimilar shadows or nudge the sensors to different angles as you try. Balancing the circuit with a single multimeter is difficult.

Wouldn't it be helpful to have something that constantly compared both pairs of sensors and turned on an LED to indicate which sensor had a higher voltage? That's exactly what you'll add to the breadboard in the next chapter.

CHAPTER 15

Comparators

You're in the midst of prototyping a line-following robot on a solderless breadboard. At this point, the breadboard has a power supply (9 V battery), a power switch, a power indicator (LED circuit), and two pairs of brightness sensors. It's time to add some brains.

In this chapter, you'll learn about a comparator chip. Upon adding it to the breadboard, it compares the sensors and illuminates an LED depending on which pair of sensors is receiving more light.

Voltage Comparator

An analog voltage comparator chip (see Figure 15-1) is somewhat like a tiny voltmeter with built-in switches. It samples voltages at two points and turns on a switch if the first point's voltage is greater than the second point's voltage. It turns off the switch if the first point's voltage is less than the second point's voltage.

Figure 15-1. 2903 and 393 analog voltage comparators

Like most chips, the comparator comes in different models and packages. To avoid intimidation, I chose the most common comparator with the fewest connections.

The least expensive model is the LM393. The LM293, LM2903, and LM193 are completely compatible with the LM393, with the added ability to operate at more extreme temperature ranges (below freezing and above 70° C). Feel free to choose any of those model numbers from any manufacturer.

Examining the LM393

The LM393's full title is "Low Power, Low Offset Voltage, Single Supply, Dual, Differential Comparators." That's a mouthful.

- The "Low Power" term indicates that the chip doesn't use much electricity. That's valuable to a battery-powered robot.

- The "Low Offset Voltage" term indicates that the chip can compare voltages that are very close to each other. That's going to be useful for the subtle differences in brightness encountered during line following.

- The "Single Supply" term indicates that the chip operates using only one power source. A "Dual Supply" chip needs two back-to-back power supplies (or circuitry) to produce a positive, neutral, and negative. Some comparators are designed to be flexible, and can operate with either single or dual supplies, depending on how you connect them.

- The "Dual" term indicates that there are two independent comparators in each chip. It's a two-for-one special! "Quad" chips contain four independent comparators.

- The "Differential" term indicates the chip has circuitry to convert the comparison between two voltages in the input voltage range to a single digital output in the power supply's voltage range. For example, the chip's output voltage won't drop when the input voltages are very small, nor will it rise when the input voltages are very large.

Turning to the Datasheet

Vital information regarding each chip or part is contained in a document called a datasheet. The datasheet is freely available from the manufacturer, often on their web site.

The datasheet begins with a brief description of the part, usually pointing out the features that have been improved over prior models. This is helpful in that it emphasizes attributes that professional engineers find particularly important (or that were previously lacking) in that kind of component.

The datasheet contains typical and maximum values for a selective list of electrical characteristics, such as: how much current it uses (battery drain), what voltage range it can tolerate, what temperatures it operates under, and so on. According to the datasheet, the LM393 can be powered from 2 V to 36 V. This generous range easily fits within a 9 V battery's voltage characteristics (5 V to 10 V).

There are a couple of significant issues revealed in the LM393 datasheets.

The first issue is that the LM393 can't compare voltages within the upper 1.5 V of the current battery level. So, if both test point's voltages are hovering in the 8 V range and the battery is 9 V, the comparator won't always make an accurate comparison.

The second issue is that the comparator can't guarantee that it has enough strength by itself to switch on a circuit that uses more than 6 mA. The datasheet indicates that the comparator can **typically** switch up to 16 mA, but you may legitimately receive a batch of chips with only 6 mA capability.

Both of these issues are compensated for in the robot's design, as will be pointed out later.

Inspecting the Pinouts

On chips, the metal wires sticking out are called pins. By far the most necessary information about a chip is how to hook up the pins to the rest of the circuit. The tiny chip case is too small a surface on which to print text descriptions or numbers for the pins. So, the datasheet provides an annotated illustration called a pinout, which shows all of the pins and their respective functions.

The pinout of the LM393 comparator chip is shown in Figure 15-2. There's a notch and/or a dot atop the physical chip as well as a notch atop the pinout illustration. Mentally number the pins starting from the notch, rotating counter-clockwise. This method makes it easy to universally reference any pin on a chip.

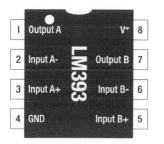

Figure 15-2. Pinout of the LM393

■ **Tip** When a bunch of chips are placed on a board, the board should be designed so that all notches are aligned in the same direction. This way, a quick visual inspection reveals if any chips have been inserted backwards.

Locating the Power Supply Pins

All chips have pins that receive power to run the chip. Think of a chip like an appliance: You need to plug it in to make it work. The power supply pins are the first two pins you should locate.

On the LM393, pin 8 and pin 4 receive power. Pin 8 is labeled V⁺, which means the positive end of the battery connects to this pin. Pin 4 is labeled GND, which means the negative end of the battery connects to this pin. At the end of this book is a list of the most common labels that indicate positive and negative power connections for chips.

Many chips have power pins on the same diagonal corners as the LM393. However, always check the chip's pinout on its datasheet to be sure.

Identifying the Comparators

Based on the chip's title, "Dual Comparators," we know that two comparators are included on this chip. Pins 1, 2, and 3 belong to the first comparator ("A") and pins 7, 6, and 5 belong to the second comparator ("B"). Notice that pin 1 (Output A) has the same name as pin 7 (Output B), pin 2 (Input A-) has the same name as pin 6 (Input B-), and pin 3 (Input A+) has the same name as pin 5 (Input B+) except that one set of pins is for comparator A and the other set for comparator B.

The comparators are truly independent: You can use them individually to measure completely different circuits or test points. The comparators function in the same manner, so once you have learned how to use comparator "A," then you know how to use comparator "B."

195

On the LM393, pin 1 is labeled Output A (see Figure 15-2). There is a solid-state switch inside of the chip that either connects the inside of this pin to the negative terminal of the battery or disconnects it.

Recall that a circuit turns off if either end of its power is disconnected. Therefore, if you connect the negative end of a circuit to pin 1 of the LM393, then the circuit can be turned on and off by the switch inside the LM393.

On the LM393, pin 2 and pin 3 are labeled Input A- and Input A+, respectively. These are connected to the test points that you'd like the chip to compare. If pin 2 has a higher voltage than pin 3, then pin 1 is switched to the battery (see left side of Figure 15-3). Otherwise, pin 1 is disconnected (see right side of Figure 15-3).

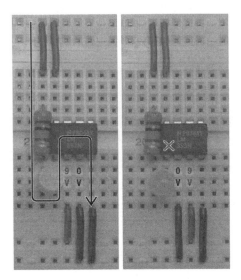

Figure 15-3. Left: *When pin 2 has a higher voltage (for example, 9 V) than pin 3 (for example, 0 V), then pin 1 is switched to the negative end of the battery, thus allowing power to flow.* Right: *However, when pin 2 has a lower voltage (for example, 0 V) than pin 3 (for example, 9 V), then pin 1 is disconnected, thus preventing power from flowing.*

Don't worry if this seems confusing. You can try it yourself with the comparator circuit coming up in this chapter.

Obtaining Comparators

Comparators are useful for many robot functions other than robot brains. They are often used to simplify sensor inputs by comparing the sensors to adjustable voltage levels. Table 15-1 shows the suppliers for the ordinary LM393 and for the more temperature-tolerant LM2903. Either is acceptable for the line-following robot.

Table 15-1. Dual Comparators

Supplier	Part Number	Price
Mouser	511-LM393N	$0.26
Mouser	511-LM2903N	$0.26
Jameco	LM393N	$0.25
Digi-Key	LM393NGOS	$0.39
Digi-Key	LM2903NGOS	$0.39

The letter "N" follows each part number in Table 15-1. The final letter(s) in a part number usually signify the chip's package size, package material, and/or temperature tolerance. For parts manufactured by National Semiconductor, the letter "N" represents a dual inline package, otherwise known as a DIP.

If you mistakenly purchase an LM393**M** ("M" not "N") chip, you'll find it encased in a different package. The SO-8 or SOIC narrow package won't fit into the solderless breadboard (see Figure 15-4).

Figure 15-4. LM393N is DIP (left), *LM393M is SOIC narrow* (right)

Brightness Comparator Circuit

The brightness comparator circuit connects to the balanced brightness-sensing circuit from the prior chapter. This is the brain that reads the photoresistor sensors and then controls the motors accordingly.

Comparing a Schematic with a Wiring Diagram

Instead of a formal schematic, the brightness comparator circuit is presented as a wiring diagram in Figure 15-5.

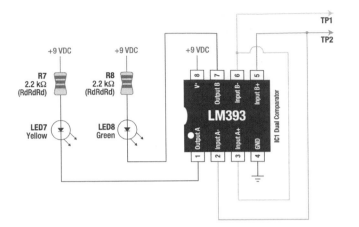

Figure 15-5. Wiring diagram of the brightness comparator circuit

In a schematic, the dual comparators would not be drawn as a chip package. Instead, each comparator would be drawn separately as symbols near the parts they are comparing. The schematic ("package-free") technique reduces the number of lines crossing over the drawing. Pin numbers are usually not shown in schematics, which make the illustration independent of the particular chip package eventually implemented.

Unlike schematics, wiring diagrams present the layout as it looks in real life. Final pin numbers and package grouping are indicated. (While I was at it, I changed the resistors to look a little more realistic, instead of symbolic. I beg the forgiveness of any old-school electrical engineers.)

A schematic is better when you're designing the functionality of the circuit, without regard to the physical layout. A wiring diagram is easier to follow when you're actually assembling the circuit.

Labeling Parts

The rules for part labeling are reasonably flexible. Because the circuit in Figure 15-5 connects to another circuit containing resistors, I chose to number the new resistors where the last circuit left off (R7, for example). For ease of reading, I switched to using "LED" instead of "D" to label the LEDs. I also numbered the LEDs to match the resistors to which they're connected (LED7 and R7).

The LM393 is labeled as IC1 for integrated circuit #1. It's called an integrated circuit because the comparators are nothing more than an ordinary circuit of resistors, wires, diodes, and transistors squished into a single part. Got it? It's a circuit that's been integrated into a small package.

By the way, for proper connections, don't forget to pay attention to the notch in the chip.

Drawing Connected and Unconnected Wire

Figure 15-5 is the first circuit presented in this book that has been complex enough that a few lines cross over each other. Sometimes the wires are connected to each other; sometimes they're just passing over.

A solid circle or dot appears on the wire near the arrow going to TP2. The dot indicates that those wires are connected.

A hop in a wire appears just above pin 5. The hop indicates that those wires aren't connected.

Some schematics and wiring diagrams don't bother with the hop. Instead they assume crossing wires aren't connected unless there's a dot. Depending on the author, you'll need to take a moment to acquaint yourself with his or her wire-connecting indicators.

Understanding the Brightness Comparator Circuit

The purpose of the brightness comparator circuit is to indicate which pair of photoresistors is receiving more light. The comparator chip accomplishes this by comparing the voltage at test point 1 to the voltage at test point 2; whichever has the lower voltage is receiving more light.

Both comparators in the LM393 are utilized. Comparator A compares TP2 (connected to Input A-) to TP1 (connected to Input A+) and turns on the LED7 (connected to Output A) when TP1 has a lower voltage (left photoresistors receiving more light). Comparator B compares TP1 (connected to Input B-) to TP2 (connected to Input B+) and turns on LED8 (connected to Output B) when TP2 has a lower voltage (right photoresistors receiving more light).

Pin 8 (V^+) connects to positive power and pin 4 (GND) connects to negative power because the comparator chip needs to be plugged in to operate. Resistor R7 protects LED7 and resistor R8 protects LED8 from the full force of the battery, just as you used a resistor for that same purpose in the LED Power Indicator Circuit.

Parts List for the Brightness Comparator Circuit

- -- – 9 VDC power supply
- **R7, R8** – 2.2 kΩ resistor (red, red, red)
- **LED7** – Yellow LED
- **LED8** – Green LED
- **IC1** – LM393 (or equivalent) dual comparator

Building the Brightness Comparator Circuit

In the last chapter, you built the balanced brightness-sensing circuit on the right side of a solderless breadboard. You should build the brightness comparator circuit in the middle of the same board (see Figure 15-6).

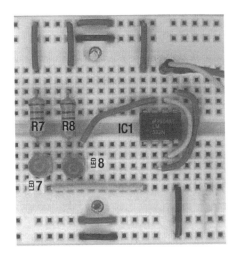

Figure 15-6. Brightness comparator circuit built on a solderless breadboard

Connect IC1 to the sensor test points (look ahead at Figure 15-7, if necessary) using reinforced jumper wire, rather than flat wire. The jumper wire crosses over other parts on the board, reaching the test points with ease. Additionally, the test-point ends of reinforced jumper wires can be pulled and positioned at other points for testing purposes.

Test point 1 (TP1) connects to IC1 input B-, which is then connected to IC1 input A+. Test point 2 (TP2) connects to IC1 input B+, which is then connected to IC1 input A-. So, both test points are connected to both comparators, except the connections are reversed on one of the comparators.

R7 and LED7 form an LED indicator circuit. As stated earlier, R7 is a current-limiting resistor that protects LED7 from the full force of the battery. This is the same simple LED circuit design that you use for the solderless breadboard power indicator. The big difference here is that the negative end of the LED circuit is connected to IC1 output A instead of the negative terminal of the battery.

When the comparator chooses to switch output A to the negative terminal of the battery, then power can flow from the positive terminal of the battery, through R7, through LED 7, through IC1 output A, and into the negative terminal of the battery. This flow of electricity turns on the LED. When the comparator chooses to disconnect output A, no power can flow and the LED turns off.

Having Fun with the LED Indicators and Light Sensors

When you turn on power, either the green LED or the yellow LED will light. One at a time, cover each photoresistor with your finger. Try waving your hand across the sensors right to left and left to right (see Figure 15-7). The LEDs should blink back and forth as each side receives more or less light.

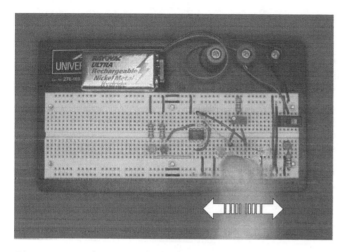

Figure 15-7. Playing with the brightness sensors; making the LEDs blink

Now you have everything you need to tune the balance between the photoresistor sensor pairs by adjusting the trimpot (R2). Turning the dial far to one side should light one LED and turning the dial far to the other side should light the other LED. At some point, toward the middle of the dial, both LEDs should be lit or they should switch back and forth with only a slight turn of the trimpot dial to the left or right.

That's the balanced position. Although not strictly impossible, you're not likely to get both LEDs to light at the same time.

With balanced sensors, the LEDs should switch back and forth with even a faint shadow across the photoresistors. I noticed that the light reflecting off of my shirt was enough to activate the appropriate LED depending on which way I leaned.

Diagnosing Problems in the Brightness Comparator Circuit

What if your circuit isn't having fun at this point? If the circuit isn't working correctly, there are a bunch of tests you can perform to pinpoint the problem.

Confirming Power Across the Board

Make sure power is on. The LED power indicator circuit installed on the solderless breadboard should be lit. If not, disconnect the battery and measure its voltage independent of the circuit. If the battery's voltage is less than 6 volts, replace it with a fresh battery.

If the battery seems to have plenty of voltage when removed from the circuit, but voltage drops significantly when installed, the circuit probably has a short. This occurs when a positive wire is mistakenly connected to a negative wire somewhere on the breadboard. In that case, the power goes straight through the shorted wires without bothering to go through the routes containing all the electronic components. Carefully compare all of your wires to the schematics and photographs.

If the battery is fine and you don't have a short circuit, check that positive and negative connections to power are being supplied throughout the buses. To do this, connect the multimeter's black test probe and red test probe to each quadrant of the board to ensure that full battery voltage is being delivered.

Check that positive power is being supplied to the top wire of R1, R7, R8, and IC1 V⁺ (pin 8). You can confirm this by connecting the black test probe to any negative bus and then (one at a time) touching the tip of the red test probe to the top wire lead of each of the resistors and to pin 8 of IC1 (see Figure 15-8). By touching the multimeter test-probe tip directly to the metal portion of the component that is supposed to be getting power, you can eliminate the possibility that the component wire is loose and not actually receiving power from the board.

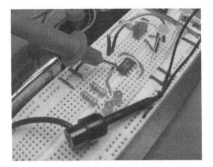

Figure 15-8. Testing the comparator's positive voltage pin with the multimeter test probe tip

Check that negative connections are being supplied to the bottom wire of R3, R6, and IC1 GND (pin 4). You can confirm this by connecting the red test probe to any positive bus and then (one at a time) touching the tip of the black test probe to the bottom wire lead of each of the two bottom photoresistors and to pin 4 of IC1. This is a slightly backwards test, since the red test probe stays in place and the black test probe moves to the points being tested. So, note that the meter displays 9 V (or whatever) if a proper connection exists, not 0 V.

Faking Input to the Comparator

For diagnostic purposes, the reinforced jumper wires connecting the comparator's inputs to the sensor test points can be redirected to ideal, unwavering test points. Connect one jumper wire to the positive bus and the other jumper wire to the negative bus to provide the highest-quality test signals (see Figure 15-9). One of the LEDs should light. You can then swap the jumper wires and the other LED should light.

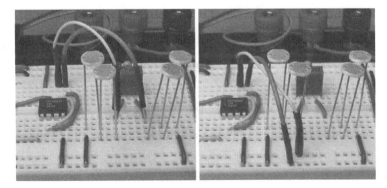

Figure 15-9. Moving the comparator input's jumper wire from the sensor test points (left) *to the power supply buses* (right)

With the jumper wires still connected to the buses (rather than the sensor test points), use a multimeter to test that the inputs of one comparator are receiving the voltages opposite from the other comparator. If the wires aren't reversed to the second comparator's inputs, then both LEDs will turn on at the same time and turn off at the same time.

Make sure neither LED is in backwards.

Adding Headlights

Currently, the sensors react to ambient (room) lighting. When installed on the robot, the sensors face down near the floor with most of the natural lighting blocked by the circuit board. By adding headlights, you can place the sensors underneath the robot and operate the robot in dim lighting or at night.

There's a special reason for adding a light source. As mentioned earlier in this chapter, the comparator can't compare voltages in the upper 1.5 V range of the battery voltage. When the photoresistor sensors are dark, their resistance gets very large. The large resistance causes the voltage at the test points to rise into the top 1.5 V. By adding headlights, the resistance remains below extreme values, thus staying away from the comparator's top-end weakness.

Understanding the Headlight Circuit's Two LEDs

The headlight circuit is nearly identical to earlier LED circuits. The major difference here is that two LEDs are sharing the current (see Figure 15-10). This is very energy-efficient since some of the voltage that was being wasted as heat in the resistor is now creating light in the second LED. Because LED10 is using the same current flowing through LED9, the additional LED has no effect on battery drain.

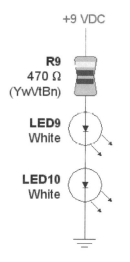

Figure 15-10. Schematic of the headlight circuit

The only trick to keep in mind when stringing on additional LEDs is that the voltage of **each** LED needs to be subtracted from the battery total before selecting the value of the current-limiting resistor (R9). Here's that formula from several chapters ago:

```
(battery voltage - LED voltage) / (maximum LED current in mA / 1000) = minimum resistor
```

White LEDs need quite a bit more voltage than do red LEDs. About 3.1 V is common. If you don't have access to the datasheet for your white LEDs, the diode test on most digital multimeters can provide a decent estimate. (Unfortunately, some older multimeters may not be able to test diodes with voltage drops as high as 3 V.)

Because LEDs are tested at low current by the diode test of the multimeter, the true voltage consumed by the LED will be larger in an actual circuit. For example, the meter's diode test might display 2.6 V for a white LED that actually uses 3.1 V.

That's okay. The current-limiting resistor formula provides an improved safety margin if calculated with the lower voltage determined by the multimeter. Of course, always provide the actual LED voltage from the datasheets or actual circuit measurements if you can.

Here's the formula for the headlight circuit with two white LEDs:

```
(9 V battery - 3.1 V white LED - 3.1 V white LED) / (30 mA maximum current / 1000) = 93 Ω
current limiting resistor
```

To be safe, I began testing the circuit with a more resistive value, 150 Ω. Even so, the white LEDs were blindingly bright! So, I continued to increase the resistor value until I was happy with the brightness, which also saves on power consumption.

Often, I'll adjust the brightness with a trimpot and then measure the trimpot resistance with a multimeter to determine the final resistor value to install. In fact, there isn't any reason you can't permanently install a 20 kΩ trimpot (like the variable brightness LED circuit) and alter the headlight brightness on the actual robot.

For the purpose of solderless-breadboard experiments, I settled on a current-limiting resistor of 470 Ω. Pick 330 Ω, 220 Ω, or even 150 Ω if you'd prefer brighter headlights. Remember that 93 Ω results in the absolute **maximum** current (30 mA), not the **recommended** current. LEDs are usually driven at currents between 2 mA and 20 mA.

Do not use any color other than white for the robot's headlights. For example, if you choose red headlight LEDs, then the robot will be unable to follow a blue tape line. The blue color of the tape reflects very little red, and the photoresistor sensors won't see any reflected light. White headlights provide the most universally satisfactory results.

Building the Headlight Circuit

The headlights should go within the cluster of photoresistor sensors. There happened to be three empty solderless-breadboard columns in the center of my sensor circuit. If you don't have enough room, just shift some parts over. Ease of rewiring is a dominant feature of solderless breadboards.

Rather than extending a wire from the upper bus above the trimpot, I chose to add the headlights with power coming from the positive bus on the lower side of the breadboard. Figure 15-11 shows the current-limiting resistor (R9) connected to positive power and then going up to the anode of LED9. This is the same technique as the LED power indicator circuit uses.

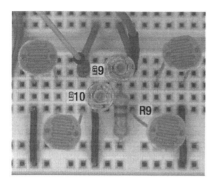

Figure 15-11. Headlight circuit built on solderless breadboard

With the headlights installed, the photoresistor sensors are no longer as sensitive to ambient shadows. That's a desirable feature for line following, as the robot won't start following deep shadows instead of the line. However, shadow ignoring takes some of the fun out of testing.

The sensors will likely need to be rebalanced. This is because the LEDs are lighting the photoresistors from behind. Some of the light is leaking through the backside of the photoresistor ceramic and contaminating the sensor values. For my finished robot, I tried to keep the heights of the LEDs the same as the heights of the photoresistors. I also painted the backs of the photoresistors black to prevent leakage.

Now that the circuit no longer needs ambient light, take the breadboard into a dark closet for hand-waving testing. Aren't you glad you're using a battery as a power source so that the breadboard is portable?

Repeating the Multiple LED Trick

You've just learned that you can add extra LEDs without greater battery consumption. Hmm. The single yellow (LED7) and single green (LED8) LEDs look a little lonely.

Determining the Number of LEDs that the Battery Voltage Can Support

Yellow and green LEDs usually require between 2.0 V and 2.2 V. We'll average it to 2.1 V for the formula. Let's see how many LEDs we can string in a row for a 9 V battery. Can the circuit support eight LEDs?

```
2.1 V LED × 8 = 16.8 V
```

No, obviously a 9 V battery doesn't have enough voltage for eight LEDs. What about four LEDs?

```
2.1 V LED × 4 = 8.4 V
```

Looks good. But wait! What happens when the battery runs down to 7 V? Oh well, not enough voltage for four LEDs when the battery runs down. Let's try three LEDs.

```
2.1 V LED × 3 = 6.3 V
```

Three LEDs are appropriate for a yellow and green LED voltage drop of approximately 2.1 V powered by a 9 V battery. Recall that only two white LEDs (not three) were used in the headlight circuit. That's because the white LED headlights require 3.1 V for each LED, for a total of 6.2 V.

Calculating the Maximum Current Draw

The yellow and green indicator LEDs need to be visible from far away in standard room lighting. Therefore, the LEDs should be run near their brightest. That calls for a higher current, which is achieved by a lower resistance.

```
(9 V battery - (2.1 V LED × 3)) / (30 mA maximum current × 1000) = 90 W current limiting
resistor
```

The most common resistor value above 90 Ω is 100 Ω. But, I'm going to use 150 Ω in case the battery voltage starts higher than 9 V. The higher resistor value provides a bit more safety. To double-check that you didn't make a math error at some point, plug the numbers into the formula for current presented a few chapters ago.

```
(V / Ω) × 1000 = mA
(9 V battery - (2.1 V LED × 3)) = 2.7 V remaining to be used by the resistor
2.7 V / 150 Ω current limiting resistor = 18 mA current
```

That's below the 30 mA maximum of the LEDs. But, there's a lurking limitation of the comparator. According to the datasheet, the typical current it can provide is 16 mA. The minimum current it assures to provide is a mere 6 mA.

The additional LEDs (much less the motors) can't be installed until this limitation of the comparator is addressed in the next chapter.

Appreciating a Simple Mind

The line-following circuit is taking shape. The comparator makes a fine brain for this simple robot. The comparator is inexpensive, fast, and accurate without being complicated to employ. However, it does have some limitations that needed to be considered during design and testing.

The headlights provide consistent lighting for the photoresistor sensors. This allows the robot to run in the dark and it eliminates the issue of the comparator failing at high values. Frankly, the headlights also garner a lot of positive praise and attention for the robot.

The left and right LED indicators are working, which allows the sensors to be tuned. When you install three LEDs for each side, the robot's thoughts should be clearly visible from across the room. In the next chapter, you'll learn how you can interface the full sets of three LEDs to the comparator.

CHAPTER 16

■ ■ ■

Transistor Switches

When a chip pin provides current like the positive terminal of a battery, it is said to "source" current. When a chip pin receives current like the negative terminal of a battery, it is said to "sink" current. These terms are reminiscent of the water analogy, where water comes out of the source and then goes into the sink.

Many chips have the same limitation as the LM393 comparator as far as their inability to source or sink significant amounts of current. Not only is maximum current an issue, but also older chips can't source as much current as they can sink. So designers connected LEDs and other circuits "backwards" to these older chips, to take advantage of the stronger draining. (That dissimilarity has disappeared in newer chips that have dedicated hardware to provide more current and at equal levels.)

A chip's low current handling capability isn't usually a serious issue, because most chips use their pins only to pass signals to other chips. When a heavier load needs to be serviced, a discrete transistor is well-suited for the job.

There are many, many kinds of transistors. Their sizes and attributes are tailored for desired amplification, switching speed, price, noise, power usage, voltage tolerance, and/or current delivery. Although intermediate and advanced robots use mixed types of transistors, only a couple of general-purpose transistors dominate beginner robots.

In this chapter, you'll learn about transistors, specifically the 2907A PNP. You'll connect transistors to your LM393 comparator so that the robot can be brilliantly lit by three LEDs on both sides.

Defining Negative Power

Most batteries' terminals are labeled with a positive ('+') and a negative ('-'). If you connect your multimeter correctly to the battery terminals, you'll see a number in voltage mode. If you then switch the probes to the opposite battery terminals, you'll see the same number with a minus sign. The battery hasn't changed, only the meter's perspective.

The technically questionable term "negative power" is used in this chapter and throughout the book because it appropriately reminds the reader of connecting to the negative terminal of a battery.

However, any voltage lower than another is relatively negative. Let's say you have two test points, the first has 9 V and the second has 4 V. If you connect something to the 9 V point, then the 4 V point is -5 V in comparison. You could say the second test point has negative voltage in comparison to the first test point. Like a battery and a multimeter, if you connect the part in the opposite direction, the voltage will be opposite.

Electrical power is more than just a difference in voltage. The term "power" is a combination of voltage and current. As used in this book, the term negative power is used to suggest that there is both a negative voltage and that sufficient electricity is allowed to flow to that negative voltage point. For example, the negative terminal on a battery has both a negative voltage and the capability for electrical current to flow to it, so it could be said to have negative power.

Focusing on the 2907A Transistor

The 2907A transistor (see Figure 16-1) is more formally referred to as the 2N2907A. It is a bipolar PNP general-purpose amplifier.

Figure 16-1. Fairchild 2907A transistor in a TO-92 package

- Bipolar indicates the type of semiconductor technology. Bipolar semiconductors are popular because they're fast, static-electricity resistant, and can deliver plenty of current. However, bipolar semiconductors use more energy (and therefore emit more heat) than field-effect semiconductors.

- PNP indicates that the transistor turns on with negative power. Just the opposite, NPN transistors turn on with positive power.

- General Purpose indicates that the transistor operates with characteristics similar to most transistors. Compare that with high-speed, low-noise, or power transistors that have special abilities tailored for specific duties.

- Amplifier indicates the transistor can magnify a signal. Some other transistors are designed more for switching, buffering, or acting as adaptors from one voltage to another.

Like all bipolar transistors, the 2907A has three leads labeled emitter, base, and collector (not always in that order). Transistor experts hook them up in bizarre ways to achieve funky abilities. However, this book focuses on the more mundane, yet popular, arrangements. For the line-following robot, the 2907A transistor will be acting as a switch controlled by the comparator's output.

Pushing the 2907A's Button

You can connect most transistors as electronically controlled pushbuttons. "Pressing" a PNP transistor's base lead with negative power turns on the circuit. Disconnecting the base lead or applying positive power turns off the circuit. (A thorough example circuit appears later in this chapter).

This may seem a little backwards. Usually something turns on when positive power is applied; NPN transistors work that way. However, since the LM393 comparator only connects its output signals to negative power, an appropriate transistor was chosen that turns on when it's connected to negative power.

So, the LM393 comparator signals to the 2907A transistor to turn on the LEDs and motor by connecting the transistor's base lead to negative power. The transistor is the muscle; the comparator is the brain.

Checking the Datasheet

Recall that a datasheet, which lists important facts about a part, is available from the manufacturer.

The 2907A datasheet indicates that it is capable of sourcing 500 mA of current continuously (as opposed to short bursts). Wow. That's a big improvement over 6 mA for the LM393 comparator. The 2907A provides plenty of electrical flow for the LEDs and the motor, with room to spare.

Just like a chip, it isn't unexpected for each part to use a little bit of power for itself. The datasheet indicates that there is a small, continuous electrical drain for enabling the 2907A transistor. There is also a slight voltage loss of 0.2 V for the circuit being switched. But these costs are insignificant on this robot.

Obtaining 2907A Transistors

Table 16-1 lists suppliers of 2907A transistors in the solderless-breadboard–compatible TO-92 package. Because bipolar transistors are so inexpensive, you can afford to reduce the individual price by purchasing ten at a time.

Table 16-1. Suppliers of 2907A Transistors in TO-92 Package

Supplier	Part Number	Price	Description
Jameco	178520	10 @ $0.05	Various manufacturers
Mouser	512-PN2907ATAR	$0.06	Fairchild Semiconductor
Digi-Key	PN2907ABU	$0.12	Fairchild Semiconductor

Plain 2907 (without the A at the end) transistors are available. They are acceptable replacements for 2907A transistors in the line-following circuit. However, the 2907 transistor has reduced capabilities in several categories (collector-emitter breakdown voltage, collector cutoff current, and gain), and, as such, is not always a suitable replacement for the 2907A in all circuits.

Testing Bipolar Transistors with a Multimeter

Depending on your multimeter, there are a couple of methods of testing a transistor. The more informative testing method requires a multimeter with a transistor test socket. The other testing method is for multimeters with a diode test function. Later in this chapter, a sample circuit is provided that allows a transistor to be tested even if your meter has neither a transistor test socket nor a diode test mode.

The following instructions should be applicable to most meters. However, it's best to follow the specific instructions provided with your meter.

Testing with a Multimeter that Has a Transistor Socket

When using a meter with a transistor test socket, you'll need to test the transistor differently depending on whether you have access to the transistor's datasheet.

Testing a Transistor When You Have the Datasheet

If you have access to a transistor's data sheet, then you already know a lot about the transistor. You know whether it is NPN or PNP. You know which lead is the emitter, the base, and the collector. You also know approximately how much it can amplify, which is called "gain."

Since you already know the transistor type and pinouts, you'd probably be testing to determine if the transistor is working and to compare its gain to other transistors in the same batch.

1. Turn the multimeter dial to h_{FE} (see Figure 16-2) or the appropriate function for your meter.

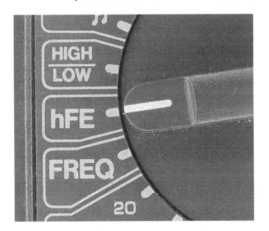

Figure 16-2. Dialing the transistor gain test (h_{FE}) on a multimeter

2. For a 2907A transistor, Figure 16-3 shows the correct insertion. All of the transistor leads are inserted on the PNP side of the socket. The emitter connects to 'E,' the base connects to 'B,' and the collector connects to 'C.'

When looking at a datasheet, pay attention to the rounded and the flat sides of the transistor's package. Otherwise, you might connect the leads in reverse by mistake (however, no damage will result if improperly inserted into a multimeter).

3. For the 2907A, the meter should display a number between 75 h_{FE} and 300 h_{FE}. This is the unique amount of gain for this individual transistor.

Figure 16-3. Inserting the 2907A into the multimeter transistor test socket (examples from two different sockets found on various meters)

Understanding the Importance of Transistor Gain

Current applied to the transistor's base is multiplied by the h_{FE} to determine the amount of current the transistor will produce. A transistor with 30 h_{FE} gain and 2 mA current on its base lead allows 60 mA of current to flow between the emitter and collector.

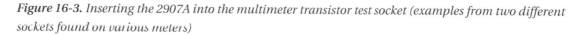

2 mA × 30 h_{FE} = 60 mA

The circuit attached to the collector isn't required to use all of the current, but it is restricted to that maximum (in this case 60 mA).

By varying the amount of current provided to the transistor's base, you can control the amount of current provided to the attached circuit. This technique is used in some battery chargers to limit the maximum current that the battery can draw, thus preventing the battery from overheating or exploding.

A transistor is a current-controlled device. Just like an LED, the output of a transistor depends largely on the current provided to it.

Gain Varies from Transistor to Transistor

The h_{FE} varies from transistor model to transistor model. It even varies from transistor to transistor within the same batch from the factory. In a lot of ten 2907A transistors, I got results from 151 h_{FE} to Q 173 h_{FE}. The datasheet guaranteed a minimum of 75 h_{FE}, so the actual numbers were very good.

The variations in gain cause headaches to stereo manufacturers as they result in speaker outputs with different sound volumes. However, since the LM393 comparator is going to be giving at least 6 mA to the base of the transistor, even a minimum gain of 75 is going to result in 450 mA available to the attached circuit.

Switching Off and On Rather Than Amplifying

When a PNP transistor is used as a switch, the base lead is provided either no current to turn the transistor completely off or plenty of negative power at the base lead to turn the transistor completely on. Putting a transistor into a fully powered state is called saturation. This is a legitimate and common technique.

When a transistor is used as an amplifier, for example for an audio speaker, the transistor is provided user-adjustable levels of current to the base lead through a potentiometer. This results in audio volume control.

Testing a Transistor When You Don't Have the Datasheet

If you don't have access to a transistor's data sheet, then you'll need to try various combinations of insertions into the multimeter's transistor test socket.

1. Turn the multimeter dial to h_{FE} (see Figure 16-2) or the appropriate function for your meter.

2. Try each of the combinations of the NPN holes. On my multimeter, the transistor can fit into the socket with EBC or BCE (E for emitter, B for base, C for collector). Then, I can flip the transistor in the opposite direction and get CBE and ECB. This allows for all combinations with either the base or the collector in the middle.

3. If you encounter the correct combination, the meter should display a number between 10 h_{FE} and 600 h_{FE}, with the extremes being more atypical. Numbers below 10 h_{FE} or above the maximum of the meter usually signify the transistor is installed incorrectly.

4. After trying the NPN combinations, try each of the combinations of the PNP holes.

5. One of the connections in the NPN or PNP holes should have resulted in a gain between 10 h_{FE} and 600 h_{FE}. The other combinations should have displayed values below 10 h_{FE} or above 600 h_{FE}. The set of holes that worked tells you whether the transistor is NPN or PNP, and which lead is the emitter, base, and collector.

Even if you have the datasheet for a transistor, trying the other combinations of holes can indicate that the transistor is damaged if it gains too much when installed in the wrong holes. Often, a damaged transistor won't provide useful gain despite being installed correctly in the multimeter's transistor socket.

If the transistor's gain isn't within the reasonable range for any of the holes, it may be because:

- the transistor wasn't fully inserted into the test socket

- the transistor isn't a bipolar semiconductor (perhaps it's field-effect)

- the transistor is damaged

- the transistor is designed for really high gain

- the transistor is designed for really low gain

Testing with a Multimeter that Has a Diode Test

If your multimeter doesn't have a transistor test socket, you can still determine the transistor type (NPN or PNP) and which lead is the base. For this experiment, you can pick either a PNP (like the 2907A) or NPN transistor. I've produced test results for both types, so that you can compare your transistor to my samples.

1. Turn the multimeter dial to diode test mode and prepare the test probes like you were going to test an LED (see Figure 16-4).

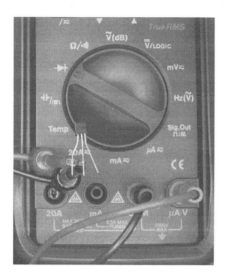

Figure 16-4. *Setting up a multimeter for testing a transistor with the diode test function*

2. With a pair of transistor leads at a time, connect each of the leads to the multimeter test probes and write down the value. For example, connect the transistor's first lead to the **red** test probe and connect the transistor's second lead to the **black** test probe and record the value.

3. Continue until you've tested all lead combinations as shown in the first column of Table 16-2.

Of all the combinations, only two should have a voltage drop of between 0.5 and 0.7. All of the other combinations should be infinity. Sample results appear in Table 16-2.

Table 16-2. *Example Diode Test Results for Two Different Bipolar Transistor Types*

Leads	Sample PNP	Sample NPN
1 red & 2 black	0.623 V	infinity
1 red & 3 black	infinity	infinity
2 red & 3 black	infinity	0.606 V
2 red & 1 black	infinity	0.610 V
3 red & 1 black	infinity	infinity
3 red & 2 black	0.619 V	infinity

The transistor lead that is present in both conducting lead combinations is the base lead. Referring to Table 16-2, for Sample PNP, the base lead is 2 (the middle lead) because it appears in test combinations 1 & 2 and 3 & 2. For Sample NPN, the base lead is also 2 (the middle lead) because it appears in test combinations 2 & 3 and 2 & 1. Although these examples both had base leads in the middle, that won't be the case with all transistors.

Furthermore, if the base lead conducted when it was connected to the red test probe, the transistor is NPN. Otherwise it is PNP. For Sample PNP, the base lead conducted when it was connected to the black test probe, so it is a PNP transistor. For Sample NPN, the base lead conducted when it was connected to the red test probe, so it is an NPN transistor.

If you'd like to reproduce the test results, Sample PNP is a 2907A transistor (no surprise) and Sample NPN is a 2222A transistor. The 2222A has very similar attributes to the 2907A, and is often used to replace the 2907A when a positive-power—activated transistor is needed.

The diode test can only determine the base lead. In order to determine the emitter and collector, a test circuit needs to be made on a breadboard.

Bipolar Transistor Test Circuits

A couple of example circuits may be helpful in understanding how a transistor can act as a switch. The first example that will be presented is for PNP transistors, which take negative power to turn on. The second example is for NPN transistors, which take positive power to turn on.

You can place a transistor in these test circuits and determine:

- whether the transistor is NPN or PNP

- which lead is the emitter, base, and collector

- the transistor's gain (h_{FE})

Examining the Schematic for the PNP Transistor Test Circuit

Figure 16-5 is a schematic of a PNP transistor test circuit. LED1 turns on when a PNP transistor is correctly inserted for Q1. NPN transistors or incorrectly inserted PNP transistors won't work, but no harm will be done.

■ **Note** In a schematic, the letter 'Q' is used to label transistors because the letter 'T' usually labels transformers. Transformers existed long before transistors were invented.

The direction of the arrow in the schematic symbol for a PNP transistor indicates that it is PNP. The arrowhead inside the symbol's circle points toward the base pin (marked with a 'B'). The arrow indicates the direction electricity must flow. Therefore, the emitter (marked with an 'E') must connect to positive power. The electricity then flows from the emitter, through the base and collector (marked with a 'C'), and eventually out to negative power.

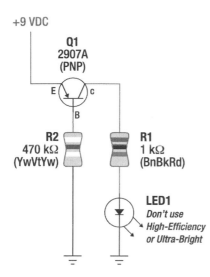

Figure 16-5. Schematic for a PNP transistor test circuit

Resistor R1 and LED1 should be familiar to you. They form a simple LED indicator circuit. No matter how much of the battery's current is made available by the transistor (Q1), the resistor (R1) limits the amount of current LED1 actually receives.

Resistor R2 also provides a current-limiting function. It prevents the transistor (Q1) from having too much current flow through it. Not only does R2 prevent too much current flowing from the emitter to the base, but it also controls the maximum current that the LED Indicator circuit can have.

Dimming the LED for Reverse Connections

Most transistors have some gain (3 h_{FE} to 5 h_{FE}) even when connected backwards. We want a circuit that only lights the LED significantly when the transistor is wired correctly (gain of over 75 h_{FE}). To achieve this, R2 is a very large resistor value and LED1 is restricted to being a standard LED (not high efficiency or high brightness).

With the large resistance of 470 kΩ, R2 doesn't allow much current to flow through the base. The amount of current flowing through the base is multiplied by the transistor's gain to determine the maximum current that is permitted to flow through the collector. Low gain (if the transistor is connected backwards) multiplied by low base current means LED1 will be limited to a low maximum current.

Unfortunately, a high-efficiency LED can still illuminate with very little current. So, that's why you should use an ordinary LED.

■ **Note** Usually you'll want to use high-efficiency or ultra-bright LEDs because their low current appetites save battery power. These LEDs work perfectly well with transistors. It's just that in the case of the transistor testing circuit, we want a current hog.

Building the PNP Transistor Test Circuit

You can build the PNP transistor test circuit to look very much like the schematic. See Figure 16-6 for a photograph.

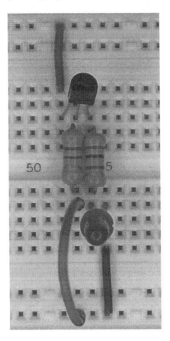

Figure 16-6. PNP transistor test circuit built on a solderless breadboard

Correcting Problems with the PNP Transistor Test Circuit

If the LED doesn't light, you can temporarily pull Q1 and connect a jumper between the positive bus and the top of R1. This is safe because R1 and LED1 form a complete LED indicator circuit by themselves. If it doesn't light with a direct connection to power, you've probably got the LED in backwards.

After you've determined that the LED indicator circuit portion is functioning, you should check that the bottom of R2 is connected to negative power. If it is, try flipping Q1 around, paying attention to the flat side. If you insert Q1 backwards or if R2 isn't connected to negative power, the LED won't turn on.

Experimenting with the Functioning PNP Transistor Test Circuit

Whatever you do, don't remove or bypass either R1 or R2. Without the resistors, the amount of current flowing through either Q1 or LED1 would exceed their maximum rating. They would quickly be destroyed.

With a functioning circuit, try flipping Q1 around to see the LED turn off.

Rather than using a flat jumper between R2 and ground, try a reinforced jumper. After seeing the LED turn on, you can pull the reinforced jumper from the bottom of R2 and see that that LED turns off. Connect the jumper to positive power to see that the LED stays off. The base lead of a PNP transistor must be connected to negative power to turn on the circuit that is attached to its collector.

Gathering Data About the PNP Transistor

When you insert a bipolar transistor with the leads in the proper orientation, the LED lights. Assuming it is a bipolar transistor, the circuit is now telling you that the transistor is a PNP. You also know which lead is the emitter, base, or collector, as the LED only lights when the leads match the schematic.

With power applied to a functioning circuit, try measuring the current flowing through R2. If you used a reinforced jumper at the bottom of R2, simply disconnect the jumper from negative power and instead connect it to the red test probe of the multimeter. Connect the black test probe to negative power. My meter indicated only 0.0164 mA (or 16.4 µA) flows through R2.

Try measuring the current flowing through R1. My meter indicated 3.1 mA. These numbers allow the calculation of the gain of the transistor.

```
3.1 mA collector current / 0.0164 mA base current = 189 h   transistor gain
                                                         FE
```

That's higher than the 171 h_{FE} indicated by my multimeter test for this transistor. However, gain varies a little depending on how much current is applied.

This PNP test circuit will become the circuit actually used in the line-following robot. It will take the 6 mA of negative power from the LM393 and will provide hundreds of mA to the three LED indicators and motor.

Examining the Schematic for the NPN Transistor Test Circuit

The NPN circuit is an upside down version of the PNP circuit. Compare Figure 16-7 to Figure 16-5. All of the components and their values stay the same except for Q1.

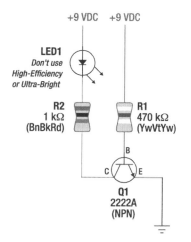

Figure 16-7. Schematic for an NPN transistor test circuit

Q1's collector has flipped to the other side of the transistor, but the LED indicator circuit (LED1 and R1) is still connected to the collector lead. The arrow remains on the emitter of the transistor symbol, but the arrowhead no longer faces the base. The arrow shows the direction of electrical flow.

R2 is connected to positive power, as is LED1. This is the most significant difference between PNP and NPN transistors. NPN transistors turn on via positive power to the base, and they connect the attached circuit to negative power. PNP transistors turn on via negative power to the base, and they connect the attached circuit to positive power.

Building the NPN Transistor Test Circuit

If you've built the PNP transistor test circuit (see Figure 16-6), rotate the breadboard upside down and hold it near Figure 16-8. It looks almost exactly the same! All the parts are in the same place and orientation, except the notch in LED1.

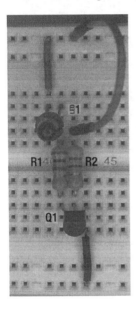

Figure 16-8. NPN transistor test circuit built on a solderless breadboard

I can't think of a more concrete example to demonstrate that PNP and NPN transistors are generally identical in function except the negative and positive are reversed.

Pay attention to the flat side of the NPN transistor (Q1). You may mistakenly want to install it with the label facing you. Also, as with the PNP transistor test circuit, you can follow the same steps with the NPN transistor test circuit to determine the transistor's emitter, base, collector, and gain.

Brightness Comparator Circuit with Transistors

Recall the brightness comparator circuit from the prior chapter. The diagram shown in Figure 16-9 is very similar to that earlier circuit, except that transistors now switch the LEDs.

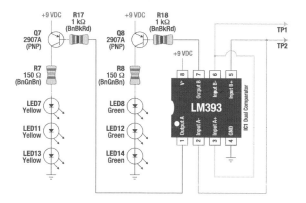

Figure 16-9. *Wiring diagram of a brightness comparator circuit with transistors*

Calculating Current-Limiting Transistors

R17 and R18 are current-limiting resistors. They protect transistors Q7 and Q8 from too much current flowing through them. The 1 kΩ resistor values are much lower than the 470 kΩ current-limiting resistor used in Figure 16-5. Here's the formula for determining how much current will flow through the base lead:

```
((V battery - 0.6 V bipolar transistor uses) / Ω base current-limiting resistor) x 1000 to
convert to mA = maximum base current
Thus: ((9 V - 0.6 V) / 1000 Ω) x 1000 = 8.4 mA
```

Based on this math, 1 kΩ resistors allow up to 8.4 mA to flow through the base lead. Notice that the transistor uses up a bit of voltage (0.6 V) for itself. Now that you know how much current is supplied to the base, you can determine how much maximum current is supplied to the attached circuit.

```
8.4 mA base current x 75 h_FE minimum transistor gain = 630 mA
```

Identifying Stresses Beyond Official Limitations

There are a couple of potential issues with the choice of 1 kΩ for current-limiting resistors R17 and R18.

Taking Into Account the LM393's Worst-Case Minimum Limit

The LM393 comparator officially only guarantees it can provide 6 mA, not the 8.4 mA permitted by the resistors. The values of R17 and R18 could be made a little higher (more resistive) to prevent stressing of the comparator outputs.

■ **Note** There are a number of potential outcomes when a circuit design exceeds the minimum and maximum values listed on a component's datasheet: The first scenario, and the most likely, is that the component will continue to perform even moderately beyond the official limitations. This is because the manufacturer understates capabilities in the official datasheets so that the manufacturer can confidently guarantee performance within the specified ranges.

The second scenario is that the component would simply not provide any greater amount, but wouldn't be damaged either. For example, the comparator would simply provide 6 mA even though the resistors would allow up to 8.4 mA.

The third scenario is that the component would not work at all, or at a significantly reduced level, but would not be harmed. For example, a chip run at lower than minimum voltage might slow down, provide incorrect output, or temporarily cease operating.

The fourth scenario is that the component would wear or age more rapidly. For example, a motor run faster and hotter than the limits might slowly become less and less efficient and then fail earlier.

The last scenario is that the component would fail utterly, perhaps being destroyed or significantly damaged. For example, a 30 mA LED dies when run at 300 mA.

The trick is in knowing how a component is going to behave outside the official limits. Although you can take an educated guess, there's usually no way to be sure in advance.

```
((V battery - 0.6 V bipolar transistor uses) / mA desired base current) × 1000 to convert
from mA = Ω desired current-limiting resistor value
((9 V - 0.6 V) / 6 mA) × 1000 = 1400 Ω
```

Oops. That didn't take into account that the battery might start as high as 10 V.

```
((10 V - 0.6 V) / 6 mA) 1000 = 1566 Ω
```

If you happen to find some resistors at or above 1566 Ω, you could design the circuit for the worst case. However, according to the datasheet, typically the comparator provides 16 mA. So, 1 kΩ resistors limiting current to 8.4 mA is fine. Additionally, as the battery voltage declines with use, the current will also drop.

Looking Out for Heavy Current Through the Attached Circuit

The other issue with an 8.4 mA base current is that some manufacturers only guarantee their 2907A can provide a maximum of 500 mA through the collector to the attached circuit. The 8.4 mA base current was calculated as being able to drive 630 mA.

It gets worse. The transistor's datasheet claims the transistor's gain could be as high as 300 h_{FE}.

```
8.4 mA base current × 300 h_FE transistor gain = 2520 mA collector current
```

2520 mA? A TO-92–encased bipolar transistor supplying that much current is going to melt!

Because the gain varies from transistor to transistor (even within a batch), it isn't reliable to design a circuit based on a particular gain. Instead, make sure the circuit attached to the transistor limits its own current below the transistor's maximum as listed in the transistor's datasheet. In this circuit, R7 and R8 protect the transistor as well as the LEDs.

Building the Brightness Comparator Circuit with Transistors

When building the circuit, leave a little room on the breadboard between the left and right indicators (driven by Q7 and Q8) shown in Figure 16-10. Motors will be attached to the transistors in a future chapter.

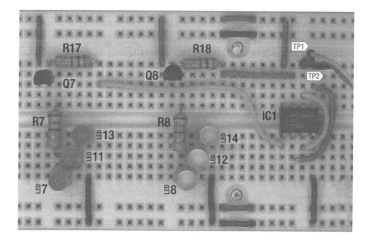

Figure 16-10. Brightness comparator circuit with transistors built on a solderless breadboard

The finished circuit should perform the same as the original brightness comparator circuit, but with the addition of more LEDs. Wave your hand in front of the photoresistors to test it.

If any of the LEDs are backwards, the other LEDs in that strand won't light. Interestingly, properly installed LEDs light even with the transistor installed backwards. This is because not much gain is needed yet. However, with the motors installed, a backwards transistor isn't going to be able to supply enough current to light the lights and engage the motors.

Summarizing PNP and NPN Transistors

When your robot needs to provide more power to a circuit than an ordinary chip can provide, attach a transistor. When the chip is providing positive power, use an NPN transistor at the negative end of the circuit you wish to control. Otherwise, use a PNP transistor at the positive end of the circuit you wish to control.

Transistors can turn all kinds of circuits and devices on and off. The examples in this chapter only involved LEDs, but there's no reason a variety of circuits couldn't be attached to a transistor's collector. In fact, that's how many power-saving devices are designed. When the brains decide enough idle time has passed, the base current provided to various transistors is stopped, thus turning off unneeded circuits.

The line-following circuit is nearly complete. By connecting transistors to the comparator, you can install three LEDs on both sides of the robot. In fact, the transistors drive enough current under the control of the comparator that the board is now ready for motors.

CHAPTER 17

DC Motors

Motion is one of the primary differentiators between a robot and a computer. More robots get their motion from DC (Direct Current) motors than from any other mechanism (see Figure 17-1).

Figure 17-1. Ordinary DC motor

This chapter details the different varieties of DC motors and their characteristics. If you don't find this subject interesting, you can skim this chapter and move on to the next. Motors won't be selected and attached to the line-following robot circuit until the next chapter.

How DC Motors Work

In an electric motor, electricity is converted to motion by magnetism.

Most people have played with a pair of magnets. Placing the magnets facing each other causes the magnets to attract and pull together. Turning one of the magnets around causes the pair to repel each other and push apart.

One magnet can attract with enough strength to drag the other magnet across a surface. This technique can be improved by adding a third magnet. The first magnet attracts the second magnet, while the third magnet repels from the rear.

When magnets are mounted around a pole, the combination of pulling and pushing can result in a rotating motion. A magnet on the shaft or pole is attracted to a magnet mounted nearby, while simultaneously being repelled by another magnet mounted on the opposite side. As soon as the shaft rotates to the magnet pulling it, the shaft magnet flips polarity and starts pushing away.

The key to making this mechanism operate is that flowing electricity can create a magnetic field. Instead of physically flipping over a magnet to change from attract to repel, the flow of electricity can be flipped forwards and backwards.

Looking Inside an Iron-Core Permanent-Magnet DC Brush Motor

An iron-core permanent-magnet DC brush motor (see Figure 17-2) consists of two major sections: the stationary parts (stator) and the rotating parts (rotor). The cap, also called the endcap or assembly, at the end of the motor is connected to the stator and doesn't move.

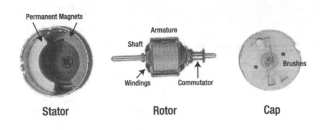

Figure 17-2. Guts of an ordinary DC motor: (left to right) *stator with permanent magnets mounted near the outside walls; rotor with shaft, armature, windings, and commutator; and cap with brushes*

Stator

The classic stator (the stationary part) includes two permanent magnets mounted opposite each other in a metal can (see Figure 17-3). The term "permanent magnets" indicates that the magnets remain magnetized even when the electricity is turned off. The magnetic field created by the electricity is going to push and pull against these two permanent magnets.

Figure 17-3. A pair of permanent magnets removed from the metal can. The clip in the foreground keeps the magnets from sliding together.

At high enough temperatures (Curie temperature), permanent magnets lose their magnetic field, resulting in reduced performance or even complete failure. Therefore, it's important not to abuse a motor by allowing it to overheat during use. Provide for adequate ventilation and, if possible, mount the motor body against other metal objects to provide a large thermal path to wick away the heat.

Interestingly, the metal container that makes up the body of the motor acts as a return path for the magnetic field. As such, less of the magnetic field is "leaked" into nearby components.

Rotor

The rotor (the rotating part) is built around a shaft. The shaft sticks out the end of the motor body so that wheels, belts, fan blades, or gears can be connected to it.

To limit friction, only a small portion of the rotor touches the motor body. High-quality motors and large motors often include ball bearings at those locations to improve carrying strength and decrease friction.

Rotor Windings

In the middle of the shaft is an armature containing many windings of wire (see Figure 17-4). The wire carries the electricity around and around an iron core in an oval loop. This increases the magnetic field that pushes and pulls against the permanent magnets on the stator.

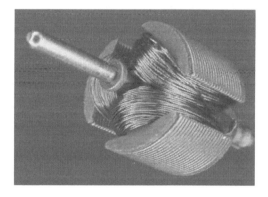

Figure 17-4. Motor shaft and armature with wire windings and an iron-based core

Besides generating and transmitting the magnetic field, the iron core also dissipates and evenly distributes heat, allowing for hard running. However, the relatively heavy iron core makes it more difficult to start or stop the shaft because of inertia.

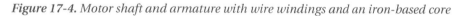

■ **Note** Almost all motors have three or more windings. Motors with only two windings wouldn't necessarily rotate in the same direction at power up, nor would they necessarily rotate all the way around. For example: Initially the shaft would rotate toward the first magnet, but then the windings reverse, so it might rotate back the way it came. Hopefully, inertia would carry the rotor around in the direction it was already going.

Rotor Shoes

At the ends of the armature are metal plates; each group is called a shoe. Motors with only a couple of shoes tend to start up unevenly and settle oddly when stopping. The irregular rotation is called cogging.

With power disconnected, it's easy to feel for cogging by gently turning the shaft with your fingers. Spin the shaft and watch it slow down. Better motors have smoother operation by increasing the number of shoes and by slanting the shoes' angles so one end overlaps the other relative to the magnets.

Rotor Commutator

At the end of the shaft is a commutator (see Figure 17-5). It contains two or more segments to receive the electricity for the armature windings. Because the commutator segments are electrical contacts, it's important that they do not become soiled or coated in any non-conductive lubricant.

Figure 17-5. Motor commutator

The commutator is necessary because power wires need to be attached to the armature windings. However, the wires can't be attached directly because they'd tangle up as the rotor turned. Instead, the commutator slides between metal brushes (see Figure 17-6) to make an electrical connection between the power wires coming in from the cap and the wire windings in the armature.

Figure 17-6. Shaft installed in the cap with brushes pressed against the commutator

As the commutator rotates around, sometimes a winding is connected to the positive and negative terminals of the battery, and sometimes a winding is connected in reverse. This feature flips the electrical flow forwards and backwards. Thus, the magnetic field flips between attract and repel.

A great thing about the commutator mechanism is that the flipping automatically speeds up as the motor turns faster!

Rotor Brushes

The "brush" term in "DC brush motor" indicates that the motor has brushes. The brushes connect directly to the battery or other power source. As stated earlier, the brushes press against the commutator to make the connection between the battery and the armature windings. The brushes must press firmly (see Figure 17-7) or else the electrical connection breaks and the electrical flow ceases.

Figure 17-7. Brushes with pads pressed against each other because the motor shaft has been removed

There are a couple of downsides to brushes. First, the pressing of the brushes against the rotor adds friction, thus slowing down the motor and increasing heat. Second, the constant making and breaking of contacts generates electrical noise (like television static when a vacuum cleaner is run) and causes sparking. Last, but most important, the brushes wear out.

Even the most well-made, well-maintained brush motor is eventually going to encounter brush failure. Brush degeneration is caused more by sparking than by friction. High-end brush motors have capacitors to absorb sparks and the motors are designed to be serviceable to replace the brushes.

Looking Inside an Iron-Core Permanent-Magnet DC Brushless Motor

Recall that brushes are required to make the electrical connection to the windings because the windings are on a rotating portion of the motor. If the windings could be located on the stationary portion of the motor (the stator), then the power wires could be directly affixed to the windings. Such a configuration would eliminate the need for brushes.

This is the case with a brushless motor (see Figure 17-8). The magnet is on the rotor and the armature with windings is on the stator. No brushes are necessary.

Figure 17-8. Guts of a brushless motor for a fan: (left to right) *rotor with permanent magnet, stator with armature, pair of bearings, compression spring, and a retaining ring*

Living Longer Without Brushes

Brushes are usually the first part to wear out on a brush motor. The lack of brushes on a brushless motor means dramatically increased lifespan and significant reduction in electrical noise. The lack of brushes eliminates sparking, and as such may be important in some scientific or hazardous situations.

For these reasons, brushless motors are very popular for computer fans. The brushless motor fan can run constantly for the life of the computer and the fan doesn't generate significant electrical noise that could interfere with the computer's digital operations.

Switching with Brushless Circuitry

Since a commutator doesn't exist on a brushless motor, the windings are not mechanically switched as the rotor rotates. Instead, a non-trivial circuit (see Figure 17-9) monitors electrical current or the position of the rotor's magnet to electronically determine when to flip the flow.

Figure 17-9. Circuit built into brushless motor

Limitations of Brushless Motors

Because of the voltage requirements of the chips and components on a brushless motor, it accepts a narrow range (around ±15%) of voltages for motor operation. On the other hand, the brush motor consists of wires and magnets that are usually perfectly content to accept the wide power ranges available from ordinary consumer batteries.

Aside from the more rigorous voltage requirements, other downsides of robot movement by brushless motors are that brushless motors tend to be less available, more expensive, and provide lower pushing power (torque). For these reasons, the robots in this book use brush motors.

Looking Inside a Coreless Permanent-Magnet DC Brush Motor

The first motor type examined in this chapter was a brush motor containing an iron core. A coreless variation (also called ironless) exists that is very similar in all other aspects. Note that this is a brush motor, not brushless.

A coreless permanent-magnet DC brush motor (see Figure 17-10) consists of roughly the same sections, materials, and parts as the classic iron-core motor. The permanent magnets are still attached to the stator, although they're mounted towards the center rather than near the outside walls.

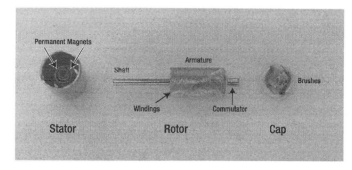

Figure 17-10. Guts of a coreless DC brush motor: (left to right) *stator with permanent magnets mounted near the center; rotor with shaft, armature, windings, and commutator; and cap with brushes*

The armature shows the biggest change. Instead of individual shoes and windings, the armature consists of overlapping windings. There is an empty space between the shaft and the windings so that the permanent magnets on the stator can slide in between.

Comparing Coreless vs. Iron Core

Without the heavy iron core, the coreless rotor is much more nimble. Motor acceleration and deceleration is improved. Without the shoes, the rotation is very smooth: no cogging.

Then again, without the massive iron core, the motor can't dissipate heat as well. A high enough temperature destroys the motor by melting the plastic that holds the windings in shape. (Overheating should never occur during normal operation, as long as the robot provides adequate ventilation and power usage within manufacturer's specifications.)

The shape of the windings in a coreless motor provides greater efficiency. In an iron-core motor, the ends of the loops are not in the proper orientation to provide magnetic forces that contribute to the rotation. The thin edges of the coreless windings waste very little mass or resistance in non-productive directions.

Simple DC Motor Circuit

DC brush motors are very easy to experiment with. You only need a motor, battery, and red and black alligator or IC hook jumper leads. No resistors or other components are necessary.

Selecting a Motor for the Simple DC Motor Circuit

The motor must have only two wires or connector terminals. If the motor has more, it's probably not a permanent-magnet DC brush motor and therefore isn't appropriate for this experiment. You don't want a brushless, stepper, or servo motor, usually indicated by attached electronics or more than two wires.

Small, two-wire DC brush motors are all basically the same (see Figure 17-11). Some motors have long wire leads but other motors only have metal connectors. Some have gears or pulleys attached to their shafts, while others have plain shafts. Despite these cosmetic differences, they're all fine for this experiment.

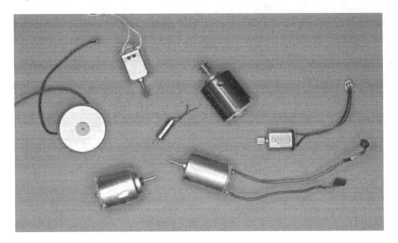

Figure 17-11. Various DC brush motors.

It's easy to identify a DC brush motor if the selected motor is labeled something like "DC Motor," "DC 3V," or "DC 12V." You're unlikely to find a label that indicates the motor is a definitely a "brush" or "permanent-magnet" motor, because that's usually assumed unless the motor is marked otherwise. However, a motor marked "brushless," "servo," or "stepper" is definitely not correct for this experiment. Obviously it's reassuring to have a copy of the datasheet for the motor just to be sure, but it isn't necessary.

You can purchase ordinary DC motors for around $1. Table 17-1 lists a couple of sources for assorted grab bags. You can purchase individual DC motors from almost any electronic store or catalog company. You can also salvage motors out of toys.

Table 17-1. Suppliers of DC Motor Assortments

Supplier	Part Number	Price	Quantity
Electronic Goldmine	GP21	$2.49	3 assorted
Jameco	18294	$7.95	5 assorted

Selecting a Battery for the Simple DC Motor Circuit

You must exercise a little care when selecting the battery. Most toy motors are designed for operation at 3 V. Although you can connect a 3 V motor to a 9 V battery for a dozen seconds or so, the motor starts heating up (you can feel it). Give the motor a minute to cool off between 9 V bursts. There are plenty of rugged DC brush motors designed to continuously accept 6 V, 12 V, 24 V, and higher.

If you only have a 9 V battery, that will do for this experiment. If possible, check with the voltage setting on your multimeter to select a 9 V battery that has run down a bit in voltage. Even better, get two AA-size cells and a holder (see Figure 17-12); they'll provide the appropriate 3 V.

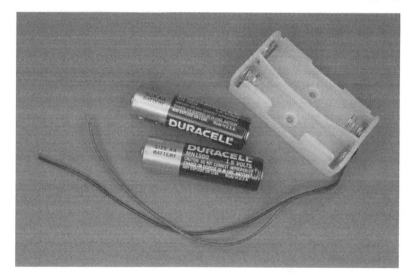

Figure 17-12. Two AA-size cells and holder

Building the Simple DC Motor Circuit

The schematic for the simple DC motor circuit is quite simple, indeed (see Figure 17-13). B1 is 3 V of battery power and M1 is a DC brush motor. Note that the schematic symbol for a DC motor is an underlined letter 'M' within a circle.

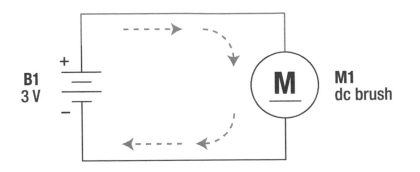

Figure 17-13. Schematic of simple DC motor circuit

Connect one end of the red jumper lead to the positive battery terminal and the other end of the red jumper lead to the positive terminal of the motor (see Figure 17-14). If the motor isn't labeled with positive or negative, then select the red wire coming from the motor. If no wires are coming from the motor or neither is red, pick either wire or terminal. If you connect the motor backwards, no big deal, it runs backwards.

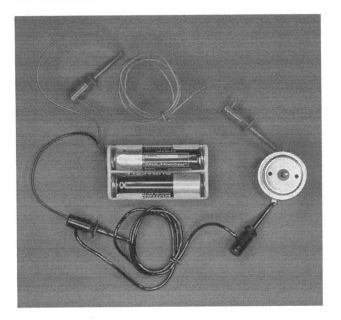

Figure 17-14. Simple DC motor circuit built with IC hook jumper leads

Connect one end of the black jumper lead to the negative battery terminal and the other end of the black jumper lead to the negative terminal of the motor. The motor should start spinning! If you swap the ends of the red and black jumpers on the battery terminal, the motor spins in the reverse direction.

Primary Characteristics of DC Motors

DC motors have many significant attributes worth examining. Which characteristic matters the most to you depends on how you are going to use the motor. Some of the more technical material may only matter to you in more advanced stages of your hobby.

Rotational Speed Characteristic of DC Motors

A popular unit for measuring motor speed is RPM, which stands for revolutions per minute. This indicates how many times the motor will rotate the shaft (and anything connected to it) in a minute.

For example, the second hand on an analog clock rotates around once every minute (see Figure 17-15), for a speed of 1 RPM. If you want to get a sense for 1 RPM, just watch a clock. That's slow!

Figure 17-15. The second hand on a clock rotates at 1 RPM

Most DC motors spin at 3000 RPM to 8000 RPM. At the high end, that means the motor can rotate its shaft around 8000 times before a clock's second hand completes a single rotation. That's really fast!

Initially it may seem that faster is better, but that's not the case. For a line-following robot with slow-reacting sensors, fast speed could drive the robot off the line before the brain has time to react. On the other hand, too little speed could put your audience to sleep. Sandwich runs its motors at around 137 RPM.

Even though DC motors naturally spin at thousands of RPM, there are some good ways to alter the final output speed. In fact, designers are rarely forced into accepting the base speed of a motor. Information on an effective speed manipulation technique, gear reduction, appears at the end of this chapter.

Common robot wheel-driving speeds are between 40 RPM (precision movement) and 250 RPM (very fast). Cooling fans usually rotate at between 3000 RPM and 6500 RPM. Robot arms or directional sensors are often rotated well below 60 RPM.

Measuring RPM

By attaching a piece of tape or half-colored disc to a motor shaft (see Figure 17-16), you can measure the number of times the shaft rotates in a minute. Depending on your brain-eye coordination and propensity towards distraction, you are unlikely to be able to count speeds faster than 120 RPM by eye. Even toy motors running at 3 V can quickly make the target a blur.

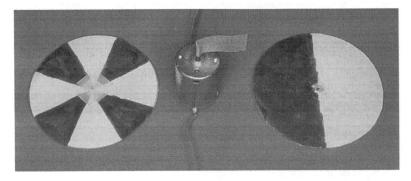

Figure 17-16. Black and white segmented discs and a masking tape flag can help in measuring RPM

However, you can measure even tens of thousands of RPM very accurately by a device called a tachometer. For short, it's often called a "tach," which is pronounced "tack."

Most cars have tachometer displays built into the dashboard. The gauge usually goes from 0 to 8, with numbers over 6 in the red portion of the dial. Multiply the number by 1000 to get the RPM. Therefore, the gauge is actually displaying 0 RPM to 8000 RPM.

"Contact" tachometers are physically connected to the motor shaft, which can reduce speed, thus providing an inaccurate reading. "Non-contact" tachometers usually employ brightness sensors to detect rotations. Some non-contact tachometers, like those placed on car hoods during emissions testing, take advantage of the expected period of vibrations.

Figure 17-17 shows a DC brush motor running at 4038 RPM being measured by a homemade tachometer. The motor spins a half-black and half-white disc attached to the motor shaft. A motionless image of the disc is pictured at the far right of Figure 17-16.

Figure 17-17. Homemade tachometer measuring a DC brush motor

The tachometer illuminates the rotating disc with an LED. The tachometer sees the disc change from light to dark by the amount of light reflected into a brightness sensor. A chip on the tachometer counts the amount of time it takes the disc to complete a light-to-dark-to-light transition (one rotation). This measurement permits the tachometer to mathematically determine the speed.

Professional handheld laser tachometers can be purchased for as low a price as $100.

Mounting Putty Aids Motor Experimentation

Poster tack or mounting putty is a rubbery clay-like substance. This reusable putty is reasonably sticky yet it rarely leaves residue and it doesn't dry out. It's primarily used for cleanly attaching posters to walls.

I find the putty to be ideal for holding motors upright while experimenting. The putty also quickly affixes the testing disc to any motor shaft. You may be able to spot that I used a bit of putty for both purposes on the top and the bottom of the motor in Figure 17-17. Of course, the putty is too soft for permanent mounting in a robot.

Figure 17-18. Putty for holding tachometer discs to motor shafts

Mounting putty is available at local hardware stores, office supply outlets, and even some supermarkets. Blue, white, and yellow colors are available.

Converting RPM to a Metric Unit

The metric unit for angular velocity is radian per second, or rad/s. Even though it doesn't appear often in advertisements, rad/s sometimes shows up in datasheets. For motors, RPM and rad/s are used to measure the same thing, but rad/s is an internationally accepted unit in the metric system.

To convert RPM to rad/s, multiply by 0.10472 (which is an approximation of $\pi/30$).

```
RPM × 0.10472 = rad/s
137 RPM (Sandwich's motors) × 0.10472 = 14.34664 rad/s
```

To convert rad/s to RPM, multiply by 9.54929 (which is an approximation of $30/\pi$).

```
rad/s × 9.54929 = RPM
14.34664 rad/s (Sandwich's motors) × 9.54929 = 137 RPM
```

Torque Characteristic of DC Motors

Torque is the amount of twisting force that can be performed by a motor. This indicates how heavy of a load the motor can turn. Torque is very important as it determines how weighty the robot can be, how steep of a hill the robot can climb, and how much the robot can push or pull.

Speed and torque are not the same things. An electric screwdriver has large amounts of torque so that it can drive a screw into or out of strong material. But the screwdriver has fairly slow speed because otherwise the tip of the screwdriver would likely slip out of the groove at the head of the screw.

Contrast the electric screwdriver with a computer fan. The computer fan has lots of speed, but the fan blade can be stopped or jammed easily (very little torque). Or take the circular saw, which has a powerful combination of speed and torque.

The Significance of Distance in Torque

It is easier to hold an object by your sides than it is to hold the object with your arms outstretched. Therefore, torque must be measured in both how much mass can be turned and how far away that mass is.

Motor torque is specified in newton meters (N·m). The little dot between "N·m" is often omitted.

Lots of other units specify torque, although they're all measuring the same thing. A common unit is pound-force foot (lbf-ft). Some imperial-system terms were specified in reverse to distinguish between torque and work, but motor advertisements specifying "foot pound" mean the same thing as "pound foot," and so on.

The letter "f," for force, is often omitted from advertisements. So, instead of seeing lbf-ft, the motor could be listed as lb-ft, ft-lb, or even ft-lbf. They all mean the same thing. To recognize a motor's torque specification, look for any force/mass (like N, g, lb, or oz) combined with a length (like m, cm, ft, or in).

Table 17-2 lists the other most-common torque units and how to convert them to N·m. For example, to compare a 3.2 lbf-ft torque motor to a 4 N·m torque motor, multiply 3.2 lbf-ft by 1.355817948 to get 4.338617434 N·m. Based on that conversion, the 3.2 lbf-ft motor has a greater maximum torque than the 4 N·m torque motor.

Table 17-2. Table for Converting Between Other Common Torque Units and the International Standard N·m

Known Unit	Multiplier	Desired Unit
kgf-m	x 9.806 650 029	= N·m
lbf-ft	x 1.355 817 948	= N·m
lbf-in	x 0.112 984 829	= N·m
kgf-cm	x 0.098 066 500	= N·m
N·cm	x 0.01	= N·m
ozf-in	x 0.007 061 552	= N·m
mN·m	x 0.001	= N·m
gf-cm	x 0.000 098 066 5	= N·m
dyn-cm	x 0.000 000 1	= N·m

Table 17-3 shows how to convert from N·m to the other most-common torque units. For example, to compare a 0.4 N·m torque motor to 50 ozf-in torque motor, multiply 0.4 N·m by 141.6119327 to get 56.64477308 ozf-in. Based on that conversion, the 0.4 N·m motor has a greater maximum torque than the 50 ozf-in torque motor.

Table 17-3. Table for Converting Between the International Standard N·m and Other Common Torque Units

Known Unit	Multiplier	Desired Unit
N·m	x 0.101 971 621	= kgf-m
N·m	x 0.737 562 15	– lbf-ft
N·m	x 8.850 745 795	= lbf-in
N·m	x 10.197 162 1	= kgf-cm
N·m	x 100	= N·cm

N·m	x 141.611 932 7	= ozf-in
N·m	x 1000	= mN·m
N·m	x 10 197.162 1	= gf-cm
N·m	x 10 000 000	= dyn-cm

I find gf-cm the most graspable torque unit for small robot motors. Table 17-4 lists other common torque units and how to convert them to gf-cm. (You can reach the same results by converting a unit to N·m with Table 17-2 and then converting N·m to gf-cm with Table 17-3.)

Table 17-4. Table for Converting Other Common Torque Units to gf-cm

Known Unit	Divider	Desired Unit
kgf-m	/ 100 000	= gf-cm
lbf-ft	/ 13825	= gf-cm
N·m	/ 10197	= gf-cm
lbf-in	/ 1152	= gf-cm
kgf-cm	/ 1000	= gf-cm
N·cm	/ 102	= gf-cm
ozf-in	/ 72	= gf-cm
mN·m	/ 10.2	= gf-cm
dyn-cm	/ 0.001	= gf-cm

Sliding Torque

A full can of soda is about 380 grams. A motor with 380 gf-cm of torque can rotate a 380-gram mass connected 1-centimeter away (380 gf × 1 cm = 380 gf-cm).

Torque isn't restricted to a 1-centimeter distance. A 9 V battery is a little over 38 grams. That same motor could rotate 38 grams connected 10 centimeters away (38 gf × 10 cm = 380 gf-cm). Torque allows for less mass farther out or more mass farther in, as long as the numbers multiplied together are less than or equal to the motor's torque.

This has practical implications. If you build a robot arm that the motor can't move, you can either get a motor with higher-rated torque, you can shorten the arm (the length), or you can reduce the mass (the weight).

The example of a soda can connected one centimeter away isn't totally accurate because the can itself is longer than one centimeter. In reality, you need to be careful to determine exactly the force from a large or odd-shaped object. At the very least, measure from the center of the mass to help determine the distance the mass is "connected" as far as the torque is concerned.

Calculating Torque Needed for a Robot

The proper calculations involved in determining the minimum torque needed for a robot-driving motor are complex. It depends on where the mass is located, If the mass shifts, how steep of an angle the robot must climb, and the other forces being generated against the robot (such as an attacking opponent).

Luckily, torque is not a major concern for motors that drive the wheels of lunchbox-size robots. If the speed (RPM) and other factors (availability, price, dimensions, weight, voltage) of the motor fit the design, torque is likely to be acceptable.

You can always begin an experiment with one kind of motor and then swap in a lower-or higher-rated torque motor until you're happy with the outcome. Compare advertised motor torque specifications using the torque conversion tables provided in this chapter.

Extra motor torque isn't a problem as long as the other factors of the motor meet your robot's needs. In fact, it's best to leave a safety margin by providing motors rated at a higher torque. If the motor can provide triple or more of the necessary torque continuously, not only will the robot run cooler and more efficiently without damaging the motors, but also the robot will have strength to spare if you decide to add new parts or loads.

Be aware that other parts on your robot are likely to break (wheels, gears, treads, body structure) if they are not strong enough to support the forces acting on the robot. That is, even with properly rated motors, the physical energy must be transmittable through wheels, treads, or legs.

Voltage Characteristic of DC Motors

In datasheets and advertisements, motor specifications are disclosed at "nominal voltage." That's the voltage the manufacturer expects the motor to run at. Common voltages are 3 V, 6 V, 12 V, 18 V, and 24 V. Larger motors can support even higher voltages.

Most DC brush motors can be run between 50% and 125% of their nominal voltage. For example, a 12 V motor could be run at any voltage from 6 V to 15 V. Below 50% of the nominal voltage the motor may not turn. Above a certain voltage the motor may overheat or breakdown.

That being said, many scientific or high-precision motors run at even 10% of their nominal voltage. At the other extreme, many motors in combat robots are run at 200% of their nominal voltage.

Try to pick a motor that has a voltage that most closely matches your batteries. Unless you're a particularly crafty expert, don't design a robot with a 9 V battery and 3 V motors. Likewise, don't build a robot with a 3 V battery and 24 V motors.

Understanding the Relationship Between Voltage and Speed

The greater the voltage, the greater the speed, up to the maximum permitted by the motor. For example, if you have a 12 V motor and it is running a little too slow, try 14 V. If it is running too fast, try 9 V.

Speed changes in direct proportion to the change in voltage. Figure 17-19 shows a graph of a test performed on an escap brand motor (made by Portescap). As voltage is increased by 1.5 volts at a time, the speed increases by about 530 RPM. Of course, the amount of speed change in other motors will be different.

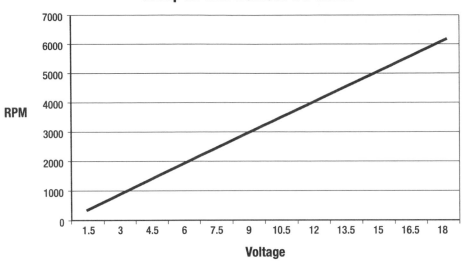

Figure 17-19. Graph of escap 26 mm DC motor showing speed increases linearly with voltage

The escap motor was received second-hand, so I don't know the nominal voltage. Assuming 12 V, this high-quality motor exhibited operation from 12.5% voltage to 150%. I would have tried up to 200%, but my previously mentioned mounting putty starting flying all over the room at 6000 RPM.

Unfortunately, controlling speed with voltage only works well when you have the ability to swap in different batteries. Furthermore, the voltage to the escap motor would need to be around 0.39 V to provide the 137 RPM speed needed by Sandwich. There are better ways (gears and pulse-width modulation) to vary the speed of the motors than directly controlling the voltage provided to them.

Watching Out for the Relationship Between Voltage and Speed

As the robot wanders around, the batteries will drain. As the batteries drain, their voltage decreases. As you've just learned, as the voltage decreases, so does the motor speed.

For many robots, the loss of speed is inconsequential to viable operation. A line-following robot still works. In fact, the line-follower will be able to turn tighter corners and complete more difficult courses since the brains and sensors can more easily outpace the motors.

For other robots, the loss of speed can be disastrous. Robots that follow preset courses using timing no longer operate because the slower motor speed doesn't carry them the same distance in a same amount of time. If necessary, the declining speed can be counteracted, such as by receiving feedback as to the actual extent the wheel has turned.

Current Characteristic of DC Motors

Recall that the amount of current flowing through a circuit has a direct impact on how long the batteries last. Look out! Electric motors really suck up the juice.

You may spend hours tweaking resistor values on your LEDs and circuits. You're proud to save a few mA here and there. And then, you discover that even a single motor drains more than the entire rest of the robot combined.

Larger DC motors rate in the amp range, such as half an amp to hundreds of amps. Lunchbox-size robot motors consume a fraction of that amount, with a usual range from 4 mA to 250 mA for each motor.

The quality of the motor makes a big difference. Case in point: When connected to 3 V, a toy motor (see Figure 17-20) uses 125 mA but an escap motor uses only 4.5 mA. At 12 V, the escap motor has superior speed and torque, yet still only uses 7 mA.

Figure 17-20. *Escap motor* (left) *and toy motor* (right)

To be fair, the escap motor costs 10 times as much, weighs 2.5 times as much, has ¼ the RPM at 3 V, and is about 25% longer than the toy motor. But, that low current draw of 4 mA to 7 mA is enormously appealing.

Examining Periods of Widely Changing Current Consumption

The amount of current consumed by a motor changes a lot during operation. As you'll soon see, the amount of current flow during start-up and stall is very different than no-load or load current.

Start-Up Current

The exposed motor guts presented early in this chapter showed that an ordinary brush motor doesn't contain any resistors or other similar parts inside of it. If you connect your multimeter in Ω mode (like when you measure resistors) to the two leads of a motor at rest (not spinning), you'll see there is a resistance.

■ **Note** It isn't always possible to accurately measure the resistance of assembled motor coils using a multimeter. If the brushes are dirty or aren't making full contact or if the motor is under mechanical stress, the resistance values vary wildly.

Although wire can usually be thought of as having practically no resistance, the lengths of wire in a motor are long enough to act like a resistor.

Big motors have a thick wire inside, so big motors usually have tiny resistances, below 1 Ω. However, small motors have an extremely skinny wire, which is more resistant. Small motors have resistances usually between 6 Ω and 150 Ω.

At the moment power is applied to a brush motor at rest, the only things resisting the flow of electricity are the coils of wire in the rotor. Here's a worst-case formula:

```
(V battery / Ω motor coils) × 1000 = mA maximum current
escap example: (12 V battery / 16.4 Ω motor coils) × 1000 = 732 mA
```

Luckily, it's not that bad. There's a property called inductance that doesn't like to see a sudden change in current. So, although there is a nasty blast of current (see Figure 17-21) in the interval of start-up, it isn't quite as bad as the simple formula indicates.

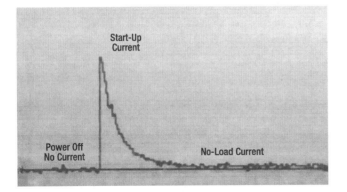

Figure 17-21. Oscilloscope trace of current flow through an escap motor

The surge of electricity from the battery can be a problem for any electronics attached to the same battery. It is possible for chips and LEDs to be temporarily starved while the battery feeds the engaging motors. There are simple techniques, like adding capacitors, which provide local energy storage during the energy crisis.

Depending on the motor, the start-up current diminishes to no-load current in about one-tenth of a second.

No-Load Current

As the motor comes up to the appropriate RPM based on the voltage provided, the amount of current flowing through the motor declines. Why? Because it is easier to keep something spinning than it is to get the thing spinning in the first place.

Let's take the escap motor as an example. At first, a lot of power is applied to make the rotor change from 0 RPM to 4000 RPM. But, thereafter the rotor has some inertia and is going the desired speed. The only continued electrical investment needed at that point is to overcome a bit of friction, noise, vibration, and sparking.

Let's say the motor would drop down to 3900 RPM in a tenth of a second if power were disconnected. So, in that tenth of a second, a motor with power needs only change from 3900 RPM to 4000 RPM, rather than 0 RPM to 4000 RPM. It obviously takes less power to speed up 100 RPM as opposed to 4000 RPM, which is why a spinning motor uses less power than a motor starting up.

When a motor is up to speed and the motor shaft is **not** connected to anything, the amount of current flowing is called the "no-load" current. This is the least amount of current the motor uses.

No-load current is easy to measure. Simply connect your multimeter in amp mode (like when you measured current in the LED Circuit) between the battery and the motor. When the number settles down after a second or so, that's the no-load current.

At 12 V, the escap motor has a no-load current of a mere 7 mA. It's as though the coil resistance went from 16.4 Ω at power-off to 1714 Ω at no-load spinning. An almost magical property called back EMF or induced EMF (Electromotive Force) resists the flow of more electricity than is needed to keep the motor going.

The important thing to keep in mind is that an already-spinning motor takes less power than getting a motor to start spinning. That's no-load current.

Load Current

As force is added to the shaft of the motor, by attaching wheels or driving a robot uphill, the amount of current increases. Even attaching an RPM measuring disc to a motor adds enough drag that the motor consumes a bit more current than it did by itself.

The increase in current stays at that level as long as the load is there. When the load is removed, the motor current decreases.

Stall Current

As more and more of the motor's maximum torque is required to rotate more and more massive or forceful loads, the motor's current increases until the motor doesn't have the twisting strength to turn anymore. When the motor stops turning but is still receiving power, that's called a stall.

Since power is fully applied but the motor's rotor can't turn, almost no inductance is generated. This is because there isn't a change in current like when the motor was starting to turn. Also, no back EMF is generated because the motor would choose to go faster if it could. It's physically stopped from turning; it's not settled into its natural speed-per-volt ratio.

A stall is the very worst state for a motor!

During a stall, the only thing resisting the current is the resistance of the coil windings. When the motor shaft is held in place, the current flow in the escap motor rockets from 7 mA to over 600 mA.

That's bad for battery life, but worse for the motor. None of the electricity is being converted to motion through magnetism. Almost all of the electricity flowing through the motor coils is producing heat. The motor could be destroyed by heat if allowed to stay in a stalled state for too long.

The dangers present in a stalled motor explain the phenomena of robot builders leaping to save their creations when the robot gets stuck against a chair leg or a wall. If the wheels aren't turning but the motors have power, those motors are stalling.

Robots can be designed to watch their wheels and to pulse, reverse, or cut power if the wheels aren't turning. Fuses or self-resetting circuit breakers can turn off power in the event of large current drain due to a prolonged stall. Adequate ventilation helps cool down the motors if they do stall briefly. By choosing strong enough motors, the safety margin should provide more than enough torque to avoid stalling during expected loads of operations.

Planning for Current Consumption

Here are some thoughts on planning for the electrical-current consumption of motors:

The robot's chips must be able to continue working during the start-up current draw of the motors. This usually means adding some capacitors. However, Sandwich has only one comparator chip whose datasheet says capacitors aren't necessary.

If a robot's motors are turning on and off a lot, like they are in the line-follower, you can assume the batteries will deplete faster due to start-up current. No big deal. However, if the motors stay on for longer periods of time, you can almost ignore the start-up current's effect on battery life.

No-load current tells you the absolute minimum current that the motors consume. This is one of many criteria for comparing motors, but a "no-load" situation is unrealistic for calculating battery life.

Load current is a much more practical value to determine battery life and heat dissipation. Of course, the robot will almost be complete, with motors and wheels installed, before you can use the multimeter to get a load-current reading. You'll also look a little weird following a robot around your house, bent over with a multimeter.

Robust robots should be designed to be able to continuously provide more than the start current or stall current of all motors. This takes care of worst-case scenarios. The impact of the design is negligible in that the electronics and batteries need to be a little beefier and the motors must be properly ventilated. The robot you spend tens of hours making (if not hundreds of hours) will be safe and capable.

Efficiency Characteristic of DC Motors

Regardless of how efficiently a robot utilizes a motor, the motor itself has an efficiency associated with its ability to convert electrical energy into mechanical energy. Well-designed motors can be as much as 90% efficient. That means almost all of the electricity is turned into useful motion, with only 10% wasted.

Wasted electricity can take many forms, such as noise, vibration, sparks (light, sound, heat, physical damage), and magnetic fields. However, the motor expends most wasted electricity as heat. Therefore, a more efficient motor not only permits the robot's batteries to run longer, but also permits the motor itself to run cooler.

Because motors usually guzzle the largest portion of the robot's power supply, more efficient motors may be worth the extra cost. This extends the robot's run time before needing a recharge.

Toy motors hover at around 30% efficiency or less. Precision motors, like escap or Maxon, are around 75% efficient or better. The motor's datasheet provides a specific number along with a curve representing the efficiency under various speeds and loads. Motors are usually most efficient when carrying a load about $1/7$ their maximum torque.

Audible Noise Characteristic of DC Motors

A squeaky motor can be annoying. Perhaps it just needs some lubrication. Maybe the motor has a defect. Or, perhaps the motor is wearing out.

In any case, the unpleasant grinding or squealing of motors can be a detractor from your robot. Before ordering a large quantity of a particular motor, it is worth sampling a couple to make sure they don't have any unadvertised negatives such as noise.

Oiling the Rotor Shaft

Motors that squeal can often be quieted (with a bonus of increased performance) by applying a tiny dab of light oil to the places where the shaft rests on the motor body. This is normally at the front and back of the motor body, just where the shaft sticks out.

Don't apply oil or other lubrication if the motor is working correctly, as the existing lubrication may be a special formulation or it may be incompatible with your choice of lubrication.

Electrical Noise Characteristic of DC Motors

Electrical noise is not the same as audible squealing and squeaking. Electrical noise appears as rapid, spiked fluctuations in voltage in attached circuitry or nearby components. The most common human experience of electrical noise is static on a television when someone is vacuuming.

Robots can have big problems with electrical noise. Noise can scramble information as it is being communicated throughout a circuit board. The chips can reset as though power had been turned off and on.

The affected board doesn't even need to be in close proximity to a noisy motor. Electronics and motors sharing the same power source (battery) can transmit the electrical noise throughout all attached circuit boards.

More efficient motors tend to produce less electrical noise. (Likewise with motors that have built-in capacitors.) Figure 17-22 shows lots of spikes generated by the brushes connecting and disconnecting from a toy motor's rotor commutator segments.

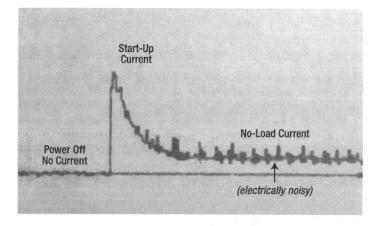

Figure 17-22. Oscilloscope trace of current flow through toy motor

Little noise ripples do exist even in the power-off state, but contrast them with the no-load spikes. Look back at Figure 17-21 and notice how small the no-load spikes are on the escap motor—especially relative to the power-off-state spikes in that same figure.

The capacitors that protect chips during motor start-up can also dampen electrical noise generated during normal motor operation. Some robot designers go farther by providing separate batteries for the motors and electronics. The designers add special optical isolators to communicate commands to the motors without a common electrical connection.

Until recently, none of my robots had ever suffered a glitch due to motor noise. My circuit boards tend to have a lot of capacitors and I tend to choose nicer quality motors whenever possible. It could also be that my robots are fairly small, so the amount of wasted power going towards electrical noise is not enough to trip up modern chips.

I solved the one problematic experience that I encountered with motor noise by switching from an ultra-low power chip to a normal (not as efficient) chip. Despite my best efforts, I could not reduce the noise coming from the inexpensive motor, so I simply opted for more tolerant electronics.

Mass Characteristic of DC Motors

Motors weigh a lot. It wouldn't be unexpected for motors to represent a third of a robot's mass. Sandwich's motors are 37% of the line-follower's mass.

When building a robot for a contest or some application where the robot's mass is restricted to a maximum, avoid selecting motors with a combined weight of more than 40% of the total. Otherwise, there won't be enough weight available for the batteries or a structurally decent robot body.

Dimension Characteristic of DC Motors

DC brush motors come in a variety of shapes and sizes. As long as the other characteristics of the motor aren't totally out of whack, the physical size of a motor is probably the most important characteristic.

Motor size usually dictates the robot's size, rather than the other way around. Many builders snap up decent motors whenever they appear in surplus sales. As such, builders have a private stash of motors that they select from at the beginning of a project. The motors available then dictate the minimum dimensions of the robot body. The maximum torque of the selected motors then dictates the maximum weight of the total robot.

Summarizing the Characteristics of DC Motors

When examining an advertisement or datasheet for a motor, here are the things to think about.

Speed – Does the RPM at the given voltage (or scaled proportionally) meet the robot's needs?

Torque – It is unlikely that you'll be sure of your robot's exact torque needs. Yet, torque is still useful in choosing between otherwise equal motors in a potential purchase. One way to get a feel for the torque of a motor you are considering is to compare it with a known motor that has either been adequate or inadequate for you in the past.

Voltage – Is the motor's specified voltage within 50% to 125% of the voltage the robot's batteries are prepared to provide? Consider the voltage of the batteries when fresh and when declared exhausted.

Current – Can the robot's electronics handle the maximum (start up/stall) current? How long will the battery last based on the minimum current (no-load) of the motors?

Efficiency – If the speed and torque of the motor is a good match for the robot, then the highest efficiency motor has, by definition, the lowest current for a given voltage. High efficiency suggests high quality, which may be true for other characteristics of that same motor.

Audible Noise – Although every motor can be expected to generate some audible noise, excessive noise can indicate a problem or, at the very least, be an irritant.

Electrical Noise – Every brush motor generates some electrical noise, but it shouldn't be so bad as to interfere with the electronics. Motors that are high efficiency or have multiple windings/commutator segments are less likely to disturb circuitry. Liberal use of capacitors in the robot's circuitry helps immensely.

Mass – Pick a motor whose weight can be supported by the body materials you're comfortable using. Where mass-limit rules apply, watch out for running out of weight due to motors, thus being forced to skimp elsewhere in the robot.

Dimensions – The motors must fit into the selected robot body, or else select a body for the chosen motors. Unless gearing or a fancy drive train is included, motors are usually positioned end to end, thus dictating the minimum width of the robot.

DC Gearhead Motors

Gearhead motors are sometimes called gearmotors or geared motors. They usually consist of a DC brush motor (either iron core or coreless) with a gearbox attached to the shaft. You can immediately identify a motor as a gearhead by two distinct segments connected together (see Figure 17-23).

Figure 17-23. Gearhead motor

Gearhead motors almost always reduce the speed of the motor in exchange for increased twisting force (torque). Recall that at optimal voltage, a DC motor rotates way too fast to be useful to most robots. With a gearhead reduction, the robot can carry heavier loads while moving at the desired speed.

Because the DC motor still has the same two wires coming from it, a gearhead motor is just as easy to use as a plain motor.

Looking Inside a Spur Gearhead Motor

A spur gearhead motor (see Figure 17-24) begins with an ordinary DC motor. A series of smaller gears touching larger gears is placed within a rigid frame called a box. The gears are usually greased and then protected with a cover to prevent dirt, grime, and stray wires from getting jammed in the works. Screws hold the gearbox tightly on top of the DC motor.

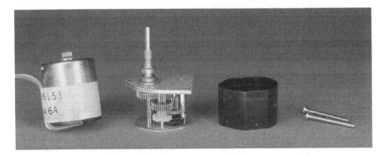

Figure 17-24. Spur gearhead motor consists of: (left to right) *DC brush motor, spur gearbox, gearbox cover, and joining screws.*

Revealing Pairs of Smaller and Larger Gears

A spur gear is a circle with pointy teeth on the perimeter. The teeth push against the teeth of other gears to make them move (see Figure 17-25).

Figure 17-25. Smaller spur gear with 12 teeth rotates only 12 teeth of the larger spur gear, which has 40 teeth total

On a spur gearhead motor, the DC motor shaft turns the first smaller gear against the first larger gear. Because the smaller gear has fewer teeth, each time the smaller gear rotates once the larger gear only rotates partially around.

For example, if the smaller gear has 12 teeth but the larger gear has 40 teeth, then the smaller gear rotates around three and a third times ($^{40}/_{12}$) before the larger gear has been pushed around once. In this example, if the smaller gear were connected to a motor running at 6000 RPM, the larger gear would only be spinning at 1800 RPM.

```
smaller gear RPM × smaller gear teeth / larger gear teeth = larger gear RPM
6000 RPM × 12 teeth / 40 teeth = 1800 RPM
```

Three and a third teeth push the same "distance" that only a single tooth previously pushed. If each little twist comes from three and third teeth pushing, then the twisting force (torque) of the larger wheel has been increased by $3\,^1/_3$ times.

This seems fair. If the motor is being fed the same voltage and the same current but only producing 1800 RPM, the missing energy must be going somewhere. It goes into increased torque. By placing a series of smaller gears and larger gears together in the gearbox, the motor speed can be reduced more and more with torque increased more and more.

Gearbox Shaft

A shaft is connected to the last gear. The end of this new shaft appears out the top of the gearbox for wheels and things to be connected to it. This new shaft out of the gearbox replaces the old shaft coming out of the motor.

When examining a motor, if the shaft doesn't come out of the center, it's likely that the motor is a gearhead motor (see Figure 17-26). Standard motors naturally put the shaft in the center of magnets. But, many gearhead motors connect the new shaft wherever the last gear fits into the gearbox. Note, however, that the last gear could be in the center, so a centered shaft doesn't guarantee the motor isn't a gearhead.

Figure 17-26. Centered shaft on a plain motor (left) *versus the offset shaft on a gearhead motor* (right)

Describing Gear Ratios

When all of the teeth of the larger gears have been added up, and all of the teeth of the smaller gears have been added up, the comparison between them is called the gear ratio. Usually, there are a greater number of larger teeth than smaller teeth. In that case, the gear ratio can also be called the gear reduction, since the speed is being reduced.

Absolute Gear Ratio

Let's say a gearbox has 1535 larger gear teeth compared to 65 smaller gear teeth. This gearbox would have an absolute gear ratio of $^{1535}/_{65}$. A motor spinning at 6000 RPM and connected to this gearbox would spin at 254 RPM with lots of additional torque.

```
6000 RPM × 65 teeth / 1535 teeth = about 254 RPM
```

Absolute gear ratios can get pretty bizarre. For example, an extremely reduced motor could have an absolute ratio of $^{63950067}/_{21125}$.

Simplified Gear Ratio

To make the ratio easier to comprehend, the fraction is usually mathematically reduced. Like $^{4000}/_{100}$ could be described as $^{40}/_{1}$. This makes it easier to say to yourself, "The speed of this motor has been reduced by 40 times and the torque increased 40 times."

Simplified gear ratios are almost always reduced to the lowest term, even if the value isn't exactly accurate. So, $^{1535}/_{65}$ would not be reduced to $^{307}/_{13}$, but is usually stated as $^{24}/_{1}$. That's not quite right, but it is more understandable.

■ **Tip** You can be sure you're looking at a simplified ratio when one of the values is "1", because no spur gear is going to have only one tooth.

Odd Gear Ratios

Gear ratios rarely reduce exactly to the lowest term. This isn't bad luck; it's by design.

A 40-tooth gear and a 10-tooth gear always have the same pairs of teeth rubbing against each other. If either gear has a slightly flawed tooth, the other gear's matching tooth is going to get rubbed down or damaged more quickly since it must mesh with the bad tooth every time.

On the other hand, a 40-tooth gear and an 11-tooth gear would rotate through all pairs of meshing teeth. The wear would be equally distributed across all teeth, causing the gearhead to last longer. Tooth #1 on the 11-tooth gear visits the following teeth on the 40-tooth gear: #1, #12, #23, #34, #5, #16, #27, #38, #9, #20, #31, #2, #13, #24, #35, #6, #17, #28, #39, #10, #21, #32, #3, #14, #25, #36, #7, #18, #29, #40, #11, #22, #33, #4, #15, #26, #37, #8, #19, #30, and then back to #1.

Indicating Both Absolute and Simplified Gear Ratios

Simplified gear ratios are easier to read and comprehend, but absolute gear ratios reveal how many teeth it actually took to reach that value. This gives a sense of how much friction is involved, how heavy the gearhead may be, and how likely the gearhead is to break.

The more teeth involved in reducing the RPM, the more friction there is. However, each tooth is having to push less, and therefore may be able to endure more.

Using a Colon

To make gear ratios easier to read, they're often written with a colon between the values. Instead of $^{40}/_1$, the gear ratio is usually written as 40:1.

Looking at Real Gears

Earlier, I used an example of 1535/65. I suppose it is possible to have 1535 actual teeth and 65 actual teeth, but that's usually not the case. Let's look at the actual number of gears and teeth inside a real motor (see Figure 17-27).

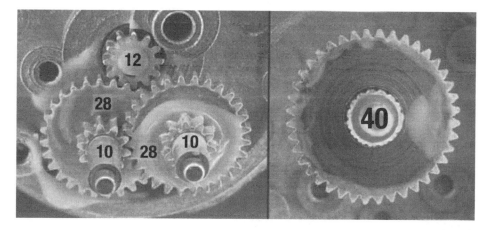

Figure 17-27. Count of teeth for actual gears inside of a Hsiang Neng motor's gearhead

The gear attached to the motor shaft has 12 teeth and it meshes with a larger gear that has 28 teeth. That is attached to a gear that has 10 teeth, which meshes with a larger gear that has 28 teeth. That is attached to a gear that has 10 teeth, which meshes with the final output gear (right side of picture) that has 40 teeth.

The gear ratios of each stage are therefore:

$$^{28}/_{12} \times {}^{28}/_{10} \times {}^{40}/_{10} = {}^{31360}/_{1200}$$

The absolute gear ratio would be described as 31360:1200, even though there really aren't that many actual teeth. That fraction could be reduced to 392:15.

The simplified gear ratio is calculated as follows:

$$^{31360}/_{1200} = 26.13333$$

The simplified gear ratio would be described as 26:1. The datasheet claims the gearhead is 30:1, which (according to my calculations) is not really the case.

Imperfect Speed to Torque Conversion

All of the gears meshing together and pushing on each other involves a lot of friction. As such, gearboxes are usually from 40% to 90% efficient.

The lack of complete efficiency means that gearboxes aren't able to convert all of the reduced speed into torque. You learned earlier that a gearbox with 2:1 gear ratio converts a 4000-RPM motor to 2000 RPM, with 2 times the torque. However, if the gearbox is only 90% efficient, the torque is closer to 1.8 times.

That being said, gearhead motors convert motor speed more effectively than lowering voltage, with the additional benefit of a lot of increased torque.

Disadvantages of Gearheads

Some disadvantages of gearboxes are:

- increased overall noise

- increased overall mass

- increased overall length

- increased no-load current

None of those factors should dissuade you from the overriding advantages of gearhead motors.

Comparing Planetary Versus Spur Gearhead Motors

There are actually two major types of gearhead motors. Spur gearboxes are the most common, but planetary gearboxes are also available. Planetary gearboxes contain the same smaller spur gears, except now the smaller gears rotate within the **insides** of the larger gears (see Figure 17-28).

Figure 17-28. Planetary gears

Stacking layers of planetary gears builds a full gearbox (see Figure 17-29). Just like a spur gearbox, the planetary gearbox is then attached to the top of a plain DC motor. A planetary gearhead motor remains as simple to control as a plain DC motor.

Figure 17-29. Exposed cross-sections of a Tamiya planetary gearhead motor

Because multiple smaller gears work in parallel for each larger gear, the planetary gearbox can operate at higher torque that would otherwise damage the solitary smaller gear in a spur gearbox. Alas, the increased maximum torque limit comes with reduced efficiency due to friction.

The output shaft comes out of the center of a planetary gearhead, rather than set off-center like most spur gearheads. Sometimes this is desirable, sometimes not, depending on where you want to place the wheels on your robot. A centered shaft on a gearhead motor usually indicates a planetary gearbox.

Choosing a Gearhead Motor

The same criteria that apply to selecting a plain DC motor also apply to selecting a gearhead DC motor. Check out the voltage, dimensions, weight, and final RPM.

For heavy-duty torque applications, look for planetary gearboxes with metal gears and metal gearbox frames. However, plastic gears are preferable for lower-torque, quick-action applications, with significantly lighter weight.

Examine the gearbox to see that the output shaft is located at the angle and placement desired. Some gearboxes have unusual shapes, such as rectangles, which add to the overall height of the motor.

Depending on your robot's needs, look for the word "reversible." Most gearheads are designed to allow the motor to continue to operate forward and reverse. However, some gearboxes only allow forward rotation. Non-reversing gearheads are acceptable if you want the robot's wheels to refuse to be pushed backwards.

Moving Forward

Hopefully you've now been exposed to enough information about DC brush and gearhead motors to get a sense for their characteristics. There are other varieties of motors common to robotics, such as stepper and servo motors. Although useful in their own ways, they weren't covered in this text simply because they aren't necessary for the robot featured in this book.

In the next chapter, you'll complete your primary education on DC motors by actually attaching them to the line-following circuit.

■ ■ ■

CHAPTER 18

Adding Gearhead Motors

In this chapter, we will select and install motors in the line-following robot circuit. You'll also learn a little about diodes.

Selecting Gearhead Motors

In choosing motors for the line-following robot, consider the following criteria:

- The motors should operate at voltage ranges provided by a 9 V battery. That's slightly less than 10 VDC, down to 7 VDC.

- The motors should be small enough to fit abreast within a sandwich container. That means each motor may be no more than 6 cm in length and 4 cm in diameter. Motors with smaller dimensions are even better, as you can add tubes or other ornamentations.

- The loaded motor speed should not be so slow as to bore people, but not so fast as to drive the robot off of the course. Depending on the wheel size, this equates to rotational speeds of roughly between 50 RPM and 125 RPM. Such slow rotation at 9 V requires a gearhead motor.

- The motor must not draw more than 500 mA of current at any time, because that's the maximum the 2N2907A transistor can support.

- There were a couple of additional criteria I considered:

- Because the motors are integral to a project that you can build yourself, I selected motors that are inexpensive and available to consumers in small quantities.

- Because the motors appear in my book, which will be available for years, I selected motors that are currently in production and are available from a major supplier. (This ruled out surplus sales.)

Obtaining the Gearhead Motors

The motors selected are 12 V, 225 RPM gearhead motors made by Hsiang Neng (see Figure 18-1). The motors are rated at voltages from 4.5 V to 12 V, which is perfect for a 9 V battery.

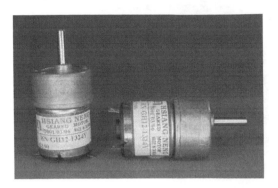

Figure 18-1. A pair of Hsiang Neng gearhead motors

Since speed decreases linearly with voltage, the 9 V RPM can be estimated as:

```
(RPM nominal / V nominal) × V desired = RPM at desired voltage
(225 RPM / 12 V) × 9 V = 168 RPM
```

That's a little faster than sought after, but it's also the no-load speed, which is unrealistically fast. The torque required to move the load of the robot decreases the RPM. Still, a slightly slower motor would be better.

The motors are available from Jameco, part #162191, manufacturer's part number #HNGH12-1324Y-R, for $17.95 each. Or, ServoCity part #GH12-1324Y for $18.95. These were the least expensive gearhead motors that met the criteria. Even so, at almost $36 a pair, the motors are more expensive than all the other line-following parts combined. You'll face this reality again and again. Motors generally make up the largest portion of a robot's cost.

If you decide to purchase different motors, or use some you already own, make sure the motors meet the first four criteria listed at the beginning of this chapter.

Solarbotics provides a wide variety of lower-cost motors. They selected their GM2 motor for their Sandwich kit. The motors are slower (which improves line following), half the weight, and cost less than $^1/_3$ of the price (only $5.75 each when purchased in pairs).

Furthermore, Solarbotics sells matching-colored wheels (see Figure 18-2), part #GMPW, for as little as $2.25 each when purchased with the motor. This allows you to tear out Chapters 19 (selecting wheels) and 20 (attaching wheels) of this book.

Figure 18-2. Solarbotics GM2 motor with matching wheel

The Solarbotics motors aren't the same shape and size as the Hsiang Neng motors. Therefore, you'll need to use your own creativity to attach them to your robot.

The downsides to the GM2 motors are that they consume slightly more power, are moderately louder, are more electrically noisy, and theoretically would have a shorter lifespan if you ran the robot continuously every day. For this application, those tradeoffs are worth it for the significant reduction in cost.

Inspecting the Gearhead Motor

Looking inside the Hsiang Neng motor, the pieces are found to be as expected for a low-price motor. Referring to Figure 18-3, the parts are (left to right): stator with permanent magnet, three-shoe iron-core rotor, cap with pleasantly thick brushes, spur gearbox, metal gearbox cover, and joining screws.

Figure 18-3. Exploded view of a Hsiang Neng gearhead motor

It's a shame the gearbox cover isn't plastic. This motor doesn't produce a lot of torque, so metal probably isn't necessary. Plastic would save a lot of mass and quicken responsiveness. The gearbox is 73% efficient, which is reasonable.

Although you can open the gearhead portion easily, don't try disassembling the motor portion. I had to permanently grind off several metal pieces to open the motor portion for the photograph featured in this book. Therefore, the brushes obviously aren't meant to be user-serviceable. When the motor wears out, toss it.

The motor is 3.8 cm long with a diameter of 2.6 cm. That's nice and small. The output shaft is offset. That means the shaft doesn't come out of the cap's center. An offset shaft is actually beneficial for mounting wheels closer to the ground, as you can rotate the motor into a position with the shaft nearest the bottom of the robot. The shaft is 1.5 cm is length, providing lots of room for attaching wheels.

Current Usage of the Gearhead Motor

As part of a motor's inspection, you should measure motor current. By connecting a multimeter between a 9 V battery and the motor (see Figure 18-4), you can determine the actual current used by the motor without a load and the amount of current used when stalled. Make sure the multimeter is in the highest current mode, so that a fuse isn't blown in the multimeter during peak current usage.

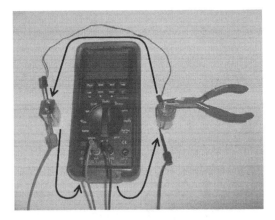

Figure 18-4. Testing motor current with a multimeter and pliers

Determining the Least Current (Best Case)

The no-load current of the selected motor (after a breaking-in period) at 9 V measures 31 mA. Simply connect the motor to a battery to experience this test case. A 150 mAh 9 V rechargeable battery would last almost five hours powering this motor when allowed to turn freely.

```
150 mAh battery capacity / 31 mA no-load motor = 4.8 h (hours)
```

Determining the Most Current (Worst Case)

By briefly applying pliers to stop the motor shaft from turning, the stall current at 9 V measures 380 mA. A gentler approach is to measure the resistance of the motor coils and then calculate stall current.

With a stall current of 380 mA, a pair of these motors that are prevented from turning (like if the robot was stuck against a wall) would drain the battery in less than 12 minutes.

```
150 mAh battery capacity / (380 mA stalled motor × 2 motors) = 0.2 h
0.2 hours × 60 minutes in an hour = 12 minutes
```

Of course the robot also has lights and chips that consume power, so the battery would actually drain in less than 12 minutes. The 150 mAh battery-capacity rating is based on a fairly slow drain, so the battery would exhaust very quickly when drained at over 800 mA.

■ **Caution** Battery manufacturers warn you to not draw so much current from a battery that it lasts significantly less than one hour. For example, a 150 mAh battery shouldn't be drained at more than 150 mA. Greater currents may damage the battery. In practice, most radio-control models and robot designs push this guideline, draining fresh batteries in as short a time as 15 minutes.

Fortunately, these motors have enough torque (twisting force) that they don't ever stall on Sandwich. Even if the robot is pushing against a wall, the wheels spin in place.

Determining the Actual Current (Average Case)

The average current of the motor is going to be somewhere between 31 mA (best case) and 380 mA (worst case). By connecting the multimeter to the robot and following it around, the load current turned out to fluctuate between 40 mA and 120 mA. Counting the chips and lights, and assuming only one motor turns at a time, the robot should last a little under an hour.

Adding Motors to the Brightness Comparator Circuit

The schematic illustrated in Figure 18-5 is a portion of the previously presented brightness comparator circuit with transistors, with the addition of a diode (D1) and a motor (M1). To reduce visual complexity, only one branch from the comparator's two outputs is shown. Imagine that the branch with transistor Q8 (not shown) also has a diode and motor attached.

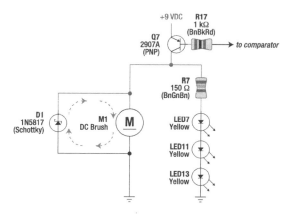

Figure 18-5. Schematic of motor and Schottky diode added to brightness comparator circuit

Motor M1 has its positive terminal connected to the output of transistor Q7. The motor's negative terminal is connected to the negative terminal of the battery. Because the transistor provides power to the motor, the motor turns on when the transistor turns on.

Introducing the Diode

A diode is very similar to an LED (Light-Emitting Diode) except an ordinary diode isn't designed to emit light. However, like an LED, the diode only works in one direction. Also like an LED, the arrow in the diode's schematic symbol (see D1 in Figure 18-4) points the direction current is allowed to flow.

Most diodes physically resemble resistors, but without the multiple color bands (see Figure 18-6). There is only one band, located at the end of the diode, which indicates the cathode. The other end, the end without the band, is the anode. Current can only flow from the anode (positive) to the cathode (negative). You can think of the band as a wall that prevents current from entering from that direction.

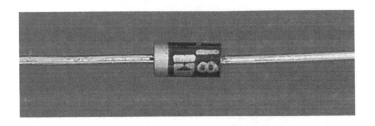

Figure 18-6. A 1N5817 diode, typical looking of many diodes

Like LEDs, diodes consume or drop some voltage as power passes through them. The voltage drop of most diodes is between 0.4 V and 1 V, as opposed to 1.2 V or more for LEDs. In exchange for this voltage cost, a diode acts as a one-way valve (a check valve).

Protecting the Transistor with a Flyback Diode

Wait a minute! Diode D1 is facing in the wrong direction in the schematic in Figure 18-5. The arrow is going up toward positive, unlike the LEDs in that same schematic, whose arrows point toward the negative battery terminal.

Diode D1 is purposely installed in this circuit in a direction that doesn't allow power to flow through it during normal circumstances. However, when power is disconnected from a motor, a large reverse voltage suddenly appears (see the following note). The diode allows the reverse voltage to flow around and around in the motor to be safely consumed.

If the diode wasn't installed, the reverse voltage in the motor could damage transistor Q7. A diode utilized to reroute reverse-induced voltage is called a flyback diode. The diode intentionally provides a short circuit for the leftover motor juices.

■ **Note** The reverse-voltage phenomenon is not limited only to motors. It also appears in coils, switches, and anywhere a current suddenly shuts off. If a large enough current flows through a motor, then the reverse voltage may potentially damage connected electronics.

Think of the reverse-voltage effect as a washing machine or dishwasher that rapidly shuts off its water supply and a loud jerk reverberates through the pipes. Suddenly the rushing water doesn't have anywhere to go, so pressure builds against the closed end of the pipe and is released backwards.

Picking the Schottky Barrier Diode

There are two specific characteristics required of a flyback diode.

First, a flyback diode should act as a barrier, not as a path, when current is going in the correct direction. Some diodes are too leaky in reverse to be good-quality barriers. In this circuit, a leaky flyback diode would waste some current that otherwise would zip through the motor and provide motion.

Second, when the motor generates current in the wrong direction, the flyback diode should be the least-resistant path (lowest voltage drop). That way, the electricity will choose the path through the flyback diode rather than breaking down a path through another component. Schottky diodes have this desired characteristic.

Technically, Schottky-type diodes aren't necessary for this circuit because the transistor's (Q7) minimum reverse voltage is 5 V. Non-Schottky diodes have a voltage drop of around 1 V, and thus would still provide the least-resistant path for the reverse current. Using a Schottky diode (about 0.4 voltage drop) provides a safety margin in case some other transistor type is used that isn't as robust as the 2907A transistor.

The little squiggly "S" atop the arrow in the diode schematic symbol indicates a Schottky diode. A plain bar would have indicated a standard diode. A "Z" shape would have indicated a Zener diode.

Obtaining Schottky Barrier Diodes

Depending on the targeted application, sometimes a diode is called a rectifier. Either way, 1N5817, 1N5818, and 1N5819 are popular Schottky barrier diodes. Any of them will do for flyback purposes.

The 1N5817 has the least-resistant path and can handle 20 V in reverse (see Table 18-1). The 1N5818 and 1N5819 (available from the same suppliers) have slightly more resistant paths but can handle 30 V and 40 V, respectively. Choose one of those higher-voltage diodes if you want to drive a robot with 24 V motors.

Table 18-1. Suppliers of Axial Lead Schottky Barrier Diodes

Supplier	Part Number	Price
Mouser	821-1N5817	$0.09
Mouser	625-1N5817	$0.12
Jameco	177949	$0.10
Electronix Express	11 1N5817	$0.25
All Electronics	1N5817	3 for $1.00
Digi-Key	1N5817FSCT-ND	$0.39
Digi-Key	1N5817DICT	$0.42

Building the Motors onto the Brightness Comparator Circuit

Only four components need to be added to the brightness comparator circuit: one diode and one motor are connected to each transistor (Q7 and Q8). See Figure 18-7 for an example.

Figure 18-7. Motor and diode added to the brightness comparator circuit on a solderless breadboard

Connecting the Diode in the Proper Orientation

You must connect the cathode end of a diode (the end with the band) to the collector (output) of the transistor. Don't mistakenly insert the diode in a different direction, or the motor and lights won't work. If the diode's anode were connected to the transistor's emitter, it would create a high-current path harmful to the diode, transistor, battery, and even the breadboard.

You must connect the anode end of the diode (the end without the band) to the negative bus. A diode connected this way won't normally conduct current.

Connecting the Motor

Use a pair of IC hook jumpers to connect each end of the motor to each end of the diode. The motor is marked underneath with a plus (+) sign to indicate the positive terminal. Using an alligator jumper or IC hook jumper, connect the motor's positive terminal to the cathode of the diode. Connect the other terminal of the motor to the anode of the diode.

Although there's no harm in connecting the motor backwards, the motor would run in reverse. In the final robot, such a mix-up could cause the robot to run backwards or to spin.

Repeating the Setup for the Other Transistor

Connect the second diode and second motor to the other transistor. In this way, one motor and diode should be attached to Q7 along with the yellow LEDs. And, one motor and diode should be attached to Q8 along with the green LEDs.

Testing the Motors

Upon powering up the circuit, one motor should spin depending on which sensors see more brightness. By moving your hand across the front of the sensors, the circuit should alternate between lighting up one set of LEDs and motor, and then the other set of LEDs and motor.

Only one motor should be enabled at a time unless the brightness is extremely balanced or unless you move your hand very quickly in front of the sensors. The robot makes tight turns with only one motor enabled, with one rotating wheel pivoting around the stationary wheel.

Completing the Electronics

Congratulations, you've finished prototyping all of the electronics necessary for the line-following robot!

Admittedly, there is one piece missing. Currently the left motor engages when the left side is brighter and the right motor engages when the right side is brighter. When the robot's board is finally built, a line-following switch will be added that can swap the motor connections to the opposite sides. In doing so, the robot can either pivot toward brightness or pivot away from brightness. Thus, it can follow either dark lines or light lines.

You can also toggle the line-following switch into the center position to disconnect the motors. In this state, you can place the robot on the starting line without it running away. This also keeps the robot stationary, but alive, during debugging.

Unfortunately, I could not locate an appropriately sized DPDT-center-off switch to prototype on a solderless breadboard. But, other than the switch, your breadboard now contains all of the components in the final configuration, ready to be soldered together.

Now that the motors are ready, it's time to add some wheels.

CHAPTER 19

■ ■ ■

Wheels

At this point, you have some wonderful motors that are only spinning themselves. In this chapter, you'll be introduced to a variety of wheels and some criteria to aid you in selecting a pair of wheels for the line-following robot.

Anatomy of a Wheel

Most wheels consist of two parts (see Figure 19-1). First, there's the tire, which is the rubbery part that grips the surface. Then, there's a sturdy core, which distributes the motor force and retains the wheel's shape.

Figure 19-1. An ordinary wheel with the rim partially pulled out

The portion of the tire that usually contacts the ground is called the tread. The sidewall is the portion of the tire that runs perpendicular to the tread, forming the shape of the tire. The shoulder is the transition area between the tread and the sidewalls. The bead is a lip designed to fit snuggly into the rim.

The rim is a made of a firm material that the tire rests against. On some wheels, individual spokes connect the rim to the hub. The hub attaches the wheel to the motor shaft or drive train.

Of course, there are many types of wheels that don't exactly fit this model. Even so, most of the basic terminology is still applicable.

Characteristics of Robot Wheels

The role of the wheel is to transfer the mechanical force from the motor to the ground. The robot's function, expected road conditions, and the abilities of the motor must be considered in determining the most suitable wheel.

Creamy Air Filling

Tires range from air-filled to solid (see Figure 19-2).

Figure 19-2. Left to right: *Sealed pneumatic, semi-pneumatic, foam, and solid tires*

Tires that are filled with air or a compressed gas are called pneumatic tires. A sealed-pneumatic tire often has air in the middle completely surrounded by rubber, like a donut-shaped balloon. Pneumatic tires become flat under a load if they lose their air pressure.

A semi-pneumatic tire holds its shape from a combination of air and the strength of the sidewalls. The bead of the tire fits into and against the rim to resist air from squeezing out when the tire deforms upon hitting a bump. However, if air escapes, the tire doesn't become flat. Usually the tire is designed to allow the air to return as the bumped portion of the tire returns to its proper shape.

Foam tires are somewhat like sponges. They have tiny bubbles of air distributed throughout the tire material. Puncturing a foam tire won't cause it to flatten since very few air pockets are affected.

Solid tires have little or no air in them. They are difficult to puncture, with no effect on shape when they are punctured.

Effects of Air

Air-filled tires tend to conform themselves to surfaces, thus providing maximum contact for traction. Air-filled tires compress on contact with small objects and particles, unlike solid tires that skip and lift up. The air acts as a shock absorber, which reduces wear of the motor and bearings.

Sealed pneumatic tires are rare in small sizes because most tire material is capable of retaining its shape against the forces present at that small a size without the need for air pressure. If sealed tires were more available, their performance would probably be equal to semi-pneumatic, with the risk of deflation with aging.

Solid tires wear well but don't grip as well, nor do they absorb bumps as well as pneumatic tires. However, because they don't squish, they add fewer errors to precision movements.

Tire Shapes

Tire shape makes a significant difference in traction and resistance. Look at the shape of the curve of the top of the tires in Figure 19-3. Some have broad, sloping shoulders; others have brief, square shoulders.

Figure 19-3. Left to right: *Rounded, balloon, hybrid, and flat*

A rounded cross section tire, similar to a bicycle tire, only has a tiny portion touching the ground at any point. Because there is less contact with the surface, these tires are easy to turn and have a low-rolling resistance. Rolling resistance is the amount of friction generated against the road, which determines how easily the tire rolls forward and backward. Because of the limited road contact, rounded tires are more energy efficient, and thus a good choice for long-endurance runs.

Balloon tires protrude a bit over the sides of the rims. Balloon tires absorb shock well and can handle uneven surfaces. They're preferred for off-road and rough surfaces.

There are some in-between tire shapes on which the center portion is slightly flattened, but drops off at the shoulders. This offers a balance of characteristics, not being the best or worst performer in any category.

Flat tires provide the greatest traction on flat surfaces. This makes them great for delivering motor power to the road, although with the expense of having the highest-rolling resistance. Choose a flat tire shape for maximum pushing, pulling, and acceleration on smooth surfaces.

Tire Width

Greater width usually provides greater stability and traction to a tire, no matter what its shape (see Figure 19-4). Wide tires are also less likely to become stuck in parallel-aligned surface grooves.

Figure 19-4. Four tires of decreasing widths from top to bottom

On the other hand, skinnier tires have lower rolling resistances and can turn much more easily. They weigh less and don't take up as much room on the robot.

Tread Designs

The style of the tread on the tire (see Figure 19-5) should be picked to match the surface and weather conditions the robot is expected to experience.

Figure 19-5. Tread designs (left to right): *Slick, grooved, and knobby*

Slick tires provide maximum contact in dry, flat conditions. For this reason, professional racecars use slicks. But, under wet, gritty, or uneven conditions, slicks tend to lift up and lose traction. That's why most professional races are immediately halted (or delayed for tire changes) upon rain.

Grooved tires are similar to slicks, but with strips and patterns cut out of the tread. They provide decent traction on flat surfaces. On gritty or wet surfaces, the grooves direct particles away from the contact points and the grooves allow the tire to flex a little more. Because of this balanced performance in wet and dry weather, grooved or pattern-treaded tires appear on almost all street automobiles.

Knobby tires have aggressive bumps throughout. They're fantastic in uneven or loose soil conditions. Because household terrain isn't designed for lunchbox robots, knobby tires provide surprisingly good performance throughout the home. However, the bumpy tread leads to noisy, side-to-side walking behavior on flat surfaces. Knobby tires wouldn't be appropriate for precise, calculated movements or for pushing contests on flat surfaces.

Tire Diameter

Believe it or not, the diameter (think "height"—see Figure 19-6) of the tire is probably the most important characteristic of a robot's tires. The obvious effect is on how tall the robot will be. But, there is a much more significant effect.

Figure 19-6. A variety of tire diameters

The diameter of a tire radically affects torque and speed. The larger the diameter of the tire, the greater the resulting speed. The smaller the diameter, the greater the twisting (pushing, pulling) force.

If your robot is going too fast, switch to smaller diameter tires. If your robot is unable to move due to a large mass or lack of motor power, again, switch to smaller diameter tires. Conversely, if your robot is going too slowly or tends to spin its wheels when starting to move, switch to larger diameter tires.

Calculating Linear Speed

Here's the formula for linear speed:

```
(RPM of loaded motor / 60 seconds in a minute) × wheel circumference in meters = linear
speed in meters per second
```

Let's use Sandwich, the line-following robot, as an example. I don't really know the loaded RPM, so I'll use the no-load value of 137 RPM. This number was determined using a tachometer when the motor spun freely. Because the motor will actually be carrying a heavy load when placed down on the ground, the robot won't go any faster than the calculation indicates, but it almost certainly will go slower.

Determining the wheel circumference is easy with a cloth tape measure (see Figure 19-7). If you don't have access to a tape measure, wrap a strip of paper around the tire. Mark the spot of overlap and unroll the paper. You can then use a ruler to determine the length of the flat piece of paper with the mark. Sandwich's wheel circumference is about 16 cm, which is 0.16 m.

Figure 19-7. Measuring wheel circumference with a cloth tape measure

Plugging the numbers into the linear speed formula results as follows:

Sandwich example: (137 RPM / 60) × 0.16 m = 0.365 m/s

The robot should be able to complete a straight, 4-meter course in about…

linear course length in meters / linear speed = number of seconds to complete
Sandwich example: 4 m / 0.365 m/s = 11 s

The calculation indicates 11 seconds. In reality, it took the robot about 15 seconds. The difference between the calculated value and the measured value is the difference between no-load RPM and loaded RPM. You can work the measured value backwards to determine the approximate loaded RPM.

((linear course length in meter / number of seconds to complete) / wheel circumference in meters) × 60 seconds in a minute = RPM of loaded motor
Sandwich example: ((4 m / 15 s) / 0.16 m) × 60 = 100 RPM

That means the loaded RPM is about 100 RPM. Of course, the robot wiggles a bit rather than going in a straight line. So, the true loaded RPM is a little higher, but 100 RPM is accurate enough for predictive calculations. Now that we know the loaded speed, let's plug it back into the original formula to make sure it will now predict a 15-second course time.

Sandwich example: (100 RPM / 60) × 0.16 m = 0.267 m/s
Sandwich example: 4 m / 0.267 m/s = 15 s

What happens if larger (22 cm) wheels are installed?

Sandwich example: (100 RPM / 60) × 0.22 m = 0.363 m/s
Sandwich example: 4 m / 0.363 m/s = 11 s

Both calculations used the same values, except for the circumference of the wheels. The total course time decreased from 15 seconds to 11 seconds. Thus, by increasing the wheel diameter, the robot's speed increases proportionally.

Selecting Robot Wheels

The best choice of wheels depends on the terrain, but here are some suggestions.

Indoor explorer: Needs balanced abilities. Select wheel characteristics of pneumatic or foam, medium width, grooved tread, and large diameter.

Outdoor explorer: Needs shock resistance and traction on uneven surfaces. Select wheel characteristics of pneumatic, balloon shape, wide, knobby tread, and large diameter.

Smooth-surface pushing robot: It's all about torque and traction. Select wheel characteristics of pneumatic, flat shape, wide, slick tread, and small diameter. (As far as the number of wheels on a pushing robot: the more the merrier! See Figure 19-8.)

Figure 19-8. A mini-sumo robot with eight wheels selected for maximum pushing

Line-following robot: Needs adept turning. Select wheel characteristics of solid, rounded shape, thin, slick tread, and medium diameter.

Reasons for Choosing LEGO Wheels

LEGO is very supportive of the robotic community. Their building blocks are of the finest quality and their wheels are no exception. LEGO rubber semi-pneumatic tires and firm solid tires are made in a variety of shapes and sizes (see Figure 19-9).

Figure 19-9. *A selection of LEGO wheels*

Here are some advantages of using LEGO wheels on your robot:

- High quality

- Wide selection

- Classic and high-tech styles

- Relatively inexpensive at about $3 for a large wheel (new), less for smaller wheels

- Available online and at local stores

- Consistently precise sizes make for flawlessly matched pair and sets

- Interchangeable (almost all use the same size axle)

Based on all of these advantages, there's little reason to make your own wheels. It's very difficult to make a perfectly round wheel with a perfectly centered hub, much less make a matching pair. Wobbly wheels introduce tracking errors and don't look professional.

Wooden wheels are heavy and don't grip well. Like wooden tires, plastic tires slip because their material also has a lower coefficient of friction than do rubber tires. Additionally, both wooden and plastic tires don't conform themselves to the ground, causing less friction because of reduced contact area. Silicone coatings for treads don't match the conforming performance or looks of molded rubber.

Making your own decent wheels is painstaking and can be quite frustrating. And what happens when one breaks? With a LEGO wheel, they're always available from the manufacturer or from a collector.

Wheel Choice for Sandwich

A couple of factors go into selecting appropriate wheels for the line-following robot. To begin with, a minimum and maximum diameter must be considered.

Determining Minimum and Maximum Diameter

Sandwich's motor shaft can be positioned as low as approximately 1.75 cm above the underside of the robot (see Figure 19-10).

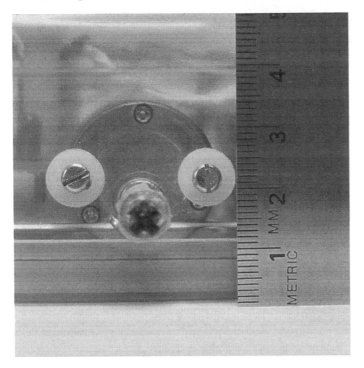

Figure 19-10. A ruler measuring the height from the surface to the center of the motor shaft

Therefore, to lift the robot up with margin for error, the wheels should have a radius of at least 2 cm.

```
radius × 2 = diameter
2 cm × 2 = 4 cm
```

The minimum wheel diameter must be no less than 4 cm.

The distance between the front of the robot and the center of the motor shaft is a little less than 10 cm (see Figure 19-11). A wheel with a diameter of 20 cm would lift the entire robot off the ground. When the motors kicked in, the robot would likely start spinning around and around the center of the shaft, jerking forward and backward.

Figure 19-11. A ruler measuring the distance from the front of the robot to the center of the motor shaft

It seems that 19 cm is the maximum diameter you could use and still have part of the robot's body touch the surface. Although this is technically correct, it would still present problems. Not only would the robot pop wheelies when starting up, but also the sensors would need to be angled strangely to face the floor.

Determining the Maximum Diameter Based on Speed

Since larger wheels result in greater speed, the maximum diameter of the wheels is probably limited most by the reaction time of the motors, sensors, and brains. After all, the robot will drive off of the line if it moves too quickly for the electronics and motors.

The primary factors that determine speed have already been identified: raw motor speed, motor voltage, motor gear ratio, robot mass (load), and wheel diameter. (More complicated electronics can manipulate the pulses of power to the motors to reduce speed in spite of the factors stated here.)

Sandwich's gearhead motors were selected on the basis of size, cost, availability, and final shaft speed. Although a slightly slower-speed motor would have been desirable, we're stuck with the limited selection of motors that met the other criteria.

The most common occasions when a robot's mass is altered with respect to speed is when a robot's mass is lightened to make it faster. Adding deadweight to slow down a robot is an energy-inefficient method.

That leaves motor voltage and wheel diameter as the best remaining factors that we can vary to control Sandwich's speed. All of this is a long-winded way of saying that the maximum appropriate diameter of the wheels is going to be determined by the size at which the robot's speed begins to cause it to stray off of the course. Some experimentation is necessary to pick this diameter.

My Choice of Wheels for Sandwich

Based on the previous paragraphs, the wheel diameter is the most significant factor for this robot. The best choice for a line-following robot is solid, round, thin, and slick-treaded wheels.

I performed numerous experiments with different diameter wheels to see at what point Sandwich veered off a reasonable track. A wheel of approximately 4.5 cm seemed to provide the best combination of speed and agility.

Sandwich rides on a pair of "49.6 × 28 VR" LEGO wheels (see Figure 19-12). They are about 5 cm in diameter. Despite the lack of other characteristics that would have been desirable for line following, I ended up picking semi-pneumatic, flat, wide, and grooved wheels simply for their diameter (and thus resulting speed).

Figure 19-12. LEGO wheels selected for Sandwich. 49.6 × 28 VR: rim #6595 and tire #6594.

If you can locate some, you should feel free to select 4.5 cm wheels that are solid, round, thin, and slick treaded.

At the time of this writing, new "49.6 × 28 VR" LEGO wheels don't seem to be available as separate items from LEGO, and the kits are all discontinued. See Table 19-1 for a list of known kits that contained these wheels.

Table 19-1. Some Kits That Contained 49.6 × 28 VR LEGO Wheels

Part Number	Description
2556	Shell Promotional Set / F1 Ferrari
3804	Robotics Invention System 2.0
3808	Shadowstrike S70
8286	3 In 1 Car / Amphipower
8440	Formula Flash / Formula Indy Racer
8445	Indy Storm
8456	Fiber Optic Multi Set / Multi Racer Set
8471	Nitro Burner
8472	Street 'n' Mud Racer
8473	Nitro Race Team
8479	Barcode Multi-Set
8482	CyberMaster
8483	CyberMaster
8516	RoboRiders The Boss
8520	Millennium/Millennia Throwbot
9719	Robotics Invention System 1.0
9747	Robotics Invention System 1.5
9794	Team Challenge Set

Although LEGO no longer sells these particular wheels, there are plenty of other sources. If you don't happen to have these wheels in your personal collection, you can find them online on eBay and other auction sites.

BrickLink.com is a fantastic source for all LEGO parts. For example, Sandwich's tire and hub can be found for less than a dollar from over 500 sellers. You can search by part number or description. (Note that BrickLink uses the term "tyre" instead of "tire" and that part #6594 also matches a Gas Transit set.)

BrickLink's sellers are independent and worldwide. So, you'll want to pay attention to reputation and location. You should try to purchase as many items as possible from the same seller to optimize the shipping cost.

Alternative Choices of Wheels for Sandwich

Recall that, besides wheel diameter, the other option for controlling speed is battery voltage. Larger diameter wheels can be installed on Sandwich if a battery voltage less than 9 V is chosen.

Compensating for Larger Wheels with Lower Voltage Batteries

LEGO rim #32057 and tire #32076 meet nearly all of the best characteristics for line following, although they have a slightly grooved tread design (see Figure 19-13).

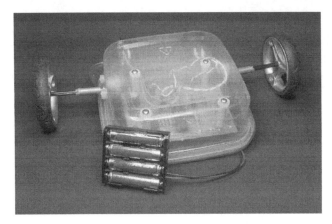

Figure 19-13. Sandwich's brother with larger diameter wheels and 6 V battery pack

The wheel has a diameter of 7 cm. The circumference can either be measured, or it can be calculated by the following formula:

```
π × diameter = circumference
3.1416 × 7 cm = 22 cm
```

By using 22 cm circumference wheels instead of 16 cm circumference wheels, the linear speed increases proportionally.

```
22 cm / 16 cm = 137.5%
```

To counteract the 37.5% increase in speed, the 9 V NiMH rechargeable battery can be replaced with a 6 V pack of four AAA-size cells. (Specifically, I used Rayovac rechargeable alkaline cells.) The reduction in voltage from 9 V to 6 V decreases speed proportionally.

```
6 V rechargeable alkaline rated voltage / 8.4 V actual NiMH rated voltage = 71.4%
```

Overall, the speed is about the same:

```
(22 cm / 16 cm) × (6 V / 8.4 V) = 98%
```

Not only does this give the robot more appropriate wheels, but also the AAA pack lasts seven times longer! The difference in mass between the two configurations is only about 5 grams more for the battery pack, or about +2.5 %.

If you choose 6 V (AAA pack) instead of 9 V (9 V battery) to permanently run your line-following robot, be sure to recalculate resistor values for the circuits. Otherwise the LEDs are going to be pretty dim.

Obtaining New Alternative Wheels

LEGO currently manufacturers another wheel size that is an excellent alternative (see Figure 19-14). The rim is 30.4 × 20 (#56145) and the tire is 43.2 × 22 ZR (#44309). The narrower diameter improves line-following accuracy and the narrower width reduces friction.

Figure 19-14. Out-of-production 49.6 × 28 VR (left) *compared to current-production 43.2 × 22 ZR* (right)

Table 19-2 lists some of the kits that include the 42.2 x 22 ZR wheel.

Table 19-2. Some Kits That Contain 43.2 × 22 ZR LEGO Wheels

Part Number	Description
4893	Revvin' Riders
4895	Motion Power
4955	Big Rig
6752	Fire Truck
6753	Highway Transport
8140	Tow Trasher
8143	Ferrari 1:17 F430 Challenge
8156	Ferrari FXX 1:17
8166	Wing Jumper
8167	Jump Riders
8271	Wheel Loader
8292	Cherry Picker
8354	Exo Force Bike
8355	H.O.T. Blaster Bike
8365	Tuneable Racer
8547	Mindstorms NXT 2.0
8645	Muscle Slammer Bike
8652	Enzo Ferrari 1:17
8667	Action Wheelie
8671	Ferrari 430 Spider 1:17

8969	Wheeling Pursuit
9648	Education Resource Set
10196	Grand Carousel

Cleaning Tires

Before long, the tires on a robot accumulate dirt and grime. Soiled rubber doesn't grip as well as clean rubber. One of the secrets to winning a robot sumo contest is to wipe off the tire surface after every match.

You can remove large chunks of dirt with an old toothbrush and water. Soaking in a bit of liquid dishwashing soap also helps.

To remove embedded contaminants, place the tires in an ultrasonic cleaner (see Figure 19-15). Micro-Mark sells the pictured ultrasonic cleaner, item # 82413, for $89.95. That particular model is fairly small, but is satisfactory for all LEGO wheels and circuit boards up to about 7 cm by 11 cm.

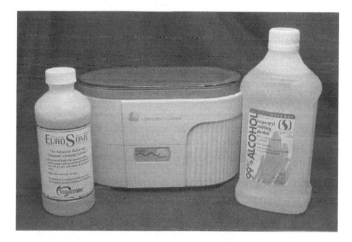

Figure 19-15. Ultrasonic cleaner (middle) *with cleaning solution* (left) *and 99% isopropyl alcohol* (right)

Ultrasonic cleaning machines vibrate with ultrasonic (above human hearing) waves. Millions of tiny bubbles form and pop, scrubbing every crevice of the immersed material.

Use either the cleaning solution designed for the machine or some water with a few drops of liquid dishwashing soap. Ultrasonic cleaning machines do a fantastic job of scrubbing by themselves. However, the surfactants in cleaning solutions significantly improve performance by binding the loosened particles to the fluid, so that they don't return to the object being cleaned.

Isopropyl or rubbing alcohol may degrade certain rubber and plastics over time. It's best to avoid using alcohol on wheels, just in case. You can clean circuit boards using 99% pure isopropyl alcohol. It's available at drugstores and supermarkets. Don't use "rubbing" alcohol or anything less than the full 99% purity, as oils, perfumes, or damaging chemicals may have been added.

Rolling Along

There are other ways of providing movement for your robot, such as tractor treads and legs. But, wheels are more likely to result in a successful design when you're first starting out in the hobby.

Over the years, you'll probably amass a collection of wheels, just as you'll amass a collection of motors and other parts. When a robot idea strikes, you can then lay out the major parts in front of you, swapping pieces until the robot's body matches the fuzzy blueprint in your head.

If you've chosen LEGO wheels or wheels that have a standard hub, it will be easy to swap different sizes and shapes, even after the robot is finished. That allows for rapid prototyping and experimentation. In the next chapter, you'll learn how to make a coupler to connect any standard LEGO wheel to a motor shaft.

■■■

CHAPTER 20

Coupler

A coupler connects two things together. This chapter consists of step-by-step instructions for making a coupler that, in this case, connects the selected gearhead motor's shaft to a LEGO cross axle. The general nature of this coupler is applicable even if you choose a different motor or a different type of wheel.

A coupler is needed because the shaft of the chosen motor is neither the correct shape nor the correct size to accept a LEGO wheel. Even if glue or solder could adhere them together, the robot would probably need to be disassembled or experimentally modified at some point. This would rule out permanent adhesion of the wheels to the motors. The coupler presented in this chapter makes it easy to remove or change wheels at any time.

The line-following robot has two wheels. It needs one coupler for each wheel. Therefore, the robot needs two couplers in total.

Alternatives

These instructions require some light machining with a handheld rotary tool. Most beginners are uncomfortable with machining or metal-working tools. Initially, so was I!

Yet, one of the most fascinating and enjoyable aspects of robotics is creating your own custom body parts. I highly encourage you to at least attempt the relatively simple coupler project in this chapter. It may open your heart to the human-ingrained discipline of physically working with tools.

Buying ready-made parts instead of making a coupler, you can purchase a motor and wheel that are designed to fit together. For example, Chapter 18 suggests the Solarbotics "#GMPW Deal" motor and wheel combination.

If you prefer the Hsiang Neng motors, ServoCity.com sells several different types of ready-made mounting hubs and matching wheels (see Figure 20-1). The motor has a 4 mm shaft. Therefore, buy either a pair of the 4 mm Bore Set Screw Hubs (3470H for $4.95 each) or a pair of the 4 mm Bore Clamping Hubs (3120CH for $7.95 each). The clamping hub is a superior design that holds onto the motor shaft more securely and does not mar the shaft, but it is more expensive.

Figure 20-1. The set-screw hub (first motor) *and clamping hub* (second motor) *connect the motor shaft to a ready-made wheel* (right)

Matching wheels screw onto the hubs. The wheels are available in a variety of sizes and colors. The two-inch diameter acrylic wheels (#2.00ACR for $3.99) and two-inch diameter foam wheels (#2.00TMD for $16.95) are the correct size for Sandwich. The wheels come in pairs, so don't make the mistake that I did by buying two of them (because you'll end up receiving four wheels).

Making Couplers If You Have Metal-Working Equipment

If you have access to a lathe or a milling machine, you may want to consider an alternative to the instructions in this chapter. In fact, a lathe is the perfect machine to produce the highest-precision LEGO couplers. Instructions are posted at http://www.robotroom.com/LatheCoupler.html.

For readers with a milling machine, Chapters 3 and 4 of *Intermediate Robot Building* by David Cook (Apress, 2010) provide complete instructions.

Tubing

At this point, let's assume you've decided to make the LEGO couplers using the instructions in this chapter. The first step is to acquire the raw material.

The coupler consists of a metal tube. One end of the tube has the appropriate inner diameter to accept a standard LEGO cross axle. The other end of the tube has the appropriate inner diameter to accept the selected motor's shaft. The LEGO axle is permanently glued to the coupler, but the motor shaft is held in place by a screw to allow for disconnection.

Choosing Between Brass and Aluminum Tubing

You can make the couplers out of either brass or aluminum (see Figure 20-2). Brass is three times heavier, about 6 grams for each coupler. Brass is stronger than aluminum, and thus is more likely to retain its shape during metal-working. Most importantly, brass is the easiest to machine. For this reason, I recommend working with brass for your first attempt at making the couplers.

Figure 20-2. Two brass couplers (left) *and two aluminum couplers* (middle) *made with tubing. Two plastic couplers* (right) *made on a lathe or milling machine out of solid rod.*

Aluminum's light weight is a definite advantage for competition robots. Even though it is a softer metal, it is unlikely to break, as the forces exerted on it are trivial on small robot sizes.

Specifying and Obtaining Tubing Sizes

Both brass and aluminum tubing are available in display cases at most hardware stores (see Figure 20-3). For this project, you'll need a total of four tubes; one each of diameters $^{3}/_{16}$ inch, $^{7}/_{32}$ inch, $^{1}/_{4}$ inch, and $^{9}/_{32}$ inch.

The tube walls must be 0.014-inch thick. "Wall size" is the thickness of the metal.

K&S Engineering manufactures the specific tubing on my couplers, stock numbers #129, #130, #131, and #132. The tubes average around $2.00 each. You can purchase similar tubing online at McMaster-Carr, Online Metals, or MSC Industrial Supply.

One pair of couplers requires only 5 cm of length, but the tubes come in lengths of 12 inches. Plenty remains left over for other robot projects or additional couplers.

If you don't have access to these diameters of tubing, you'll see how the sizes were determined in a moment. That way you can choose appropriate tubing based on what is available to you.

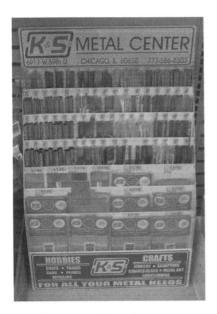

Figure 20-3. Hardware store display case of brass, aluminum, and copper in the shape of tubes, angles, channels, strips, and sheets

Telescoping Tubing Required

With the diameter and wall thickness specified, each tube fits neatly inside the next larger size (see Figure 20-4). This is called telescoping tubing. At the store, try sliding one tube into the other to make sure they fit snugly.

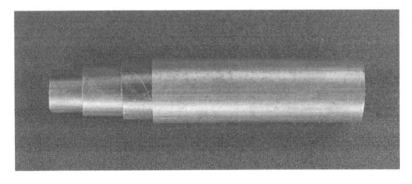

Figure 20-4. Four pieces of tubing, each inserted inside the next

Fitting the LEGO Cross Axle into a Tube

A LEGO cross axle must fit into one side of the coupler. By inserting a LEGO axle into various tubes, the closest match is found to be a $^7/_{32}$-inch diameter tube (see Figure 20-5).

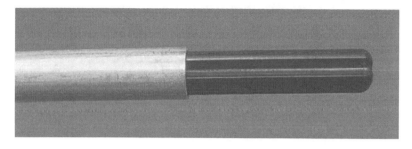

Figure 20-5. *LEGO cross axle inserted into $^7/_{32}$-inch diameter tubing*

Fitting the Motor Shaft into a Tube

The shaft of the selected motor must fit into the other side of the coupler. By inserting the motor shaft into various tubes, the closest match is found to be a $^3/_{16}$-inch diameter tube (see Figure 20-6).

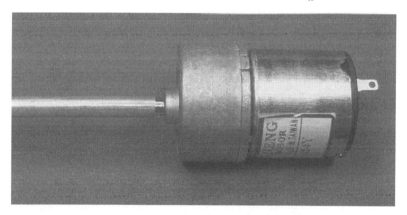

Figure 20-6. *Motor shaft inserted into $^3/_{16}$-inch diameter tubing*

Because the tube diameters differ on each end of the coupler, a single metal tube can't connect the axle and the shaft. Luckily, a $^3/_{16}$-inch diameter tube with 0.014 inch walls fits snuggly within a $^7/_{32}$-inch diameter tube with 0.014 inch walls. The $^3/_{16}$-inch diameter tube is cut to half the total length of the coupler and inserted into the $^7/_{32}$-inch diameter tube. This way, one half fits the motor shaft and the other half fits the LEGO axle.

This explains how the wall size and two of the four tube sizes were determined. The other two tubes have larger diameters. Those tubes slide over the smaller tubes for added strength and to provide enough thickness to add a screw hole.

Measuring and Cutting the Tubing

The tubing comes in lengths longer than needed for the coupler. The desired length of the individual tubes needs to be determined and then cut accordingly.

Determining and Marking Tube Lengths

The motor shaft sticks out 15 mm. The motor-shaft half of the coupler should be a bit shorter, say 13 mm, to avoid rubbing against the gearbox cover as the shaft rotates.

Measure two 14 mm lengths on the $^3/_{16}$-inch diameter tubing. Mark the two locations to cut with a fine-point felt-tip permanent marker (see Figure 20-7). Why 14 mm? Didn't we just decide we wanted a 13 mm length? Yes, but about a millimeter is going to be lost during cutting and sanding, so a 14 mm mark results in a 13 mm cut and finished tube.

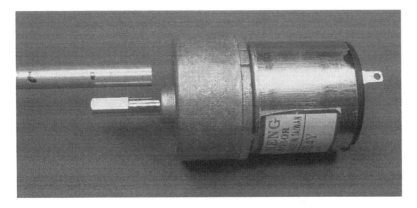

Figure 20-7. $^3/_{16}$*-inch diameter tubing held beside the motor shaft to mark the desired length*

Measure two 23 mm lengths on the three larger-diameter tubes. These tubes will span the entire length of the coupler, about 22 mm, after cutting and finishing. Cut the tubes longer if desired, but a wider robot will result.

Cutting Tubing

There are a number of tools that can cut tubes. A fine-toothed hacksaw works, although the thin walls of the tubes usually bend or deform. You can insert a suitably sized wooden dowel within the tubing during cutting to reduce warping, but there are tools that are superior to a hacksaw for cutting small tubes.

Tube Cutter Tool

A tube cutter is a tool designed specifically for cutting tubes (see Figure 20-9). A tube is placed between a rotating blade and two rotating rollers. Twisting a knob pushes the two rollers against the tube, forcing the tube into the blade. By rolling the tube and twisting the knob over and over, the blade eventually cuts through the entire circumference of the tube.

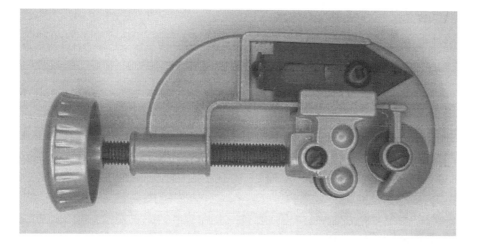

Figure 20-8. *Mini tube cutter*

Although this tool cuts very straight, the ends of soft tubing curl in slightly after being cut. With this reduced diameter on the ends, the tubes no longer fit inside of each other. You can sand the curled ends down or core them out, but it isn't worth all the effort.

Variable-Speed Rotary Tool

A variable-speed rotary tool is like an extremely fast power drill (see Figure 20-9). But instead of only making holes, you can add various discs and attachments to sand, carve, route, and cut.

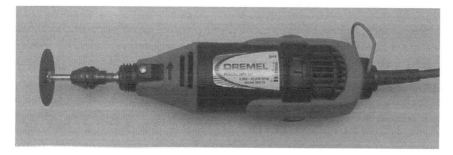

Figure 20-9. *Dremel variable-speed rotary tool with cut-off wheel accessory*

■ **Caution** Always wear a dust mask and safety glasses when operating a rotary tool.

Variable-speed rotary tools are available at most hardware stores. The tool runs from $35 up to $200 depending on the features and included accessories. Dremel manufactures the most popular brand. There's nothing wrong with starting with the least-expensive model, although a mid-price kit is a better investment.

In robotics, a variable-speed rotary tool is as irreplaceable for bodywork as a multimeter is for electronics. It is worth obtaining and practicing with this valuable tool.

Securing the Tubing in a Vise

A vise consists of a pair of heavy metal blocks, called jaws, connected via a screw (see Figure 20-10). Turning the screw handle causes the jaws to come together, clamping the material in between. This firmly holds the piece on which you're working.

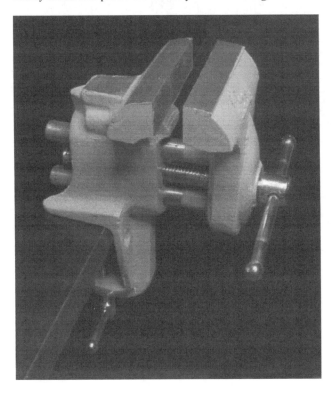

Figure 20-10. Small bench vise

A small bench vise is fairly inexpensive and is a necessary tool in robotics.

Cutting the Tubing with a High-Speed Rotary Tool

To cut the tubing with a rotary tool, first place the tubing in a vise (see Figure 20-11). Gently tighten the vise, but make sure it's not too loose or the tubing will slip during cutting, and not too tight or the tubing will be crushed.

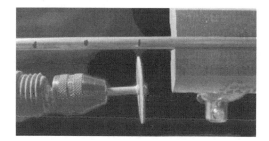

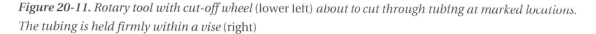

Figure 20-11. Rotary tool with cut-off wheel (lower left) *about to cut through tubing at marked locations. The tubing is held firmly within a vise* (right)

Insert a heavy-duty or fiberglass-reinforced cut-off wheel attachment into the rotary tool. Bring the rotary tool to the lower range of its speed and lightly maneuver the blade through the tubing at the marked location.

The picture in Figure 20-11 was taken for illustrative purposes. You actually want to start cutting at the first mark on the tube, with the remainder of the tube firmly in the vise. If the tube is hanging way out of the vise, it's going to vibrate a lot, marring the cut. If a middle mark is cut before the first mark, half of the tubing is going to fall on the floor.

The bulbous front of most rotary tools sometimes gets in the way of cutting straight across the tubing. To make things worse, the cut-off wheel shaves down over time, becoming smaller with use. A fresh cut-off wheel helps, as does a flexible shaft extension. However, don't be overly concerned with the angle of the cut, as it can be corrected with sanding and, in any case, it doesn't cause the coupler to wobble.

Finishing the Cut by Sanding

Depending on the method chosen for cutting, freshly cut tubing commonly contains hanging metal particles called burrs. Rubbing the cut face in a circular motion against sandpaper cleans the rough ends of the tubing (see Figure 20-12). You can use a fine single-cut or Swiss-pattern file, but sandpaper seems gentler.

Figure 20-12. Freshly cut tubing showing scratches and burrs (left). *Finished tubing sanded flat and clean* (right).

291

Sandpaper is usually available in assorted packs of different grades of coarseness. Choose a variety pack labeled for use on metal, like aluminum-oxide sandpaper. It should contain sheets from medium (100 grit) through extra fine (225 grit). For a beautiful finish, also pick up some sheets of super fine (400 grit) silicon-carbide sandpaper, or even finer.

■ **Caution** Always wear a dust mask and safety glasses when sanding.

Lower grit numbers remove more material more quickly, but scratch the workpiece. Start with coarser sandpaper (100 grit) to straighten out the cut or remove large chunks. Then, work the piece through finer and finer sandpaper (225 grit) until you achieve the desired smoothness. Other than aesthetics, there's no reason to put a mirror finish (even finer than 400 grit) on the tubing. But, at the very least, remove all burrs and sharp edges.

Testing the Cut Pieces

To make one coupler, you should now have three 22 mm long tubes of diameters $^{7}/_{32}$ inch, $^{1}/_{4}$ inch, and $^{9}/_{32}$ inch. You should also have a 13 mm long tube of $^{3}/_{16}$-inch diameter.

Combine the three 22 mm long tubes by pushing the tubes into each other to form one thicker 22 mm long tube (see far left of Figure 20-13). If any of the tubes don't slide in easily, carefully sand the blocked tube or replace any damaged tubes. Don't worry if the tube lengths vary a little bit, and are not completely even. You can either ignore it or sand the end down as a group.

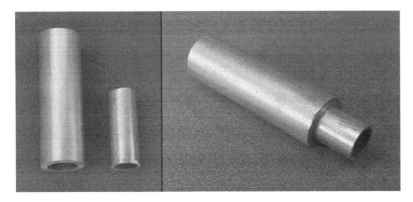

Figure 20-13. Left: *Three 22 mm tubes inserted together* (left side of left panel) *placed beside a 13 mm tube* (right side of left panel). Right: *13 mm tube partially inserted to test the fit*

Insert the 13 mm long tube into one end of the 22 mm long combined tube. Again, test for a smooth fit. When satisfied, separate the tubes again (the end of a small screwdriver or the remaining stock of tubing helps push the inner tubes back out).

LEGO Cross Axles

A LEGO cross axle is long thin black beam that looks like a plus sign (+) or the letter "X" when viewed from the end. LEGO axles are designed to insert into the hubs of wheels, gears, and other LEGO parts. Although the connection is achieved only by friction, the fit is firm and usually doesn't shift or separate during use.

Selecting a LEGO Cross Axle Length

LEGO pieces are commonly measured in comparison to the number of studs on top of a standard LEGO brick. For example, the cross axles in Figure 20-14 are 4, 5, and 6 LEGO units in length. (That translates to 31.8 mm, 39.7 mm, 47.6 mm.) LEGO cross axles are available in LEGO unit lengths of 2, 3, 4, 5, 6, 8, 10, and 12.

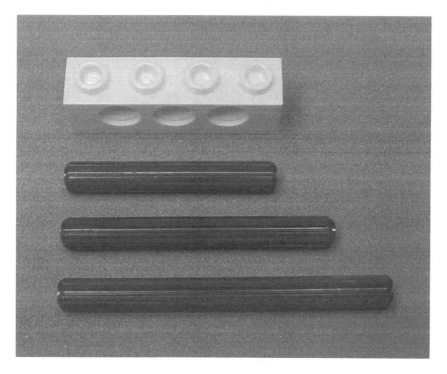

Figure 20-14. *Three example lengths of LEGO cross axles beside a 4 LEGO unit brick* (top) *for comparison purposes*

The minimum length of axle that should be installed in a coupler is about 2.5 LEGO units long (a 5 LEGO unit axle cut in half). Anything less than that either isn't long enough to connect to a LEGO piece or has too little of the axle supported within the coupler's metal tubing. Properly supported, even a 12 LEGO unit axle can be attached to a coupler.

Sandwich's coupler has a 3 LEGO unit cross axle. Actually, the coupler was made from a 6 LEGO unit cross axle cut in half because that size of axle is a more common part. If you decide to cut an axle in half (use the rotary tool cut-off wheel accessory), be sure to place the cut end into the coupler and leave the official tapered end sticking out. The taper makes it easier to slide on a wheel.

Axles longer than 3 or 4 LEGO units tend to stick out farther than necessary for a wheel. That length is usually reserved for axles intended to reach wheels or gears in a frame (see Figure 20-15). Placing a wheel at the end of a long unsupported axle runs the risk of bowing or snapping the plastic axle.

Figure 20-15. A 6 LEGO unit cross axle installed in a coupler for connecting a wheel inside of a frame.

Obtaining LEGO Cross Axles

Because of their usefulness, LEGO includes cross axles in most kits. If you don't already have some extra cross axles in your LEGO collection, you can obtain them easily from eBay or BrickLink.

Gluing the Coupler Together

Glue adheres best to parts that are free of dust and oil. Be sure to clean the individual tubes and the LEGO cross axle before gluing. An ultrasonic cleaner works well, but hand cleaning in soap and water is perfectly acceptable. Let the parts dry completely before gluing.

Coming Unglued

Until recently, I always skipped the step in directions that said, "Clean and dry parts completely." Then, I ran across a LEGO cross axle that would not glue.

LEGO axles are made of polypropylene thermoplastic (the same as Sandwich's body container). Both polypropylene and polyethylene are beloved for consumer containers due to their incredible resistance to chemicals. That same property makes those plastics almost impossible to glue. After all, what substance do they make glue containers out of?

Polypropylene has an inherently low surface energy. With oil, grime, and dirt coating the surface, there are even fewer available binding locations for the glue. By thoroughly cleaning the axle of all contaminants, the glue has additional opportunities to grab hold. For best results, immerse the axle in isopropyl alcohol and wipe with a cotton ball.

Some special glue kits on the market contain a separate bottle of hexane, which acts as an accelerant. Cyanoacrylate adhesive (super glue) dries extremely quickly on hexane-treated surfaces, thus locking the glue in sharp shapes that grab at the surface, rather than allowing the glue time to pull away like water beads on a freshly waxed car. Hexane is a last resort—a clean surface usually does the trick.

Notching the Cross Axle

Before cleaning the axle, consider using a file to cut notches into the end of the axle (see Figure 20-16). The glue will fill these voids. When hardened, the glue in the notches will prevent the axle from being pulled out, even if the glue didn't adhere to the axle surface.

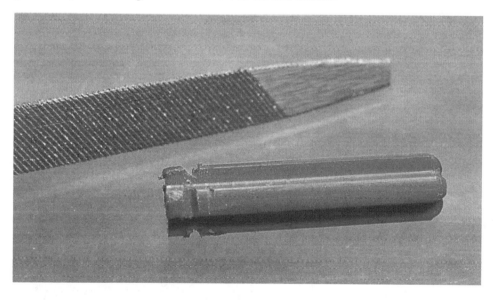

Figure 20-16. Notch the coupler-inserted end of the cross axle with a file. Don't disturb the tapered end where the wheel fits

Using Epoxy

Two-part epoxy resin works well for gluing together the entire coupler. Epoxies are thick, strong, and appropriate for filling voids. There are a variety of epoxies available from hardware stores. Try to find one that dries clear (see Figure 20-17).

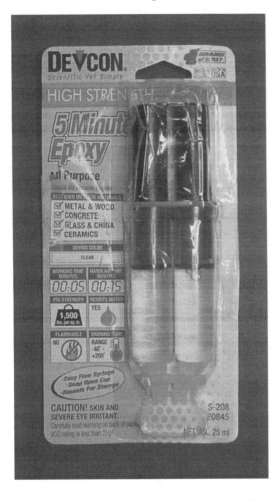

Figure 20-17. Devcon All Purpose 5 Minute Epoxy

■ **Caution** During gluing, wear vinyl or nitrile (not latex) gloves. Enough skin exposure to epoxy resin leads to an allergic reaction.

Follow the directions on the package. Mix the epoxy on a scrap piece of paper. Spread a thin coat on the outside of a cut tube and insert it into a larger tube. As each tube is inserted, twist the tube to spread the epoxy evenly throughout.

When the coupler tubing is completely assembled, twirl the end of the LEGO axle in the epoxy on the scrap piece of paper. Get a big glob of epoxy on the end and make sure it fills the notches in the axle. As the axle is inserted into the tubing, twist and pump the axle to distribute the epoxy throughout the inside of the tubing. The idea here is to have the epoxy fill all the space between the "X" shape of the axle and the "O" shape of the tubing.

Give the epoxy plenty of time to dry. The package on the epoxy I use reads, "full strength in 1 hour."

Removing Extraneous Epoxy

After drying, sand or chip off extra epoxy as desired. Notice how easily the epoxy chips off the plastic LEGO axle? Don't worry! If the axle was very clean and you made notches with a file, the axle should hold quite strongly in the coupler. If the axle falls out for some reason, a nice reverse "X" of epoxy remains in the coupler. Try some hexane and cyanoacrylate adhesive to adhere the axle back in place within the epoxy reverse "X".

Fortunately, the axle doesn't get tugged on very much as it gets rotated. Most of the motor force transmits to the axle through the reversed epoxy "X". As such, the epoxy's shape and adherence to the tubing are more important than adherence to the axle.

If you applied plenty of epoxy, it's likely that some got forced down into the motor shaft's side of the coupler. Drill out the invading fragments with a rotary tool and a $^1/_8$-inch drill bit. As long as the chips come out white, you haven't hit the black plastic LEGO axle yet. The axle is much harder and resists drilling. If the drill feels like it has bottomed out or black chips start coming out, you've drilled deeply enough. Some epoxy sticking to some of the sides of the tube may still need attention from the drill.

Adding a Setscrew to the Coupler

The coupler is almost complete. Something needs to be added to hold the coupler on the motor shaft, yet still allow removal.

A setscrew is a small screw that applies pressure against the flat portion of the motor shaft. Not only does the screw prevent the shaft from sliding out of the coupler, but it also forms a "D" shape within the coupler. The flat side of the "D" shape gives the flat portion of the motor shaft something to push against, so that the shaft spins the coupler rather than the shaft just spinning within the coupler.

Marking a Hole for the Setscrew

Hold the coupler beside the motor shaft to determine a good location for the hole in the coupler. Aim for the end of the flat portion of the shaft that's nearest the motor. That tends to be around 6 mm or so from the end of the coupler. Mark the spot with a fine-point felt-tip permanent marker (see Figure 20-18).

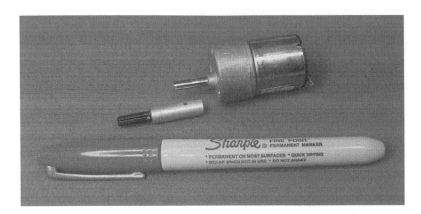

Figure 20-18. *Marking desired location for the setscrew hole on a coupler using a fine-point permanent marker*

Drill Press

A drill press is a device that holds a drill firmly and completely perpendicular to the work piece (see Figure 20-19). A lever on the side of the press lowers the drill straight down. Notches on the lever indicate the depth drilled, for precise control.

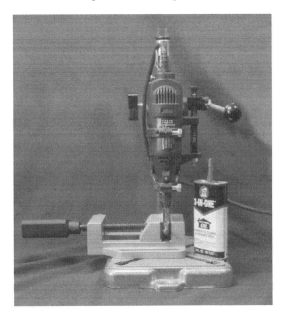

Figure 20-19. *Dremel rotary tool installed on a Dremel drill press. Optional oil and drill-press vise also pictured.*

With the drill turned off, you can position the workpiece and lower the lever to show exactly where the hole would be drilled. Thus, a drill press insures that a hole will be drilled straight, in the exact location, and to the exact depth intended.

Maybe I'm sounding like a broken record, but this is a third tool (rotary tool and vise being the other tools) that I couldn't build decent robots without. The Dremel drill press or Dremel Rotary Tool Work Station is available at hardware stores and Amazon.com.

Drill-Press Vise

The Dremel drill press comes with instructions for making clamps to hold the piece being worked on. A drill-press vise is a superior solution for small items. The Wolfcraft vise has a V groove in the jaw to hold round items, which is perfect for the coupler (see Figure 20-20). The vise is available from Micro Mark, item #82546, for $26.50.

Figure 20-20. Wolfcraft Quick-Jaw vise with a small V groove on the right side

Drilling the Hole for the Setscrew

Simply drill in the location marked earlier. Use a #43 drill bit. If you don't have that size, you can substitute a $^5/_{64}$-inch diameter drill bit for shallow holes. But, for deeper holes or stronger materials (like steel), you really must use a #43.

Drill all the way through the tube wall, but not through the tube wall on the other side.

Aluminum drills easily with a Dremel. Brass is slightly more difficult and may require a drop of oil to aid cutting and chip removal. In fact, after drilling the start of a straight hole in brass using the rotary tool, I switch to a power drill to finish the job.

Tapping the Hole for the Setscrew

A T-handle tap wrench is the tool that makes the internal threads in a hole for a screw or a bolt. A 4-40 taper tap (size 4, with 40 threads per inch) is required to finish the setscrew hole in the coupler. Tap and die sets are available at most hardware stores. Make sure the set includes the standard 4-40 taper thread tap or, if necessary, purchase it separately.

Carefully insert the taper tap into the start of the hole that was already drilled (see Figure 20-21). Try to keep the tap as straight and square as possible to the hole. By slowly turning, the taper tap begins to dig into the metal on the sides of the drilled hole. Be firm, but don't force it. It twists in, not pushes.

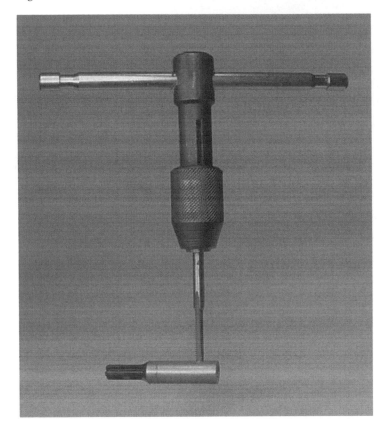

Figure 20-21. By turning a T-handle tap wrench, the taper tap starts cutting internal threads in the sides of the hole in the coupler

Every turn and a half, turn backwards a half turn or so to work excess metal out of the hole. If turning becomes a struggle, rotate the tap completely out and remove the chips from the tap and hole with a piece of cloth (not your fingers). A little oil or cutting fluid helps, too.

Inserting the Setscrew

From a hardware store, purchase some #4-40, $\frac{1}{8}$-inch long panhead machine screws (see Figure 20-22). Panhead refers to the shape at the top of the screw. Panhead screws are flat and wide, keeping them near the shaft while being easy to grasp by hand. Choose either slotted or Philips screw head styles.

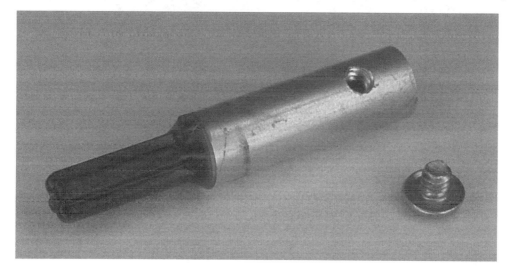

Figure 20-22. Finished coupler displaying beautiful screw threads. Alongside, a #4-40, $\frac{1}{8}$-inch long panhead machine screw.

Admiring the Coupler

The setscrew makes it simple and quick to install and remove the coupler from the robot. Equally beneficial, the LEGO cross axle allows for a variety of LEGO wheels to be slid on (see Figure 20-23). The LEGO axle accepts LEGO gears and other parts as well, so you can use the coupler to motorize more than just wheels.

You can modify this coupler design for other types of wheels and different-sized motor shafts. Using telescoping tubing ensures that the wheel hub and motor shaft are perfectly centered, eliminating any up and down play or wobble during operation.

Because of all the tools and components required to make the couplers, I usually build more than I need at a time. With half a dozen extra couplers floating around the home laboratory, you can build robots quickly when inspiration strikes.

Figure 20-23. Sandwich with the coupler attached to the motor shaft and a LEGO wheel about to be pressed on

CHAPTER 21

■■■

Soldering Equipment

Solder is the shiny silver-gray metal seen in tiny blobs on almost all circuit boards (see Figure 21-1). Soldering is the process of melting the solder onto the desired joints to connect the joint materials together both physically and electrically.

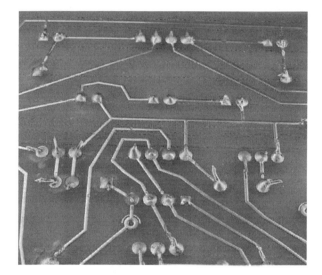

Figure 21-1. Circuit board featuring numerous solder points

At first, soldering may seem messy, complicated, or even dangerous. The perceived permanency may bother some beginners. But, after a little practice, it turns out that soldering is easy and effective!

Soldering requires solder wire, flux, a soldering iron, a soldering-iron stand, a tool for removing excess solder, and some type of vise for the item being soldered. An economical soldering kit can cost as little as $30. This chapter describes the items you'll want for your soldering kit.

Solder Wire

Electrical solder wire is a thin, malleable metal (see Figure 21-2). Solder conducts electricity well, thus providing a low-resistance path for current to flow from one component to another. Unlike solderless breadboards, solder physically holds the components together firmly and permanently.

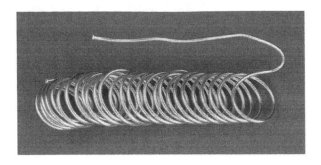

Figure 21-2. Lead-free solder wire

For circuit-board work, look for solder wire with a thickness of #21 AWG or #22 AWG (American wire gauge), usually stated as around 0.75-millimeter or 0.032-inch diameter. For health reasons, always use lead-free solder, which is commonly a mix of tin, silver, and copper.

Solid-core solder consists only of solder throughout the entire wire, whereas cored solder contains flux in the center. Flux is a chemical that dissolves oxides on the metal during soldering. The removal of surface oxides greatly improves the joint connection. Choose solder containing a core of mildly activated rosin flux or no-clean rosin flux.

■ **Caution** Never use acid-flux core solder on electrical components. Also avoid organic or highly activated rosin flux unless the circuit is then thoroughly cleaned according to the flux manufacturer's instructions. Unless completely removed, those fluxes can erode or degrade electrical components and their connections over time.

Table 21-2 lists a couple of sources of 0.031-inch diameter, no-clean, flux core, lead-free, solder wire. The same type of solder in a slightly larger diameter is an acceptable substitute.

Table 21-1. Suppliers of Lead-Free Solder Appropriate for Robot Circuit Boards

Supplier	Part Number	Price	Quantity	Description
SparkFun	TOL-09163	$3.50	10 grams	Solder Lead-Free 10-gram Tube
SparkFun	TOL-09325	$7.95	100 grams	Solder Spool - Lead-Free
Mouser	738-14048	$40.31	1 pound	SAC305 Glowcore
Digi-Key	KE1137	$56.15	1 pound	0.031-Inch Lead-Free No-Clean Core Solder

Flux

Besides appearing in the core of solder, liquid and paste flux is also available separately (see Figure 21-3). Applying a bit of flux to grungy or stubborn joints is the secret to high-quality soldering. Whenever I am unable to solder a particular location, I'll dab a little bit of flux onto the spot and try again.

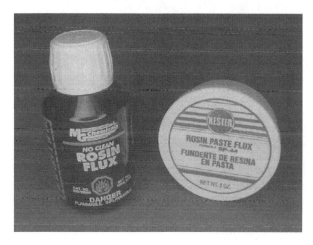

Figure 21-3. Liquid flux (left) *and paste flux* (right)

Table 21-2 lists suppliers for liquid flux. Paste flux stays in place, but liquid flux leaves fewer residues. I prefer liquid flux.

Table 21-2. Suppliers of Liquid Flux

Supplier	Part Number	Price	Description
Electronix Express	060722	$4.50	"No-Clean" Flux Pen Formula 951
Electronix Express	25835-4OZ	$7.95	Liquid Rosin Flux No-Clean
Digi-Key	KE1804	$4.38	Kester Low-Residue No-Clean Liquid Flux Pen
Mouser	590-835-100ML	$6.95	Liquid flux 125 mL
Mouser	533-0951	$7.40	Kester Low-Residue No-Clean Liquid Flux Pen

Flux only removes oxides. Solder and flux won't work if the metal is dirty. Contaminants prevent heat and solder from reaching the bare metal, causing intermittent or failed connections. Before soldering, clean dirty contacts with a scrubbing pad or fine sandpaper and then wash to remove all chemicals, oils, or grime, thus exposing clean bare metal that bonds well.

Soldering Iron

A soldering iron heats up at its tip to transfer heat to the metal joint being soldered. Choose a low-wattage soldering iron (25 W to 40 W). Inexpensive stand-alone stick irons or soldering pencil-shaped models run as low as $10.

Don't use a soldering gun on robot circuits. The gun's thicker tip is obtrusive and the more substantial heat can damage small electrical components. Soldering guns are designed for water pipes, stained-glass windows, and larger metal objects.

Most soldering irons have tip temperatures from 600°F to 900°F (about 315°C and 480°C). In practice, temperatures between 700°F and 800°F (about 370°C and 425°C) are preferred. Expensive soldering irons have adjustable temperatures and have displays that show the current tip temperature (see Figure 21-4).

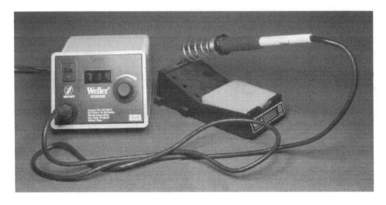

Figure 21-4. Temperature-adjustable soldering iron with sponge and stand

Some soldering irons have tips that are safe from ESD (electro-static discharge), usually labeled "ESD safe" or "grounded tip." The spark or shock from static electricity is only an annoyance to human beings, but can ruin sensitive chips. For most hobbyists, an ESD-safe tip, temperature display, and adjustable temperature are unnecessary features.

If possible, select a fine-point tip (see Figure 21-5). Most inexpensive soldering irons end in a larger, chiseled tip that is satisfactory. But, as you master robotic circuits, you'll discover that a fine point improves targeting of small joints and tiny chip leads.

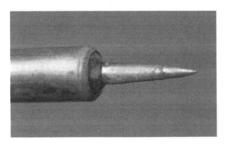

Figure 21-5. Fine tip of soldering iron

Soldering Stand

Because a soldering iron gets very hot, a coiled metal stand is required to hold the soldering iron when not in use (see Figure 21-6).

■ **Caution** Don't ever rest, set down, or store the soldering iron in any place but the manufacturer's specifically designed holder. The soldering iron is hot enough to start a fire, even after power is disconnected.

Figure 21-6. Soldering stand with metal coils to safely hold a hot soldering iron

Soldering Sponge

During soldering, the soldering iron tip coats in oxides and cakes with contaminants. As this occurs, it becomes more difficult for the tip to effectively transfer heat to the metal joints and solder.

The soldering stand usually includes a special sponge (see Figure 21-7) for cleaning the soldering iron's tip. Only use a sponge specifically designed for soldering iron tips, as other sponges may melt or give off fumes when the hot tip is applied.

Figure 21-7. Moistened sponge for cleaning a soldering iron's tip

The sponge should be heavily moistened, but not quite soggy, with distilled water. Ordinary tap water works just fine, but contains impurities that reduce the amount of time between tip cleanings. Don't put chemicals or soaps into the sponge or on the soldering iron tip, as the residues will remain in the solder joints and on the tip as the chemicals are burnt off.

Some people prefer waterless brass sponges, such as SparkFun #TOL-08965 for $9.95. Brass is a relatively soft metal, so it won't damage the soldering iron tip. Don't try substituting steel wool. It will scratch the soldering iron and fine steel wool catches on fire (no kidding).

Helping-Hand Tool

Soldering requires two hands, one to hold the soldering iron and the other to hold the solder. A tool called a "third hand" or "helping hand" steadily holds the circuit board or parts during soldering (see Figure 21-8).

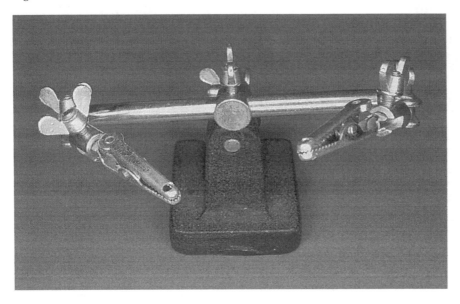

Figure 21-8. Helping hand with adjustable alligator clips to hold pieces being soldered

Although a bench vise could be substituted for a helping-hand tool, the helping hand has two or more hinged alligator clips that you can adjust to a wide variety of positions around the circuit board. If you're having trouble with the helping hand tipping over, you can grip the base of the helping hand in a bench vise to keep the work piece steady.

Table 21-3 lists suppliers of the helping-hand tool. A two-inch magnifying lens is included with some models, but I don't find it clear enough or powerful enough to be particularly useful.

Table 21-3. Suppliers of the Helping-Hand or Third-Hand Tool

Supplier	Part Number	Price	Attachments Included
Electronix Express	060834	$3.50	Two alligator clips
All Electronics	HELPH-M	$4.50	Two alligator clips and magnifying lens
Jameco	26690	$5.95	Two alligator clips and magnifying lens
SparkFun	TOL-09317	$9.95	Two clips, magnifying lens, and iron holder
Micro-Mark	21120	$9.95	Three alligator clips

Desoldering Vacuum Tools

Sometimes you'll apply too much solder to a joint. The solder blob has either spread to another wire or circuit, or is perilously close to doing so. Sometimes you'll discover a part is wired backwards.

For whatever reason, there are times that some solder needs to be removed. Desoldering pumps and desoldering bulbs are tools designed to suck up molten solder (see Figure 21-9).

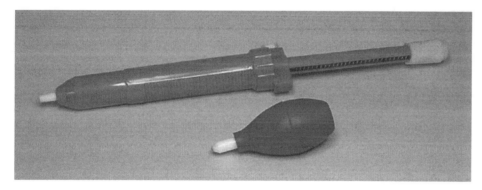

Figure 21-9. Desoldering pump (top) *and desoldering bulb* (bottom) *remove unwanted or excessive solder through vacuum suction.*

1. Squeeze the desoldering bulb or push in the desoldering pump's spring.

2. With the soldering iron, heat the solder that is currently on the joint.

3. With the soldering iron still heating the joint, place the nozzle of the bulb or pump into the molten solder.

4. Release the pressure on the bulb or push the pump button to cause the molten solder to be drawn by suction into the desoldering tool.

5. Repeat steps 1 through 4 as necessary until the desired amount of solder is removed. Note that it may not be possible to remove every bit of solder, but you can usually remove enough so that the part can be pulled free when the remaining solder is molten.

Sometimes it actually helps to add some fresh solder to a joint before attempting to remove it. If the solder at the joint still won't remelt, try adding some flux.

Over time, the desoldering tool's nozzle may clog and need cleaning. At some point, it may become worn enough to merit replacement.

Table 21-4 lists suppliers of desoldering bulbs. The desoldering pumps are fine, but I find bulbs less cumbersome to operate with one hand.

Table 21-4. *Suppliers of Desoldering Bulbs*

Supplier	Part Number	Price
Electronix Express	060825	$2.35
Mouser	384-1002	$2.79

Steps of a Typical Soldering Session

The following is an example of a typical soldering setup and breakdown routine:

1. Set up the soldering equipment in a location with adequate ventilation, away from combustible (flammable) materials.

■ **Tip** You can't go wrong by investing in a small fire extinguisher for your home or laboratory. Having it nearby may save your robot and your home.

---

2. With the soldering iron stored in the stand and turned off, moisten the sponge with distilled water.

3. Put on goggles and an apron or other protective clothing.

4. Plug in and turn on the soldering iron.

5. Wait two to five minutes for the soldering iron to heat up.

6. Remove the heated soldering iron from the stand and wipe and roll the tip against the moist sponge to remove contaminants.

7. If necessary, apply a little flux to the soldering-iron tip to remove oxide build-up.

8. Touch the soldering-iron tip to some solder wire so that a thin, shiny layer of solder forms over the tip. Not only does this protect the tip, but the molten solder also improves heat transfer to the joint. This is called "tinning."

9. Proceed with soldering (details discussed in the next chapter).

10. As the tip becomes soiled during soldering, repeat tinning (steps 6 through 8).

11. At the end of soldering, give the tip a final tinning before storing.

12. Return the soldering iron to the stand. Turn off and unplug the soldering iron.

13. After the soldering iron has cooled, remove the sponge from the stand and wash the sponge.

14. Place the cool soldering iron, stand, and all other soldering supplies in a locked cabinet or out of reach of children and other untrained personnel.

15. Thoroughly wash your hands with soap and water.

Get Ready to Solder

Soldering requires a few more tools than many other operations in robotics. But when you think about it, the equipment quantity isn't that much different than what's required for metalworking, such as for making the wheel couplers. The value of each tool and part in a soldering operation will become clearer in the next couple of chapters as you actually begin to solder.

■ ■ ■

CHAPTER 22

Soldering and Connecting

This chapter covers soldering, with emphasis on soldering smaller pieces, like the motors and the line-following switch. This chapter also describes instances when it's better to not solder certain wires together, but instead to use a connector.

Putting Together the Motors and Switches

Before attempting to solder the line-following circuit (next chapter), it's prudent to practice on less complicated parts. For example, each motor only needs two wires soldered to it.

The switches, motors, and a few other items (see Figure 22-1) are all independent from each other and from the main circuit board. That makes them short and easy projects to work on.

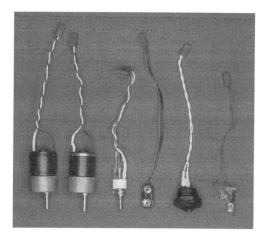

Figure 22-1. (left to right) *Motors, line-following switch, battery snap, power switch, and tube LEDs. They're all soldered to Molex KK connectors and insulated with heat-shrink tubing.*

You'll begin by soldering wires to each component and then protecting the component terminals with heat-shrink tubing. After that you'll attach connectors to the ends of the wires and twist the wires around themselves. If you don't quite understand the instructions that follow, refer to Figure 22-1 to remind yourself of the final result.

Putting Together the Motors

The following steps describe how to attach wires and connectors to the DC gearhead motors. When complete, you can quickly attach and remove the individual motors from the line-following circuit.

Preparing and Attaching the Motor Wires

Solid wire was selected for the solderless breadboard because it doesn't fray on the ends when being inserted into the breadboard holes. However, **stranded** wire is a better choice for a soldered circuit because stranded wire is more flexible and it readily twists around the joint to be soldered.

1. Obtain some white and some black stranded #22 AWG wire to be soldered to the positive and negative motor terminals, respectively.

2. Cut two pieces of white wire and two pieces of black wire to about 15 cm in length each (four 15 cm pieces total).

3. Using wire strippers, remove about 1.5 cm of plastic insulation from one end of each wire, and about 0.35 cm of insulation from the other end of each wire (see Figure 22-2).

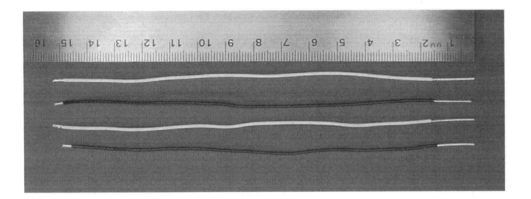

Figure 22-2. Two white and two black wires cut to the correct length with their ends stripped

4. Loop the 1.5 cm stripped end of a white wire through the eyelet (hole) in the positive terminal of a motor (see the left side of Figure 22-3).

5. Twist the wire around itself to provide a firm grip on the terminal (see the right side of Figure 22-3). Serrated needle-nose pliers work well for this task.

Here is the first rule of soldering: Whenever possible, the pieces to be joined should hold themselves together and have as much contact with each other as possible.

The solder should be a bonus. Don't try to connect pieces that aren't touching by creating a solder bridge. Don't rely solely on the holding strength of solder to connect pieces that will undergo mechanical strain.

Figure 22-3. Stranded wire looped through the eyelet in the positive motor terminal (left). Wire twisted around itself to hold firmly and provide multiple points of electrical connection to motor terminal (right).

6. Attach the black wire to the negative motor terminal in the same manner.

Although it might seem that these connections are firm enough as is, these connections would eventually loosen and pull apart during use unless soldered.

Holding the Motor Firmly and Preparing the Soldering Iron

7. Place the motor in a helping hand (see Figure 22-4) or vise, so that it doesn't move during soldering.

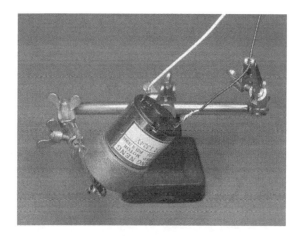

Figure 22-4. Helping hands holding motor and wire in preparation for soldering

8. Follow the steps listed in the previous chapter for preparing the sponge, heating up the iron, cleaning the tip, and tinning.

Soldering the Motors

9. Touch the soldering iron tip to one side of the motor terminal and wire, directly at the point of connection (see Figure 22-5). It is important to make as much contact with the clean, tinned tip so that heat transfers to the wire and motor terminal.

Figure 22-5. Soldering iron tip on one side of the wire, solder on the other side of the wire

10. Press the solder wire against the other side of the motor terminal and wire.

Here is the second rule of soldering: the solder to be applied should be touched against the heated joint, not the soldering iron tip.

Because the solder wire is heated by the joint instead of the soldering iron tip, the solder-wire flux core cleans the heated metal and then the molten solder flows over, into, and around the joint.

Sometimes, I'll briefly place the solder wire at the location where the soldering iron tip meets the joint, so that a small amount of molten solder provides a high-quality thermal path between the soldering iron tip and the joint. Then I'll switch the solder wire to the other side to insure that the joint has been heated up enough and that the molten solder flows throughout the entire joint.

Beginners often try to apply solder to the soldering iron tip and then brush the molten solder against the joint. Although this appears to work, the solder wire's flux core cleans only the soldering iron tip and burns off before reaching the joint. Also, the solder coats only the surface of the joint; it doesn't flow into all the nooks and crannies.

With a properly cleaned and heated tip, the solder wire should melt from the other side of the **small** joint in three seconds or less. If it isn't melting, pull back and let the area cool. On the next attempt, make sure the tip is clean and is making firm contact against the joint. A bit of molten solder between the tip and the joint may help.

Thicker leads and larger metal pieces take longer to heat up. This is because the heat is absorbed by the metal and conducted away before the solder can melt. In these situations, slide the solder wire nearer the soldering iron tip and the joint. Be a little more patient, it may take up to five seconds for the solder to flow on larger or thicker metal.

11. After the solder first starts to flow, it should only take a second or two more to completely flow around and through the entire joint. Now you can remove the solder wire from the joint.

12. After you have removed the solder wire, you can then remove the soldering iron tip from the joint. If you remove the soldering iron tip *before* the solder wire, the solder wire cools and sticks to the joint or deforms the solder joint's shape as the solder wire is pulled off.

13. You should be pleasantly rewarded with a shiny, strong, rounded, encompassing solder joint (see Figure 22-6).

Figure 22-6. *Wire and terminal soldered together*

If you aren't happy with the shape or shine of the joint, simply reheat it with the soldering iron tip and let the joint cool again. Additional solder is not necessary, just the soldering iron tip. This usually corrects mistakes and allows the molten solder to reflow thoroughly.

If you've applied too little solder, reheat the joint and apply additional solder wire. If you've applied too much solder, reheat the joint and use the desoldering bulb to remove excess. Occasionally it's cleaner to remove almost all of the solder at the joint and then apply the desired amount of fresh solder from the solder wire.

14. Repeat these steps to solder the black wire to the negative terminal.

15. Repeat these steps to solder the white and black wires to the other motor.

16. Test that the wires are attached correctly by connecting them briefly to a 9 V battery. The motor should spin.

In Soldering, Practice Makes Perfect

How did the soldering turn out? If it didn't turn out as well as you hoped, don't despair. Good soldering takes practice.

One of my first soldering experiences was to construct a 32-byte read-only memory panel out of 256 diodes (see Figure 22-7). It took 816 solder joints to complete. During testing I discovered half a dozen disconnected or intermittent solder joints. After carefully reheating each one (and a few I didn't trust), the board worked like a charm.

Figure 22-7. Array of 256 diodes requiring 816 solder connections.

I find my soldering skills improve with each robot. Sometimes I'll get overconfident or sleepy and mess up a few joints, which is frustrating and tedious to find later. So, be patient with yourself; give yourself time and plenty of experience to learn how to solder.

Protecting Soldered Joints with Heat-Shrink Tubing

Heat-shrink tubing is marvelous stuff. It's flexible, hollow plastic that slides over solder joints or other exposed connections. When heated, the tubing permanently shrinks firmly around the joint, protecting it against the elements and errant contact with other circuits. Additionally, the tubing provides strain relief, which prevents the wire from breaking at the otherwise uninsulated location near the solder joint.

You'll find heat-shrink tubing so valuable that you'll use it on all of your robots. I use $^1/_{16}$-inch and $^3/_{32}$-inch inner-diameter tubing the most often.

Obtaining Heat-Shrink Tubing

See Table 22-1 for a list of $^3/_{32}$-inch inner-diameter colored heat-shrink tubing needed for this project. For a wider selection, I recommend that you pick up the kit instead, which includes a seven-color assortment of eight diameters. Heat-shrink tubing is also available from many other electronics suppliers.

Table 22-1. Color Heat-Shrink Tubing

Supplier	Part Number	Price	Length	Inner Diameter	Color
Digi-Key	FP332W-5	$2.02	5 feet	$^3/_{32}$-inch	White
Digi-Key	FP332K-5	$2.02	5 feet	$^3/_{32}$-inch	Black
Digi-Key	FP332R-5	$2.02	5 feet	$^3/_{32}$-inch	Red
Digi-Key	FP332Y-5	$2.02	5 feet	$^3/_{32}$-inch	Yellow
Digi-Key	FP332G-5	$2.02	5 feet	$^3/_{32}$-inch	Green
Digi-Key	FPC-KIT	$79.95	5 feet	$^3/_{64}$-inch to $^1/_2$-inch	Black, Clear, Blue, Green, Red, White, and Yellow

Protecting the Motor Terminals with Heat-Shrink Tubing

You should cover the motor terminals and soldered joints with heat-shrink tubing. Although it isn't absolutely necessary for Sandwich, it's a good habit to get into.

1. Cut two pieces of white $^3/_{32}$-inch diameter heat-shrink tubing to a length of

   1.5 cm (see Figure 22-8). You will use one white tube on each motor.

2. Cut two pieces of black tubing to the same length (again, see Figure 22-8).

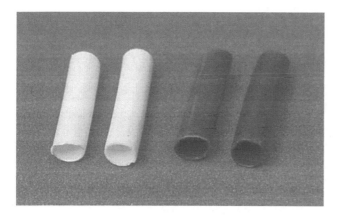

Figure 22-8. White and black $^3/_{32}$-inch diameter heat-shrink tubing cut to 1.5 cm lengths

3. Slide one of the white tubes over the soldered white wire on the positive motor terminal (see Figure 22-9). It should slip on without a struggle. If it staunchly resists being pushed on, pick a larger diameter of heat-shrink tubing.

319

Figure 22-9. Heat-shrink tubing placed over soldered motor terminal in preparation for shrinking

With heat, the tubing shrinks to about half the original diameter. So, don't use too large of a diameter because it won't shrink tightly enough.

4. Slide one of the black tubes over the soldered black wire on the negative motor terminal.

5. Add the white and black tubes to the other motor.

6. Before shrinking the tubing in place, be sure you've tested the motors. Although it is possible to remove the shrunken tubing by cutting it across its length, it's a bit of a pain to do so.

7. Obtain a hair dryer or a heat gun (see Figure 22-10).

Figure 22-10. Ordinary hair dryer and paint stripper heat gun

Heat guns are often available at hardware stores for stripping paint. They get very hot and are capable of starting fires (as can hair dryers). However, heat guns are faster and do a better job of shrinking the tubing completely.

8. Take the motors and hair dryer (or heat gun) to a location away from combustible materials. I use my concrete basement floor.

9. Turn on the hair dryer and position a motor so that the heat-shrink tubing is near the front grill of the hair dryer. If you're using a heat gun, keep the motor (and your hands) at a more comfortable distance. You may need to experiment to discover the optimal location.

10. The heat-shrink tubing contracts within four or five seconds with a heat gun, a bit longer with a hair dryer. Rotate the motor in the hot air stream to shrink the tubing equally on all sides.

11. Let the motor and the tubing cool. The tubing should conform to the shape of the terminals and solder (see Figure 22-11). It shouldn't be loose at all. Reapply heat if necessary.

Figure 22-11. Heat-shrink tubing after heating; protecting and insulating soldered terminals

12. Repeat the process for the other motor.

13. Unplug the hair dryer or heat gun. Set it someplace where it can cool safely.

During heating, the heat-shrink tubing may pull away a bit from the end cap of the motor. That's all right, but in general, the heat-shrink tubing should be covering almost all exposed metal. Because the tubing shrinks in length to some extent, remember to cut pieces that are longer than the joint you want to cover.

Not only does heat-shrink tubing make your robot guts look more professional, it also provides some short-circuit protection from wires touching during the inevitable spills, falls, and crashes.

Adding Connectors

It would be possible to solder the motors directly to the line-following circuit board. However, this would make it difficult to assemble and disassemble the robot. Additionally, if a motor needs replacement or the motor is going to be borrowed by another robot (the horror!), the motor would need to be desoldered from the circuit board.

There is a better way. The motor wires can conclude in a connector, which you can then attach or detach from a board as necessary without soldering.

Molex KK Connectors

There is a huge variety of connectors available. I happen to be partial to Molex KK connectors. They're reasonably small, come in widths that allow from 2 to 15 pins, and are available to fit in standard 0.100-inch-spaced breadboard holes. Figure 22-12 shows a Molex KK housing being pushed into the matching Molex KK header on the circuit board.

Figure 22-12. Molex KK female housing (top) *connecting with male header* (bottom) *on the circuit board*

A Molex KK connector consists of three parts (see Figure 22-13). First, there's a male header, whose bottom portion is soldered to the circuit board. Then, there's a metal terminal that is crimped (bent around) onto stripped wire. The terminal with attached wire is slid into the last part, which is the plastic female housing.

There are a couple of variations to the housing. Choose the housing with polarized ribs and locking ramp. The polarized ribs are small rectangular ridges on the ends of the housing. These ribs prevent the housing from accidentally being inserted onto the header either facing backwards or shifted over a pin. The locking ramp on the housing clips into the header so that the connection is unlikely to vibrate loose or to fall off if turned upside down.

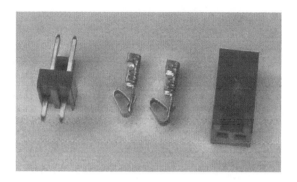

Figure 22-13. *A Molex KK 2-pin connector consists of:* (left to right) *2-pin male header, pair of terminals, and female housing*

A tool is necessary to force the metal terminal to wrap around and hold the wire for attachment (see Figure 22-14). You can use the crimp tool on a variety of connectors, not just the KK series.

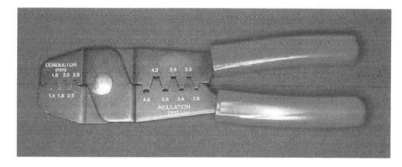

Figure 22-14. *Molex universal crimp tool (Molex #63811-1000)*

Note that the metal terminal is not soldered to the wire. It's pressed into a shape that embraces the wire. Interestingly, industrial strength motors or components that consume many amps of current can actually heat up solder enough to liquefy it. In those circumstances, crimped connections are the way to go.

Some builders do solder the terminal to the wire after crimping. Additionally, they add heat-shrink tubing to protect the terminal and keep it firmly in place in the housing. However, these steps are optional.

Obtaining Molex KK Equipment

In total, the line-following robot requires the following connector parts:

- 5 two-pin headers
- 5 two-pin housings
- 1 four-pin header

- 1 four-pin housing

- 14 terminals (but, get some extra)

- 1 crimp tool

In all cases, the headers and housings should be 0.100-inch center (2.54 mm). The housings should all have locking ramps and polarizing ribs.

When you add up the total cost per connection, connectors are not inexpensive. Table 22-2 lists a few suppliers of the necessary Molex KK equipment.

Table 22-2. Suppliers of Molex KK Equipment and Parts

Supplier	Part Number	Price	Description
Mouser	538-08-50-0114	$0.11	Terminal
Mouser	538-22-23-2021	$0.24	Two-Pin Straight Friction-Lock Header
Mouser	538-22-23-2041	$0.39	Four-Pin Straight Friction-Lock Header
Digi-Key	WM2000	$0.15	Two-Pin Housing with Locking Ramp and Polarizing Ribs
Mouser	538-22-01-3027	$0.15	Two-Pin Housing with Locking Ramp and Polarizing Ribs
Digi-Key	WM4200	$0.25	Two-Pin Straight Friction-Lock Header
Digi-Key	WM2002	$0.30	Four-Pin Housing with Locking Ramp and Polarizing Ribs
Mouser	538-22-01-3047	$0.29	Four-Pin Housing with Locking Ramp and Polarizing Ribs
Digi-Key	WM4202	$0.44	Four-Pin Straight Friction-Lock Header
Digi-Key	WM2200	$1.24	10-Pack Terminals
Jameco	304928	$47.95	Universal Crimp Tool
Digi-Key	WM9999	$50.75	Universal Crimp Tool

Attaching Molex KK Connectors to the Motors

The wires coming from the motors should already have about 0.35 cm of their plastic insulation stripped off, exposing bare wire.

1. There are two sets of "flaps" on the metal terminal. Insert the wire into the terminal so that the bare wire is located at the inner set of flaps and the insulated portion of wire is located at the flaps on the end (see Figure 22-15). This is so that one set of flaps will be crimped over the bare wire to make an electrical connection and the other set of flaps will be crimped over the plastic insulation to mechanically hold the wire securely.

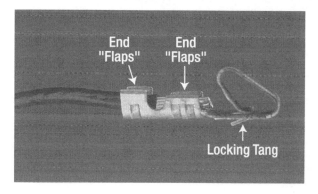

Figure 22-15. Wire inserted into terminal with plastic insulation in end flaps and bare wire in inner flaps

2. Carefully insert the wire and terminal into the 1.6 mm diameter slot of the crimp tool, so that only the flaps over the bare portion of the wire will be crimped (see Figure 22-16). The flaps should point toward the numbers printed on the crimp tool.

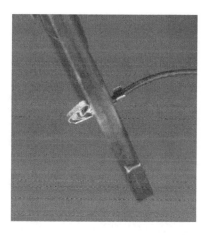

Figure 22-16. Crimping the inner set of flaps on the terminal onto the stripped portion of the motor wire, while the outer set of flaps remains open over the plastic insulated portion of the motor wire

3. Gently squeeze the crimp tool handles, causing the flaps to be curved over the stripped portion of the wire.

4. Remove the terminal and wire.

5. Insert the terminal and wire into the 1.8 mm diameter slot of the crimp tool, so that only the flaps over the insulated portion of the wire will be crimped. Again, the flaps should face toward the numbers. To do so, I need to flip the terminal upside down on my crimp tool.

6. Gently squeeze the crimp tool handles, causing the flaps to be curved over the insulated portion of the wire.

7. When complete, the terminal and wire should look like Figure 22-17. Because there are two sets of flaps being crimped over two thicknesses of wire, you have to crimp each set of flaps individually in different-size diameter slots of the crimp tool.

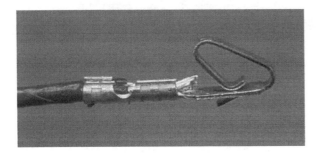

Figure 22-17. Two crimps attaching wire to terminal

8. Repeat the process to add terminals to all four wires on the pair of motors.

9. Insert the terminals into the housing with the loop facing the polarizing ribs (see Figure 22-18).

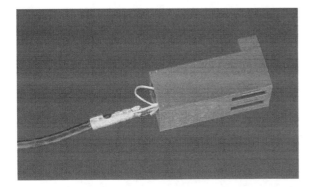

Figure 22-18. Terminal being inserted into KK housing

10. On the underside of the terminal is a tiny piece of metal bent outward, (not the big loop, but the fragment on the reverse side) called a locking tang. The tang snaps into an open window at the bottom of the housing. You'll hear a click when the terminal has been pushed all the way in, and the entire tang will be viewable in the housing's window.

Until the tang is completely visible, the terminal isn't fully seated in the housing. You can tug on the wire and pull it out. Without the locking tang in place against the housing window's shelf, the terminal and wire would be pushed out when the housing is connected to the header on the circuit board.

What happens if you discover you've accidentally inserted the wired terminals in a different arrangement than you soldered the header on your circuit board? With a tiny screwdriver, you can push against the tang in the window of the housing while simultaneously pulling on the wire (see Figure 22-19). The terminal and wire will slide back out. Afterwards, you'll need to bend the tang outward again in order for it to lock back in the housing.

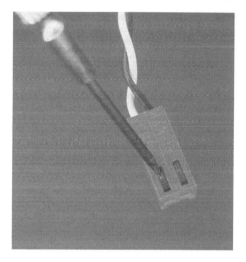

Figure 22-19. Pushing down on locking tang to remove terminal from housing

11. Insert the remaining wired terminals into their housings.

Facing the windows in the housing with the wires pointed downward, I choose to connect the negative wire from the motor on the left side, and the positive wire on the right. It doesn't matter so long as you're consistent with your circuit board and both motors.

12. Hold the motor in one hand and the connector housing in the other hand.

13. Twist the housing about ten times, so that the pair of wires twist together (see Figure 22-20). Not only does this prevent the wires from becoming tangled with other wires in the robot, but also it cancels out some of the electrical noise generated by the motors.

327

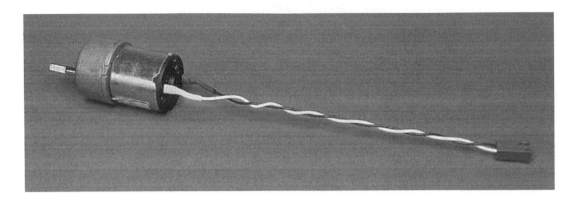

Figure 22-20. Motor with heat-shrink tubing protecting soldered terminals and twisted wire ending in KK connector

Congratulations, the motors are complete! The motors now have color-coded wires soldered to them, the terminals and solder joints are protected with plastic heat-shrink tubing, and the wire ends in a finger-friendly connector.

Putting Together the Line-Following Switch

The line-following switch was the only part of the circuit that wasn't prototyped on a solderless breadboard. This is because the switches available with the necessary switching characteristics have thick and widely spaced terminals that don't fit in a solderless breadboard.

The purpose of the line-following switch is to connect the motors to the transistors. In different switch positions, the motors will be hooked to different transistors, if at all.

When the switch is toggled to the center position, both motors are disconnected. This aids debugging and allows the robot to be placed on a starting line.

When the switch is toggled to the left position, the motors are connected in a straightforward manner, with the left motor connected to the left transistor and the right motor connected to the right transistor. This causes the left motor to activate whenever the left sensors detect brighter light.

When the switch is toggled to the right position, the motors are connected in the opposite way, with the left motor being connected to the right transistor and the right motor connected to the left transistor. This causes the left motor to activate whenever the right sensors detect brighter light.

The robot follows a dark line or a bright line based on whether the motors connect to the sensors on the same side or opposite side. Graphic details of this motion will be revealed in a later chapter.

Obtaining the Line-Following Switch

The line-following switch is a DPDT (double-pole double-throw) center-off toggle switch. Some suppliers list the switch as "on-off-on."

Don't purchase a switch for the line-following robot that has parentheses around one or more of the terms, such as "(on)-off-on." The parentheses indicate a momentary position returned to the center by a spring. That's beneficial for some projects, but, for this robot, you want the switch to stay in position even after your finger is removed.

The meaning of the "center off" term is obvious. The switch is turned off (no connections are made) when the switch is in the center position.

"Double pole" means that the switch can control two separate components at the same time. This is important, since the line-following robot has two motors that need to be controlled through the same switch.

"Double throw" means that each pole can be switched to make two different connections. This is important, since each motor needs to be connected to either the left transistor or the right transistor.

Table 22-3 lists suppliers of appropriate switches. However, sometimes it's better to see and feel a switch in person, before buying. The size, shape, and color of external switches define the look and feel of the robot. Pick a switch that is consistent with the style of your robot.

Table 22-3. Suppliers of Subminiature DPDT Center-Off Toggle Switches

Supplier	Part Number	Price
Jameco	21952	$1.55
Jameco	22841	$1.49
Jameco	317421	$2.49
Jameco	317490	$2.49
Electronix Express	17TOGDDC-M	$1.75
Digi-Key	EG2413-ND	$4.31

"Subminiature" refers to the approximate size of the switch. Even though it sounds small, you'll be surprised at how big subminiature really is.

Don't buy cheap or smaller (micro-miniature) switches. The plastic melts as you attempt to solder on the wires. You're left with a switch that either doesn't toggle at all or fails intermittently.

Preparing and Attaching the Switch Wires

Like the motors, the switch terminals need to have stranded wires soldered to them and then be covered with heat-shrink tubing (see Figure 22-21). Unlike the two-pin Molex connector attached to each motor, the switch ends in a four-pin Molex connector. The four pins are wired as follows: right motor, right transistor, left transistor, and left motor.

To make the wires more identifiable, use different colors. I chose yellow and green for the transistor outputs, which matches the LED colors. I chose white and red for the motors, since they're both receiving positive voltage.

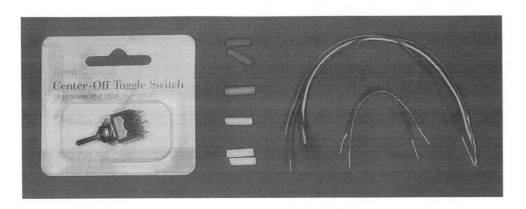

Figure 22-21. *DPDT center-off switch* (left), *heat-shrink tubing* (center), *and various lengths of wire* (right)

To make the wires fit into the small eyelets in the switch terminals, use thinner wire than was used with the motors. Instead of #22 AWG, I chose #26 AWG (bigger numbers indicate smaller wire) for the switch.

1. Cut four wires total (one each of white, yellow, green, and red) to a length of 15 cm.

2. Strip 0.75 cm of plastic insulation from one end of each wire.

3. Strip 0.35 cm of plastic insulation from the other end of each wire.

4. Cut two more wires (red and white) to a length of about 6 cm.

5. Strip 0.75 cm of plastic insulation from both ends of both 6 cm wires.

6. Cut one piece of yellow, one piece of green, two pieces of red, and two pieces of white heat shrink tubing (six pieces total) to a length of 1.5 cm.

Soldering the Line-Following Switch

A DPDT switch has six terminals: Three terminals for the first pole and three terminals for the second pole. Depending on the position of the switch, the center terminals can be switched to connect to the first terminals, no terminals, or the third terminals.

7. Loop the green wire through the eyelet in a center terminal, twist the wire together, and solder (see Figure 22-22). This is the same technique used to connect wires to the motors.

8. Loop the yellow wire through the eyelet in the other center terminal, twist the wire together, and solder.

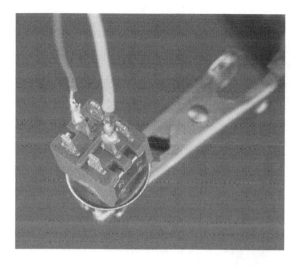

Figure 22-22. Left and right transistor outputs soldered to the switch's center terminals

The center terminals will have power rushing from the transistors to the motors. At the present time, since nothing is connected to the remaining switch terminals, the power doesn't reach the motors, so the robot won't move. The same thing occurs when the switch is in the center position: The switch doesn't internally connect the center terminals to either side terminals, thus the motors aren't connected to transistor power and the robot won't move.

9. Loop one end of the 6 cm red wire and one end of the 15 cm red wire together to the same terminal. You can pick any of the remaining terminals. I arbitrarily chose the lower right terminal in Figure 22-23. Twist together and solder.

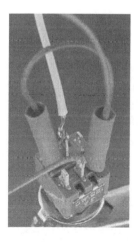

Figure 22-23. Diagonal side terminals covered in heat-shrink tubing and connected to left motor

Got it? You have two red wires, one long and one short, connecting to the same terminal.

10. Slide both pieces of red heat-shrink tubing over the pair of red wires.

11. Loop, twist, and solder the other end of the 6 cm red wire to the terminal on the diagonal across the switch.

If one neglects to slide the heat-shrink tubing onto the red wires in step 10, the tubing can't be added after step 11 because both ends of the short wire will be soldered to the switch.

Figure 22-23 shows the state of the switch as of completing step 11. The yellow and green wires are soldered to the center terminals. Two red wires are soldered to the lower right terminal of the switch and are covered by a piece of heat-shrink tubing. The other end of the shorter red wire is soldered to the terminal diagonally opposite it, and covered in heat-shrink tubing.

Reasoning Behind the Diagonal Cross Over

Let's say the 15 cm red wire is connected to the left motor. It's very important that the red wire leading to the left motor is connected to opposite terminals on each pole (the diagonal crossover).

Here's why: Electricity flows into the green wire from the left transistor. When the switch is toggled in one direction, the green and red wires are electrically connected and power from the left transistor flows into the left motor. When the switch is toggled in the other direction, the yellow and red wires are electrically connected, and power from the right transistor flows into the left motor.

If the two red wires were connected to each terminal on the same pole, then the left motor would always be connected to the left transistor no matter whether the switch were toggled left or right.

If the two red wires were connected to each terminal on the same side of the switch, then the left motor would be connected or disconnected to both left and right transistors at the same time.

The crossover forces each motor to be connected to only one transistor at a time and the opposite transistor when the switch is flipped. If none of this makes sense, just trust me and follow the directions.

Finishing Soldering the Line-Following Switch

Follow the same steps with the white wire and the two remaining terminals. That is:

12. Loop one end of the 6 cm white wire and one end of the 15 cm white wire together to the same terminal. You can pick any of the remaining terminals. I arbitrarily chose the upper right terminal as it appears in Figure 22-23. Twist together and solder.

13. Slide both pieces of white heat-shrink tubing over the pair of white wires now soldered to the switch.

14. Loop, twist, and solder the other end of the 6 cm white wire to the terminal on the diagonal across the switch.

All six terminals on the switch should now be wired (see Figure 22-24).

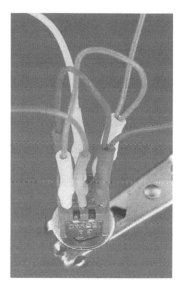

Figure 22-24. Finished switch with transistor outputs in center, left, and right motors connected to diagonally opposite terminals

You can test the arrangement by hooking a multimeter to either center wire and testing the continuity to the red and white wires while toggling the switch. Does the green wire connect to the white wire, off, and then red wire? Does the yellow wire connect to the red wire, off, and then the white wire?

15. Shrink the tubing in place using a hair dryer or heat gun.

16. Crimp Molex terminals onto all four of the switch wires.

17. Insert the terminals into the Molex KK four-pin housing.

Facing the windows in the housing with the wires pointed downward, I choose to connect the wires in the following left-to-right order: white wire (right motor), yellow wire (right transistor), green wire (left transistor), and red wire (left motor). It doesn't matter so long as you're consistent with those connections on your line-following circuit board.

The switch is complete.

Putting Together the Tube LED Circuit

The headlights and left/right brightness-indicator LEDs light up when the robot's power switch is turned on. So, there isn't really a need for a power indicator light. However, the plastic tube connecting the motors gave me an idea.

There is diverse assortment of colors of mini M&M candy tubes available. Sandwich has a yellow tube. By tossing a couple of red LEDs in the center of the tube, it's dull yellow when power is off but glows red whenever power is on (see Figure 22-25). It looks magnificent!

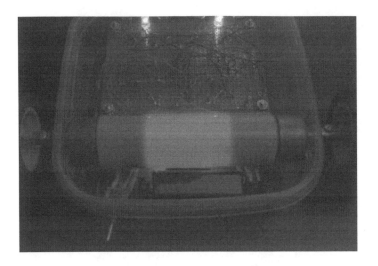

Figure 22-25. *Glowing center tube*

Examining the Tube LED Circuit Schematic

You can skip the tube-glowing circuit if you want, since it's purely for aesthetics. However, the schematic in Figure 22-26 shows how easy it is to make.

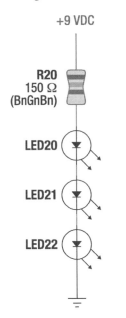

Figure 22-26. *Schematic of the tube LED circuit*

The LED colors aren't listed on the schematic, but you'll want to select an LED color that contrasts with the color of the plastic tube you choose. Choose the highest-brightness LEDs you can find because the opaque plastic of the tube absorbs much of the light. Wide-angle LEDs are desirable, as they'll light the tube evenly rather than having a few obvious bright-spots.

Building the Tube LED Circuit

The resistor and LEDs chain together in a column. Considering that, and the small number of parts, you can solder the circuit together without a circuit board. See Figure 22-27 for an example.

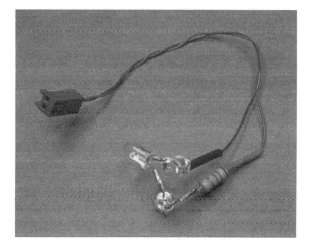

Figure 22-27. Tube LED circuit implemented with three LEDs and a 150 Ω resistor soldered to a Molex KK connector

Try to solder the LEDs facing different directions, so the light won't be focused on a single spot within the tube.

There is a possibility of the component leads accidentally touching each other in their scrunched-up state within the tube. To avoid that, cover the exposed joints with heat-shrink tubing. At the very least, cover the joint that connects the resistor to positive voltage. That way, even if a short circuit occurs down the line, power must always pass through the resistor.

Finishing Up

Besides the main circuit board, only a couple of components remain to be completed. The 9 V battery snap doesn't require soldering, only a Molex connector needs be crimped on the end.

Obtaining the Power Switch

The power switch is as easy to prepare as the motor: Solder two wires, cover with heat-shrink tubing, add a Molex connecter, and twist the wires together.

Because of the relatively low voltage and current consumed by the robot, almost any type of switch will do. Most power switches are rated at several amps (A) and 125 VAC or 250 VAC. That's more than rugged enough to handle 0.5 A at 9 VDC.

If you want an illuminated power switch, be sure the built-in light's voltage is appropriate for the robot. If the voltage rating is too high, it'll just waste the low-level DC power it receives without providing sufficient light. If the voltage rating is too low, the bulb will pop. Maybe it's better to avoid an illuminated power switch.

It's worth selecting a switch in person rather than through a catalog so you can find one that looks cool and feels good. Table 22-4 shows the part numbers of some power switches that fit nicely with Sandwich's body.

Table 22-4. Attractive Power Switches for Sandwich

Supplier	Part Number	Price	Description
Mouser	612-RR3130A	$2.79	SPST Rocker Switch Black
Digi-Key	EG4564	$3.48	SPST Rocker Switch Black
Digi-Key	EG1889	$3.48	SPST Rocker Switch Black w/Markings
Mouser	612-RR3402A	$2.48	SPST Paddle Switch Black
Digi-Key	EG1892	$3.09	SPST Paddle Switch Black

Assuming you are going to mount the power switch inside of a plastic sandwich container instead of soldering it to a board, be sure to purchase a panel mount switch that has threads and a nut (see Figure 22-28). All of the switches in Tables 22-3 and 22-4 meet those criteria. Avoid a "snap in" style switch, as they are designed for a rigid structure (usually metal) of a specific thickness.

Figure 22-28. Rocker switch (left) *and paddle switch* (center) *with threads and nut. Avoid "snap in" style switches* (right) *for Sandwich.*

Soldering Experience

Review Figure 22-1 (presented at the beginning of this chapter). Make sure that you've finished each item and that your finished parts look similar to those in the photograph.

Hopefully, learning to solder has been a positive experience for you. Soldering is a powerful skill with which you can create a whole new class of robot circuits. With practice, not only will you produce better joints, but also you'll gain an intuitive sense for when a joint isn't quite right.

Including connectors in your arsenal of robot parts complements soldered connections. The time spent in crimping pays off tenfold in serviceability. As your robots grow in complexity, connectors lend themselves to modularity. You'll begin designing parts that you can swap between robots.

The main circuit board awaits you as your next soldering challenge. After all, you need something to connect to all of those parts.

■ ■ ■

CHAPTER 23

The Motherboard

Throughout the book, you've slowly been building and testing a line-following circuit on a solderless breadboard. That's a good way of designing and proving a circuit, because there's no reason to solder something together until it appears to be functional.

Some builders attach their solderless breadboard to a mobile platform and pronounce their robot complete. Unfortunately, the vibrations and handling can cause the wires and components to slip out of the holes, either intermittently or completely. Ultimately, the robot functions poorly (if at all) and has a limited lifespan.

In this chapter, you'll transfer your line-following circuit to a board and solder it all together. Don't attempt this until you've finished soldering the parts in the prior chapter, as you'll perform better with some experience.

The Line-Following Circuit

The final line-following circuit is presented as a wiring diagram in Figure 23-1.

Figure 23-1. (next page) *Wiring diagram of the final line-following circuit.*

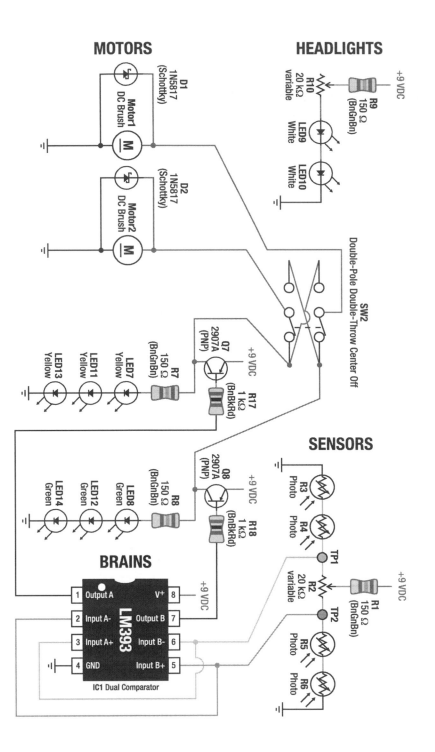

The final line-following circuit consists of identifiable modules of circuits from prior chapters.

- The sensor module is the balanced brightness-sensing circuit

- The headlight module is the headlight circuit

- The brains and LEDs modules are the brightness comparator circuit with transistors

- The motor module is the motor and Schottky diode circuit

A couple of minor changes were made to make the robot "kit friendly" or "production friendly:"

1. Two 470 Ω resistors (R1 and R9) were replaced with 150 Ω resistors to make it less complicated for someone to offer this line-following robot as a kit. Now, only 1 kΩ and 150 Ω resistors are in the circuit. The reduction in values shouldn't pose a problem, since the resistor values are still large enough to limit current extremes.

■ **Note** Recall that resistor value selection can be an art. Earlier in the book you had to choose a resistor value that either leaned toward making an LED brighter with shorter battery life, or saved power but made the LED dimmer.

The change presented in Figure 23-1 represents another potential resistor value selection methodology: You can consolidate on common values in a design so that components can be purchased in bulk. Schools or companies producing multiple copies (or kits) of this robot can save money by purchasing greater quantities of just a few resistor values, rather than lesser quantities of many resistor values. Additionally, the person assembling the robot has fewer opportunities to insert the wrong value resistor, because there are fewer resistor values from which to choose.

---

2. A 20 kΩ variable resistor (R10) has been added to the headlights to allow their brightness to be adjustable on the robot. The value of 20 kΩ was chosen so that R10 and R2 are matching parts. Again, this makes it "kit friendly." However, because you are unlikely to ever dial down the headlights to be that dim, a 2 kΩ value would have been preferable if not for the kit advantages.

Feel free to test these modifications on your solderless breadboard before committing them to a soldered circuit.

Tweaking For Better Performance

Before we continue, let's discuss the opposite strategy for selecting resistor values for R1 and R9. Instead of designing for a kit, what optimal values should you select if you want to tailor the resistors for the unique components sitting in front of you now?

You would want to find a value for R9 that permits your headlight LEDs to be as bright as safely possible and select a value for R1 that is correlated with your sensors. These customizations help ensure that the sensor voltages for your specific robot are in the range that IC1 can compare. That means your robot will be able to accurately follow a line at faster speeds.

Because different types of white LEDs vary significantly in voltage drop and brightness, and because cadmium-sulfide sensors vary significantly even in the same batch, there is no way to select a "perfect" value in a book. Yet, the kit values work just fine for most people.

If you want to try to determine the best value for your white LEDs, set up the headlight portion of the circuit in Figure 23-1 on a solderless breadboard (you don't need the other parts of the circuit for these tests). Then, proceed as follows:

1. Temporarily replace R9 with a low resistance, say 40 Ω to 50 Ω.

2. Dial R10 to any value over 200 Ω.

3. Insert a multimeter in mA mode between R10 and LED9. That is, R10 and LED9 should NOT be connected together. The multimeter's red lead should be in the mA socket and it should attach to the bottom of R10. The black lead should be in the COM socket and should attach to the top of LED9. Electricity has no choice but to pass through the bottom of R10, into the multimeter to be counted, and out to the top of LED9.

4. Apply power from a **fresh** battery (usually near 9.6 V). You're trying to find the absolute maximum brightness.

5. Carefully adjust the dial on R10 until the meter reads 30 mA. The dangerous thing about this is that R10 could accidently get adjusted to zero ohms, and with R9 so low, the battery could fry the LEDs. Therefore, adjust the dial very slowly.

6. Disconnect power from the circuit.

7. Remove the multimeter and attach the bottom of R10 to the top of LED9. They are now reconnected like it shows in the schematic.

8. Change the multimeter to resistance mode. The red lead should be in the Ω socket and the black lead in COM.

9. Connect the multimeter's red lead to the top of R9 and the black lead to the bottom of R10. This measures the combined resistance of R9 and R10. That's the final value you want to use for your robot's R9.

Using the white LEDs in the Solarbotics kit, and adjusting R10 until 30 mA flowed through them, I measured the resistance for R9 and R10 to be 106 Ω. That's close enough that I'll use a 100 Ω resistor for R9. Now, if the robot struggles to follow a line, I can adjust the headlights to be significantly brighter with a 100 Ω resistance, instead of 150 Ω resistance.

The second optimization, choosing a value for R1, is almost all mathematical.

1. One at a time, measure the resistance of your cadmium-sulfide sensors under a desk or in a relatively dark place. Don't completely cover them up. You want an idea for the maximum resistance when they are looking at a black line or black surface.

2. Assuming you're going to evenly distribute the sensors, calculate the "dark" values of each pair. My examples were 150 kΩ, 500 kΩ, 400 kΩ, and 550 kΩ. So, 550 kΩ is the maximum. I'd pair 150 kΩ with 550 kΩ = 700 kΩ, and 500 kΩ with 400 kΩ = 900 kΩ

3. Now use this formula: R1 = ((pair1 * pair2) / (pair1 + pair2) - (R2 / 2)) * 0.25. This calculates the resistance of the sensors in parallel, minus the resistance of the potentiometer for one of the sensor branches, with an approximate percentage that would provide the comparator's required top-end 1.5 V when the battery is almost exhausted (7 V). For my example: R1 = ((700 kΩ * 900 kΩ) / (700 kΩ + 900 kΩ) - (20 kΩ / 2)) * 0.25 = 96 kΩ.

Wow! 96000 Ω is much greater than the book's default 150 Ω. Remember, this proposed change is to handle the extreme case where all of the sensors are looking at a dark surface. Usually, at least one of the sensors sees a bright line. The potentiometer resistance provides more than enough voltage drop during normal operation. If you're at all concerned about making such a major change, particularly given that it may alter the normal performance, you have some choices:

- Leave R1 with the 150 Ω resistor. You can always turn up the headlight brightness.

- Compromise and install 10 kΩ. (Probably the best choice.)

- Install a 100 kΩ resistor but be prepared to solder a 10 kΩ or smaller value resistor on top of it. This trick works because electricity is lazy. It will take the less-resistant path. (You'll end up with a total resistance of around 9 kΩ.)

- Leave the 150 Ω resistor and replace the LM393 comparator with a LMC6772BIN comparator (Digi-Key $2.60). The LMC6772 can compare voltages over the entire range, and thus won't be affected if the sensors all see darkness.

Point-to-Point Soldering Versus a Printed Circuit Board

At this point, you have built and tested the line-following circuit on a **solderless** breadboard with either the default or custom values. There are several methods of creating a **soldered** circuit. You can obtain a blank, solderable breadboard (see left side of Figure 23-2), insert the components, and solder wires from each component lead to the other. This is called point-to-point soldering.

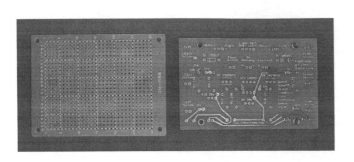

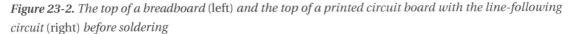

Figure 23-2. The top of a breadboard (left) *and the top of a printed circuit board with the line-following circuit* (right) *before soldering*

The other method is to obtain (or make) a printed circuit board (PCB, see right side of Figure 23-2) where all the wiring is built onto the surface of the board. In that case, the parts need only be inserted into the correct holes and soldered into place.

Point-to-point soldering is faster and cheaper for one-time small circuits. After all, there's up-front effort required to design and etch a printed circuit board yourself. Also, since ordinary wires in a point-to-point board connect all of the parts, you can arrange (or fix) the circuit somewhat more easily by desoldering and resoldering the wires.

Obviously, buying a pre-printed circuit board with the line-following circuit is much easier and faster. There's a lot less soldering to do. Not only that, but if the circuit has been previously verified as being correct on the board, then you don't have to be concerned about miswiring the circuit.

Looking at the end results, there are a couple of other factors that make printed circuit boards better than point-to-point-soldered circuits. As illustrated in Figure 23-3, the point-to-point circuit (on the left) is much messier, takes up more space, and is more likely to fail (due to loose wires) than is the printed circuit (on the right).

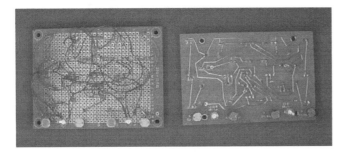

Figure 23-3. Underside of breadboard showing point-to-point wiring (left) *and printed circuit board* (right) *after soldering*

I've created the line-following robot both ways: with point-to-point soldering and with a printed circuit board. Because there aren't an overwhelming number of connections and because you can build the board up in modules, any beginner should be able to create the circuit using point-to-point soldering. Point-to-point instructions follow in the next sections of this chapter.

However, I highly recommend purchasing a printed circuit board with the line-following circuit from Solarbotics (#SandPCB $12), even if you don't buy the full kit. This will save you soldering, frustration, and debugging, so that you can more quickly reach the goal of experimenting with your finished robot. It's not cheating to use a PCB since you've already built the circuit on a solderless breadboard. It's an optimization of your time.

Instructions for stuffing the ready-made PCB are posted at http://www.robotroom.com/SandwichPCB.html

Point-to-Point Soldering the Line-Following Circuit

Soldering the line-following circuit is the most arduous part of building Sandwich. But, the soldering practice you've had with the motors and switches should help a lot. Be patient.

If possible, obtain a second set of parts so that the original parts from the tested circuit can remain on the solderless breadboard. The line-following circuit components should cost less than $10.

1. If you're not buying the PCB, obtain a **perforated** breadboard (also called perf board, stripboard, or prototyping board) that is approximately 7 cm (or less) by 10 cm (or less), with 700 or more holes spaced at 0.100 of an inch. Each hole should have copper plating around it. Examples are: All Electronics #PC-4 $2.00 or WrightHobbies.net #expboard2 $2.49.

Laying Out the Line-Following Circuit Components

A grid-style solderable breadboard is more freeform than a solderless breadboard. You can change the positions of components considerably from the rigid 5-position groups imposed by the solderless breadboard. Since the robot is going to be stuck with whatever arrangement you solder together, take some time to carefully plan the positions of the components.

Placing Components with a Helping Hand

2. Place the board on a Helping Hand tool (see Figure 23-4).

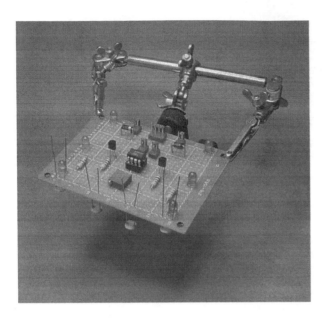

Figure 23-4. Helping Hands makes laying out a circuit board much easier

3. **Highly Recommended:** Test components with a multimeter before placing them on the breadboard. This gives you a sense of confidence in their quality and values before permanently soldering them in place. At the very least, measure the trimpots and center them to their middle resistance.

■ **Note** After being soldered into a circuit, it isn't always possible to accurately measure the resistance or diode test the individual components using a multimeter. This is due to the fact that the components to which they are connected may loop back electricity to the opposite multimeter test probe, thus skewing values.

---

4. Lay out the components onto the breadboard (see Figure 23-5). Try to place components so that they are nearest the other components to which they will connect. This reduces the length of the wires and reduces the number of wires that cross over each other.

Example Layout

A suggested layout appears in Figure 23-5. Notice that the LEDs are distributed on the far sides to increase visibility. The comparator is in the center flanked by transistors because the comparator connects to the greatest number of components. The brightness balancing and headlight brightness-adjusting trimpots are far forward to make them easy to reach from the front of the robot.

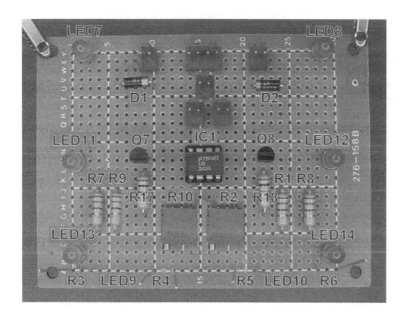

Figure 23-5. *Breadboard with line-following circuit laid out. R3, R4, R5, R6, LED9, and LED10 are on the underside of the board.*

All of the Molex connector headers are located at the rear of the board. This makes sense since all of the switches, motors, and other parts are at the back of the robot body. The locking ramp of each header faces away from the center of the board to provide strain relief and help retain the connector in place if the wires are pulled away from the board.

Obtaining an IC Socket

Use an IC socket (see Figure 23-6) instead of soldering the comparator chip directly to the circuit board. That way, the comparator is spared the heat and abuse of the soldering process. Also, you can substitute a more capable or advanced comparator (such as the TLC393, TLC372, TLV3402, or the LMC6772) in the circuit, as long as the new comparator is pin-compatible with the LM393.

Figure 23-6. *8-pin DIP IC socket to allow chip removal*

Notice the notch on one side of the DIP (dual inline package) socket. This corresponds to the notch in the chip to indicate the direction in which the chip should be aligned. Table 23-1 lists suppliers of 8-pin DIP IC sockets.

Table 23-1. *Suppliers of 8-Pin DIP IC Sockets*

Supplier	Part Number	Price	Description
Jameco	51571	$1.20	10 Per Package, Single Wipe
Jameco	112206	$1.30	10 Per Package, Dual Wipe
Electronix Express	ICL08	$0.10	Low Profile
Digi-Key	3M5473	$0.18	Dual Wipe
Solarbotics	DC-8 Pin	$0.25	Dual Wipe
Jameco	105620	$6.95	100 Assorted (may or may not have 8-pin)
Jameco	135386	$14.95	1-Pound Grab Bag Assorted (may or may not have 8-pin)

Keeping the Components on the Board During Soldering

After all the work you've invested in carefully laying out the components on the breadboard, you don't want the parts spilling out when you turn the board upside down for soldering. Here are a couple of common techniques to prevent that.

Gluing the Molex KK Headers to the Circuit Board

The pins of Molex KK headers are slightly loose in the holes of standard breadboards. When the board is turned over for soldering, the Molex headers slip out slightly or even fall out completely. (This won't occur with appropriately sized holes of custom PCBs.) It is very important that the headers are soldered completely flat against the board, otherwise they may wiggle or rip out when attempting to make a connection to the housing.

5. With a disposable toothpick, apply a bit of adhesive to the edges (not the metal leads) of the Molex headers (see Figure 23-7). This will keep them fully seated on the board during soldering.

Figure 23-7. Adhesive being applied to edges of Molex connnector

I prefer clear silicone adhesive for gluing components to circuit boards (see Figure 23-8). Many adhesives simply don't stick well to the resin circuit board substrate. Silicone adhesive is a tacky gel, so it's easy to apply exactly where you want it, it stays put, and keeps the part from sliding around too much before it is dry. Actually, because silicone adhesive doesn't dry instantly, you can still shift or nudge the part if your initial placement wasn't accurate.

Additionally, silicone adhesive can stand high temperatures, which is a good idea for anything that holds a part to be soldered. Silicone adhesive dries to a rubbery consistency, so you can peel it off if the component needs to be desoldered.

6. Reinsert the headers into the desired location on the board.

7. Let the adhesive dry for five minutes (or whatever time period is instructed on the package). Don't solder around adhesives that may still be expelling fumes or that are listed as flammable!

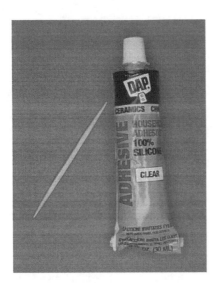

Figure 23-8. *DAP clear silicone adhesive with a toothpick for applying*

Bending Component Leads

Fortunately, most component leads are much more pliable than the rigid metal pins of connectors. Leads can be bent to hold the component in place so you don't need to glue them.

8. Carefully bend the component leads toward the back of the board so that the components won't fall out during soldering (see Figure 23-9). Bend the leads only as much as necessary to keep the components in place during soldering; don't bend the leads completely flat against the board. Solder tends to wick under the flattened leads and contact other pads or components. Also, it's more difficult to trim off excess length of flattened leads.

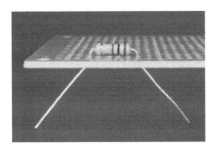

Figure 23-9. *Side view of a breadboard with a component's leads bent slightly to hold it in place during soldering*

However, with long leads or nearby components, sometimes you can bend a lead enough to reach the lead to which it needs to be soldered. Of course, then you don't gain the protection of the plastic insulation that a wire would provide.

Creating Power Distribution Buses

Most solderless breadboards have long rows at the top and the bottom to distribute positive and negative voltage to locations near all of the components. Although some solderable breadboards have these buses built on the board surface with copper traces, many breadboards do not.

In any case, it's not hard to make your own power distribution buses. What's more, you're free to design the placement, length, and pattern of these buses yourself.

9. Obtain some #22 AWG bare wire. You can always strip off the plastic insulation from wire you already have. However, it's faster and cleaner to obtain a spool of the bare stuff. Figure 23-10 shows some uninsulated copper wire that has a thin coating of tin to improve solderability.

Figure 23-10. Spool of #22 AWG bare (no plastic insulation) tin-coated copper wire

10. Loop some bare wire starting at the positive pin on the Molex header that receives power from the power switch (see Figure 23-11). This bare wire is the beginning of the positive distribution bus.

Figure 23-11. Bare wire shaped to connect to underside of Molex KK connector

11. Loop the bare wire up to the top of the board and back down again (see left side of Figure 23-12). Not only does this provide a mechanically strong starting point for the bus wire, but also makes a nice little loop that is perfect for hooking a multimeter probe.

Figure 23-12. Loops atop breadboard to allow attachment of multimeter IC hook probe tips for positive voltage (left) *and negative voltage* (right)

12. Back on the underside, make a long stretch with the bare wire (see Figure 23-13) and solder in place.

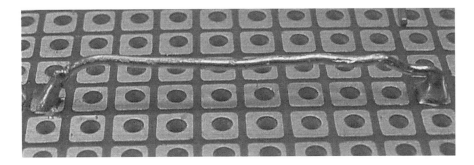

Figure 23-13. Underside of breadboard showing long bare wire to provide a distribution bus that can accommodate many connections of wire

13. Now, whenever a module circuit needs access to positive power, simply solder a wire to the bare wire that forms the positive-voltage distribution bus (see Figure 23-14).

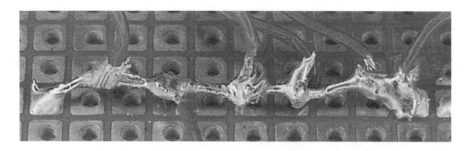

Figure 23-14. *Positive-voltage distribution bus on which many wires are soldered*

> 14. Repeat the same technique to form a negative-voltage distribution bus.

Soldering the Remaining Components

The components are laid out on the breadboard and held in place. A positive and negative distribution bus is now available, just as it is on the solderless breadboard. All that remains is to connect the components together, using the solderless breadboard as a model and checking the wiring diagram as necessary.

> 15. Working on a module at a time, pick a component lead and determine where it needs to be connected.
>
> 16. Determine the approximate distance of the connection and cut a piece of stranded, insulated wire to the desired length, plus some extra length for slack. Any wire diameter from #22 AWG to #26 AWG is acceptable, although I prefer thinner (#26) wire.
>
> 17. Strip a bit of insulation from both ends of the wire.
>
> 18. Wrap one end of the wire around the component lead. Alternatively, sometimes you can stuff the end of the wire into the same hole as the component, providing some mechanical strength and lots of electrical contact. Either way, make sure the joint to be soldered has plenty of bare metal exposed for both the wire and the component lead.
>
> 19. Solder the joint.
>
> 20. Repeat steps 18 and 19 for the other end of the wire.
>
> 21. Slowly, but surely, make your way through each circuit module and solder every component. Take breaks as needed.

Soldering the Cadmium-Sulfide Photoresistors

Before soldering the photoresistors, it's beneficial to paint their backs with black paint. The thick, dark paint prevents direct light from the headlights from leaking from behind and affecting the sensor readings.

Testors Flat Black Enamel #1149 works well (see left side of Figure 23-15). Alternatively, instead of using black paint with a paintbrush, try a black paint marker. They're easier to guide, which reduces the chances of accidental brush strokes on the face of the sensor. You can find paint markers at local hardware stores or McMaster-Carr (part #16625T25, 3mm black paint marker, $3.53).

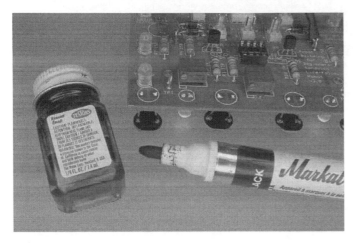

Figure 23-15. Black paint (left and bottom) *and photocells raised 12 mm from circuit board surface* (top right)

When installed in the robot's body, the circuit board is about 20 mm above the floor, so the photoresistor and headlight LED leads need to be trimmed short. After soldering, their tips should be about 12 mm from the circuit board surface (see top-right side of Figure 23-15). At the very least, try to keep all of the photoresistors at the same level.

Trimming Leads with Wire Snips

After everything is soldered, use a pair of wire cutters to trim the excess leads from the board. Long leads are likely to catch or tangle, and can accidentally touch other long leads, which causes circuit failure. Be sure to wear safety goggles during lead trimming!

Cleaning the Board

Depending on the flux in the solder you used, it may need to be cleaned from the board. No-clean flux and many of the newer rosin fluxes don't require cleaning. Read the product label or check with the manufacturer.

Specialty flux cleaning solutions are available if you really want to remove the flux.

Testing the Robot's Electronics

When everything has been soldered, you may be tempted to immediately install a battery to see the fruits of your labors. However, there are a couple of simple tests you should perform first that may save your battery and circuit board from damage.

The Dangers of a Low-Resistance Circuit

If you accidentally soldered a positive wire to a negative wire, electricity would rush from the positive terminal of the battery, through the shorted connection, to the negative terminal of the battery. The remainder of the circuit won't receive any current because electricity always takes the short path (direct positive to negative). In that case, the robot won't do anything.

It's also possible to have a bad (or missing) part or partially shorted circuit, where one path in the circuit has a very low resistance. In that case, a current-sensitive component, like an LED or chip, may not be getting the protection it was supposed to be receiving from a resistor.

In any case, a shorted or very low resistance in a circuit consumes battery power quickly and generates excessive heat. The heat is likely to damage components on the board, and finding the newly damaged parts can be difficult.

Checking for Unsoldered Leads

Examine each part to ensure that it has been wired to something. A two-lead part with only one end hooked-up indicates something is amiss. Every pin and every lead in Sandwich's circuit should be connected to a bus or another part.

Checking All Leads that Connect Directly to Positive Voltage

Electricity needs a path from the positive battery terminal to the negative battery terminal in order to flow. By examining all the connections made to positive voltage, you can be sure that each of the paths starts out correctly.

Begin with the 9 V battery. Make sure that the red wire from the battery snap is hooked up to the positive pin on the Molex connector. The positive pin on the Molex connector should be wired only to the power switch connector. That is, power from the battery should not be allowed to enter the circuit unless it first passes through the power switch.

Note When the power switch is off, absolutely no current can flow from the battery because nothing else but the power switch is connected to the battery's positive terminal. Therefore, the robot doesn't consume any power at all when the power switch is off. It's as though the battery weren't installed.

Even so, it's a good idea to remove the battery if the robot is going to be stored for long periods of time. Aging batteries can leak corrosive chemicals.

The other pin of the power switch's Molex connector should be wired to the positive voltage bus. Double-check all wires connected to the positive voltage bus. Most of them should be going to resistors. In Sandwich's circuit, the exceptions are the collector pins on two transistors and pin 8 on the comparator IC. Everything else runs through resistors.

Measuring the Resistance of the Entire Circuit

After completing the visual inspection, here are a few quick multimeter tests that can spot some problems.

Note: Toward the end of the book, I recommend the addition of a diode between the power switch and the rest of the circuit that protects against damage from a battery installed backwards. The resistance tests described in this section won't work through the diode. So, if you choose to include the diode, you'll need to temporarily install a wire (alligator or hook jumper) to both ends of the diode so that the multimeter power can skip around it during resistance testing.

Measuring the Power Off Resistance

1. Attach all of the parts that have Molex connectors to the finished circuit board (see Figure 23-16). That means the motors, power switch, battery snap (without battery), line-following switch, and tube LEDs (if desired) should now be connected to the circuit board.

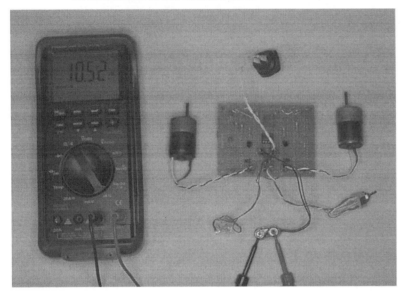

Figure 23-16. Testing resistance of circuit through 9 V battery snap connector

2. Connect the multimeter's test probes to the positive and negative snaps of the battery connector (it helps to use alligator clips or IC hooks). Note that the battery is not installed! The multimeter is pretending to be the battery.

3. Dial the multimeter to measure resistance (Ω).

4. Turn on the multimeter.

5. Toggle the robot's power switch back and forth. In one direction, the resistance should be infinite. That's power off.

If you don't get an infinite resistance in either switch position, something is wrong with the power switch or its connections. Recall that in an off state, the positive entrance to the circuit is completely disconnected, thus the infinite resistance to electricity trying to enter the circuit.

Measuring the Power On Resistance

6. Toggle the robot's power switch to the power on position.

7. The resistance should be between 5 kΩ and 50 kΩ.

A value of infinity, with the power switch on, suggests a wire is missing or broken between the battery, power switch, and either power bus.

A value below 1 kΩ suggests a partial short circuit or bad component. Then again, a trimpot could be dialed to a minimum value.

Anything below 10 Ω indicates a serious short circuit! If you find that's the case, absolutely do **not** connect the robot to a battery. Trace each circuit and wire to find the cause. Switching the multimeter to continuity mode and touching the test probes between stretches of components can help find the problem.

Measuring the Sensor Resistance

8. Cover the photoresistors with your hand. The resistance of the circuit should be quite high. Sandwich measures 45 kΩ.

9. Expose the photoresistors to light. The resistance of the circuit should be lower. Sandwich measures about 5 kΩ when held against a light bulb.

If the resistance doesn't vary with the amount of light the photoresistors are receiving, then the sensor circuit isn't correctly wired to the positive and negative bus. Or, maybe there's a bad solder joint somewhere in the sensor circuit.

Measuring the Voltage Drop

There are some semiconductors in the circuit that won't pass significant current until the voltage from the meter exceeds 0.5 volts or better.

10. With the meter test probes still connected to the battery snap, switch the multimeter dial to diode mode.

11. When the robot's power switch is in the off position, the meter should display "open" or "infinity."

If the meter indicates that any voltage is being dropped through the circuit when the robot's power switch is in the off position, that should warn you that the power switch isn't completely disconnecting the robot's circuit from positive voltage. It is not safe to connect the circuit to a battery until you're sure that the power switch works.

12. When the robot's power switch is in the on position, the voltage coming from the multimeter should be high enough to cause diodes, chips, and transistors to conduct. For Sandwich, the multimeter displays "good" or 0.742 V.

Your meter may give slightly different readings, but there should be a noticeable change from the robot's power off switch position. In diode test mode with the switch in the on position, anything above 1.6 V or below 0.4 V is suspect.

Reheating Solder Joints

If at some point during testing you discover a weak or loose solder joint, it might be worth briefly reheating all of the solder joints on the board to ensure they're completely bonded. You probably don't need any more solder, just touch the soldering iron tip to each joint until it melts completely. That should cause the solder to flow through and coat the joint.

Unlike wire stripping, wire attachment, and soldering, the reheating process is fairly quick. Five minutes spent guaranteeing clean joints saves a lot of frustration in debugging.

■ **Caution** Never solder or reheat joints when a circuit is powered on. The combination of heat from the soldering iron and heat generated by electrical flow permanently melts apart the tiny bonds and leads within semiconductor component cases. Also, brief short circuits can result from the edge of a molten solder blob accidentally contacting multiple traces, leads, or wires.

Holding Your Breath

After the multimeter tests verify an acceptable resistance and voltage drop, it is finally time to connect the battery to the line-following circuit board. The power switch is in the off position, isn't it?

Power up and chant the mad scientist's creed, "It's alive! It's alive!"

If everything went well, you should be rewarded with a soldered circuit that performs as well as the circuit on the solderless breadboard. If not, follow the paths on the modules that aren't working. Is a component in backwards? Is a nasty solder joint spilling onto other wires or leads? Do the voltages at each point in each module on the soldered circuit match the voltages at each point in each module on the solderless breadboard?

The robot is nearing completion. All that remains is to build a body to protect the electronic guts and hold it all together.

CHAPTER 24

■ ■ ■

Body Building

A robot's body provides a framework to which you can attach various components and circuit boards. The body protects the robot's innards against battering damage as well as environmental harm. The body can make a robot convenient to carry and straightforward to store. Often overlooked as a consideration, the robot's body strikingly affects the way humans perceive the robot.

This chapter begins with some common approaches to developing robot bodies. The rest of the chapter explains how you can create a body like Sandwich's for your line-following robot.

Approaching Robot Bodies

Sometimes you'll run across a wonderful enclosure, container, or case that you feel you must build a robot around. In that case, you're done with body selection! However, most of the time you'll perform a careful, deliberate body-selection process. Often, form follows function.

Ethereal Drafting—Thinking About the Robot

When beginning a project, you'll probably have a basic idea of what you want the robot to accomplish. The work to be performed by the robot dictates the approximate quantity and complexity of the sensors, circuits, and motors.

At first, body designs are explored mentally. With infinitely strong, inexpensive, and moldable material, what would be the ultimate shell for the robot you have in mind? After many iterations of shapes are considered and discarded by the brain, the rough body figure (including width and height) and variety of the materials (metal and plastic) are subsequently constrained.

Sometimes rough sketches on napkins or on the reverse side of boring meeting agendas further focus the potential benefits or pitfalls of conceptual designs.

Vision Revision—Accepting Constraints Based on Available Parts

At some point, cold reality sets in. It's time to peruse the home-laboratory stockroom (junk pile) and read through catalogs to determine which parts are realistically attainable.

Available motors, wheels, and batteries tend to have the largest reductive impact on potential robot bodies. It's helpful to physically lay out all of the major parts, including candidate breadboards, and to rearrange them like puzzle pieces until a harmonious configuration emerges.

The width and mass of the motors play a significant role in the robot's shape. The selected motors specify the minimum battery voltage and current. The total mass and sizes of the motors and batteries combined suggest whether metal or plastic is required.

When you have a sense of the weight requirements and dimensions, the robot body's characteristics are clear enough that you can begin selecting materials and shapes that are likely to be sufficient. At this point, you can either build a custom body that approaches your particular vision or you can select from existing mass-produced bodies (whether designed for robots or not).

Designing Custom Bodies

The overriding philosophy of building a custom robot body is that the body is made to fit the robot, rather than the robot fitting the body. If you're a skilled or patient artisan with the proper tools and materials, a proud and capable robot will result.

Plastic Prototyping—Constructing Models with LEGO Bricks

LEGO bricks are God's gift to robot builders. Honestly, they're serious prototyping tools. Don't let a loved one knock you for playing with your LEGOs.

With LEGO bricks, robot designs can be invented, altered, refined, discarded, recovered, and ultimately born. LEGO bricks hold together well under light to moderate loads. They're readily available in a huge variety of shapes, colors, and sizes. Although moderately expensive, their reusability and time-saving qualities make them a worthwhile investment.

When first designing a robot for this book, I began with a pair of elegant Maxon motors and a pair of homemade aluminum couplers (like the ones described a couple of chapters ago). With a box of LEGO Technic bricks, gears, and tires, I established a basic frame (see Figure 24-1).

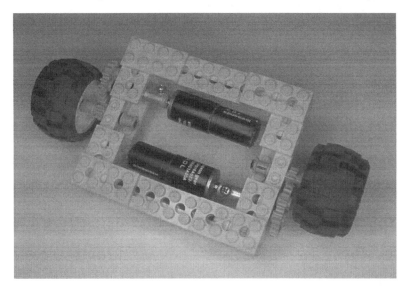

Figure 24-1. Prototype for Wavy, designed with LEGO bricks

Material Substitution—Transitioning Out LEGO Parts

Although LEGO frames can be instantly glued together with cyanoacrylate adhesive (super glue), it's more cost-effective to use materials other than LEGO bricks. Metals provide greater strength and give the robot a rugged look.

With a marking pen, I traced the LEGO frame onto a stock piece of aluminum. I then cut out the aluminum, sanded the edges, and drilled some screw holes (see Figure 24-2). This reduced the quantity of LEGO blocks to two side bars for wheel and gear alignment.

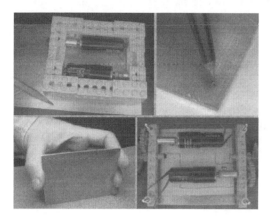

Figure 24-2. Preparing an aluminum base to replace much of the LEGO Technic frame

Origami Helper—Bending Paper Before Bending Metal

Here's a trick that works well for brackets, cowls, or other parts that you can form by bending a flat material. Begin by folding and cutting the piece out of paper. Paper is cheap, plentiful, and easy to cut and bend.

Wavy's motors needed to be firmly attached to the base; otherwise, the motors would spin in place instead of spinning the wheels. I cut and folded several test brackets out of paper until the shape was exactly what I needed (see Figure 24-3).

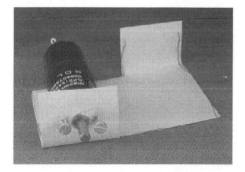

Figure 24-3. Design with folded paper before cutting complex metal shapes

Then, I flattened the paper and traced the outline onto a thin piece of aluminum. Because it takes a lot of time and effort to cut, drill, sand, and bend aluminum, it was reassuring to know that the approximate outcome had already been tested.

Embracing Prefabricated Platforms

Entirely custom bodies, built from the ground up, take a lot of work. You may not want to devote that much to the body of every robot you build. Sometimes it's more fun to concentrate on the electronics, software, assembly, or tweaking. There are reasonable alternatives to making your own body from scratch.

Commercially Available Robot Platforms

A decent selection of base platforms is readily available for robots. Some commercial platforms are made from metal and some from plastic. Most have plenty of screw holes, brackets, and wire passages built in. Some platforms come with motors and wheels; others are designed with compartments and spaces ready for those parts to be installed.

You can find ready-made robot platforms at most web sites that carry robot parts. Lynxmotion is a good source: http://www.lynxmotion.com/.

Converting and Recycling Everyday Items for Robot Bodies

Other sources for ready-made robot bodies are the toy store, hardware store, grocery store, and the recycling bin. You'll never look at packaging the same way again.

I purchased a couple sets of inexpensive plastic containers (see Figure 24-4) to store my mid-project robot parts away from curious little human hands (you know who you are). Late at night, it's easier to toss unfinished piles of electronics into a container rather than return every component to the organizers.

Figure 24-4. Various reusable/disposable containers

At some point, the motors and sensors for Wavy were serendipitously sitting almost in perfect robot position in the plastic container. It occurred to me that the container made a more protective, cheaper, more easily obtained, and less difficult-to-customize robot body than the aluminum body I had already constructed for Wavy.

And that's how a Ziploc container came to become Sandwich, the line-following robot.

Transforming the Sandwich Container

The following instructions are based on the out-of-production Ziploc 591 ml (2.5 cup, 20 fluid ounce) square reusable/disposable plastic container with lid. However, there are so many similar products that you may choose another container and still find the instructions applicable.

Creating Motor Holes

Let's begin by making the screw and shaft holes for the motors.

Marking and Determining Space Required By the Circuit Board

1. Lightly tape the breadboard or PCB you've chosen to the inside of the container. Make sure to place the board flat against the bottom of the container and as far forward against the front of the container as it will go (see Figure 24-5).

■ **Note** At this point in the instructions, you may be a little irritated with me if you finished soldering your only board in the last chapter. It's difficult to tape a board full of parts against the plastic. But, you can still measure the locations of the holes with a ruler and then mark them on the container that way.

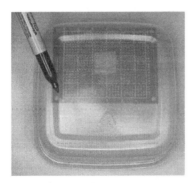

Figure 24-5. Breadboard taped inside the container to mark drill points and determine the amount of space it needs

2. Mark the location of the screw holes on the outside of the container.

Notice the amount of space taken up by the breadboard. The motors are going to be placed to the rear of the breadboard. The reason for inserting and marking the location of the breadboard before the motors is that the breadboard determines the proper location for the motor holes.

Creating a Template Sticker for the Motor Holes

You can measure the dimensions and placement of the screw holes and motor shaft of the gearhead motors by hand with a ruler and calipers. Or you could read them from the manufacturer's datasheets.

Figure 24-6 illustrates the dimensions of the motor shaft cap and screw holes for the Hsiang Neng motor described several chapters ago. The two screw holes are 2.6 mm in diameter. The cap around the motor shaft is 7.6 mm in diameter. The centers of the screw holes are 22 mm apart, 4 mm above the center of the motor shaft.

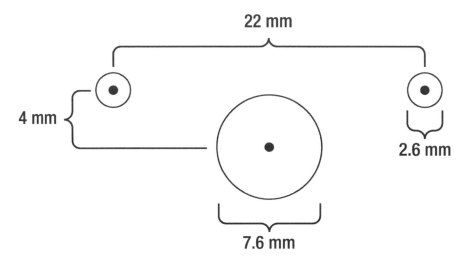

Figure 24-6. Outlines and center points of the holes needed for the Hsiang Neng motors

3. Create the exact motor profile in a drawing program. Or, use the Hsiang Neng motor label drawings, which are available at
    http://www.robotroom.com/SandwichStuff.html

4. Print a pair of the drawings onto a sheet of address labels stickers. Use a ruler on the printout to double-check that the software and printer didn't resize the dimensions.

Positioning the Template Stickers on the Container's Sides

5. Cut the labels and closely trim the edge on the side nearest the motor shaft cap circle (see the side below the largest circle in Figure 24-7).

Figure 24-7. Outlines printed on a sticker and placed on the container. Push pin being inserted into each center dot to create pilot holes

6. Place one label on each side of the container. The motor shaft cap circle should be far enough toward the rear of the container to allow the breadboard to fit toward the front. Also be sure that the larger circle is placed directly against the inner edge of the container lip (again, see Figure 24-7). For Sandwich, the center of the motor shaft ended up about 4.5 cm from the rear lip of the container.

Place the motor shaft against the inner edge of the side lip to get the motor shaft as low to the ground as possible, without damaging the container lip or obstructing the lid. This is important as it determines the minimum diameter of wheels that you can install. If the motor shaft were higher in the body, larger wheels would be required, causing the robot to move faster (possibly too fast).

The location of the motors must provide enough space in the front for the line-following circuit board and enough space in the rear for switches and a 9 V battery.

7. After attaching the stickers, manually position the motors, breadboard, and 9 V battery in the container. This is to make sure everything fits with the location you've chosen for the motor holes.

Making Pilot Holes and Drilling Screw Holes

8. Insert and remove a pushpin into the center of each circle on the sticker (again, see Figure 24-7). This creates tiny pilot holes that guide the drill into the centers.

■ **Note** The plastic container is slippery. Without a pilot hole, the drill slides around, marring the surface and causing the hole to be drilled in an inaccurate location.

---

9. Remove the circuit board, motors, pushpin, and any other parts from the container. Leave the stickers in place.

10. Insert a 2.6 mm (or $^7/_{64}$-inch) drill bit into a variable-speed rotary tool.

11. Using the pilot holes and stickers as guides, drill the screw holes and the **center** of the motor shaft circle. Even though the motor shaft circle will eventually be made larger, it helps to start small.

The stickers may come off at some point during drilling, but that isn't a problem since you have already indicated the centers of the holes with the pushpins.

The plastic bends easily, making it difficult to drill. It also tends to grab and twist rather than drill out cleanly. If necessary, place a piece of scrap wood behind the container wall to firm up the location for drilling.

12. Drill the holes for the circuit board that you marked way back in step 2.

I use #4-40 screws to hold the circuit board, so at step 12, I swap down to a $^1/_8$-inch drill bit.

You can roughly determine the desired drill-bit size for the screws you've chosen by holding different bits against the screws and comparing diameters by eye. If you want the screws to twist in and hold firmly against the plastic, use a slightly smaller drill bit (my preference). If you want the screws to drop straight in for easier insertion, use a bit the same diameter as the screw plus threads.

Introducing the Grinding Stone Accessory

A tiny drill bit rotating at high speed produces acceptable holes on plastic. However, larger bits walk all over the piece and become entangled in the hole. Fortunately, there's an easier way.

Obtain an aluminum-oxide grinding-stone accessory for your variable-speed rotary tool (see Figure 24-8). Get a stone that has a tapered tip. They're available at hardware stores, hobby shops, and online.

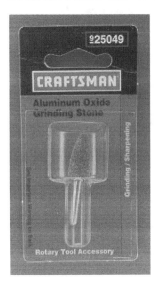

Figure 24-8. Aluminum-oxide grinding-stone accessory for variable-speed rotary tool

You'll be amazed at how cleanly and quickly you can remove and shape thin plastic with a grinding stone! This is the secret to making medium and large holes in thin plastic (see Figure 24-9).

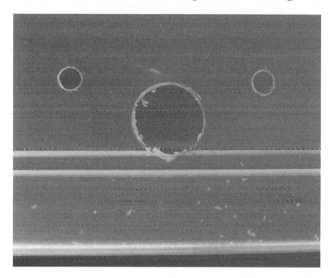

Figure 24-9. Nearly perfect motor holes in container after drilling and grinding

13. Grind out the motor shaft cap holes on each side of the robot body to the desired size. Centering the grinding-stone accessory in the motor shaft cap target area is made easier by the screw-size hole you drilled in its center, back in step 11.

The golden rule of drilling and grinding: If you're at all unsure, drill the hole smaller than you think you need. It's easy to drill and grind out additional material, but impossible to restore material if you removed too much.

Don't select drill speeds that are so fast that the plastic melts. Just work the stone through the piece at low to medium speeds, at a moderate pace.

14. Insert the motor to test the alignment of the holes and to make sure the motor presses completely against the plastic container's wall. (There is a raised section on the gearbox cap around the motor shaft. Upon inserting the motor into the holes, the raised section of the cap should stick out of the container; otherwise, the remainder of the motor cap won't screw flat against the plastic.)

Mounting the Motors

There are a number of ways to attach motors to a robot. Some people use double-sided foam mounting tape. Also not unheard of are hook-and-loop fasteners, cable ties, duct tape, and hot glue. Usually the best solution is to mount the motors in the manner in which they were designed: using the mounting screw holes.

Obtaining Metric Screws

The Hsiang Neng motors have two screw holes for M2.6 ISO metric screws. It would almost seem that an American standard, UNC (Unified National Course) #3-48 screw size would be acceptable. But, metric threads and UNC threads are not interchangeable.

Metric screws are standard outside of the United States. Most American hardware stores have at least one drawer with miniature metric screws (see Figure 24-10).

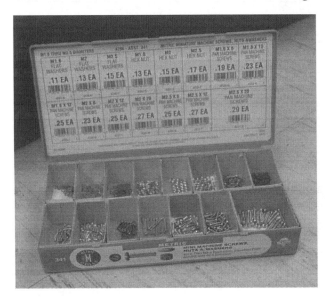

Figure 24-10. Hardware-store display case (#341) of Hillman Miniature Metric Machine Screws

Purchase four M2.6 x 6 mm screws. Unfortunately, all I could find in the Hillman case were M2.5 x 8 mm screws, which are satisfactory when washers are added. Micro Fasteners sells M2.6 x 6 mm screws (see Figure 24-11), part #MSPPS2606, $2.60 for 50 pieces. McMaster sells 100 for $5.00 (#90353A112).

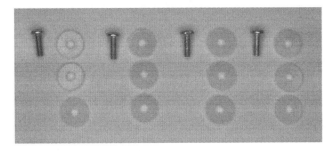

Figure 24-11. Four M2.6 x 8 mm screws with three nylon washers each

Needing Washers

You could drive the screw until the screw head is completely pressed against the container wall. But then, all of the forces acting on the motor and wheel would be exerted on a tiny, thin area of plastic. After the robot has a couple of solid hits against a wall or chair leg, one or more screw heads may rip through the plastic wall, ruining the robot body.

Washers are flat discs with holes in the center (see Figure 24-11). By inserting a washer between the screw head and the container wall, the forces are spread out across the surface covered by the washer. In this way, washers provide added strength to the location under the most stress.

Because of the thin plastic throughout the container, all screws on Sandwich have nylon washers added to them. You can purchase 100 nylon #4 screw size flat washers for $4.85 from Digi-Key (part #3158K). These washers are 0.047-inch thick.

15. Add one washer to each screw if you obtained 6-mm long screws. If you're using 8-mm long screws, add three washers to each screw (see Figure 24-12) since the motor holes aren't deep enough to drive the 8 mm screws in all the way.

Figure 24-12. Test fit of motor with screws and washers

16. Test both motors to see that they fit in the container holes and that the screws and washers hold the motors firmly in position. (Don't forget to remove the motors before drilling any more holes in the container.)

Creating the Motor Tube

Because each heavy motor is attached on only one side with two screws, the motors droop down on the unsupported side. It isn't a huge deal, although it causes the bottom of the wheels to tilt a bit outward (negative camber). You can overcome this by adding a center tube to support the mass across the entire motor's body, which keeps the motors straight and level.

Obtaining the Motor Tube

This is by far the most delicious part in the whole book.

1. Purchase a mini M&M's candy tube. Not the short package, but the "mega" variety, 55 g (see top of Figure 24-13).

Figure 24-13. Unopened mini M&M's candy mega tube (top) *and finished tube* (bottom)

There are a wide variety of M&M's candy tube colors to choose from: red, pink, orange, yellow, green, and blue. Select the color you prefer.

2. Consume all of the candy eagerly.

3. Rip off the plastic label.

Cutting the Motor Tube

4. With a hacksaw or rotary tool cut-off wheel accessory, cut off the lid and rim (see Figure 24-14).

Figure 24-14. Lid and rim cut off from the top of the tube

Take a closer look at the diameter of the tube. Oh, no! The top diameter of the M&M's candy tube is slightly wider than the bottom diameter. The gearbox cover of the motor can slide completely into the top of the tube but not into the middle or the bottom of the tube. Oh, well.

This means that one contiguous tube can't envelop both gearbox covers across the width of the robot. So, for symmetrical aesthetic reasons, you'll want to cut the tube down so that only the motor portions (not the gearhead cover portions) are contained within the tube. Notice the finished tube at the bottom of Figure 24-13 is much shorter than the original tube, and that the finished tube consists of the wider end of the original tube.

5. From the top of the tube after the lid is removed, measure 9.5 cm and cut. Retain the 9.5 cm piece (the one with the larger diameter) and discard the smaller end.

6. Midway across the tube, use the grinding stone accessory to grind a 1-cm diameter or slightly larger hole (see the bottom of Figure 24-13). This is where the connectors for the motors will pass through to the circuit board. If you discover later on that the connectors and wires are difficult to insert in this hole, feel free to make the hole larger.

Sanding the Motor Tube

The cutting process creates burrs on the ends of the tubes. Additionally, you may not have made the cut evenly straight across.

7. With a circular motion, sand the ends of the tube with medium to fine sandpaper to level the cut (see Figure 24-15).

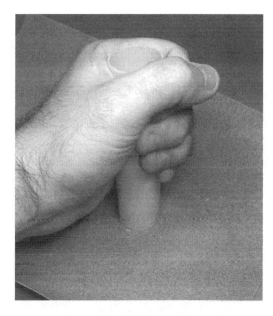

Figure 24-15. Removing burrs and shaping ends with a circular motion on sanding paper

8. Switch to extra-fine sandpaper to remove the burrs and smooth the edges of the ends of the tube.

Removing the Label Residue

Some adhesive likely remains on the tube after removing the label.

9. Use a dab of acetone (nail polish remover) on a cloth to quickly wipe away the label adhesive residue (see Figure 24-16).

Figure 24-16. Removing sticker adhesive residue with acetone

Be aware that acetone can destroy some types of plastics, but the M&M's candy tube is unaffected because it is made out of polypropylene thermoplastic, as you can see from the recycling symbol on the bottom (see Figure 24-17). Polypropylene is very resistant to chemicals. So, acetone doesn't harm the tube.

Figure 24-17. Recycling symbol indicates tube is polypropylene

The LEGO cross axles, the M&M's candy tube, and the Ziploc container are all polypropylene. By the way, the chemical resistance of polypropylene means it is nearly impossible to paint or permanently attach stickers to those portions of the robot's body.

Standard LEGO bricks are made of ABS (acrylonitrile butadiene styrene) thermoplastic. Don't try cleaning your LEGO bricks with acetone; they'll decompose (see Figure 24-18). Also unlike polypropylene products, LEGO bricks are not dishwasher safe; they'll melt.

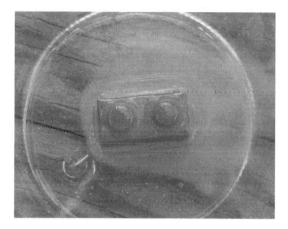

Figure 24-18. *Acetone destroying a standard LEGO brick*

Widening the Motor Diameters

To reduce vibration and tilt, the motors should be made to fit snuggly in the tube by wrapping them with masking tape (see Figure 24-19).

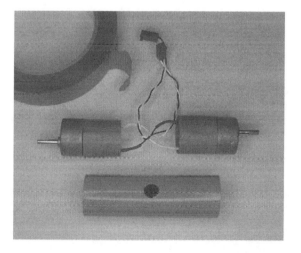

Figure 24-19. *Masking tape enlarging motor ends to fit snugly in the tube*

A negative consequence of the tape is that it is a thermal insulator, meaning it will be more difficult for the motors to dissipate heat. That's not an issue for this robot because the metal gearboxes remain exposed and the motors aren't being run at excess voltages or extreme loads. But, think carefully before adding tape to the motors of other robots.

10. Obtain a roll of low-adhesion masking tape, 1-inch (2.5 cm) wide. Scotch-brand Long Mask #2090 works well.

11. Wrap approximately 68 cm of tape around the motor portion of one of the gearhead motors.

12. 12.   Try inserting the motor into the larger end of the tube to see how it fits. Although it should now be snug, the motor should still be able to be completely inserted (including the gearhead) into the larger end of the tube. After testing, remove or add tape as necessary.

You don't want to use double-sided tape or anything that causes the motors to stick to the inside of the tube. You are only using the tape as padding and to widen the diameter for a cushioned fit.

13. Wrap approximately 39 cm of tape around the motor portion of the other gearhead motor.

14. Try inserting the motor into the smaller end of the tube to see how it fits. The motor should be able to be inserted, but the gearhead won't fit. After testing, remove or add tape as necessary.

Installing the Motors and Tube

15. Feed the Molex connector of the 39 cm taped motor through the smaller end of the tube and out the center hole (see Figure 24-20).

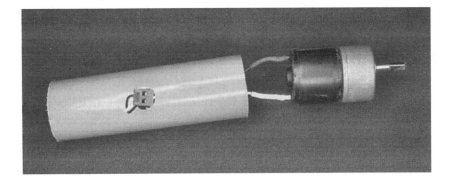

Figure 24-20. Motor's Molex connector emerging from hole in middle of tube

16. If you're going to include LEDs in the tube, insert them now into the other end of the tube and feed their Molex connector out the center hole.

17. Feed the Molex connector of the 68 cm taped motor through the wider end of the tube and out the center hole.

At this point, there should be one motor on each end of the tube with the LEDs inside the middle of the tube. All three connectors should be popping out in the center hole.

Insert the motors and tube into the robot's container body and test the fit. To aid insertion, you can push the motor on the wider end in all the way. Either add the washers and screws to hold the motors and tube in place, or remove the motors and tube and wait until you have drilled the holes for other parts in the container.

Adding the Switches and Battery Holder

Using the grinding stone accessory, grind suitably sized holes at the rear of the container for the power switch and line-following switch (see Figure 24-21). Be sure to leave enough room between the switches to install a 9 V battery and battery clip.

Figure 24-21. Large hole ground out for power switch (upper left) *and small hole ground out for line-following switch* (upper right)

The diameters for the holes for the switches depend on the sizes of the switches you choose. To avoid removing too much plastic, drill smaller holes than you think are necessary and then test the fit of the switches. It would be lousy to have to be gentle with your switches because you're afraid they might fall in due to holes that are too large.

Installing the Power Switch

Attach your power switch to the robot's body.

I really like the shape and feel of the rocker switch. The faceplate on the outside complements the large nut that steadfastly holds the power switch to the robot's body (see Figure 24-22).

Figure 24-22. Locking nut being screwed onto rear of power switch

Installing the Line-Following Switch

Threaded-bushing toggle switches usually come with four circular pieces: two nuts, a keyway washer, and a lock washer (see Figure 24-23). Sometimes the pieces ship pre-installed on the switch's bushing (the neck).

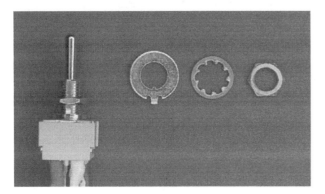

Figure 24-23. Power switch with nut installed on bushing (far left), *keyway washer* (left), *internal-tooth lock washer* (right), *and nut* (far right)

Screw one nut onto the switch's bushing to a point that allows the desired amount of the bushing to stick out of the robot's body. Too little bushing doesn't leave enough room for all the other pieces to be screwed on. Too much bushing looks gangly.

Then, place the keyway washer (also called a "locking ring") against the positioning nut. The keyway washer has a tiny internal tab that fits in a groove (called a "keyway") on the switch's bushing. The keyway washer also has a larger, external tab that presses against the container wall. When securely fastened, the tabs on the keyway washer prevent the toggle switch from twisting and rotating when the user switches the actuator back and forth.

On the outside of the container are the lock washer and another nut (see Figure 24-24). The lock washer helps prevent the nut from loosening and coming undone.

Figure 24-24. *Line-following switch installed. Inside the container: switch body, nut, keyway washer.*
Outside the container: lock washer, nut, and switch toggle actuator.

Don't forget that one of the most significant benefits of all washers is to spread the forces and load across more of the surface. Appropriately, the switch has two washers (keyway washer and lock washer) sandwiching the plastic container between two nuts.

Installing the 9 V Battery Holder

Sandwich holds its battery with a preformed metal clip (Mouser 534-080 or 534-095). Add some masking tape to the ends of the clip to prevent the sharp metal edges from scratching the battery.

With a washer on the outside, install the battery clip inside the robot's body between the power switch and line-following switch (see Figure 24-25). You'll need to drill a hole for the screw.

Figure 24-25. *9 V bracket battery holder with taped tips*

Adding the Circuit Board

On the recommended breadboard, there are four holes to attach the line-following circuit board to the robot's body. At the beginning of this chapter, you marked and drilled holes for the mounting screws.

Circuit Board Mounting Hardware

To hold the circuit board onto the robot's body, you'll need:

- Four #4-40 1½-inch long machine screws (available at local hardware store)

- Four #4-40 nuts with built-in lock washers (available at local hardware store). Plain #4-40 nuts with separate lock washers are also acceptable.

- Eight #4 screw-size nylon flat washers (same washers as used on the motors)

- Four 1-inch long spacers

See Figure 24-26 to get a look at them all.

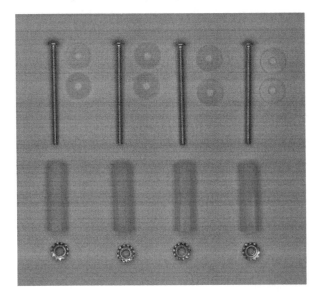

Figure 24-26. Four #4-40 1½-inch machine screws with two #4 washers each (top), *four hex threaded standoffs* (middle), *four #4-40 nuts with integrated external-tooth lock washers* (bottom)

Selecting and Obtaining Spacers

Spacers position the line-following circuit board away from the container so that the Molex connectors can fit in the space in between. Additionally, the spacers position the circuit board about 20 cm from the floor, giving the sensors ample, nearby views of the line to follow.

Shorter-length spacers are commonly used on computers, stereos, and other products with circuit boards to allow airflow on both sides of the board for heat dissipation.

Hex (six-sided) threaded spacers, like those shown in Figure 24-26, have holes with screw threads that grip the #4-40 screw. These types of spacers, with threads or integrated screws, are often called standoffs. The thread's grip on the screw reduces rattle and permits the circuit board to be removed without the screws and standoffs falling out. Unfortunately, some of the longer threaded spacers are not threaded all the way through in the very center, which must be laboriously corrected with a tap.

Round thru-hole spacers are also available. Sometimes they're called "clear" spacers or "non-threaded." Not only are they less expensive than the threaded variety, but also they have the advantage of simply slipping onto the screw without all the effort of turning them (no threads). But, of course, they fall off just as easily when the nuts and circuit board are removed.

To compromise, you could select two ½-inch spacers, one threaded and the other thru hole. Put the thru-hole spacers on first and then add the threaded spacers to the ends to keep everything in place.

Aluminum, nickel-plated brass, and ceramic spacers are common. But nylon is cheaper and lighter. Table 24-1 lists suppliers of various lengths of nylon spacers.

Table 24-1. Suppliers of Spacers

Supplier	Part Number	Price Per Ten	Length	Description
Digi-Key	878K	$1.94 for 10	0.500 inch	#4 Round Thru-Hole
Digi-Key	882K	$2.55 for 10	1.000 inch	#4 Round Thru-Hole
Mouser	561-K4.50	$0.20 each	0.500 inch	#4 Round Thru-Hole
Mouser	561-TSP3	$0.30 each	0.500 inch	#4-40 Round Threaded
Mouser	561-TSP5	$0.34 each	1.000 inch	#4-40 Round Threaded
Mouser	561-K41.00	$0.39 each	1.000 inch	#4 Round Thru-Hole
Mouser	561-L4.50	$0.55 each	0.500 inch	#4-40 Hex Threaded
Digi-Key	1902CK	$5.76 for 10	0.500 inch	#4-40 Hex Threaded
Digi-Key	1902EK	$8.51 for 10	1.000 inch	#4-40 Hex Threaded
Mouser	561-L41.0	$0.73 each	1.000 inch	#4-40 Hex Threaded
Jameco	55968	$14.95	Various	100 Assorted Aluminum and Nylon, Various Shapes and Sizes
Jameco	135423	$29.95	Various	1-Pound Assorted Aluminum and Nylon, Various Shapes and Sizes

Installing the Circuit Board

When installation is complete, the mounting hardware for the circuit board looks like Figure 24-27.

Figure 24-27. *Mounting hardware installed. Top to bottom: screw head, washer, container, washer, spacer, circuit board, lock washer, nut, end of screw*

Here are the steps for installation:

1. Place a nylon washer on the 1½-inch long #4-40 screw. This washer prevents the screw head from ripping through the thin plastic of the container.

2. Insert the screw into one of the holes previously drilled in the container for the circuit board.

3. Place a nylon washer on the other side of the screw so that the thin plastic of the container is sandwiched between nylon washers on the screw.

4. Add a 1-inch long spacer or two ½-inch spacers.

5. Complete steps 1 through 4 for the other screws.

6. Attach all of the switches, motors, and other parts to the circuit board via the Molex connectors.

7. Place the circuit board into the body, nudging and positioning so that all four of the screws pass through their corresponding holes on the circuit board.

8. Place the nuts with integrated lock washers onto the screws. The lock washers should be against the surface of the circuit board.

9. There are a number of options for tightening the nuts onto the screws. You can use needle-nose pliers, your fingers, a small crescent wrench, or a nutdriver (see Figure 24-28).

Figure 24-28. Nutdriver tightening nuts onto standoff screws

A nutdriver looks like a screwdriver, except a nutdriver's center is hollow and the tip is shaped to fit around a nut. Simply place the nutdriver over the nut and twist to tighten or loosen the nut (see Figure 24-29). Nutdrivers are inexpensive and available at local hardware stores. Because of the head-on accessibility of the nuts on this robot, I prefer a #4 nutdriver to a wrench or pliers.

Figure 24-29. Close-up of nutdriver tip

Be sure to firmly tighten down each nut. When the robot is turned over to follow lines, the nuts are facing the ground. Therefore, if a nut is loose, it'll eventually fall off. If desired, you can purchase anti-vibration nuts with built-in nylon centers, such as McMaster #90715A005. Or, you can install an additional nut on top of the first nut. These are called jam locknuts.

Drilling Holes for the Trimpots

The final line-following circuit has two trimpots, one for headlight brightness and the other for balancing the left and right pairs of sensors. With the circuit board in place, drill the necessary holes to be able to adjust the trimpots with a small screwdriver (see Figure 24-30).

Figure 24-30. *Tiny holes drilled into container front to allow a small screwdriver access to the headlight brightness and sensor-balancing trimpots*

Carving Out a Window in the Container Lid

The Ziploc container comes with a blue lid. Technically, the robot works fine without the lid. However, the lid looks nice, adds structural stability, raises the sensors up a bit for a better view, and catches any robot parts that fall out during operation (*gasp*).

Using the grinding-stone accessory on a variable-speed rotary tool, carve out a window in the lid for the sensors to be able to see the floor (see top of Figure 24-31). The robot can run without the window, but not as well since only blue light will pass through the lid.

Figure 24-31. *Window ground out of front of container lid*

It would be beneficial to attach some clear plastic, like a piece of an overhead transparency, into the window so that dirt, small objects, and fingers don't bend or soil the sensors when the lid is in place on the robot. Unfortunately, polypropylene's amazing chemical resistance characteristics and the lid's flexibility make it difficult to glue anything in place.

Finishing Touches

Add any remaining parts, like the couplers and wheels, to the robot. Install a 9 V battery and put the lid on.

Now's a good time to add stickers, a nameplate, pipe cleaners, or funny eyes. Perhaps stick an army man to the top to lead the way, or a racecar driver to steer. There's also enough room on the inside to toss in some knick-knacks.

Ready to Roll

In this chapter, you've seen one option for a robot body for the line-following robot. By all means, experiment with other fun and interesting robot body materials.

Although it may seem that the robot is now finished, there's still some effort you need to invest in testing and tweaking. In the next chapter, you'll enter the final, critical stage of robot building.

■ ■ ■

CHAPTER 25

Launching the Line-Follower

This chapter begins with last-minute checks followed by a qualifying run of your line-following robot. I provide you with simple tests for diagnosing and solving likely problems, and data to compare your robot to mine. The chapter concludes with line course ideas and potential robot enhancements.

Correcting and Tweaking

Don't expect your robot to run perfectly on the first try. There will be bad connections, loose screws, burrs, and things rubbing. Because of an early collision, Wavy stalled every few feet. After days of wasted effort concentrating on the electronics, it turned out that a cross axle hadn't been glued properly in a coupler and was slipping. These things should be expected.

Be prepared to spend as much time tweaking the "finished" robot as you did in other phases of the project. Logically, a properly adjusted robot performs better than an unadjusted robot. Minor alterations are often the difference between success and failure.

Preliminary Examination

Before setting the robot onto a track, there are some important basic tests and calibrations to perform. This ensures the robot is road-worthy.

Checking the Power Supply

1. Test the circuit board with a multimeter before applying power. For a list of tests to perform, see the end of Chapter 23.

2. Toggle the line-following switch to the center (off) position.

3. Turn on the power switch.

If neither the headlights, brightness indicator LEDs, nor tube LEDs turn on, then something is wrong with the power supply module. Check the voltage of the battery, battery connector, power switch, and power switch connector. Measure the voltage at different points in the circuit to see where it may be dropping off.

The board has four deliberately-added test points (TP+, TP-, TP1, TP2) for testing battery and sensor voltage. However, every exposed solder point, component lead, and connector pin can be considered a test point. It is often helpful to probe the voltages of each point with a multimeter. Is pin 4 of IC1 (the comparator) around 0 V and pin 8 around 9 V?

If only the headlights or tube LEDs don't light, it could be that one or more of the LEDs are backwards. The tube LED connector may be loose or have its wires reversed. The trimpot for the headlights might be set at too high of a resistance.

In a modular robot or in a robot that uses a lot of connectors, a great diagnostic trick is to disconnect everything that is unnecessary. You can test each part on its own. And, you can reinstall one part at a time until the robot stops working again. For example, the motors and tube LED can be disconnected while diagnosing a headlight issue.

Parts can also be swapped. If the motor on the left side doesn't work, try swapping it with the motor on the right side. If the motor suddenly starts working on the left side, then you know the issue is with the motor that you exchanged. If neither motor works on the left side, but both motors work on the right side, then you know the issue is with the left side of the circuit.

At no time should any of the parts become hot. If the transistors, comparator chip, or any other component seem to be heating up, disconnect power immediately. Make sure errant solder blobs or metal leads aren't resulting in unintentional connections.

Checking the Sensors

4. Place the robot on a solid, evenly lit, non-patterned surface, such as a large white piece of paper. The goal is to make sure the sensors are seeing the same amount of light.

5. Slide a thin dark piece of paper back and forth under the sensors. The brightness-indicator LEDs on the left and right sides of the robot should light up alternately.

If neither sets of brightness-indicator LEDs light, compare the wiring of the soldered circuit board to the solderless breadboard. Is the comparator chip or any of the LEDs in backwards? Is the comparator damaged? Since the comparator is socketed, it's easy to pull it out and put it into the solderless breadboard version of the line-following circuit for testing.

If both sets of LEDs turn on and turn off at the same time (rather than alternating), then check the wiring between the sensor test points and the comparator. Perfectly balanced sensors may appear to light both LEDs at the same time, but putting your hand under one set of LEDs should be enough to break the tie.

If one set of LEDs turns on and off, but the other set always stays off, there's likely a broken connection or reversed LED in the set that stays off.

If one set of LEDs always stays on and the other set always stays off, then maybe the trimpot (R2) for balancing the sensors is not near the center. At the extremes of its range, the trimpot will imbalance one set of sensors so much it always seems to be brighter or darker.

Balancing the Sensors

6. Remove the dark piece of paper. With only the evenly lit piece of white paper beneath the sensors, dial the trimpot so that the left and right brightness indicators light up at the same time.

Sometimes it isn't possible to get both sets of LEDs lit at the same time. A tiny nudge of the screwdriver causes one side to light, and a tiny nudge the other way causes the other side to light. But, that's close enough, and it indicates the sensors are evenly balanced.

7. Place a dark piece of paper under the right-side set of sensors. The left set of brightness-indicator LEDs should light.

8. Move the dark piece of paper to be under the left-side set of sensors. The right-side set of brightness-indicator LEDs should light.

If the indicator LEDs are lighting up the opposite way, you can either start calling them "darkness" indicators (no, don't do that) or swap the comparator outputs to the transistors.

Checking the Motors

9. Prop the robot on top of something so that the wheels don't touch the ground. An unused container is perfect for this.

10. Flip the line-following switch to either side to enable the motors. Move your hand back and forth under the sensors to verify each motor is able to turn.

If neither motor turns, check the motor connectors, motor wiring, and line-following switch. If both motors always turn and stop at the same time (rather than alternating), check the connections to the line-following switch. If one motor turns and stops, but the other motor doesn't turn at all, check the failed motor's connector and wiring.

Another possibility is that the battery is weak or that the custom motors you picked require more power than a 9 V battery can supply. As a test, you can wire an LED and 1 kΩ resistor to a Molex connector to temporarily replace each motor. If the LEDs light, then the battery or motor are most likely to blame.

Due to the variety of battery chemistries, it is difficult to specify an exact voltage at which a 9 V battery would be considered "dead." Instead, it is easiest to swap in a fresh battery for test purposes.

11. Put a short piece of tape on the sides of each wheel. This will help you to be able to see in which direction the motors are turning.

12. Place your hand under the left or right sensors to make the left motor spin. The left motor should spin counter-clockwise (see Figure 25-1).

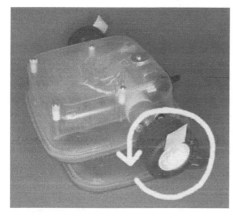

Figure 25-1. The robot's left motor spins counter-clockwise. Notice the extra container underneath the robot keeping the wheels off the ground.

13. Place your hand under the opposite set of sensors so that the right motor spins. The right motor should spin clockwise (see Figure 25-2).

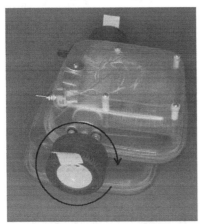

Figure 25-2. The robot's right motor spins clockwise

Having a motor spin backwards is the most common mistake in building this robot. It's confusing since one motor has to spin in the opposite direction than the other motor. Think about it this way: the tops of both motors must spin toward the front of the robot to move forward.

If both motors spin in the wrong direction, try swapping them to the opposite Molex connector headers on the board (so the left motor housing is attached to the right header connector on the board, and vice versa). Depending on how you wired the circuit, this may fix the problem. If that doesn't work, use a tiny screwdriver to pop both terminals out of each motor connector housing and re-insert the wires in the opposite order.

If only one motor spins in the wrong direction, you've got two possibilities. If the order of the terminals in the Molex connector housing of the "bad" motor are the opposite of the "good" motor, then pop and flip the terminals of the "bad" motor. However, if both motors are wired the same way, then the Molex header on the circuit board that connects to the "bad" motor should have its wires desoldered and flipped around.

Determining the Light and Dark Positions of the Line-Following Switch

14. Toggle the line-following switch to the left.

15. Place a dark piece of paper under the right side of the robot's sensors. The left brightness LEDs should be lit up.

If the left motor spins, then the line-following switch is in the position to follow dark lines. If the right motor spins, then the line-following switch is in the position to follow light lines.

16. Toggle the line-following switch to the right. The opposite motor should spin.

If the same motor spins as when the switch was toggled in the opposite direction, then the line-following switch is miswired. Most likely the motor wires don't diagonally cross over the center of the switch.

17. Label which position of the line-following switch is for light lines and which for dark lines.

To label the switch, I printed and cut out a 2 cm square piece of paper (see Figure 25-3).

Figure 25-3. A printed piece of paper inserted inside the container for labeling the line-following switch

I cut a hole in the center of the paper with an ordinary paper punch. The switch bushing goes through the center of the paper so the paper is sandwiched between the switch's locking washer and the inside of the plastic container. If the paper had been mounted on the outside of the container, the paper would have become torn and soiled over time.

■ **Tip** You can add decorations or a nameplate to your robot in the same manner as the line-following switch label. Simply put the piece of paper on the inside of the container, sandwiched between the washers of the standoffs that hold the circuit board.

Trial Run: Following a Straight Line

The first test track for the robot should be a straight line.

1. On an indoor, flat, non-patterned, evenly lit, light-colored floor, place more than 4 meters length of 2.5 cm wide dark tape in a straight line.

A line-following robot couldn't ask for better racing conditions. The course may seem rigged for success, which is exactly the point.

It's like the high jump. Competitors start with the bar at lower levels, which they rightfully expect that they can clear. After you're assured that the robot is fully operational, then start increasing the difficulty of the course and conditions.

■ **Note** As appealing as a sidewalk may look in daytime, the bright sun overwhelms the sensors, resulting in very small voltage differences to compare. Covering the container in thick, opaque tape helps. But, it is still a tough challenge for a robot designed for indoor lighting. So, avoid outside courses.

---

2. With the line-following switch in the center (off) position, place the powered-on (yet motionless) robot on the floor, centered on the dark line.

You can tell when the robot is truly centered by observing the left and right brightness indicator LEDs. Either they'll both light up or they'll alternate with the slightest nudge in either direction.

3. Toggle the line-following switch to the dark-line position and watch the robot go!

Sandwich takes between 12 and 15 seconds to complete a straight 4-meter course. The time varies based on battery voltage. The speed decreases about a quarter of a percent per trial due to battery-voltage decline.

Correcting Common Problems

There are a couple of common problems that you might encounter during trial runs of the robot on a straight course.

Line-Following Switch Toggled to Incorrect Position

If the robot doesn't center on the line, but sort of hugs the outside or inside of it, the line-following switch is probably toggled in the wrong direction. It's an odd effect (and worth trying purposely for fun).

If the line-following switch is set to follow a light line but the robot is actually placed on a light surface with a dark line, then the robot sees the light surface as a massively wide light line. The robot moves into the light area until the light is balanced under both sensors. The robot believes it is now centered over the white "line."

But, no matter how balanced the trimpot adjustment may seem, at some point one set of sensors is still a little less resistive than the other set and one motor has a bit more spunk than the other. So, the robot drifts until it hits the side of the dark line. Because it wants to center over the nonexistent white "line," it turns away from the dark line because the white "line" is no longer centered under the robot.

As long as the robot's default drifting side turns toward the dark line, the robot will hug the outside of the dark line, basically following it. Then again, if the robot's default drifting side turns away from the dark line, the robot will either wander away aimlessly, centering over this massive light "line," or the robot will spin in a circle because it has nothing to follow.

The correction is simple; just toggle the line-following switch the other way.

Sensors Placed Too High or Too Low

The headlights must be high enough off the floor to have enough distance for the emitted light to illuminate the floor and bounce into the sensors (see Figure 25-4).

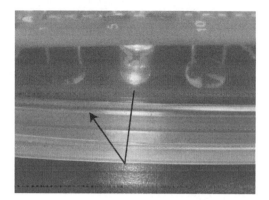

Figure 25-4. Sensors placed at the optimal height to see the light reflected off the floor

If the headlights and sensors are too near the floor, only fringe amounts of light (if any) can bounce off the floor and into the sensors. The sensors will be unable to tell the difference between a light-colored surface and a dark-colored surface; everything will look dark due to lack of light.

If the headlights and sensors are too far from the floor, stray ambient light from the room will bounce off the floor and affect the sensors more than the light from the headlights does. As such, the robot may begin following bright spots and room shadows, which is admittedly amusing. Placing some opaque tape across the front of the robot helps a lot, but doesn't look as stylish.

If you determine that the headlights and sensors are too high or too low, you can adjust the circuit board's mounting hardware. You can add additional washers above the circuit board to bring the sensors nearer the floor. To move the sensors away from the floor, remove the inside upper washer or either cut the spacers/standoffs shorter or substitute them with shorter pieces.

Headlights Too Dim or Too Bright

Take a closer look at the bottom of the photograph in Figure 25-4. Notice that the surface beneath the robot is black. But, directly beneath the headlight, the glossy black surface appears mottled white. If the headlights are too bright, the sensors will be unable to tell the difference between a light-colored surface and a glossy dark surface reflecting too much light; everything will look light.

On the other hand, if the headlights are too dim, they won't be contributing a reliable and predominant light source to the sensors. The room's ambient lighting and shadows will negatively affect the robot's line-following ability.

Fortunately, it's easy to adjust the brightness of the headlights with the associated trimpot (R10). After adjusting the headlight brightness, it may be necessary to rebalance the sensors using trimpot R2. This is because each headlight LED likely produces a different amount of light than the other LED. Adjusting the amount of current flowing through the headlight LEDs may alter the total difference in brightness between them.

Objectively Evaluating the Sensors and Headlights

Adjusting trimpots and circuit board position by intuition may seem a little unscientific. For measurable results, you need to be able to test the voltage at the sensor's test points, TP1 and TP2. After all, that's what the comparator is looking at.

Grind a hole of approximately 1 cm in the side of the robot's body. Or, you could put the hole in the rear. Thread three IC hook jumper leads through the hole (see Figure 25-5). One jumper lead should be connected to the negative power bus (or negative power test point).

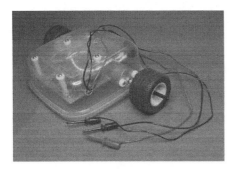

Figure 25-5. *Hole in the side of the robot's body with IC hook jumper leads inserted for measuring the voltages on the board during operation*

The other two jumper leads should be hooked to TP1 and TP2, respectively. If you didn't specifically make a loop of wire for each test point (see Figure 25-6), simply connect the hooks to the first and third leads of trimpot R2.

Figure 25-6. *A multimeter test lead IC hook firmly grasps a loop of wire for a sensor test point*

With the robot powered up but with the line-following switch in the center position (motors off), manually place the robot over various points in the course. With a multimeter, measure the voltage at the test points to determine how easy it would be for the comparator chip to compare them.

To measure the voltage of the test points, the black test lead of the multimeter must be connected to the IC hook jumper lead of the robot's negative power bus. The red test lead of the multimeter can be hooked up to the IC hook jumper lead for either TP1 or TP2, but not both at the same time.

Adjust the brightness-balancing trimpot (R2) and the headlight-brightness trimpot (R10) and observe the effect on the measured voltage of each sensor test point. With an external light, such as a flashlight, light up the floor and cast shadows under the sensors to determine if the ambient contamination significantly affects the outcome.

The results of these experiments are not applicable if you lift up the robot from standard course position. You want to test what the robot is experiencing under racing conditions.

Expected Voltages at the Sensor Test Points

After balancing the sensors and adjusting headlights, what follows are the voltages I measured on Sandwich. Compare your voltages to mine. Recognize that depending on how fresh or drained your battery is, your robot is unlikely to have the same voltages that Sandwich did. Simply scale the numbers to determine if your robot is roughly similar.

■ **Note** I covered Sandwich with a cardboard box during testing to avoid deviations due to ambient lighting and shadows. During these tests, Sandwich is actually supplied power from a wall transformer, because a dropping battery voltage would skew the values of the last tests performed.

```
Positive power bus:     9.07 V
```

Be sure to measure the voltage at the power bus, not at the battery. A battery disconnected from a circuit produces higher voltages than it does under load. Also, if a diode is added to the line-following circuit to protect from reverse installation of the battery, then a bit more voltage is dropped before reaching the rest of the circuits.

```
TP1 and TP2 on white paper:     2.036 V and 2.034 V
TP1 and TP2 on black paper:     7.54 V and 7.40 V
```

Sandwich's brightness-balancing trimpot (R2) was adjusted on white paper. Notice how the static value fails to balance the sensors at darker levels. The white-paper test-point voltages are similar to each other, but the black-paper test-point voltages are not as similar to each other. No big deal. Just remember to rebalance the sensors on the course at race day under local lighting and surface conditions.

```
1-inch wide blue masking tape beneath right sensors on black paper,
TP1 and TP2:     4.43 V and 7.13 V
1-inch wide ordinary masking tape beneath right sensors on black paper,
TP1 and TP2:     3.098 and 7.02 V
1-inch wide strip of shiny aluminum foil beneath right sensors on black paper,
TP1 and TP2:     2.374 and 7.21 V
1-inch wide strip of white paper beneath right sensors on black paper,
TP1 and TP2:     2.134 and 6.88 V
```

A couple of interesting results:

- The robot can see the difference between blue tape and black flooring. The blue tape is a little above the middle of the robot's brightness range.

- Ordinary masking tape (slightly tan) is less bright than white paper.

- Aluminum foil doesn't diffuse as much light as white paper.

- The lower resistance of the photoresistors on the right side has a voltage-reducing effect on TP2. However, light reflecting off the surface in front of the right headlight also seems to be reaching the left sensors depending on the surface material. Note the fairly low TP1 voltage, but fairly high TP2 voltage, for aluminum. Perhaps a physical barrier between the two sets of sensors might improve performance?

```
1-inch wide blue masking tape beneath right sensors on white paper,
TP1 and TP2:    3.604 V and 2.065 V
1-inch wide strip of black paper beneath right sensors on white paper,
TP1 and TP2:    4.93 and 2.075 V
```

Acceptable Ranges of Voltages at the Sensor Test Points

The comparator will not switch correctly if both test-point voltages exceed the positive power bus's voltage minus 1.5 V. For example, a 9.07 V bus permits comparisons up to 7.57 V (9.07 V – 1.5 V). The sensors are not getting enough light if a line exists but both test-point voltages are that high.

In Chapter 23, the section "Tweaking for Better Performance" includes instructions for optimizing R9 and R1 for your robot's white LEDs and sensors. If you previously chose to stay with the default 150 Ω values, but your sensor test points routinely exceed the upper 1.5 V limit, then you probably need to remove those resistors. Replace R9 with 100 Ω for increased brightness and replace R1 with 22 kΩ for a larger voltage drop.

The comparator won't differentiate precisely if both test-point voltages are too similar to each other. That's desirable if the surface has the same brightness (a blank piece of paper) and the sensors are properly balanced. But, that's a big problem if the line to follow is beneath one set of the sensors! Look for a difference of at least ±1 V between the set of sensors with the line and the set of sensors without the line.

If both sensors are below 1 V most of the time, the sensors are getting too much light.

After fine-tuning the trimpots and the circuit board's position, be sure to move the robot into the brightest, darkest, most shadowy, most contrasting, and least contrasting situations to ensure the voltages meet the comparator's requirements under all conditions.

Does This Look Straight to You?

Now is a good opportunity to observe and explain that the robot doesn't quite drive straight.

Except for brief moments when both sets of sensors are receiving exactly the same amount of light, both motors are not turned on at the same time. This means the robot rarely drives straight forward. Instead, the robot shuffles left and shuffles right so the overall direction averages out to be straight.

Following a Dark Line

Figure 25-7 consists of three frames showing the motion of the robot following a dark line. The robot's angles in these pictures are exaggerated for illustrative purposes.

Figure 25-7. Composite photograph of exaggerated movements of the robot following a dark line

The first frame shows the robot perfectly centered over the black line. Both sets of sensors see white floor with a bit of black at the inner edge. The overall brightness is balanced, so both sets of LEDs and motors are enabled.

But floors, tires, and motors are naturally uneven. Eventually the robot drifts off course.

The second frame shows that the robot has drifted and that the black line is beneath the right-side set of sensors. That means the left side is brighter, so the left LEDs and motor kick in and the right LEDs and motor are disabled. With only the left motor spinning, the robot's left side will rotate toward the line.

At some point the sensors become balanced again, but because the left side is already in motion, the robot overshoots the line a little before the right motor can come up to speed.

The third frame shows that the robot has overshot and that the black line is now beneath the left set of sensors. That means the right side is brighter, so the right LEDs and motor kick in and the left LEDs and motor are disabled. With only the right motor spinning, the robot's right side will rotate toward the line.

This pattern repeats over and over very quickly but without such radical overshoots in reality. That's how the robot keeps centered over the line!

Following a Light Line

Figure 25-8 consists of three frames showing the motion of the robot following a light line. The robot's angles in these pictures are exaggerated for illustrative purposes.

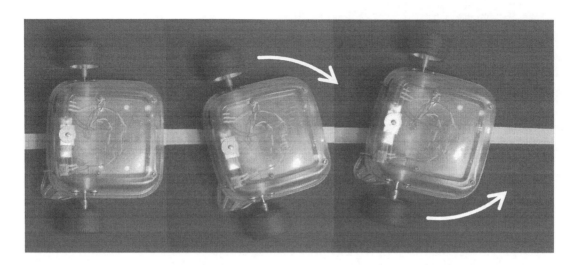

Figure 25-8. *Composite photograph of exaggerated movements of the robot following a light line*

The robot proceeds in the same manner as it did for following a dark line. The vital difference is that the line-following switch has swapped the motor wires.

The first frame shows the robot centered, with the sensors balanced. Both sets of LEDs and motors are enabled.

The second frame shows the robot has drifted and that the white line is beneath the right-side set of sensors. That means the right side is brighter, so the right set of LEDs are enabled, but the line-following-switch swap causes the left-side motor to engage. The left side of the robot will rotate toward the line. If the right motor had been engaged instead, the robot would have continued moving off course.

The third frame shows the robot has overshot and that the white line is beneath the left set of sensors. That means the left side is brighter, so the left set of LEDs are enabled, but the line-following-switch swap causes the right-side motor to engage. The right side of the robot will rotate toward the line.

Very sneaky!

The Maiden Voyage

After you have checked the robot over and calibrated, it's time for the maiden voyage.

Laying out a track with masking tape is fun, because you can rapidly extend the course or quickly make changes to turns or intersections. Oval or "8" shaped courses allow you to sit back and admire your work, rather than having to pick up the robot and return it to the starting line.

Forks and splits in the road are interesting. Obviously the robot isn't making an intelligent decision about which road to take, but it's entertaining to alter the split until the robot starts taking different branches at random.

Don't forget to add tunnels to drive through or block walls to knock down. Hang bells on strings for the robot to ring as it drives by. Maybe a finish line?

Solving Steering Problems

If the robot is struggling to complete certain turns, there are three simple changes that you can make to significantly improve performance.

Reducing Battery Voltage

A fresh alkaline battery produces around 9.5 V. In comparison, after a couple of runs around the track, a low-end NiMH battery produces a nominal voltage of around 7.2 V. The fresh alkaline battery causes the robot to drive 32% faster.

As the battery voltage drops, so does the robot's speed. This gives the sensors more time to adjust to the changing surface brightness and prevents overshoot due to motors engaging and disengaging. Ultimately, the slower the robot proceeds, the better it turns.

This causes an interesting phenomenon. Upon discovering that the robot can't complete a certain turn, the builder makes adjustments to the robot and the course. After a number of attempts, the robot starts to consistently make the turn. The builder congratulates himself or herself on the alterations, only to discover the robot can't make the turn the next morning. The actual source of improvement was likely the decline in battery voltage.

At first, you may be offended at the thought of intentionally slowing down the robot. After all, doesn't greater speed imply greater capability? Well, if you find yourself disappointed with the robot's line-following aptitude, then perhaps the ability to follow a line is in fact a greater indicator of capability than is pure speed.

Potential solution: Replace those old 9 V batteries in your smoke detectors with fresh ones and use the depleted batteries to follow lines. Alternatively, switch the robot to a 6 V battery pack consisting of 4 AA or 4 AAA cells. With such a pack, the robot runs more accurately and lasts longer.

Reducing Wheel Size

This is an easy one. If your robot is popping wheelies (the front end is lifting up temporarily at the start of the course), the wheel diameter is too large.

Wheel size makes a tremendous difference in speed, which makes all the difference in the ability to turn. The most successful change I made in Sandwich during development was to switch to smaller-diameter wheels.

Modifying the Course

Let's face it; you're a cruel course designer.

At first you may not think that you're being unfair or unkind to the little robot. But, consider this: How well could you make a turn in your automobile if all you were allowed to look through were a slit in the floorboard? You'd sure miss a lot of those 90° turns! Especially if you were driving fast.

Review the course requirements presented toward the beginning of the book. Keep the course turns gradual and with high contrast.

Potential Improvements

Several potentially beneficial design changes to the line-following robot have already been mentioned throughout this book:

- Cover the clear plastic body with something opaque so that ambient light won't affect the sensors as much.

- Switch to a 6 V rechargeable alkaline battery pack for improved cornering (due to reduced speed) and longevity.

- Use an improved yet completely compatible comparator chip such as the National Semiconductor LMC6772 to accept sensor voltages in the upper 1.5 V region.

- Place an opaque barrier in the middle of the robot between the left set of sensors and the right set of sensors. This should reduce the light coming from the surface of the opposite side of the robot.

- Switch to wheels that are solid, round shouldered, thin, have a slick tread, and medium diameter for reduced rolling resistance and improved cornering.

- Switch to more efficient motors for longer running time.

- Add clear plastic to cover the window that was ground out of the lid. The plastic will prevent damage and dirtying of the sensors.

- Use modern, smaller surface-mount components to reduce the circuit board to a quarter of its present size.

Obviously, you could completely redesign the robot circuit around a smart microcontroller. But there are a couple of other enhancements that you can make more simply.

Protecting Against a Reversed Battery

The line-following circuit is fairly robust. It can operate within the entire voltage range of the battery's lifespan without the need for a voltage regulation module. The transistors can handle the current to the motors, even if the motors stall. Flyback diodes protect the transistors from motor spikes. Resistors protect the circuitry attached to trimpots from the operator dialing extreme values.

There is one common error that can harm the robot's circuits: inserting the battery the wrong way. If the 9 V battery is touched, however briefly, to the battery snap with the positive terminal and negative terminal reversed, and the power switch is turned on, the comparator chip could be destroyed.

There is an easy solution to protect against battery reversal. Between the power switch and the positive power bus, insert a diode (see Figure 25-9). Recall that diodes are one-way valves. As long as the battery power is going in the correct direction, the diode (D3) will let it pass. If the battery power is reversed, the diode blocks it.

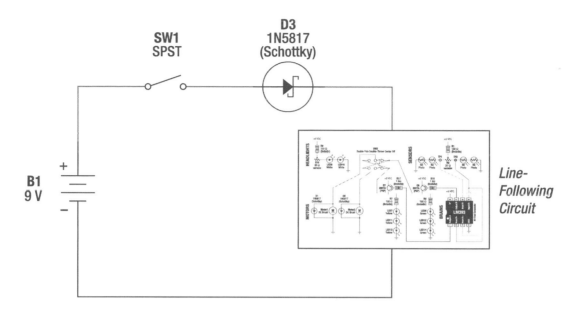

Figure 25-9. *Schematic of reverse battery protection circuit*

Be sure to place the diode so that the anode (plain end) connects to the power switch and the cathode (banded end) connects to the positive power bus. The diode should be the only "wire" connecting the switch and the bus.

There is a small cost or another benefit to adding the diode, depending on how you look at it. A Schottky diode drops up to 0.45 V in exchange for the service of passing current through it. This means the motors would receive a little less power, and would move at a slower speed.

Eliminating Surges with Capacitors

Because this robot has a simple brain without memory, doesn't require voltage regulation, and has fairly insensitive circuitry, the robot isn't harmed by brief losses of power. That being said, I have noticed the LEDs dim a bit when both motors kick in at the same time.

Think of capacitors as tiny rechargeable batteries. They charge up when voltage is available, and discharge when voltage drops down. Although they don't hold much electricity, they can be used as local power sources when power has been diverted from the battery to the motors.

The electrical location and storage capacity of a capacitor determines its effectiveness in filtering spikes, electrical noise, and sudden current draws. For example, a large-value capacitor (thousands of microfarads) placed across the power buses can supply current to the entire circuit. Whereas a smaller-value capacitor can charge and discharge more quickly than a larger-value capacitor (thus smoothing out higher-frequency transitions), it has a lower capacity, and is therefore more suited for caring for only a few chips. The filtering effect is most pronounced on the chips nearest the small-value capacitor.

There are two appropriate locations for capacitors in the line-following circuit. You can attach the leads of a large-value capacitor, say 330 μF (microfarad), to the positive and negative power buses. That capacitor would be called C1. It can supply large amounts of power more quickly than the battery can, thus temporarily providing more than enough current for the entire robot each time a motor starts-up.

And, you could attach the leads of a tiny, 0.1 μF capacitor to the positive and negative pins of the comparator. That capacitor would be called C2.

Although they aren't necessary for this robot, capacitors are vital in more complicated circuits. Chapters 7 and 8 of *Intermediate Robot Building* by David Cook (Apress, 2010) discuss capacitor values, circuit locations, and capacitor chemistry in detail.

Improving Line-Following

Cadmium-sulfide photoresistors react fairly slowly to changes in light. Phototransistors respond 1000 times more quickly. That suggests that substituting phototransistors for photoresistors would improve line following.

Figure 25-10 shows the photoresistors (R3, R4, R5, and R6) replaced with phototransistors, such as part #120221 from Jameco for $1.95 each. R2 must then be replaced with a 500 kΩ trimpot to retain the same levels of voltage division.

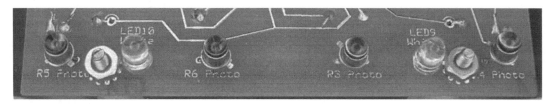

Figure 25-10. Phototransistors replace photoresistors on Sandwich's brother

Surprise! After substitution, no noticeable improvement in line following was observed. That doesn't mean that the phototransistors didn't improve the responsiveness of the sensor circuit, it just means that something else was the critical factor in steering. Hmmm. What would that be?

Analyzing Cornering, Frame By Frame

To determine how the robot handles steering, I shot a video of the robot and analyzed each frame (see Figure 25-11). I apologize for the poor centering of the robot in the video, but the relevant material is still visible.

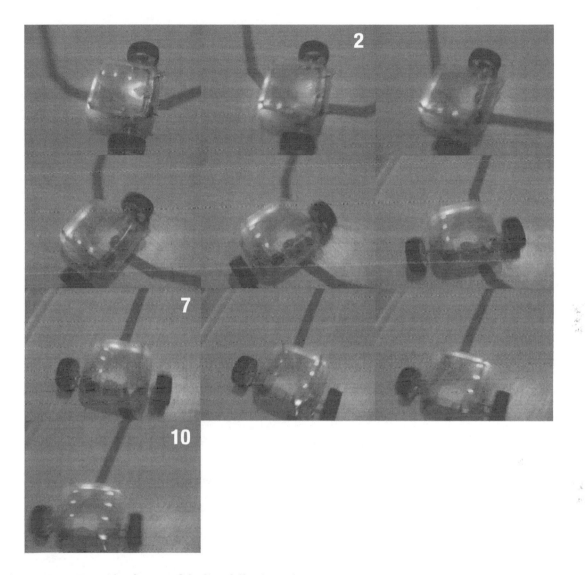

Figure 25-11. Ten video frames of the line-following robot turning a corner

In the first frame, the right LEDs are lit. Since the robot is following a dark line on a light floor, the right motor must engage when the right LEDs are lit. By frame two, the left LEDs have been turned on, and only a brief residue of light remains in the right LEDs. So, at this point, the left motors are engaged but the power to the right motors has been disengaged.

Frames three, four, five, and six all show the robot properly powering the left motor to turn the corner. The right LEDs, and hence the right motor, are disengaged at that time.

By frame seven, both LEDs should probably have been lit since the curved line appears to now be centered. Both sets of LEDs are lit in frame eight, but by then the robot has oversteered. So, in frame nine, the right LEDs are lit and the right motor corrects the course.

In frame ten, the robot has both sets of LEDs and both motors engaged and is heading straight down the straight line. Beautiful!

There's a problem, though. Check out the position of the right wheel at the time the right motor was first disengaged (frame two). Now compare that to the wheel's position before the right motor is reengaged (frame seven). The wheel has continued to roll toward the line, probably about 6 cm (see Figure 25-12), even though the right motor is turned off.

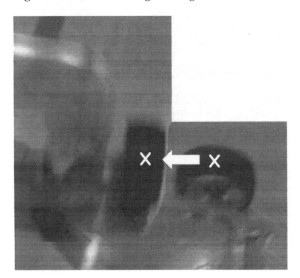

Figure 25-12. *Frames two and seven superimposed to show wheel roll. If the wheel had stayed in place, the "x" marks would be directly on top of each other. (Please excuse the quality of this image; it came from a video camera. Even so, it does show that the wheel has moved forward instead of pivoting in place.)*

To make tighter turns, the robot must pivot in place.

Braking to Pivot

In order to pivot in place rather than allowing a wheel to roll forward, the robot needs to apply an electrical brake. It's easier than it sounds. In the present circuit design, when a motor is disengaged it is simply disconnected from the positive power bus. If instead it were then connected to the negative power bus, the motor would brake.

To achieve that, two more transistors would need to be added (one for each motor), and a push-pull comparator (or a pull-up resistor and a 4069 inverter logic chip) would need to be substituted. These are just suggestions; I'm not going to add them to the line-following robot in this book.

A major downside of braking the motors is that the overall progress of the robot will be slowed when driving straight. This is because the opposite wheel no longer rolls forward. To fix that, a microcontroller could be programmed to only apply the brakes when turning.

This is getting complicated! To truly improve the performance of Sandwich, it needs faster sensors, motor circuitry that can brake, and a microcontroller for better control. Not surprisingly, the line-following robot in *Intermediate Robot Building* has these features.

Final Bow

I hope you've enjoyed reading about Sandwich. Hopefully, you've even built one of your own.

If your robot isn't working as well as you'd like, don't get frustrated. Every great scientist anticipates and appreciates the opportunity for learning from every point of failure. The investment you make objectively examining this robot is actually time spent planning your next robot.

To that end, there were actually three Sandwich robots built while writing this book (see Figure 25-13). Each one consists of improvements I made from observing the advantages and disadvantages of the prior one. The improvements were then worked back into the book, so that you, the reader, see the most advanced design.

Figure 25-13. Left to right: *Sandwich, Blue Sandwich, and Red Sandwich*

Now that you've been introduced to the fundamentals of robot building, where do you go from here? That's what the next chapter is all about.

■ ■ ■

CHAPTER 26

Encore

You've gained an understanding of the items and methods needed to get a good start at robot building. You've read schematics and hopefully experienced prototyping, soldering, and tweaking. Maybe you've even built your first robot.

Where do you go from here?

It seems that there's a never-ending stream of new parts, tricks, and technologies in the world of robotics. That's half the allure. Besides the everyday challenges that remain to be solved by robots, there are also plenty of organized contests. This chapter highlights some of the components, challenges, and contests that may interest you as next steps.

Robot Components

The line-following robot contains the primary electrical components encountered in almost all robot designs: batteries, resistors, diodes, transistors, IC chips, LEDs, potentiometers, and switches. In fact, you'd be hard pressed to build a decent robot without these pieces.

As this book is aimed at novice backyard scientists, a few noteworthy parts were excluded to reduce the complexity of the robot presented. Before closing, I decided to examine all of my robots (both real and imagined) to make a list of useful components that otherwise would have gone unmentioned.

Logic Chips

At one time, logic chips ruled the circuit board. Like the comparator used in the line-following robot, each logic chip performs a very specific function. For example, an AND logic chip turns on the third pin when the first pin is on **and** the second pin is on. An OR logic chip turns on the third pin when the first pin is on **or** the second pin is on.

A portion of the numbers printed on the chip indicates the industry-standardized function. For example, a 7404 chip (see Figure 26-1) is an inverter. When the input pin is on, the output pin turns off. When the input pin is off, the output pin turns on. This chip is useful if you need an "off" condition to turn something on.

Figure 26-1. *Logic inverter chip*

Like a six-pack of beer, simpler logic chips contain multiple copies of the same function in a single package. For the 7404 inverter chip, it has a six-pack of inverters: 6 inputs + 6 outputs + 2 power pins = 14 pins.

Beyond the Golden Age of Logic Chips

As microcontrollers and programmable logic array chips became less expensive and more powerful, most of the more complex functions (counter chips, math chips, single bits of memory, and so on) became obsolete. Besides the obvious economic incentive, you can program complex relationships inside of a single microcontroller chip instead of wiring together a board full of logic chips.

Some logic chips still have their place in modern electronics. Inverters, AND, OR, latches, transceivers, de/multiplexers, de/coders, parallel to serial, and serial to parallel chips can do a lot in robots. They're cheap, wonderful for experiments, great for learning digital electronics, and helpful companions to microcontrollers.

Microcontrollers

Without a doubt, the biggest advancement in robotics is the microcontroller. Microcontrollers contain memory and storage space, just like tiny computers. Programs are written on a PC and then downloaded to the robot usually via a USB cable to a programmer board.

If you're dreaming of building a smart robot one day, the microcontroller is a necessity.

Capabilities of Microcontrollers

Although there are sets of special-purpose pins on the microcontroller chip, the remaining pins can provide whatever functions you desire. Blinking an LED is as simple as writing a program that says, "turn on pin 4, wait, turn off pin 4, wait, and repeat."

The line-following robot could be greatly improved by replacing the comparator with a microcontroller. For example, each photoresistor could be evaluated individually to perform smooth turns (when the line is slightly off center), hard turns (when the line is under a far sensor), or to go straight ahead (when all sensors have approximately the same value).

With a microcontroller, motors can be enabled individually or at the same time. With sensors watching the wheels, the microcontroller could insert brief pauses in motor power to slow down when the battery is fresh or a turn is sharp.

With a set of switches in the front and sides of the robot, the microcontroller could stop and back up when a switch is pressed by a collision. The capabilities and creative options provided by a microcontroller make it a must-have part in modern robotics.

Microcontroller Costs

Microcontrollers are relatively inexpensive, most cost between $1 and $15 each. However, the programming boards are expensive, costing between $99 and $400. But, that's a one-time expense for a particular chip. To further reduce costs, some hobbyists sell simplified programming boards, often built into a cable, for as little as $20.

Another expense is the programming language. Some microcontrollers include a BASIC language, but most ship with assembly language, which is a more powerful but more complicated language. If you come from a computer science background, you'll be pleased to discover C, C++, and some Java compilers are generally available for most microcontrollers for an additional price.

Choosing a Microcontroller

The microcontroller market is very competitive, so most manufacturers provide equally capable products. Usually, the reason someone supports a particular microcontroller is because that's the chip family the person learned first. Once invested, it's very difficult to get a designer to discard their tools and knowledge for a different manufacturer's product line, especially for one that only proves equivalent.

I prefer Atmel 8-bit AVR microcontrollers (see Figure 26-2). My newest robots are based on them. Almost all of the ATmega and ATtiny series are available in hobbyist-friendly DIP packages.

Figure 26-2. Atmel microcontrollers: ATmega328 (top), *ATtiny84* (bottom left), *and ATtiny85V* (bottom right)

Other designers prefer Parallax Propeller (multi-core), and Microchip PIC. Another choice is Arduino, which is an open-source microcontroller platform that is compatible with a wide variety of ready-made and enthusiast-created boards.

Voltage Regulators

The major issue that complicates establishing the brightness of an LED, and other calculations of current, is that the battery voltage declines with use. That factor also makes it difficult to document test point voltages for comparison with acceptable values. Is 6 V okay at test point 1? I don't know, maybe. It depends on the voltage of the battery.

Steady voltage makes for consistent brightness, consistent motor speed, and a single set of calculations. More significantly, steady voltage provides an environment suitable, **if not strictly required**, for fussier chips or sensitive components.

Voltage Regulator Packages

Like other parts, voltage regulators come in a variety of packages (see Figure 26-3). The most basic regulators take positive power on one pin, negative power on another pin, and output a steady voltage on a third pin. Fancier regulators have additional pins that indicate a low battery or provide a power-suspend feature.

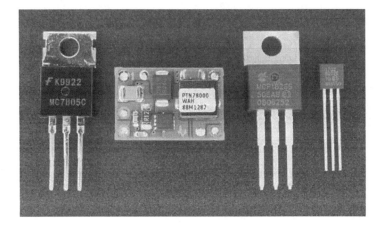

Figure 26-3. Robot-friendly voltage regulators: (left to right) *classic 7805, high- efficiency PTN78000 switching-regulator, low-dropout MCP1826, and low-dropout MCP1702 in a compact package..*

Many regulated voltage values are available, such as 1.8 V, 2.8 V, 3.3 V, 5 V, 8 V, and 12 V. 5 volts is the most common among hobbyists, as many chips operate at that voltage. To save power, lower voltages are more common with modern commercial products, such as cell phones and handheld devices. Some regulators allow you to specify any voltage within a reasonable range by attaching a pair of resistors.

Voltage Regulator Types

There are two major types of voltage regulators:

- Linear regulators require a battery voltage above the final desired voltage, with the regulator discarding the extra. That's a waste of power, but it works. So, a 9 V battery could be regulated at 5 V for its entire useful life. The voltage regulator wouldn't output 4 V when the battery was at 8 V, it would always output 5 V. The discarded extra voltage is turned into heat.

- Switching regulators conserve power by converting voltage using capacitors or inductors. Excess voltage is almost always converted into additional current. Some switching regulators are designed to step-down higher voltages, some step-up lower voltages, and others buck-or-boost (raise or lower) depending on the battery's output. Although not 100% efficient, the best switching regulators approach 90% under ideal conditions. Besides saving power (thus extending battery life), switching regulators don't get as hot as linear regulators.

Selection Criteria

When selecting a voltage regulator, look for your desired final output voltage, the minimum input voltage, the maximum input voltage, the maximum current allowed, and the typical quiescent current (how much current the regulator uses for itself).

Other beneficial features to look for in a voltage regulator include reversed battery protection, thermal shutdown if overheating, and damage protection if the attached board has a short circuit.

Capacitors

As described earlier, capacitors are power storage devices. Unlike batteries, capacitors don't hold a lot of energy, but they can charge and discharge an almost unlimited number of times. Most capacitors are small, lightweight, and inexpensive.

Almost every robot circuit requires capacitors. The line-following circuit is fairly rudimentary, but probably would require a couple of capacitors if additional chips were added.

Capacitor Roles

Capacitors have a number of vital uses:

- Absorbing small power spikes and power dips (reducing electrical noise);.often called a "decoupling" capacitor in this role

- Providing large bursts of power on demand, such as when a motor starts up

- Maintaining circuit power to a memory module or real-time clock for a short time while a battery is being replaced

- Storing regulated voltage

- Acting as buckets to increase voltage in a voltage multiplier circuit

- Creating an inexpensive oscillator or timer by charging and discharging slowly across a resistor; often called a "timing" capacitor in this role

Capacitor Characteristics

The two most important characteristics of a capacitor are the maximum amount of charge it can hold (expressed in farads, abbreviated F), and the maximum voltage it can handle (expressed in volts, abbreviated V). The maximum voltage is easy to understand; don't use a 6.3 V capacitor to store 9 V.

The amount of charge, F, is a little more difficult to comprehend, but it will be clearer once you see how it is commonly used and its capacitor ratings:

- Greater than 10000 µF: used for industrial and military machinery, and solar panel collection. Smaller voltages are used to retain memory or system clocks.

- 100 µF to 10000 µF: used to provide large bursts of power for motors or other current-hungry components. Upper values used on solar robots.

- 1 µF to 100 µF: retains a short-term supply of power from a voltage regulator or power supply.

- 0.1 µF: used to connect to the positive and negative pins of chips to reduce electrical noise.

- 1 pF to 1 µF: used in moderately accurate timing circuits.

- 1 pF to 40 pF: vital for high-accuracy crystal-based oscillator circuits, especially those for microcontrollers and microprocessors.

As would be expected, the greater the maximum voltage and the greater the capacity, the larger the physical size of the capacitor. In Figure 26-4, the second and third capacitors are the same physical size. The one on the left has a smaller maximum voltage but greater capacity; the one of the right has a larger maximum voltage but smaller capacity.

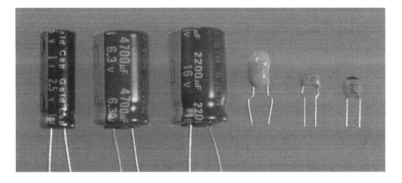

Figure 26-4. Various capacitors: (left to right) *2.5 V 1 F electrolytic, 6.3 V 4700 µF electrolytic, 16 V 2200 µF electrolytic, 10 µF tantalum, 0.1 µF monolithic ceramic, 24 pF ceramic disc*

Solar Power

A robot that continues to operate autonomously without regular human intervention seems more alive than a robot that dies when its battery runs down. The ability to independently recharge, either by returning to a power station or via solar panels, is a real milestone in robot design.

A big problem with small solar panels (see Figure 26-5) is that they don't provide nearly enough continuous power for a motorized robot. You can overcome this by having the solar panels recharge a battery or capacitor, and also by limiting motor activity to short, daylight trips.

Figure 26-5. *Various solar panels*

BEAM Robots

There's a whole class of tiny, simple robots that utilize solar panels instead of batteries. These are called BEAM robots. Because of their limited intelligence and size, they're easy to make. BEAM robots seem to attract artisans as builders, as some BEAM robots are absolutely stunning to behold.

The lack of a battery requires the robot to stand motionless for long periods at a time, charging a capacitor from its solar panel (see Figure 26-6). Then, in a rapid burst, the robot releases the power through its brains and motors, and begins the cycle again.

Figure 26-6. *Appetizer, a BEAM robot, charging its rear capacitor from its front solar panel*

Because they don't have a battery, BEAM robots often lack a power switch. Instead they wander around all day, and sleep at night.

If you're interested in learning more, check out the Solarbotics company web site, http://www.solarbotics.com/.

Resistor Networks

If a robot circuit contains a lot of resistors of the same value, purchasing a part that contains multiple resistors in the same package can save space.

A resistor network, also called a resistor array, consists of many resistors in a single part (see Figure 26-7). Depending on the package, the resistors may be electrically independent of each other, they may be wired so that one end of all of the resistors connects to a single pin, or they may have bizarre arrangements employed for bus termination. Before ordering, be sure to examine the manufacturer's schematic to determine the layout you desire.

Figure 26-7. *Resistor network consisting of nine 470 Ω resistors in one package*

Pushbuttons

Most pushbuttons are spring-loaded switches. Push down and the switch connects, let go and the switch disconnects. Other than that physical difference, the robot sees switches and pushbuttons identically at an electrical level.

Pushbuttons (see Figure 26-8) find their place on keyboards as well as mode selectors, reset buttons, start buttons (stop! buttons), and control pads.

Pushbuttons can also be used as "soft" power switches on smart devices. Most VCRs, TVs, and stereo equipment work this way. Unlike a real power switch that totally disconnects power, soft-powered devices often contain an internal chip constantly receiving power that watches the pushbutton. When the user pushes the button, the brief continuity causes the chip to enable power (via a relay, transistor, or voltage regulator) to the rest of the circuits. When the user pushes the button again, the chip disconnects power to all of the circuits but its own.

The soft-power button approach is especially valuable to circuits that can be powered remotely, can turn themselves off after a period of disuse, or can turn themselves on at a certain time (like a VCR, handheld PDA, or fancy coffee machine). A soft-power button would be very appropriate for an autonomous robot, so long as the batteries were physically removed for servicing.

Personally, I select pushbuttons on the basis of how good they look or feel to the finger.

Figure 26-8. Various pushbuttons

A word of warning with pushbuttons and switches: there's a moment during the physical transition between on and off when the switch fluctuates, turning on and off very quickly before settling. If a chip is watching a switch, it's a good idea to use capacitors or some sort of a delay to hide the indeterminate phase, otherwise the robot or device may think the user pressed the button a bunch of times. Switch filtering techniques are called "debouncing" the switch.

DIP Switches

You may recall from the comparator chip that DIP stands for dual inline package. Although not guaranteed, DIP usually implies a standard width and pin spacing.

There are groups of tiny switches available in the standard DIP size (see Figure 26-9), making them perfect for breadboards. DIP switches act like normal switches, connecting and disconnecting wires.

Figure 26-9. Collection of various DIP switches

413

Because of their small size, DIP switches are difficult to toggle without a tiny screwdriver. Also, the internal switch wiring is a bit delicate. So, they can't handle really large currents or voltages and they may break if switched too often or too aggressively.

DIP switches are excellent for making your robot configurable. I try to load as much intelligence as possible into the programming of my robots, but sometimes, especially on the day of a competition, a robot likes to play dumb. With configurable DIP switches, you can manually select certain settings or patterns to coach the robot to victory.

Think of DIP switches as the on/off equivalent of trimpots: Sometimes you need to perform a tweak or two on the track under ambient conditions.

Jumpers and Shorting Blocks

To save money, jumpers and shorting blocks often replace DIP switches for the purpose of configuration on mass-produced circuit boards.

A plastic piece, called a "shorting block" (see Figure 26-10), containing a thin strip of metal is placed over a pair of pins on the male header on the circuit board. Thus, the metal strip connects the pins as a switch would.

Figure 26-10. Male header and shorting blocks

Jumpers and shorting blocks are less expensive than DIP switches, take up less space, can handle a bit more current, and can be cut down to a single pair of pins if desired. In most cases, I prefer DIP switches for configuration, since they don't have parts that can come loose and become lost. However, shorting blocks provide multimeter access to the male header's metal pins, so current flow can be tested.

Tilt Sensor

You can imagine the futility of an upside-down robot spinning its wheels. The first step toward a robot righting itself would be to know it has tipped over (sort of a 12-step program for robots).

Figure 26-11 is a part that I've always been meaning to try out. A metal ball rolls around a bunch of metal pins. Whenever the ball touches two or more pins, they're connected together electrically. That way, a circuit could detect if the robot was upside down or tipping in some direction by checking to see which pins were "switched" together.

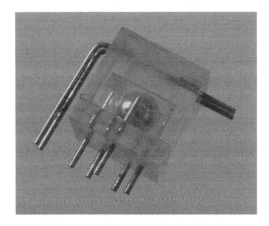

Figure 26-11. Tilt switch consisting of a metal ball surrounded by metal pins within a plastic cube

I can't imagine the part will work while the robot is moving, since the ball probably bounces around a lot. But, it might be functional when the robot pauses.

Temperature Sensors

A thermistor is a variable resistor, just like a potentiometer, but one that changes resistance with changes in temperature. For example, a negative temperature coefficient thermistor decreases in resistance when you hold it in your hand or against a light bulb. It increases in resistance when dipped in ice water.

Thermistors are very small and fairly inexpensive (see Figure 26-12). They often sit inconspicuously on circuit boards, within battery packs, or in probes.

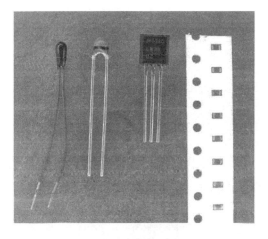

Figure 26-12. Various thermistors for measuring temperature. The first two are plain, the LM34 includes built-in electronics (center right), *and the far right side shows a strip of tiny surface-mount thermistors.*

415

A thermistor is as easy to use as a cadmium-sulfide photoresistor. Hook the thermistor up in a series with a standard resistor and test the voltage at the point where they connect. A comparator would work well with a thermistor. In fact, you could replace the photoresistors in the line-following robot with thermistors, and you'd end up with a really lame heat-seeking robot (thermistors change values too slowly and they'd all be measuring nearly the same local air temperature.)

For the best results, a thermistor should be read by a smart part, like a microcontroller. The microcontroller could contain a table of resistances with associated actions (shut down the battery charger at a certain temperature) or the numeric temperature values to display (like degrees Celsius).

Touch Sensors

Sandwich has no method of detecting a wall, and thus smacks into it. But there are some basic sensors that can provide robots with a crude sense of touch.

The simplest sense of touch is a pushbutton of some form. Appropriate pushbuttons for touch sensing have long lever arms that activate with little force (see top right of Figure 26-13). The pushbutton can electrically disconnect a motor, connect it in reverse, or signal the event to the brains.

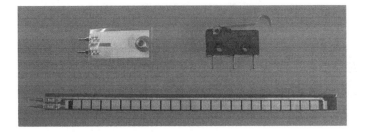

Figure 26-13. Touch sensors: vibration sensor (top left), snap-action level switch (top right), and Jameco #150551 $12.95 flex sensor (bottom)

Flex sensors are variable resistors (see bottom of Figure 26-13). As they bend, they change resistance. You can see this in action on a multimeter in Ω mode. Flex sensors work well with comparators or microcontrollers. Surrounding the robot with a ring made of flex sensors would inform the robot of the slightest warping from any side.

One form of a vibration sensor is a stubby flex sensor with a weight attached (see top left of Figure 26-13). You could put a couple of these inside a robot at different angles and determine the gross direction in which the robot is oriented. Or, knocking the robot on the head could make it say "ouch" or start moving.

Object Detection and Infrared Remote Control

A popular technique for detecting the presence of an object is to use an infrared LED to blink a signal and simultaneously check an infrared detector to see if the signal bounces back. If the signal doesn't bounce back, the area in front of the infrared LED is clear of obstacles.

There are a couple of commercially manufactured parts that perform the most difficult part of detecting a signal (see Figure 26-14). These parts usually have only three pins: one pin for positive power, one pin for negative power, and the last pin, which turns on or off depending on the presence of the signal.

Figure 26-14. Metal-encased infrared photodetector to suppress false signals due to electrical noise (left) *and standard Panasonic PNA4602M infrared photodetectors* (right)

By observing the time between the appearances of a signal, an appliance can decode commands, which is the basis for remote control. In fact, the target market for these parts is actually the remote control industry (VCRs, TVs, and stereos). That large audience has caused the standardization of the signal frequency and dramatically decreased price of the parts.

Some robots surround themselves with photodetectors. By turning on different infrared LEDs at different times, and then reading each of the photodetector's outputs, the robot can get a rough idea of the locations of nearby objects. Other robots use the photodetectors in a classic way, as a remote control, or in a fancy way, as a method of data communication.

Distance and Object Sensor

Standard and remote control photodetectors can tell a robot whether an object is nearby, but can't tell the robot exactly how far away the object resides.

Sharp makes a variety of fantastic distance sensors (see Figure 26-15) with which the robot can determine not only if an object exists, but also how far away the object is. The sensor emits an infrared beam and detects the angle of return in a lens. It can detect objects and walls at distances between 10 cm and 80 cm.

Figure 26-15. Sharp GP2D02 infrared ranger

417

The distance sensor is available with either a digital-numeric output or a variable-voltage output. You could mount a pair with variable-voltage outputs slightly forward on the sides of the robot, replacing test point 1 and test point 2 of the line-following robot's brightness sensor. In that case, Sandwich might be able to drive down a corridor, centering itself.

You can learn more about Sharp distance sensors by visiting http://www.robotroom.com/DistanceSensor.html

Oscillators and Crystals

Oscillators provide accurate timing to microcontrollers, power converters, motor controllers, or any time-sensitive circuit. The timing signal, often called "the clock," provides the drumbeat that keeps all the chips and components working together at the same pace, like clockwork.

Crystals are a portion of an oscillator circuit. The crystal itself has a natural vibration that can be converted to an electrical signal, and then amplified by other components in an oscillator circuit. A canned oscillator is a component that consists of the crystal plus the rest of the oscillator circuit inside a single piece.

For breadboard applications, oscillators are available in the space-saving half-can size (see Figure 26-16) and the full-can size. Or, you can purchase crystals separately, which is better for microcontrollers that have the ability to multiply the base crystal frequency to speed up or slow down for power savings.

Figure 26-16. Half-can oscillator (middle left), *full-can oscillator* (top right), *and crystal* (bottom)

When someone asks, "How fast is your computer?" and you answer 2.6 GHz, you're actually giving a number related to frequency of the crystal or oscillator. If your robot has a microcontroller, it must have an oscillator. To make things simpler, the newer microcontrollers often have a fairly well-timed oscillator built-in.

Sound

You can add sound to a robot to enhance the theatrical effect (with music or funny noises), to provide a friendly interface (with speaking or button feedback), or to aid in debugging (by playing a certain noise when sensor readings are in a specific range or when you need to take actions).

Buzzers are the easiest to control (see Figure 26-17). Connect them to power, like you would a motor, and they make a predetermined noise, like an alarm. Speakers are much more versatile and provide a much higher-quality sound. Although tones and basic tunes can be played on a speaker without much effort, specialized chips are usually required to reproduce digitized sounds or music.

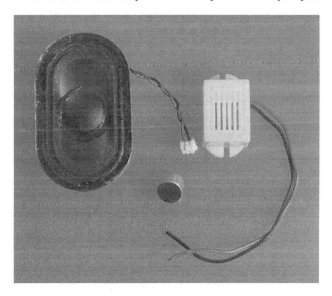

Figure 26-17. Left to right: *Speaker, microphone, and buzzer*

Voice recognition is difficult enough for high-powered computers, much less a robot. However, recording and playing back brief messages can be achieved with commercially available modules. For recognition of simple tones, a microphone and inexpensive chip will do.

Relays

One concern with transistors is the limited amount of power they can switch. Relays provide a switching function similar to transistors, but allow much higher voltages, greater current, and even different voltage types (such as DC controlling AC). Most importantly, mechanical relays allow one circuit to control an adjacent circuit that has a completely separate power source.

A typical mechanical relay (see Figure 26-18) has an electromagnet that physically moves metal plates together to connect. This physical switching explains why some relays make a distinctive clicking sound during operation. When power is disconnected, a spring, or the bent metal plates themselves, forces the metal plates back into their original position.

Figure 26-18. *Miniature relay* (left) *and solid-state relay* (right)

Because a bit of current (10 mA and up) is needed for the relay itself, a transistor often switches the power to the relay. So relays supplement switching—they don't replace transistors. In fact, because relays can be large, noisy, heavy, and relatively slow, they're usually employed only for heavy-duty jobs.

Some robots use relays for controlling large motors. That's understandable. But, for mid-sized and lunchbox-size robots, current-efficient transistors (called MOSFETs) are superior choices under most circumstances.

Adding Gears

Gearhead motors contain tiny, precisely manufactured, precisely placed gears for optimal motor performance. However, that doesn't prevent you from adding additional gears (see Figure 26-19) to the motor shaft in order to alter the final output speed or deliver the rotation to a different location.

Figure 26-19. *Assorted gears*

420

A robot tends to become fairly wide when you add wheels and couplers directly to a motor shaft with the motors placed end-to-end in the robot's body. Even if you are not trying to change the speed, you can still rearrange the shape of the robot by placing the motors side by side with pairs of gears transferring the motor power to a different location (see Figure 26-20).

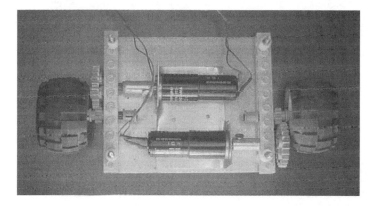

Figure 26-20. Wavy's gearhead motors and couplers fit parallel, with added gears speeding up the robot and centering the wheels

Servos

There are four major types of DC motors usually found in robots. Plain DC motors and gearhead motors were covered in this book. Stepper motors are more precise but require complicated electronics to implement well. The last major type of motor is the servo.

Servos contain built-in electronics and gearing (see the right side of Figure 26-21) that position the motor shaft at a specified angle rather than continuously rotating. Servos are often found on model airplanes and model sailboats to control the angle of the wing flaps or sail.

Figure 26-21. Servo (left) *and exposed servo showing gears and circuit board* (right)

Out of the box, servos are wonderful for positioning arms and legs or for aiming sensors. By opening the cover and cutting away a couple of plastic notches, you can make a servo to rotate continuously, much like a gearhead motor.

A servo's built-in electronics handle motor power, eliminating the need for motor-driver transistors on the robot's main circuit board. Unfortunately, the command signals to a servo are timed pulses. Thus, a special module or microcontroller is required to control a servo.

Encoders—Determining Wheel Speed

Many robots could benefit from knowing the speed at which that their wheels are rotating. For example, Sandwich could improve turning by sensing when the "off" wheel slips forward, to which it would correct the pivot point by rolling the wheel back by the same amount. Another use of rotation information is that when a wheel spins faster than the loaded robot's mass should allow, the wheel is probably slipping or perhaps even off the ground.

By multiplying the number of rotations by the wheel size, a robot could determine the distance traveled. In fact, a line-following robot could store the course distances and turns made on the first lap, and then speed up in the straight-aways on subsequent laps. Or, a roving robot could find its way home by backtracking along the turns and distances it had traveled.

An encoder disc (see Figure 26-22) is placed on a shaft or wheel. By aiming photoresistors or phototransistors at the disc, the robot can tell how much the wheels or shaft are turning. All the robot needs to do is watch and count the number of transitions from black (high resistance) to white (low resistance). The greater the number of transitions per second, the faster the wheel is turning.

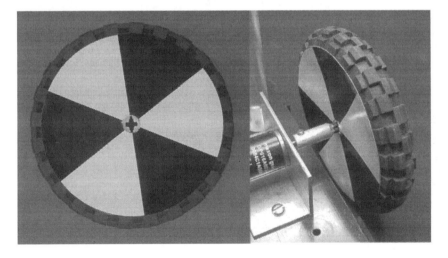

Figure 26-22. A black and white patterned disc for determining wheel or shaft rotation

There are more complicated disc patterns, like Gray coding, from which the robot can tell the exact position of the wheel and in which direction it is rotating. There are adapters for motors, called encoders, which include a sensing technology and a circuit in a single enclosed piece.

Displays

Indicator LEDs are inexpensive, lightweight, and easy to add to a circuit. But, they only convey a limited amount of information. On the other hand, multi-segment alphanumeric LEDs, character-based LCDs (liquid crystal displays), and graphic displays are much friendlier and informative.

Character-based LCDs (see Figure 26-23) are available in a number of sizes, ranging from a small display of 8 characters by 2 lines up to a display of 20 characters by 4 lines. Most character-based LCDs communicate through an industry-standard 14-pin interface. Once you've learned how to control one, there's almost nothing more to learn to control the other sizes and styles.

Figure 26-23. Standard 14-pin 20-character by 4-line LCD

■ **Tip** LCDs consume much, much less power than LEDs. That's why solar-powered calculators use LCDs.

Other than the most basic LED displays showing simple numbers and a few characters, a decent display requires a microcontroller. I highly recommend attaching some sort of alphanumeric (numbers and letters) display to your robot's microcontroller, as it makes debugging so much easier.

Wireless Data and Control

Look no further than the common garage door opener or radio controlled (RC) toys for radio frequency (RF) controllers. There are lots of good robot-ready controller boards that are sold for model airplanes, boats, trucks, and cars. As robot combat television shows made obvious, model radio controllers are easily adapted for robots.

Some modules have features that can even provide data transfer rather than just control (see Figure 26-24). With data RF modules, the robot can remotely log sensor information to a laptop or desktop machine. Or you can reprogram the robot remotely rather than with a serial cable. Or the robot can receive status information about the environment (doorbell ringing, heat source detected on the couch in front of the TV) and communicate that information to a primary location, such as a home computer.

Figure 26-24. Wireless data transmitter and receiver modules

Perhaps the coolest potential opportunity for wireless data technology is the ability for multiple robots to work together on a task. RF modules are like miniature robot walkie-talkies.

Everyday Challenges

I compiled a list of tasks that I think would be fun or helpful for a robot to perform. I constantly annoy my friends, family, and coworkers with statements like "Oh! That would be a great task for a robot." I notice that fewer and fewer people are eating lunch with me lately.

Houseplant-Watering Robot

The robot normally sits on a charging base. Every once in a while, it would drive over to the sink and extend a telescoping tube to obtain some water (perhaps a floor-level copper outlet would be easier).

The robot would then wander through the house, stopping at predetermined spots that are perhaps marked on the floor to improve positioning. The robot would extend a telescoping probe up to reach the houseplants. With the probe, the robot measures the resistance of the dirt, thus determining the approximate moisture level.

If needed, the robot dispenses water into the pot. It proceeds on, visiting each plant, returning for water and power as necessary.

Compost Cart

To weed a garden, a person normally plucks weeds and carries them along until their hands are full. The noxious weeds with seeds are disposed of as yard waste, but the majority of the plant matter is eventually deposited in a compost pile.

It would be very useful to have a robot that followed you throughout the garden. The robot would have a pair of small buckets for depositing weeds and vegetable matter. When the gardener tapped a large button (or whenever the mass exceeded a certain amount), the robot would speed away. The robot drops the first load at a predetermined location for yard waste and deposits the other load in the compost pile.

The robot would then return to the last known location of the gardener, using a heat-sensor to catch up or locate the person.

Trash Emptier

Someone with a remote control would drive the robot around the house to show the robot each of the wastebaskets. At daily intervals (or perhaps at night), the robot would repeat the pattern, either unloading the wastebaskets into a larger container located on the robot, or carrying the wastebaskets to a fixed container in a central location.

For the ultimate helper, the robot could even be given a doggy door to take the waste directly outside to the trash cans. Like in a bad sitcom, your family members would thank you for your neatness and thoughtfulness at empting the trash so regularly, and you'd just smile and wink.

Window Washer

Here's one that everybody laughed at.

You could attach a miniature robot with suction cup legs to any flat windowpane in the house while you perform other activities. The robot would be equipped with a tiny squeegee and cleaning solution. It would meander over the surface of the glass, cleaning as it went. After a while, you'd pass by and pop the robot off and put it onto a new window.

Roof Rat

You could toss a weatherproof, drop-proof robot with an integrated solar panel onto the roof of a garage or a house. It would seek the gutters and discard leaves on a regular basis. During the winter, it would scrape off snow to prevent ice dams and to expose the dark shingles for absorbing more heat from the sun.

I guess after a hard rain you'd need to go and find the roof rat on the ground and chuck it back onto the roof.

Micro Snowplow

You'd place a robot similar to the roof rat outside on the driveway when it started to snow. The robot would carry small loads of snow and deposit them in a specific location (a beacon of some kind would probably be necessary). Although the robot would relocate only small quantities at a time, usually snow doesn't fall that fast.

When I dared speak about this idea, people howled: "After a few hours, you'd walk outside to find your robot frozen into an ice block against a snow bank," and "No, no. You'd find that the robot was still working diligently, yet it's only accomplishment would be a network of snow caves and tunnels beneath a 4-foot drift."

Slug Squisher

This one isn't for the weak of heart, but it is for line-following robots.

In some areas, slugs and snails devastate home-garden vegetables. Organic gardeners are opposed to poison bait, and beer traps are only effective against lush slugs or really desperate neighbors.

You could take advantage of the slug's obvious weaknesses, its slow speed and fragile body. Place a line course across major slug trails around your grounds. The robot would sleep when it was hot or dry, like slugs. However, at night or when it was damp, the robot would speed along the line course, slicing up or smushing any slimy critters in its path.

You'd need to calculate the maximum course length based on the best-case slug speed and the robot's width.

Automatic Street mailbox

This one is actually a pretty good idea. In rural areas or certain housing developments, the mail is delivered to a mailbox that is detached from the house, usually quite a distance away.

In this scenario, the robot would look like an ordinary mailbox. After anything is loaded into the mailbox (detectable by a photointerrupter beam), the robot would wait a short period of time to avoid scaring the postal worker. Then, the robot would drive the mail into the house via a doggy door and dump the mail at a predetermined location before heading back to its post. For security reasons, the doggy door could be locked with an infrared security signal to open it.

Contests

There are a couple of United States autonomous-robot contests worth mentioning. By autonomous, I mean no human beings with remote controls. There are also some contests aimed at professional electrical engineers or graduate students, but they're not appropriate to mention here.

If you don't find any of these contests appealing, or if you are located too far away, consider establishing a contest in your own area. You'd be surprised at the positive response of local libraries or museums to the idea of hosting or providing facilities.

Worldwide Robot Sumo

Robot Sumo is a non-violent pushing contest between two robots. The robots dual in a flat black ring with a white border (see Figure 26-25). The robots can detect the white border using the same technology that detects the white line in a line-following robot. The first robot to be pushed out of the ring, or to fall out, loses.

An illustrated guide with complete details for Robot Sumo appears at `http://www.robotsumo.com/`.

Robot Sumo contests are held throughout Japan, Canada, the United States, and many parts of the world. In the United States, significant tournaments are held in Seattle, Washington; Peoria, Illinois; Portland, Oregon; San Francisco, California; Atlanta, Georgia; and in many other places. A few contests feature cash prizes, but most award wonderful parts and kits donated by commercial sponsors.

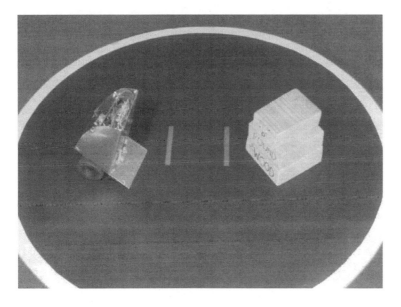

Figure 26-25. Bugdozer, a mini-sumo robot, faces off against a less capable challenger, Pound of Wood.

Trinity College Fire-Fighting

Probably the most attended and lucrative amateur contest in the United States is Trinity College Fire-Fighting in Hartford, Connecticut. Total cash to be awarded is over $10,000. The prize money is distributed among multiple divisions, so, there's a fairly good chance of obtaining an award. T-shirts and other goodies are provided to all who enter.

The goal of the contest is to extinguish a candle flame in the shortest possible time. The candle may be located in one of four rooms. The specifications for the course layout are published so that your robot may take advantage of wall mapping technology. There are optional complications that may be voluntarily selected by the robot builder to produce a better score.

You can find complete details at `http://www.trincoll.edu/events/robot/`.

Atlanta Robot Vacuuming

The Atlanta Robot Vacuuming contest may provide the excuse you've been looking for to purchase as many robot parts as your heart desires, with the full support of your spouse, mother, or roommate.

The purpose of the contest is to vacuum as much rice as possible in four minutes or less. There are bonuses awarded for returning to the start, using less than the four minutes allotted, and for lighter-weight robots. Penalties occur for pushing or knocking over furniture. It is perfectly acceptable to add some beacons to help guide the robot, which isn't the case in most other events.

You can view photographs, see past years' scores, and obtain additional information from the Atlanta Hobby Robot Club's web site (`http://www.botlanta.org/`). They don't hold the robot vacuuming contest every year (it depends on interest levels), but that doesn't prevent you from hosting a contest in your local area.

Seattle Robotics Society Robothon

Every year, the Seattle Robotics Society holds Robothon, an open house gathering of robots, robot enthusiasts, resellers, and members of the public. At that event, not only do they hold Robot Sumo and Fire-Fighting contests, but they also hold other contests such as line following and maze solving.

It's worth attending Robothon even if you don't have a robot to enter in the contest. For more information, including their newsletter, meeting minutes, and photographs, visit http://www.seattlerobotics.org/ or http://www.robothon.org/.

Dallas Personal Robotics Group Roborama

The Dallas Personal Robotics Group (DPRG) features some of the more practical contests, which are very inviting to people just getting started. Using a specified arena, four different tasks are presented, one at a time.

- Quick Trip – The robot drives straight from one end of the arena to the other, and then back again.

- Line Following – An easy course shaped a little like the outline of a letter "T" on its side.

- T-Time – The same T-shaped course without the line. The dimensions are published in advance, walls surround the arena, and solid lines appear before each corner of the T. So, there are a number of simple ways to effectively tackle the course.

- Can-Can – The most challenging, but the most interesting as well. The robot has up to ten minutes to fetch up to six empty soda cans placed upright throughout the arena.

From year to year, DPRG Roborama features additional contests. For details, visit http://www.dprg.org/competitions/index.html .

Central Illinois Robotics Club

In the Midwest, the Central Illinois Robotics Club holds an annual robot contest. They have a great turnout from many surrounding states, in a family-friendly, kid-friendly atmosphere.

Although emphasis is placed on several different-size classes of Robot Sumo (including a LEGO division), they also dabble in line following. I've attended the event in the past and plan to again in the future. Maybe I'll see you there?

To learn more, visit http://circ.mtco.com/.

Chicago Area Robotics Group (Chibots)

Last, but not least, is my hometown robotics club. Chibots holds regular meetings in the northwest suburbs of Chicago. They also hold a bi-annual event at the Chicago Museum of Science and Industry and the iHobby Expo. Chibots has defined rules for over a dozen different robot contests, which are held based on registration.

Their web site is http://www.chibots.org/.

The Great Wide Open

I hope this book has given you the confidence, knowledge, and enthusiasm to send you headfirst into robotics. There's plenty to do and lots of interesting projects to start. You couldn't have picked a better time to begin this fascinating and rewarding hobby.

Thank you for reading this book. It was a real joy to write.

CHAPTER 27

Appendix

This chapter contains notes and other items not covered in the main portion of the book.

It begins with proper credit to Ohm's law, which describes the interdependent relationship between voltage, current, and resistance. Then, I come clean about some of the mistakes I made during development, so that you can avoid them yourself. Finally, the chapter concludes with an explanation and listing of the various labels for positive and negative power.

Magical Ohm's Law

Most of the electrical formulas in the book are derived from Ohm's law. Therefore, it would be remiss not to directly describe the most valuable set of math equations for electronics.

Ohm's law describes the relationship between voltage, current, and resistance. If you have any two of those parts, you can instantly calculate the third. You can divide voltage by either of the other two parts, or multiply current and resistance together (see Figure 27-1). Let that triangle burn into your head and you'll never forget which part needs to be divided and which parts multiplied.

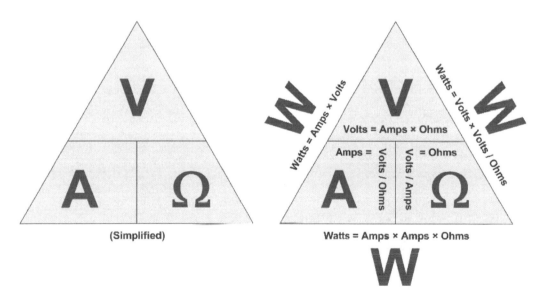

Figure 27-1. *Ohm's law expressed as a triangle, where V is volts, A is amps, and Ω is ohms*

Here are the formulas expressed in a standard way:

```
current in amps = voltage in volts / resistance in ohms
```

or...

```
resistance in ohms = voltage in volts / current in amps
```

or...

```
voltage in volts = resistance in ohms × current in amps
```

All three formulas are identical. They've only been moved around algebraically.

Ohm's Law is Helpful in Selecting a Current-Limiting Resistor

Here's a practical example. According to some datasheet, the maximum current flow that some component can accept is 0.25 amps. You've got a 12-volt battery. What size resistor should you select to limit current flow to 0.25 amps or less?

According to the Ohm's law, if you know two parts, you can calculate the third. You know 0.25 amps and you know 12 volts.

```
resistance in ohms = 12 volts / 0.25 amps
48 Ω = 12 V / 0.25 A
```

A 48-ohm resistor will never allow more than 0.25 amps to flow through it when you're using a 12-volt battery.

Help in Determining Current from a Voltage

You're worried about the robot's motors stalling and burning out. Based on the motor datasheet, the motor's stall current is 0.5 amps, but you've decided to have the robot shut off motor power if it reaches 0.4 amps, just to be safe. Unfortunately, almost all of the chips and microcontrollers only seem to be able to read voltage, not current.

Ohm's law guarantees that if you know the voltage and the resistance, then you can calculate the current. The solution is to put a known value of resistor in the same path as your motor and have the robot read the resistor's voltage to calculate the current in that path. Installing a low-value power resistor, say 0.1 Ω, should have little effect on the motor's performance.

```
voltage in volts = 0.1 ohms × 0.4 amps
0.04 V = 0.1 Ω × 0.4 A
```

When the chip detects 0.04 volts or more, then 0.4 amps or more are pouring through the motor. This must be true, since the resistor is in the same path as the motor, so any electricity passing through the motor must pass through the resistor.

Remember, this is magical, unbeatable Ohm's law. There's absolutely no way to get more than 0.4 A through a 0.1 Ω resistor unless the voltage dropped across the resistor is 0.04 V or more.

Multimeter Voltage to Current Trick

Ohm's law is helpful for measuring current on a soldered circuit board. You can't measure current directly with the multimeter unless you desolder one end of a wire somewhere to connect it through the meter in amp mode. But, if you can find a resistor with a value printed on it, then you can calculate the current after measuring the voltage across the resistor.

Let's say you find a 220 Ω resistor. You measure the voltage by touching the multimeter probes to each end of the resistor and it reads 3.52 volts.

```
current in amps = 3.52 volts / 220 ohms
0.016 A = 3.52 V / 220 Ω
```

In case you've forgotten, you can multiply amps by 1000 to get milliamps.

```
0.016 A × 1000 = 16 mA
```

16 mA must be passing through the path of the resistor, regardless of the stuff in the circuit before the resistor or after the resistor. Why? Mr. Ohm (Georg S. Ohm) guarantees it or double your money back!

The Key Point of Ohm's Law

Anytime you say to yourself, "I sure wish I knew A, but I can only measure B and C", think of Ohm's law. To assist you, I've created an online tool (see Figure 27-2) where you can enter two measurements and the site calculates all of the other values. Visit: http://www.robotroom.com/Calculators/Ohms-Law/Ohms-Law-Voltage-Current-Resistance-Calculator.aspx

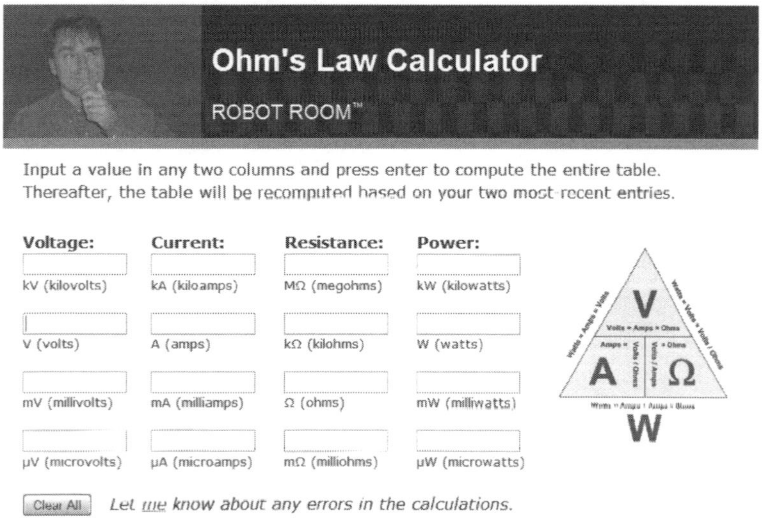

Figure 27-2. Online Ohm's law calculator

433

The Larger Implication of Ohm's Law

There is an undeniable reality to Ohm's law: In a circuit, you can't change just one of the three terms (either voltage, current, or resistance). Any change in one causes at least one of the others to change to balance.

This also means you can purposely alter one term to force a change in another.

Things I've Accidentally Destroyed While Writing This Book

Sometimes after I read a good book about robots, I get a little discouraged. I think, "Wow, this guy's a lot smarter than I am. How can I be expected to build what he built?" The truth is that most authors only publish their successes, so of course everything seems perfect. You're not there to observe the junk he flung out of an open window.

Perhaps revealing my mistakes will prevent you from repeating them. Additionally, it may offer some explanations as to why I made a change in the robot's circuit and also warned you to avoid certain parts.

Which Way Does a 9 V Battery Get Installed?

Let's face it, a 9 V battery is difficult to install backwards. But, it is possible for anyone to touch the battery to the wrong terminals of the battery snap, even briefly. That's no tragedy, unless you've left the power switch on.

In my case, the reversed voltage zipped through Sandwich's circuits. Each path with an LED was protected by the diode (one-way) nature of the LED. The photoresistors, resistors, and trimpots were safe because they're non-polarized devices, meaning they don't care in which direction current flows.

After correctly snapping the battery into place, it didn't occur to me that anything had happened. After all, I was looking at the bottom of the circuit board and the headlights and tube LEDs were now illuminated. But, frankly, something started to stink. The robot really smelled bad.

Upon flipping the robot right side up, I noticed the left and right brightness indicator LEDs weren't lit. After wiggling wires and flipping switches to no avail, I began to suspect that something was wrong with the comparator or transistors. Since the comparator was socketed, it was the easiest part to swap out. Indeed, the comparator was dead (see Figure 27-3).

Figure 27-3. A destroyed LM393N comparator

The comparator has a direct connection to the positive and negative terminals of the battery. The reversed battery with the power switch on was enough to fry the chip. This is why I introduced the Reverse Battery Protection circuit in Chapter 25 as a potential improvement.

Melting Switches

The standard-size subminiature DPDT-center-off line-following switch seems a bit large for the line-following robot. So, I experimented with smaller, micro-size switches.

After wiring and soldering up a couple of micro switches (see Figure 27-4), they were installed in the line-following robot brothers. One robot spun in circles, and the other robot followed dark lines but not light lines. The switches made nasty, horrible crunching sounds when toggled.

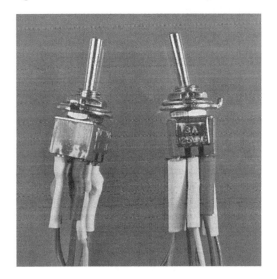

Figure 27-4. Disfigured micro switches

Upon closer inspection, I realized the switches had melted and cracked during soldering (see Figure 27-5). I don't know whether the switches were of poor quality or if I held the soldering iron against their leads for too long.

Figure 27-5. Melted (left) *and cracked* (right)

Larger pieces of metal do take longer to solder, so I believe the manufacturer should use material that can withstand being heated for a reasonable period of time. Due to this failure, I didn't end up recommending this particular model of switch in the book.

Popping Multimeter Fuses

In the years I've practiced electronics, I've never blown a fuse in a multimeter (see Figure 27-6).

Figure 27-6. Two, count 'em, two blown fuses!

In writing a book, a lot of time is spent researching and validating facts. Since it's going to be on paper for a long time, with my name associated with it, I want the information to be reliable.

For the transistor chapter, I measured transistor gain in a multimeter transistor test socket. I wanted to verify that the multimeter was displaying an accurate value and that the amount of gain multiplied by the amount of base current determined the maximum amount of current allowed from the collector to the emitter.

With the transistors in a test circuit, I dialed the multimeter to amp mode. With this higher-rated mode, I tested the amount of current coming from the battery to ensure it was below the 500 mA limit of the meter in milliamp mode. The current was well below that limit.

I switched the multimeter to milliamp mode and disconnected one end of the resistor from the base lead of the transistor. I connected the red multimeter test probe to the base lead of the transistor and the black test probe to the negative bus. Poof!

I must have been thinking about measuring voltage. Instead, I should have connected the black test probe to the disconnected end of the resistor. The resistor is there to limit the amount of current provided to the transistor. By hooking the black test probe to the negative bus, I provided a short path from the positive terminal of the battery, through the transistor's collector lead, through the transistor's base lead, through the multimeter, to the negative battery terminal. There weren't any resistors in that path to limit current.

The current through the multimeter exceeded 500 mA, blowing the fuse inside the meter. The multimeter continued to display information ("0.0 mA") and operate in modes other than milliamps. I can't tell you how long I spent trying to figure out why the milliamp mode wasn't working.

Fortunately, the multimeter contained a spare fuse, and I was able to continue testing. This time, I connected the multimeter correctly and obtained the validation of the experiment.

Fool Me, Twice

After finishing a chapter, I let it sit for a few days. Then, I proofread it and redo the experiments according to my written directions before handing the chapter to the publisher.

Guess what happened? During proofreading, I blew the fuse again making the same mistake with the test leads (see Figure 27-6, again!)

Voltage's Real Name

Throughout this book, I chose to use the term "negative voltage." It's not inappropriate, and the battery is labeled that way. It's just a bit primary school or old fashioned. Okay? It's un-cool.

As you move forward in electronics, you'll run across other terms for voltages. It's worth knowing these modern labels, as you're going to encounter them on datasheets, schematics, books, and articles.

Ground, Not Negative Voltage

Figure 27-7 shows one of the most prevalent symbols in a schematic. Recall that this indicates the conventional return path for all power in a circuit. On a battery-operated circuit, the path indeed leads back to the negative terminal of the battery. However, this symbol is actually referred to as "ground" or "common."

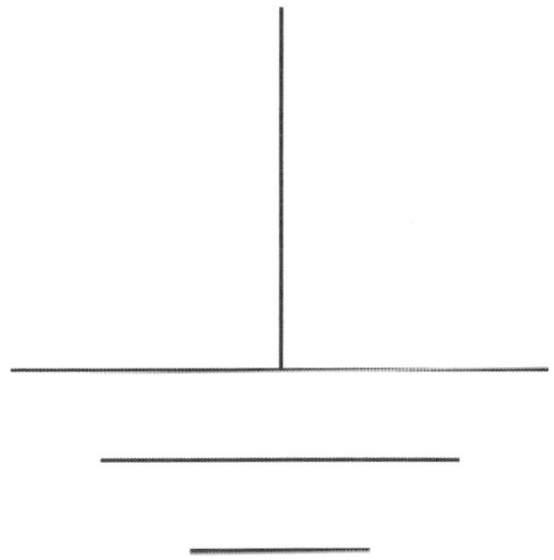

Figure 27-7. Schematic symbol for ground, usually abbreviated GND

You can think of this as the lowest voltage possible in the circuit; 0 V; the power has reached the ground. You connect your black multimeter test probe to this location in the circuit and measure all positive voltages as being "above ground."

Nowadays, negative voltage suggests three power-supply voltage levels: a positive voltage, a ground, and a truly negative voltage that ground power can flow to. When speaking informally, there's nothing wrong with saying, "Hook one end of the motor to positive and the other end to negative." However, when there are really only two connections from the power supply, you should formally refer to negative voltage as ground, to prevent confusion.

V Double Letter

With few exceptions, all integrated-circuit (IC) chips contain transistors. There are two kinds of transistors, bipolar and field effect. From an earlier chapter, you know that bipolar transistor leads are labeled collector, base, and emitter. Field effect transistors happen to be labeled drain, gate, and source.

When IC chips became popular in the 1970s, chip pin voltages were specified based on the internal part of the transistor to which they were connected. For example, the positive power supply pin would be labeled V_{CC}. The C stands for collector, and is repeated (V_{CC}) to indicate that it represents the voltage that the power supply for the collector should create. That's not necessarily the voltage at the collector (which would be V_C).

The transistor pin labeling conventions continue today. No doubt you'll see them on everything from discrete transistor circuits, logic chips, all the way up to microcontrollers.

You may consider the following voltage terms positive voltage: +, V^+, V_{BB}, V_{CC}, V_{DD}, and V_{GG}.

You may consider the following voltage terms ground (formerly "negative") voltage: -, V^-, GND, common, V_{EE}, and V_{SS}.

Practical Example

On a 74LS04 (bipolar-based) chip, the power supply pins are labeled V_{CC} and GND. The positive bus connects to the V_{CC} pin and the ground bus (formerly "negative") connects to GND.

The power supply pins of a Freescale 68HC908KX8 (field-effect based) microcontroller are labeled V_{DD} and V_{SS}. The positive bus connects to the V_{DD} pin and the ground bus (formerly "negative") connects to V_{SS}.

Index

■ M

■ S

■ W

■ Z

Made in the USA
Middletown, DE
17 July 2015